The Education–Drug Use
Connection

How Successes and Failures in School Relate to Adolescent
Smoking, Drinking, Drug Use, and Delinquency

D0864093

The Education–Drug Use
Connection

How Successes and Failures in School Relate to Adolescent Smoking, Drinking, Drug Use, and Delinquency

Jerald G. Bachman
Patrick M. O'Malley
John E. Schulenberg
Lloyd D. Johnston
Peter Freedman-Doan
Emily E. Messersmith
Institute for Social Research
University of Michigan

LEA Lawrence Erlbaum Associates
Taylor & Francis Group

New York   London

Lawrence Erlbaum Associates
Taylor & Francis Group
270 Madison Avenue
New York, NY 10016

Lawrence Erlbaum Associates
Taylor & Francis Group
2 Park Square
Milton Park, Abingdon
Oxon OX14 4RN

© 2008 by Taylor & Francis Group, LLC
Lawrence Erlbaum Associates is an imprint of Taylor & Francis Group, an Informa business

Printed in the United States of America on acid-free paper
10 9 8 7 6 5 4 3 2 1

International Standard Book Number-13: 978-0-8058-6171-6 (Softcover) 978-0-8058-6170-9 (Hardcover)

Visit the Taylor & Francis Web site at
http://www.taylorandfrancis.com

Contents

Preface

Young people in adolescence face a variety of important developmental tasks. To the extent they can succeed in those tasks, and at the same time avoid behaviors that place them at risk of immediate or long-term health consequences, their futures will be brighter. This book focuses on a key issue in adolescent development and health—the links between educational success and failure, on one hand, and substance use and other problem behaviors, on the other. It is a well-established fact that educational success and substance use are negatively related, but questions remain about the extent to which substance use in adolescence causes reduced academic attainment, versus the extent to which substance use is a consequence of earlier educational failures. The purposes of this book are to (a) examine and document the various linkages among educational experiences, delinquent behavior in general, and substance use specifically (including tobacco, alcohol, marijuana, and cocaine use); (b) estimate the relative importance of the several causal processes involved; and (c) address policy implications of the findings.

In pursuing these purposes, the book employs a unique and valuable data set from the University of Michigan's Monitoring the Future (MTF) project. The project's annual reports of drug use by youth and young adults in the United States are widely used and cited. These annual MTF reports are based on large, nationally representative annual in-school surveys of high school seniors (since 1975) and 8th- and 10th-grade students (since 1991), as well as mail surveys that follow the high school graduates into young and middle adulthood. The present book takes advantage of all of these data resources in order to place our findings in their larger context. However, our primary focus here is on a relatively new data set from the project—a longitudinal panel study that tracked eighth-grade adolescents into young adulthood, with survey content that includes family background, educational experiences, delinquent behaviors, substance use, and more. This large and nationally representative sample of eighth-grade students in the

United States (initially surveyed in 1991–1993) covers the vitally important developmental period between ages 14 and 22.

The age-14 starting point is late enough to provide a good deal of background on early educational successes and failures, but early enough to catch most adolescents before they have gone very far down the path of substance use. We are thus able to observe whether early educational experiences predict later substance use, and we can also observe whether and to what extent substance use then makes educational success less likely. We are mindful that we are reporting survey research based on the self-reports of real people in real circumstances. We thus lack the advantages of experimental designs, with their *potential* for establishing causal directions unambiguously. We also recognize that correlation does not necessarily mean causation. Nevertheless, having *panel* survey data tracking the same individuals from ages 14 to 22 provides what we consider to be strong circumstantial evidence in our effort to sort out the causal processes underlying the negative correlation between educational success and adolescent substance use.

The basic findings that emerge in this book are that educational experiences and their prior causes do have a considerable influence on delinquent behaviors in general and on substance use in particular, whereas any impacts of substance use on subsequent educational outcomes are much more limited. So rather than counting on substance-use prevention as a means of boosting academic attainment, our findings indicate that the primary policy emphasis should be on increasing early educational success not only as the means for raising longer term academic accomplishments and earnings, but also as an important step toward reducing substance use. A popular anti-drug media message has been "Parents—the anti-drug." Our findings on family background certainly support this message. But our findings also suggest an additional message: "Educational success—the anti-drug." Young people's experiences in school—acquiring the skills of learning and earning the rewards of successfully coping with the demands of school—make a critical difference to a broad range of outcomes in their lives, not the least of which is their ability to resist pressures to use drugs.

Guidelines for Using This Book[1]

This book is intended for anyone who deals with education and/or substance use. The list of potential readers includes, but is not limited to, educational psychologists, developmental psychologists, social psychologists, sociologists, epidemiologists, policymakers, and educators more generally. Because it involves the analysis of panel survey data using a variety of analytic strategies, the book also may be of interest to survey methodologists and students of quantitative methods.

We recognize that users of research monographs are often selective, sometimes wanting only the "big picture," sometimes wanting full technical details, and sometimes wanting only one particular part of the picture— in the present book, perhaps one particular type of substance use, or one aspect of educational experience. We have organized this book, including its index, to be responsive to all of those needs.

The reader seeking a brief summary of findings and conclusions finds, in chapter 1, an introduction and overview, an outline of the other chapters, and a preview and illustration of key findings. The final chapter (chap. 10) provides a more extensive summary of findings, conclusions, and implications. Both of these chapters are designed to stand alone.

Chapter 2 provides a review and discussion of relevant literature. It helps to place the present work into the context of what is already known about the issues addressed here.

Chapter 3, along with sections of the appendix, spells out our survey and analysis methods (including panel response rates and our procedures for dealing with missing data). Much of the detailed exposition of analytic methods, however, has been left for subsequent chapters, so that the applications can be illustrated with real data, rather than described in the abstract. Our analytic methods are likely to be familiar to many readers,

---

[1] Portions of this section were adapted from previous books.

and they may want to skim over some methodological portions of the text in this and subsequent chapters. Similarly, readers who would rather "just take our word for it" and get to our conclusions may also want to skip over some of the details. But for those who do want to see the evidence in detail, we have tried to provide it in the text and the appendix. We have come to some important conclusions based on this research, but we have tried to provide enough of the evidence to permit readers to draw their own conclusions.

Chapter 4 examines the academic attainment of the young people in our longitudinal panel. It explores correlates—and potential causes—of educational success and failure. It also introduces the multiple regression and structural equation modeling approaches we use, as well as the formats for tabular presentation of the analysis results. The final portion of chapter 4 develops a causal model of academic attainment that serves as the basis for subsequent more elaborated models.

Chapter 5 examines delinquent behaviors reported by our panel members and links them with the measures of educational success and failure. Chapter 5 also expands the causal model of academic attainment, first to incorporate delinquency and then to incorporate also the four types of adolescent substance use examined in this book: cigarette, marijuana, cocaine, and alcohol. This causal model, simultaneously exploring all four types of substance use, is used in the next four chapters, with each chapter focusing on different portions of the model findings.

Chapter 6 reports on cigarette use, including patterns of initiation, continuation (which is common), and cessation (which is, alas, rare). The close links with educational experiences are then examined, and the structural model is used to consider to what extent educational factors predict smoking and vice versa.

The next three chapters use procedures similar to those in chapter 6—exploring marijuana use (chap. 7), cocaine use (chap. 8), and alcohol use and occasional heavy drinking (chap. 9). The findings on each of these other drugs replicate to some extent the findings on cigarette use presented in chapter 6, but some important differences emerge as well.

Chapter 10, as just noted, summarizes and integrates the evidence from earlier chapters, reports our conclusions, and explores policy implications.

Acknowledgments

Throughout the life of the MTF project, the sponsor has been the National Institute on Drug Abuse (NIDA). We are indebted to the various NIDA directors, division directors, and project officers who provided their support and assistance during the past three decades. The data collections and analyses reported here were carried out under NIDA Research Grant No. R01DA01411.

Our project has benefited from the efforts of many individuals in the Survey Research Center at the University of Michigan's Institute for Social Research. These include members of the sampling, field, telephone, and computing facilities, as well as field interviewers throughout the nation. In addition, of course, past and present members of the MTF staff have been essential to the success of the project.

Several staff members in particular made many direct and valuable contributions to this book. Tanya Hart was our editor during the early stages of writing and did much to curb the authors' occasional errors or excesses. Kathryn Johnson took over the editor role during the later stages and provided extensive editorial support (i.e., further curbing, as needed), as well as coordination of the whole manuscript development process. Ginger Maggio contributed extensively in reviewing and improving tables and figures, as well as making sure they matched what we said in the text. Nicole Ridenour provided further skilled help, especially in the preparation of figures.

We appreciate the helpful contributions provided by Lawrence Erlbaum Associates. In particular, we thank our Senior Editors, Lori Handelman and Debra Riegert; their associate, Anthony Messina; and our Book Production Supervisor, Sarah Wright. We also appreciate the suggestions of four reviewers commissioned by LEA, who read portions of the text and encouraged publication. We also greatly appreciate the thoughtful contributions of Professor Nancy Galambos, the series editor for our previous two books, who served as a consultant on this book; she reviewed the full manuscript and provided many valuable suggestions.

We are grateful to thousands of principals and teachers, and to the great many students who participated in the MTF surveys conducted in schools. Finally, we owe special words of thanks to those individuals who were selected and participated in mail follow-up surveys, extending through their adolescence and into young adulthood. We thank them for their efforts, and we hope we have told their story well.

Chapter 1

Introduction and Overview

Consider the claims in these two "headlines":

1. *Doing well in school protects your teenager from drug use.*
2. *Drug use threatens your teenager's success in school.*

Both claims can cite, as supporting evidence, a large body of research (summarized in chap. 2) showing negative correlations between adolescent substance use and success in school. Yet the two headlines do more than assert correlations; they also make strong—and different—assertions about the causal processes underlying the correlations. The first headline asserts that school performance influences drug use, whereas the second asserts that drug use influences school performance. Either assertion can be seen as consistent with the correlations; indeed, both may be correct to some extent. This already complicated story does not end there; the correlations also may arise, perhaps in large part, because educational outcomes and substance use share common prior causes.

Which of these three possible causal processes accounts for the negative links between substance use and educational success? Our own view at the outset of this research was that all three are involved to some degree. A primary purpose of the research in this book has been to estimate just how much of each type of causation is involved. Now, after our extensive analyses of a great deal of data linking educational experiences with adolescent smoking, drinking, marijuana use, and cocaine use, we offer the following broad conclusion: *Adolescent substance use is negatively correlated with educational success (a) because both sets of behaviors share common prior causes, (b) because educational successes protect against substance use whereas educational failures are risk factors, and (c) to a lesser extent because some substance use can impair educational success.* Behind this simple and general "all-of-the-above" conclusion lies a variety of nuanced findings, reported in later chapters. The findings differ from one substance to another and from one developmental period to another.

One of the central premises of this book is that patterns of behaviors established during adolescence can have important consequences extending into adulthood. Adolescence is a time when individual differences in educational success become more manifest as course work becomes more demanding and individual talents more challenged; it is also a time when substance use is most likely to emerge. Societal-level factors influence preferences about substance use, as well as educational aspirations. Thus, we and many other researchers have observed and documented shifts in attitudes and behaviors involving substance use, as well as changes in educational aspirations, over the course of recent decades. But our primary focus in this book is not on secular trends or changes across recent decades, but rather on patterns of individual differences that show great consistency across the decades. Educational successes, as well as substance-using behaviors, reflect individual-level choices—choices that are, of course, influenced by family, peers, and many other factors. We believe that such choices, and thus their consequences, can be changed for the better. But much depends on a firmer understanding of how educational difficulties and substance use interrelate. So "getting it right" in adolescence is of critical importance, and our hope is that this book helps in this regard.

Our book is based primarily on a rich set of adolescent panel data from the University of Michigan's Monitoring the Future (MTF) project tracking a large nationwide sample of young men and women through a critical 8-year period from modal age 14 (late eighth grade, in 1991–1993) through modal age 22 (in 1999–2001). In addition, we make limited use of other sets of data from the MTF project: nationally representative annual cross-sectional surveys of 8th-, 10th-, and 12th-grade students, as well as panel data from some of those originally sampled in 12th grade (with follow-up surveys extending to age 40).

The eighth-grade panel data provide information about the ordering of the behaviors of interest; however, knowledge of chronology is not necessarily sufficient to resolve questions of causation. As one brief illustration of that point, let us preview two findings from chapter 6 in this book. The first finding is that those who were smokers at age 14 were more likely than average to become high school dropouts and less likely to go to college; that would be consistent with the causal assertion that smoking inhibits educational success (in other words, smoking stunts one's intellectual growth). The second finding is that those who reported good grades at age 14 (i.e., during eighth grade) were less likely to be smokers at age 22; and that would be consistent with the causal assertion that doing well in school protects against becoming a smoker. So panel data do not guarantee solutions to knotty problems of causal interpretation.

Although panel data are not a panacea, they can be quite helpful in narrowing the choices among plausible causal interpretations. The panel data permit us to employ structural equation modeling, along with other techniques, to examine the several alternative causal interpretations of the links between substance use and educational success. In addition to these complex analyses, panel data can provide relatively simple descriptive findings that illuminate relationships—sometimes with striking clarity. In the next section, we present several such descriptive findings based on panel data from ages 14 to 22 and from ages 18 to 40; this provides an introduction and overview of the relationships examined in greater detail in later chapters.

SUBSTANCE USE, AGES 14 TO 40, LINKED TO EDUCATIONAL SUCCESS

The findings and underlying methods in this section are reported in greater detail elsewhere (Bachman, Freedman-Doan et al., 2006). For purposes of this introductory chapter, it is sufficient to highlight key results. Here, as in the rest of the book, we present findings separately for males and females, so as not to confound any gender differences with other findings. Although some gender differences in substance use are evident, it can also be seen that the patterns of relationships are generally similar for males and females.

Daily Smoking

Figure 1.1 shows how prevalence of daily smoking, from adolescence through middle adulthood, differs according to educational attainment by modal age 21 to 22. The top portion of this figure (as well as of Figs. 1.3 and 1.4) reports findings from the eighth-grade panel; even as early as eighth grade, the proportions of daily smokers are ordered neatly according to later (age-22) educational attainment. In particular, eighth graders who would later become dropouts were about three times as likely as their age-mates (taken as a whole) to be daily smokers. Although the proportions of daily smokers increased during adolescence, the link with later educational attainment remained stable and strong.

The remaining portions of Figure 1.1 show that the link between educational attainment and smoking was also strong during adulthood, based on other MTF panel data—but this figure illustrates samples of

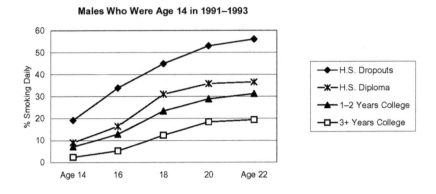

Males Who Were Age 14 in 1991–1993

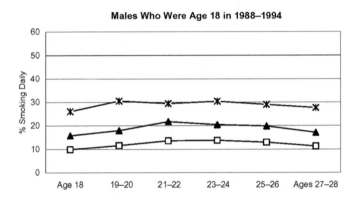

Males Who Were Age 18 in 1988–1994

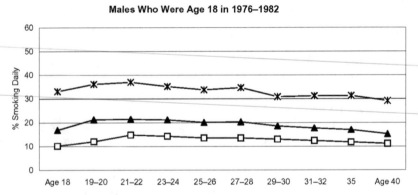

Males Who Were Age 18 in 1976–1982

Percentage values in this figure are shown in Table A.1.1a in the appendix.

Figure 1.1a. Percentage reporting any daily smoking in the last 30 days by academic attainment at modal ages 21 to 22: males.

Females Who Were Age 14 in 1991–1993

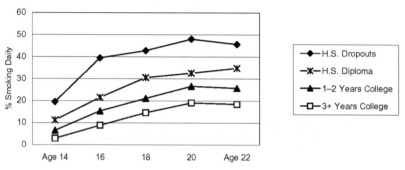

Females Who Were Age 18 in 1988–1994

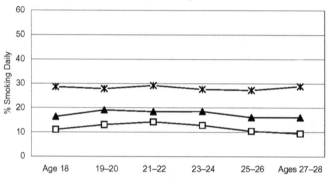

Females Who Were Age 18 in 1976–1982

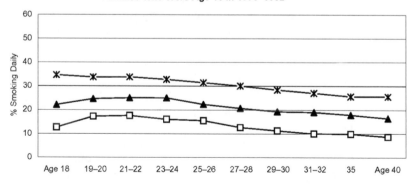

Percentage values in this figure are shown in Table A.1.1b in the appendix.

Figure 1.1b. Percentage reporting any daily smoking in the last 30 days by academic attainment at modal ages 21 to 22: females.

high school seniors who were tracked into adulthood. Fortunately, smoking rates declined among respondents from the high school classes of 1976–1982 as they moved from their early 20s to age 40. This decline likely reflects both developmental and historical effects because this was a period during which the health risks of smoking were increasingly publicized. Despite this decline, a clear, negative relationship remained between educational attainment (at modal ages 21–22) and likelihood of daily smoking (at later ages). Daily smoking was only one third to one half as prevalent among those who completed 3 or more years of college compared with those who completed no years of college. (Because these panels began at the end of 12th grade, they did not include high school dropouts; dropouts undoubtedly would have shown still higher prevalence rates for daily smoking.)

In sum, Figure 1.1 indicates that the more educationally successful a young person is at age 22, the less likely he or she was, is, or will become a regular daily smoker. This pattern of findings is robust across three sets of cohorts spanning ages 14 to 40 and covering the last quarter century—a period during which overall smoking rates changed and levels of educational attainment rose substantially. As for questions of causation—which causes which?—our best answers are based on the more complex analyses shown in chapter 6. We can, however, provide another strong hint based on the eighth-grade panel data. Figure 1.2 shows smoking rates for another set of subgroups, this time separated according to self-reported grade point average (GPA) at the end of eighth grade. The relationships show a striking parallel to those for the educational attainment subgroups shown in Figure 1.1; the A students were far less likely to be or become daily smokers, compared with the C or lower students. This is surely consistent with our focus on the importance of shared prior causes, especially those having to do with educational successes and failures.

Marijuana Use

Figure 1.3 presents prevalence rates for current use of marijuana (any use in the past 30 days). The picture for ages 14 to 18 (top portion of the figure) bears some similarity to that for cigarette use: Those who would later become dropouts were most likely to use marijuana, and those who would later complete 3 or more years of college were least likely to use marijuana. By age 22, the dropouts remained more likely to be marijuana users, especially among the males; however, among the non-dropouts, educational success appeared no longer negatively linked with current marijuana use.

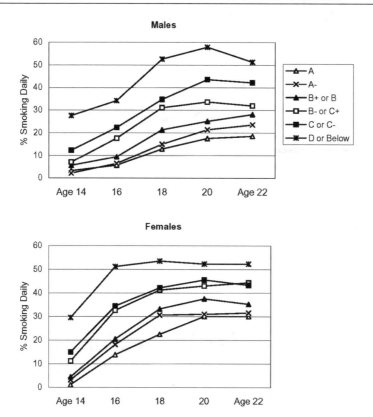

Percentage values in this figure are shown in Table A.1.2
in the appendix.

Figure 1.2. Percentage reporting any daily smoking in the
last 30 days by eighth-grade GPA: age 14 in 1991–1993.

The next older cohorts (age 18 in 1988–1994) also showed modest
negative correlations between marijuana use at age 18 and later educational attainment, but by ages 19 to 20 and thereafter, the correlations
were close to zero. Among the oldest cohorts (age 18 in 1976–1982),
the negative correlations at age 18 were a bit stronger, and the correlations at later ages were almost all negative, but often less than statistically significant.

In sum, the most academically successful individuals (as indicated
by later attainment) are least likely to use marijuana during adolescence. But these differences fade, and, except for dropouts, any such
differences in educational attainment after age 18 are small and not
entirely consistent.

Males Who Were Age 14 in 1991–1993

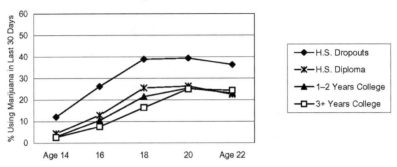

Males Who Were Age 18 in 1988–1994

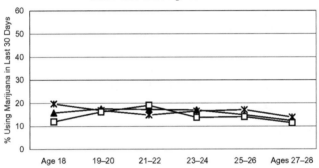

Males Who Were Age 18 in 1976–1982

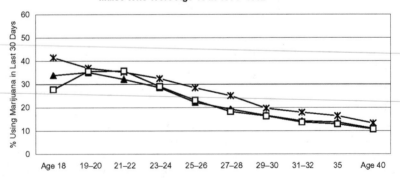

Percentage values in this figure are shown in Table A.1.3a in the appendix.

Figure 1.3a. Percentage reporting any marijuana use in the last 30 days by academic attainment at modal ages 21 to 22: males.

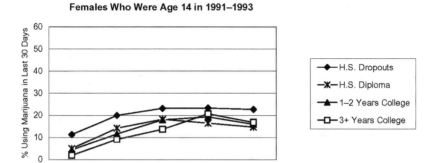

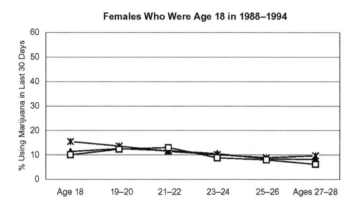

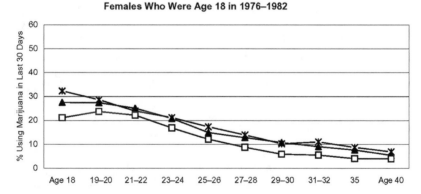

Percentage values in this figure are shown in Table A.1.3b in the appendix.

Figure 1.3b. Percentage reporting any marijuana use in the last 30 days by academic attainment at modal ages 21 to 22: females.

Heavy Drinking

Figure 1.4 presents prevalence rates for consuming five or more alcoholic drinks in a row on at least one occasion during the preceding 2 weeks. Once again the youngest respondents showed a clear negative correlation between substance use and later educational attainment. At age 14, those who would later drop out were about four times as likely to drink heavily as those who would later complete 3 or more years of college. The differences remained substantial at age 16, but by age 18 the differences had nearly disappeared. By age 22 those who had completed 3 or more years of college actually had the highest proportions of heavy drinkers among young women (42%) and also among young men (56%, essentially matched by the dropouts at 57%).

The older cohorts showed similar patterns of crossover. At age 18 those headed for college were a bit less likely than their age-mates to drink heavily, but by ages 19 to 20 that was no longer the case. Among members of the high school classes of 1988 to 1994, those who would complete 3 or more years of college were most likely to be among the heavy drinkers at ages 19 to 22, especially among women. But by the later 20s these distinctions had largely disappeared. Among the oldest cohorts, members of the high school classes of 1976 to 1982, the college years involved sharp increases in proportions of occasional heavy drinkers—essentially "catching up" with their less educationally successful age peers—but by their later 20s the correlations between heavy drinking and educational success were again negative.

In sum, heavy drinking is negatively correlated with educational success during adolescence (particularly ages 14–16). However, these negative links are reduced and sometimes reversed during the college years (ages 19–22), largely due to social role and context changes such as living arrangements in college (e.g., Bachman et al., 2002) and individual characteristics (e.g., Schulenberg & Maggs, 2002), matters discussed in chapter 9.

STUDYING COMPLEX CAUSAL RELATIONSHIPS IN NATURAL SETTINGS

The previous examples, along with the rest of the findings reported in this book, are based on self-reports of adolescents and young adults. In chapter 3, we say more about issues of accuracy in self-reports of substance use, but we and other researchers in this field are generally satisfied that respondents in surveys like ours strive to report truthfully and, to a large extent, succeed in reporting accurately. The more difficult problem is

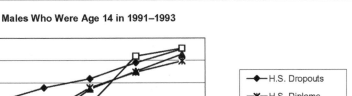

Males Who Were Age 14 in 1991–1993

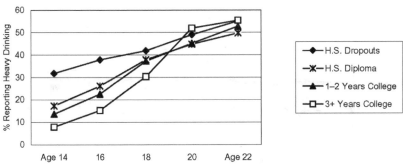

- ◆ H.S. Dropouts
- ✕ H.S. Diploma
- ▲ 1–2 Years College
- ☐ 3+ Years College

Males Who Were Age 18 in 1988–1994

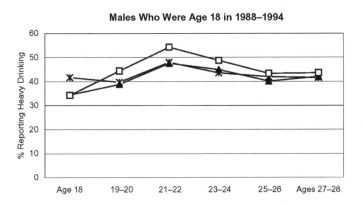

Males Who Were Age 18 in 1976–1982

Percentage values in this figure are shown in Table A.1.4a in the appendix.

Figure 1.4a. Percentage reporting any heavy drinking in the last 2 weeks by academic attainment at modal ages 21 to 22: males.

Females Who Were Age 14 in 1991–1993

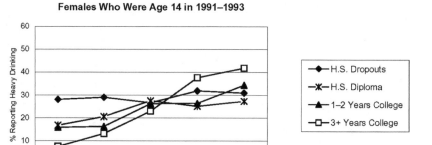

Females Who Were Age 18 in 1988–1994

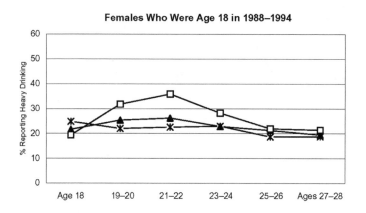

Females Who Were Age 18 in 1976–1982

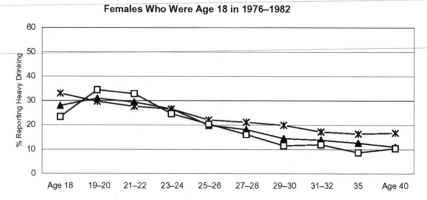

Percentage values in this figure are shown in Table A.1.4b in the appendix.

Figure 1.4b. Percentage reporting any heavy drinking in the last 2 weeks by academic attainment at modal ages 21 to 22: females.

the one mentioned at the start of this chapter—the problem of sorting out and deciding among the various possible causal interpretations of the negative links between academic success and substance use.

Research on the physical effects of substance use often employs genuine experiments, in which an independent variable (e.g., exposure to cigarette smoke) is manipulated to ascertain effects on a dependent variable (e.g., lung cancer). Most people find such research acceptable—provided it is carried out on animals (preferably rats rather than primates). Attempting to conduct a genuine experiment on how cigarette use might affect educational success is quite another matter; one might set out to examine whether and how exposure to cigarette smoke affects the ability of rats (or monkeys) to solve problems successfully, but far more difficult would be a study reversing the independent and dependent variables. Imagine the challenge of manipulating "educational success" among rats or monkeys and then testing whether that makes a difference in their "choosing to inhale" tobacco smoke.

So we are left with observations (in this case, self-report data), based on real people in the real world, from which to gain an understanding of the causal processes and mechanisms. Having panel data from the same individuals tracked over a number of years helps somewhat, as we tried to illustrate previously. Another source of help is data on some of those shared prior causes that may influence both educational success and substance use. In the chapters that follow, we examine a large number of such factors, and we attempt to control them in our more complex statistical analyses. At the same time, however, we attempt to provide enough descriptive data so that we do not lose sight of the "big picture" while immersed in multivariate coefficients.

WHAT IS THE "BIG PICTURE" THUS FAR?

We have not yet illustrated the impacts of shared prior causes. That has been left for later chapters. Suffice it to say for now that the factors examined include parental education and other family considerations, as well as early educational setbacks. Delinquent behavior is also a key potential prior cause. Some of these factors appear to make strong contributions to academic attainment, as well as to substance use during adolescence.

Throughout this book, we discuss several kinds of behavior that can be considered maladaptive or undesirable. Among these concepts, we use the terms *problem behavior* and *deviant behavior* as approximate synonyms for a broad, inclusive category of activities that are negatively related to academic attainment. At times, we discuss various forms of problem behaviors more specifically. In our study, these forms of problem behaviors include delinquency (or illegal offenses, primarily misdemeanors), substance use, and misbehaviors in school.

One portion of the big picture illustrated in this chapter (see Fig. 1.2) is that early educational successes and failures, as reflected in GPA at the end of eighth grade, are predictive of smoking. We have also illustrated that smoking, both throughout adolescence and into adulthood, remains consistently negatively correlated with later (age-22) academic attainment (see Fig. 1.1). Instances of heavy drinking and marijuana use during adolescence are similar to cigarette use in showing negative correlations with academic attainment (see Figs. 1.3 and 1.4). Moreover, early educational success (eighth-grade GPA) is negatively linked to adolescent alcohol use and illicit drug use, as reported in later chapters. Clearly, marijuana use at age 16 or cocaine use at age 18 cannot cause low grades during eighth grade. Later chapters explore the alternative causal interpretations—that early educational experiences and/or other shared prior causes may cause adolescent substance use.

Although early educational success relates negatively to all the forms of adolescent substance use we have examined, the figures presented previously illustrate that the longer term patterns of linkage differ considerably from one kind of substance to another. Most notably, the differences in cigarette use, once established during adolescence, remain largely intact throughout much of adulthood. The patterns for other forms of substance use are different, and alcohol use in particular shows effects of college-related experiences that tend to cancel and reverse (temporarily) the patterns of difference shown at younger ages. Although the story is in some respects loudest and clearest for cigarette use, with its serious long-term health risks, we want to emphasize that we do not take lightly any of the forms of substance use. Each involves risks—some more immediate and dramatic than others. The central finding that emerges from this book, in its totality, is that early educational success appears to be an important protective factor against all forms of adolescent substance use.

OVERVIEW OF CHAPTERS

Chapter 2 summarizes relevant literature, focusing on previous findings and relevant theory that informed the present work. Chapter 3 describes our panel of adolescents and provides an overview of analysis methods and issues. With this as a foundation, we then turn to an examination of how and perhaps why educational success is linked with substance use during adolescence and beyond.

We begin our analytic quest in chapter 4 with a close look at academic attainment (at modal age 22) and those factors that may be predictors of attainment. We examine bi- and multivariate correlates of attainment and then develop a structural equation model of attainment, taking advantage of the panel data to sort out chronological (and presumably causal) sequences.

In chapter 5, we expand the causal model to include a multi-item measure of delinquent behavior. We include this dimension because it is central to our notion that substance use is part of a syndrome of problem behaviors, including delinquency (Brook & Newcomb, 1995; Donovan & Jessor, 1985; Jessor & Jessor, 1977; Kandel, 1988). At the end of the chapter, we expand the model further to include cigarette use, marijuana use, cocaine use, and alcohol use.

The next four chapters consider each of these types of substance use in turn. In addition to the causal model, we employ several other analysis techniques to examine the links between the substance-use measures and other factors associated with educational success. We also compare our adolescent panel findings with data from the large-scale MTF surveys of 8th-, 10th-, and 12th-grade students, as well as adult high school graduates, which show substance-use changes in the United States in recent decades. The comparisons with these other MTF data sets place our findings within a larger context and provide further assurance that our adolescent panel data remain representative despite complexities introduced by panel attrition.

Chapter 10 summarizes our findings and presents our conclusions in greater detail than we have been able to provide in this brief introductory chapter. We are impressed by the consistencies in the findings, as well as the differences from one substance to another. Obviously, efforts to increase the educational successes of adolescents are valuable for many reasons having to do with adult accomplishments and adjustments; the findings in this book suggest that another important reason is protection against adolescent substance use and its long-term consequences.

Literature Review: Conceptual and Empirical Overview of Issues

Despite a large amount of research over the past few decades showing that academic achievement and failures are associated with substance use (see Dewey, 1999; Perkins & Borden, 2003, for reviews), the direction of the association between these behaviors is still in question. Many studies thus far have been cross-sectional, leaving researchers to guess at the mechanisms driving their findings. On one hand, substance use may decrease academic achievement by interfering with concentration, memory, and motivation, or by actually causing brain damage. Use of substances may be encouraged through associations with delinquent peers, which also provide incentive for truancy, misbehavior in school, and a devaluing of academic achievement. On the other hand, difficulty coping with school problems may lead adolescents to seek solace in substance use and associations with delinquent, low-achieving friends.

In this chapter, we review the literature regarding the connection between substance use and academic success or failure, and we consider how the current conceptual and empirical literature informs our study and interpretation of the findings. Our work in this book is guided, in large part, by a deductive approach to considering the various possible interrelations among indexes of educational success, substance use, related behaviors, and background characteristics. Our conceptual framework draws extensively from the relevant empirical and conceptual literature (exemplified by that reviewed later in this chapter) and is consistent with our own views about a developmental syndrome of adolescent difficulties (e.g., Bachman, Safron, Sy, & Schulenberg, 2003; Bachman & Schulenberg, 1993). Problem behaviors, which we view as the broader category of difficulties of interest in this book, include poor school adjustment, school misconduct (e.g., truancy, suspension), delinquent behaviors (including behaviors that may be offenses), and substance use. School difficulties typically come early in the sequence, and thus set the stage for involvement in delinquency and substance use. More detail about this general model is provided in chapters 4 and 5, and we revisit this model in our concluding chapter.

Our review of the literature in this chapter is necessarily selective. Because academic experiences begin much earlier than experimentation with illicit substances, we begin by examining the stability of educational success and failure. Then we review literature that links educational factors with various substances, as well as other related problem behaviors, and we discuss the interconnectedness of these factors in a developmental context. We conclude with a brief consideration of policy and intervention implications.

STABILITY OF EDUCATIONAL ACHIEVEMENT

Under most circumstances, educational achievement and motivation are quite stable across time (Feshbach & Feshbach, 1987; Harackiewicz, Barron, Tauer, & Elliot, 2002; Helmke & van Aken, 1995; Roeser, Eccles, & Freedman-Doan, 1999). Duchesne, Larose, Guay, Vitaro, and Tremblay (2005) examined trajectories of academic functioning and found that a large majority of French-Canadian students displayed stable levels of academic achievement from ages 10 to 13. However, their measurement of academic functioning relied on maternal perceptions of their children, rather than more objective measures such as test scores or grade point average (GPA). Chen and Kaplan (2003) used such a measure—poor grades—to show that academic achievement in middle school predicted educational attainment in early adulthood; a strong connection between achievement and educational attainment is common in other studies as well (Maggs, Frome, Eccles, & Barber, 1997).

Stability of educational achievement is facilitated by patterns in students' beliefs about themselves and their abilities. For instance, some students respond to failure in academic tasks by becoming less interested in the task and displaying less effort during subsequent similar tasks (Butler, 1999; Elliott & Dweck, 1988; Miller, 1986); students who are not interested in a task are less likely to engage in the task when given a choice (Jussim, Soffin, Brown, Ley, & Kohlhepp, 1992). Thus, early failure experiences in school can create a cycle of lowered academic motivation and performance.

Grade retention—being required to repeat a grade in school, rather than progressing to the next grade level with one's age-mates—is a strategy often used by educators to improve the performance of students who are failing or fall behind their peers. Unfortunately, early grade retention does not always allow students to catch up in their skills. Rather, early retention is associated with poorer academic achievement and school adjustment in later grades (Meisels & Liaw, 1993). Grade retention can be a stressful event for students, and many retained students report negative emotions regarding their lack of academic progression (Mantzicopoulos, 1997; Shepard & Smith, 1990). Possibly as a result of making unfavorable comparisons between themselves and peers, as well as having low academic achievement, students who have been retained are more likely to drop out of high school than their peers who could have been retained but were not (Jimerson, 1999; Roderick, 1994). Hence, just as early successes often predict later high achievement, early academic setbacks can lead to persistent poor achievement.

Long before students begin experimenting with substance use, early school experiences such as grade retention or successful completion of academic tasks guide students' academic achievement and affective reactions to school into relatively stable trajectories. Because substance use and school achievement do become related in adolescence, the early stability of achievement hints that school factors contribute to later problem behaviors or that exogenous variables contribute to both problems. However, normative stability in academic achievement may hide smaller segments of the student population whose substance use does alter their achievement trajectory. Therefore, we examine evidence for each of these causal accounts later in this chapter.

EDUCATIONAL SUCCESSES AND FAILURES ARE CONNECTED TO SUBSTANCE USE

As other researchers have noted, it is difficult to establish causal relationships between educational success and substance use (Dewey, 1999). One of the reasons a debate exists regarding the direction of effects between substance use and educational outcomes is the inconsistency of educational factors from study to study. Some studies investigate academic achievement measured by students' grades and test scores; some focus on investment, such as school bonding or academic motivation; and still others examine educational attainment with measures of high school dropout status or years of college attended. Few studies explore a variety of educational predictors or outcomes simultaneously. For the purposes of reviewing possible directional influences, the following sections make the reasonable assumption that the educational variables noted thus far are all indicators (positive or negative) of an underlying factor, akin to "success in school." At the end of this chapter, we make clear our hypotheses about the actual nature of the relation between substance use and various educational measures.

Cigarette Use

Of all licit and illicit drug use, cigarette smoking has one of the strongest relations to educational achievement, attainment, and school-related problems. In many cross-sectional studies, cigarette smoking has been positively related to suspensions from school and negatively related to academic performance (Bryant, Schulenberg, Bachman, O'Malley, & Johnston, 2000; Conwell et al., 2003; Hollar & Moore, 2004; Wright & Fitzpatrick, 2004).

Some evidence suggests that tobacco use drives down academic achievement. In a study of seventh graders, smokers were more likely than nonsmokers to be absent from school or class, and also were more likely to have low grades (Ellickson, Tucker, & Klein, 2001); longitudinal evidence from this same study showed that smoking during 7th grade predicted a greater likelihood of school-related problems and dropping out by 12th grade. Jacobsen and colleagues (2005) reported evidence suggesting that cigarette smoking during adolescence impairs working memory and attention, two cognitive abilities with important implications for academic performance. Furthermore, the negative relation between smoking and cognitive abilities continues well into adulthood (Whalley, Fox, Deary, & Starr, 2005). These studies show that smoking during early adolescence is a strong indicator of future academic problems.

Research also suggests that educational factors can predict cigarette use (Hu, Lin, & Keeler, 1998). In addition to finding that seventh-grade smokers faced later educational problems, Ellickson, Tucker, and Klein (2001) reported that these students were also more likely to have previously repeated grades in school. Low academic achievement among middle-school students has predicted concurrent cigarette use (Carvajal, Hanson, Downing, Coyle, & Pederson, 2004), use throughout adolescence (Bryant, Schulenberg, Bachman, O'Malley, & Johnston, 2000), and heavy smoking by 12th grade (Griffin, Botvin, Doyle, Diaz, & Epstein, 1999). A lack of enjoyment in school also predicts smoking among older adolescents and young adults (Brunswick & Messeri, 1983; Wang et al., 1999). Although many studies that show relations between tobacco use and school achievement use primarily White samples, poor achievement also predicts smoking initiation among adolescents of other ethnic groups (Brunswick & Messeri, 1984; Johnson & Hoffmann, 2000). In an urban, primarily African-American sample, Bryant and Zimmerman (2002) found that low achievement motivation is a risk factor for increased cigarette smoking over the course of high school, even among those students with high grades. Furthermore, across many countries, adults with low levels of education are the most likely to use cigarettes and the least likely to stop smoking (Chassin, Presson, Rose, & Sherman, 1996; Giskes et al., 2005; Werch, Dunn, & Woods, 1997; Wetter et al., 2005).

Research on cigarette use and educational success is consistent in finding a negative relation between the two, but inconclusive in the developmental story that describes which comes first. Part of the problem is that many researchers focus on only one outcome—either educational success or cigarette use—and do not attempt to model changes in both over time. We return to the discussion of causation later in the chapter. For now, we turn our attention to the possible connections between marijuana use and educational success.

Marijuana Use

As with tobacco use, some studies have shown that marijuana use negatively predicts educational success. In one prospective study of New Zealand adolescents' drug use, frequency of marijuana use predicted whether an individual left school without qualifications, which is roughly the equivalent of dropping out of high school among American students (Fergusson, Horwood, & Beautrais, 2003). Zimmerman and Schmeelk-Cone (2003) found that marijuana use during high school predicted students' high school completion status in an African-American sample.

Predicting marijuana use from educational success presents more complicated findings. For instance, although Fergusson and colleagues (2003) found a relation between leaving school without qualifications and subsequent marijuana use, after they controlled for students' background characteristics the relation disappeared. The sum of the findings in this study led the researchers to conclude that the association between marijuana use and educational attainment was not bidirectional, but rather that marijuana was the driving force behind the correlation.

Yet when educational indicators other than high school dropout status are used, a different picture seems to emerge. For instance, low grades during early and middle adolescence predict initiation to marijuana use by

Grade 10 (Ellickson, Tucker, Klein, & Saner, 2004). In addition, academic achievement appears to be a protective factor against the use of marijuana by African-American students (Wright & Fitzpatrick, 2004). Academic achievement is not the only construct that is predictive of marijuana use. Zimmerman and Schmeelk-Cone (2003) found that academic motivation predicted subsequent marijuana use among high school students, and marijuana use did not have predictive power for later academic motivation.

Research that examines the connection between marijuana use and educational success (like that which examines cigarette use) shows clearly that there is some link, but is inconclusive as to what is driving that link. On the one hand, using marijuana appears to have some impact on dropping out of high school, but poor academic achievement and motivation also appear to have some impact on marijuana use. We return to this complexity and the developmental implications later in the chapter after considering how other substances might be related to educational success.

Alcohol Use

Alcohol use should be considered somewhat differently than cigarette and marijuana use partly because it becomes statistically normative during adolescence, and also because its links with educational success become complex by late adolescence. Still, as is the case with cigarette and marijuana use, there is evidence to suggest that (a) educational difficulties contribute to alcohol use, (b) alcohol use contributes to educational difficulties, and (c) both are the result of more fundamental problems. For example, academic motivation negatively predicts initiation to drinking among sixth graders (Simons-Morton, 2004), poor academic achievement at seventh grade predicts frequency of alcohol use and heavy drinking (Ellickson & Hays, 1991), and during college having a high GPA and a high commitment to school are associated with a lower amount of binge drinking (Tibbetts & Whittimore, 2002). As an illustration of the opposite direction of influence, Hollar and Moore (2004) found that among 12th-grade students with disabilities, alcohol use and binge drinking negatively predicted their cumulative high school GPAs. As an example that both educational difficulties and alcohol use are caused by more fundamental difficulties, Braggio, Pishkin, Gameros, and Brooks (1993) administered the Peabody Individual Achievement Test to three groups: substance-dependent, alcohol-using adolescents residing in an inpatient hospital; adolescent hospital residents with conduct disorder; and nonhospitalized adolescents in a control group. They found that both patient groups scored lower on the test than the control group;

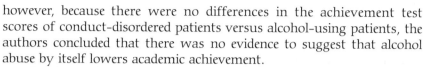

however, because there were no differences in the achievement test scores of conduct-disordered patients versus alcohol-using patients, the authors concluded that there was no evidence to suggest that alcohol abuse by itself lowers academic achievement.

What is unique about alcohol use (compared with use of other substances) is that there is literature suggesting that educational success is sometimes positively related to alcohol use. Indeed, using Monitoring the Future (MTF) 12th-grade panel data, Schulenberg, Bachman, O'Malley, and Johnston (1994) found that, although high school students' college plans were a protective factor against contemporaneous alcohol and cigarette use, they proved to be a risk factor for increased alcohol use and heavy drinking during the transition to adulthood (although they did remain a protective factor against increased cigarette use). Similarly, Maggs et al. (1997) showed that alcohol use during high school positively predicted years of education at age 20. Obviously, what is behind these relations is the fact that going to college relates both to doing well in school and to escalating drinking during late adolescence and the transition to adulthood, highlighting the reversal of the association between drinking and educational success that is seen at other ages and in other populations (Schulenberg & Maggs, 2002). Thus, although it is clear that alcohol use is associated with educational outcomes, the connection between alcohol use and educational outcomes appears to vary across development and subsamples.

Other Illicit Drugs and Multiple Substance Use

The three substances discussed previously—cigarettes, marijuana, and alcohol—are the substances most widely used and abused by adolescents (Ellickson, Hays, & Bell, 1992). Because use of these three substances is somewhat common, it is relatively easy to study the relation of their use and educational outcomes. Other substances, such as cocaine, inhalants, and narcotics, are much less likely to be used, especially during early adolescence. Of course, the lower rate of use is positive in terms of public health, but it creates problems for those who seek to conduct research on questions related to these substances. Although fewer studies have examined the relationship between educational outcomes and use of other illicit drugs, there is some evidence linking the two.

Jeynes (2002) found that being under the influence of cocaine while at school predicted lower academic achievement, but only before taking into account the additional influences of cigarette, alcohol, and marijuana use. Similarly, Block, Erwin, and Ghoneim (2002) found that stimulant and polydrug users (as well as a group of alcohol users) in drug treatment programs performed worse than a community control group on tests of verbal, math, memory, and abstraction abilities. Although this study did not include measures of academic performance in the form of grades, demonstration of such cognitive impairments suggests that achievement would likely decline among substance-dependent students.

However, reflecting the opposite causal direction, Block and colleagues (2002) also reported that the patients in drug treatment programs had lower standardized test scores in fourth grade than a community control group. Sutherland and Shepherd (2001) found that low perceived academic achievement and low expectations for educational attainment both discriminate between English youth who have used any illicit drugs and those who have not. Likewise, high academic achievement has been shown to be a protective factor against use of other illicit drugs among adolescents who already use marijuana (Stronski, Ireland, Michaud, Narring, & Resnick, 2000).

A few studies provide more mixed results regarding the relation between illicit drug use and educational factors. Guagliardo, Huang, Hicks, and D'Angelo (1998) reported that initiation of drug use at an early age predicted dropping out of high school. Yet they also found that delayed progression through school, measured as being old for grade or a dropout as opposed to being on track, was a risk factor for substance use. In another case, Ensminger, Juon, and Fothergill (2002) reported that males who had above-average school readiness scores when they were in the first grade were less likely to use cocaine in their early 30s than those with low school readiness scores. However, school readiness scores were not predictive of adult females' current cocaine use.

Previous research using MTF data has shown both direct and indirect effects of high school GPA on illicit drug use (Schulenberg et al., 1994). In this study, the indirect effects lasted into young adulthood; part of the concurrent association between achievement and drug use was mediated by truancy and evenings spent out during high school. Such a link between substance use and other potential problem behaviors is quite common, as we describe later in this chapter.

DELINQUENCY AND OTHER PROBLEM BEHAVIORS

Substance use and poor academic achievement are not only related to one another—they are also often seen in adolescents who exhibit other problematic behaviors (Luthar & Ansary, 2005; Wiesner & Windle, 2004). For instance, educational commitment and aspirations are negatively associated with delinquent behaviors in both White and Latino youth (Vazsonyi & Flannery, 1997). Similarly, academic achievement is negatively related to delinquency (Chang & Le, 2005; Luthar & Ansary, 2005; Vazsonyi & Flannery, 1997). Violent behaviors are more common among high school dropouts and students with poor grades than among students with passing grades (Beauvais, Chavez, Oetting, & Deffenbacher, 1996), and low grades predict delinquency 1 year later (Crosnoe, 2002). However, early academic difficulty does not always lead to delinquent behavior. McCoy and Reynolds (1999) reported that early grade retention does predict subsequent academic achievement difficulties, but it does not predict later delinquency. When delinquent youth perform poorly in school, their academic standing rarely improves, so delinquency during adolescence also predicts lower educational attainment by adulthood (Tanner, Davies, & O'Grady, 1999).

Deviant behavior among seventh graders predicts the frequency of their alcohol use as well as heavy alcohol use (Ellickson & Hays, 1991). Furthermore, drinking during middle adolescence predicts violent behavior during young adulthood (Wells, Horwood, & Fergusson, 2004). Likewise, delinquent behavior predicts an initiation to or an increase in marijuana use (van den Bree & Pickworth, 2005). Because deviant behaviors must be engaged in outside of conventional social settings, it is no surprise that delinquency and substance use are highly related. Some of the association can be attributed to involvement with a deviant peer group (Duncan, Duncan, & Strycker, 2000). Alternatively, a general tendency toward deviancy or risk-taking behavior might account for the relation between delinquency and substance use. We explore this last possibility further in the next section.

Unfortunately, it is clear that using substances and poor performance in school are only two aspects of a wide range of problem behaviors that may be exhibited by adolescents. Throughout this book, we acknowledge the overlap in undesirable behavioral tendencies even as we attempt to distinguish between one form and another. For instance, in chapter 5 we focus on delinquent behaviors or activities that have the potential to result in an arrest. Certainly, drinking alcohol while underage or smoking marijuana could be included in the category of delinquent behaviors, but we have chosen to make a distinction between substance use and other offenses. Although others may prefer to define constructs differently, we chose to think about problem behaviors primarily in terms of (a) substance use, (b) offenses that are not related to substance use, and (c) school misbehavior (including poor performance).

EXOGENOUS VARIABLE EXPLANATIONS

Several of the studies described so far suggest that there may be causal influences between substance use and educational success, although there are different assertions about which comes first. Of course, much of the relation may be spurious—many other factors have been empirically related to both. One of these exogenous variables, or potential confounds, is family background or composition. For instance, Pierret (2001) compared adolescents in intact families to those whose families had experienced at least one divorce; children from divorced families had lower GPAs and were more likely to use marijuana. Other studies have also shown that home environment characteristics in early childhood, such as parenting and attachment, predict educational achievement (Ferguson, Jimerson, & Dalton, 2001; Mullis, Rathge, & Mullis, 2003; Riala, Isohanni, Jokelainen, Jones, & Isohanni, 2003) as well as substance use (Caspers, Cadoret, Langbehn, Yucuis, & Troutman, 2005; Miller & Volk, 2002).

Jessor and Jessor's (1977) Theory of Problem Behavior is commonly cited as an explanation for the co-occurrence of low academic achievement and substance use. According to this view, multiple risky or problem behaviors often appear in tandem within individuals partly because some individuals have a general tendency for such activities. Rather than either low school success or substance use serving as a risk factor for the other, Jessor, Donovan, and Costa (1991) claimed that a psychosocial tendency for unconventionality would be a risk factor for both.

Research has supported this notion of a general risk factor for a constellation of several problem behaviors (Costa, Jessor, & Donovan, 1989; Ellickson et al., 2001; Ketterlinus, Lamb, & Nitz, 1994). Jessor's framework has been popular for theoretical explanations of such findings and has garnered much support and credibility. Yet it remains difficult to distinguish empirically between one or more underlying casual factors and reciprocal relations between several or all problem behaviors. Although unconventionality may increase one's likelihood of exhibiting problem behaviors, that does not preclude some problem behaviors from preceding and influencing others.

An illustration of developmental influences within a constellation of problem behaviors lies in the phenomenon of drug sequencing. It is common for youth to use some substances before initiating the use of others (Ellickson, Hays, & Bell, 1992; Hawkins, Hill, Guo, & Battin-Pearson, 2002; Kandel & Yamaguchi, 2002). Although populations differ, tobacco and alcohol are usually found to precede marijuana use, which is then initiated before other "harder" illicit drugs. In this example, it cannot be said that alcohol or tobacco use cause marijuana use, but youth who use a legal drug illegally (while underage) may then be at greater risk for further substance use. If adolescents find that their underage use presents no serious consequences, they may come to the conclusion that other substances are not as harmful as they previously believed, and they may be more likely to use those as well. Also, they may associate more often with polysubstance-using peers. Similar to drug-sequencing patterns, evidence from longitudinal studies suggests that early educational failure and poor academic achievement are not simply two of many problem behaviors in a general constellation, but rather are likely to serve as a gateway for both delinquency and substance-use initiation.

LONG-TERM RELATIONS BETWEEN EDUCATIONAL FAILURE AND SUBSTANCE USE

In previous sections, we primarily reported evidence from cross-sectional or short-term longitudinal studies; this evidence has been rather inconclusive. In the following paragraphs, we report the findings of longer longitudinal studies and research that has attempted to model bidirectional or reciprocal effects. We use this evidence to draw firmer conclusions and illustrate the theoretical model that informed our current study.

First, it appears that achievement and ability during the elementary school years are useful in predicting substance use during adolescence and even into adulthood. In a prospective study of impoverished African-American children, Crum et al. (1998) collected reports of classroom behaviors from participants' first-grade teachers. Children who were identified by their teachers as underachieving and exhibiting maladaptive behaviors had a 60% greater likelihood of predicted lifetime prevalence of alcohol use disorders at ages 32 to 33. Academic and social behaviors measured in middle elementary school predict substance use in 9th and 10th grades (Hops, Davis, & Lewin, 1999).

Second, it appears that there is some reciprocity in the relation between educational success and substance use. Andrews and Duncan (1997) modeled reciprocal relations between substance use (cigarette, alcohol, and marijuana use) and academic motivation. Over 4 years, they found that changes in adolescents' smoking and academic motivation each had direct effects on the other. Likewise, changes in marijuana use and academic motivation predicted one another, but only indirectly.

Among the studies that have looked for reciprocal relations between substance use and educational success, not all have found evidence of such effects. For instance, a short-term longitudinal study of ninth-grade students showed that grades in the first half of the school year predicted drug use at the end of the school year, but drug use in the fall was not predictive of changes in grades over the school year (Luthar & Cushing, 1997). Previous research utilizing MTF panel data has shown that, although academic achievement and school misbehavior show a negative reciprocal relation from 8th to 10th grade, and both of these variables predict cigarette use in the 10th and 12th grades, cigarette use influenced neither achievement nor misbehavior (Bryant et al., 2000). Furthermore, in contrast to their findings concerning cigarette and marijuana use, Andrews and Duncan (1997) found no relation in either direction between changes in alcohol use and academic motivation. They qualified these findings by acknowledging that, among the adolescents in their sample who were selected for being at risk for substance use, alcohol consumption was normative. Although use varied by age and time of measurement, between 61% and 80% of their sample reported drinking alcohol at least once a month. Normative use may have artificially weakened the link between alcohol consumption and academic motivation.

Certainly, educational failure, substance use, and other problem behaviors during adolescence are related. There is no doubt that exogenous variables, such as mental health problems or early home environments, may contribute to all of these phenomena. However, the evidence accumulated to this point is strong enough to warrant a belief that education and substance use are directly linked.

Although we proposed earlier that one could examine educational variables together, as an overall construct called *educational success*, these studies hint that not all educational variables have the same relation to substance use. The developmental timing of different educational measures seems to have an impact on the relation to be found with substance use. Zimmerman and Schmeelk-Cone (2003) provided an example of this by showing that low academic motivation among adolescents predicted alcohol use, and that alcohol use in turn negatively predicted graduation from high school. Our view is that if such a developmental sequence is common, then an effect of substance use on educational success may grow stronger over time through the buildup of educational failures or setbacks. Thus, substance use may have a greater impact on later-occurring, cumulative educational indicators (such as dropping out of high school or educational attainment in adulthood), rather than earlier or more immediate measures (such as school engagement).

The pattern of influence between education and substance use appears to be something close to the following: Educational failure and repetitious poor achievement generate distress and self-blame in students (Mantzicopoulos, 1997). Such distress eventually compels students to disengage from school, devaluing the academic world in order to protect their own sense of self-worth, rather than continuing their effort in the face of additional potential failure. In an attempt to cope with their distress and alienation from school, low-achieving students turn to substance use and similar-minded peers (Crosnoe, 2002; Ellickson & Hays, 1991). Involvement in delinquency and substance use—consequences of academic failure and co-occurring with low academic motivation—may interfere with academic performance and do predict lower educational achievement and attainment.

POLICY AND INTERVENTION IMPLICATIONS

This chapter is not meant to be pessimistic. Although we suggest that early educational achievement has significant implications for substance use and delinquency, students who are at risk for educational failure need not be doomed. Despite the long-term stability of educational failure and success, interventions have proved useful in altering students' educational trajectories and related problem behaviors. An evaluation of a long-running intervention program for at-risk children in Chicago, Illinois, found that preschool intervention participation was positively predictive of educational attainment at age 20 (Reynolds, Temple, Robertson, & Mann, 2001). There are also many successful alternatives to grade retention. Shepard and Smith (1990) concluded that remedial programs, after-school or summer programs, and tutoring by adults or peers are educational policies that are more economically prudent and show better results for academic achievement than grade retention.

It may sound trite to say that preventing academic failure and poor achievement will fix America's drug problem. If it were so easy to pass all children, while still ensuring rigorous learning standards, wouldn't we already do so? The truth of the matter is that we do need to acknowledge different degrees of learning and performance, and therefore we may need to give some students poor grades. Similarly, achievement tests are purposively standardized to enable comparison between students' scores; by definition, some students will have scores that are below average. Short of ridding our educational system of all accountability, some critics may argue that we cannot alter the connection between educational failure and substance use. They may claim that spending funds on drug prevention programs and treatment centers is the only way to combat the problem of substance use.

Yet educational research has shown us another way. Students' reactions to an academic failure vary. Some students are able to cope in a positive manner, staying focused on problem solving and improvement (Diener & Dweck, 1978; Hong, Chiu, & Dweck, 1999). These students may maintain an orientation toward mastery goals, which would allow them to focus on personal improvement and learning (Meece, Blumenfeld, & Hoyle, 1988; Pintrich, 2000). They may also suffer less negative affect after the failure experience (Elliott & Dweck, 1988; Mantzicopoulos, 1997). Further details regarding the relation of students' motivation and their subsequent achievement and educational attainment can be found in work by Fredricks, Blumenfeld, and Paris (2004); Pintrich (2003); and Schunk and Ertmer (2000). Luckily, there are many things that parents, teachers, and school staff can do to promote positive attitudes and academic engagement in students (Ryan & Deci, 2000; Stipek & Kowalski, 1989). A comprehensive review of educational policies designed to help students deal well with poor academic performance is not the aim of this book, but for some suggestions see Maehr and Midgley (1996). The goals promoted in schools and classrooms are influential in determining how students view their own abilities and how they react to their educational failures as well as their successes. When students are able to cope effectively with academic setbacks, we believe they will be less likely to fall into a downward spiral of educational failure or resort to substance use and other problem behaviors.

Unfortunately, the effects of educational disengagement or failure begin quite early. Poor educational achievement is not the sole predictor of substance use and other problem behaviors, but they are strongly related. Our conclusion from previous literature, which is supported by our research presented in the following chapters, is that early educational interventions, additional support for low-achieving students, and a focus on personal growth rather than social comparisons could be some of the most effective ways to decrease substance use and delinquency when students reach adolescence.

Chapter 3

Survey Methods and Analysis Strategies

The Monitoring the Future (MTF) adolescent panel is the basis for most analyses in this book. The age span covered is not limited to adolescence, of course; although the study followed young men and women through adolescence, it continued following them into young adulthood. Nevertheless, the term *adolescent panel* seems appropriate because our data collection began with adolescents near the end of eighth grade, when most had reached age 14, and because the analyses reported here focus heavily on experiences prior to or during adolescence. We link these early experiences to academic attainment in early adulthood, 8 years after the initial survey (when most had reached age 22). But our analyses pay special attention to whether substance use during adolescence (measured at modal ages 14, 16, and 18) is influenced by earlier educational successes and failures, and whether adolescent substance use in turn influences subsequent academic attainment. So although we include some events and circumstances that precede adolescence, as well as some that follow, we look most closely at ages 14 to 18—a crucial period during middle and late adolescence.

At age 14, virtually all adolescents in the United States are still enrolled in school; but well before that age, they have had many formative educational experiences, developed skills (or not), and recorded successes and failures. By age 18, some individuals have dropped out of high school, most are about to graduate, and many have arranged to enter college in a few months. As for substance use, we have already illustrated (in chap. 1) that most of the initiation into daily cigarette smoking or current (monthly) marijuana use occurs between ages 14 and 18, as does much of the initiation of alcohol use and occasional heavy drinking. Thus, the age span covered by our adolescent panel is a period of many important events and experiences, in terms of both education and substance use.

A BRIEF HISTORY OF THE MTF ADOLESCENT PANEL

The MTF project began in 1975 with a large nationally representative survey of high school seniors clustered in public and private schools throughout the coterminous United States. A new sample of high school seniors has been surveyed each year thereafter. Additionally, mail follow-up surveys of subsamples from each graduating high school cohort have been included in the study, with follow-ups now extending to age 40 (as illustrated in the figures in chap. 1).[1] Beginning in 1991, the program of annual in-school surveys was expanded to include 8th- and 10th-grade students (independent samples in separate schools), along with the continuing surveys of 12th-grade students. Extensive details on survey design and procedures are available in Bachman, Johnston, O'Malley, & Schulenberg (2006), and Johnston et al. (2005b,c).

The 8th- and 10th-grade surveys permit monitoring of behaviors at younger ages, including assessment of substance-use behaviors at earlier stages of development, as well as attitudes and beliefs relevant to substance use. Another important advantage of the surveys of lower grades is a broader inclusiveness than is possible with the 12th-grade samples. Specifically, the 12th-grade samples omit nearly all high school dropouts (the only exceptions are those who drop out very late), whereas relatively few students drop out before the end of 10th grade, and virtually none drop out as early as the end of 8th grade (see appendix A in Johnston et al. [2005b] for a discussion of dropouts and the effect of their exclusion from the study). This much greater inclusiveness of the eighth-grade samples prompted us to test whether a program of mail follow-up surveys would eventually yield representative samples of dropouts (as well as graduates, of course). An additional goal of the follow-up effort was to permit us to track important developmental changes in behaviors for representative samples of adolescents in the United States.

Given our primary goal of generating follow-up samples that included many who would become high school dropouts, our initial sampling

---

[1]Follow-ups have begun for some respondents who have reached age 45, but those data are not included in the chapter 1 figures.

procedure stratified according to several factors having to do with educational success, and our targeting for follow-up oversampled those at higher risk for dropping out of school. (Weights to correct for these differential sampling rates are always applied during analyses.) Mail follow-ups of the selected eighth graders took place at 2-year intervals. It became clear, as we expected, that the same factors that predict dropping out of high school also tend to predict nonparticipation in follow-up surveys. Intensive tracking and recruiting efforts improved matters somewhat; nevertheless, the dropout samples were not optimal for providing annual estimates of substance use in this population, and we concluded that a continuing effort to follow up new samples was not justified given the original epidemiological goal of obtaining nationally representative samples of high school dropouts. By that time, however, we had obtained follow-up data from considerable numbers of those who had been in our eighth-grade samples in 1991, 1992, and 1993—including a large number who had dropped out of high school. We had already "taken our main losses" with these panels in terms of attrition; we thus felt that continued follow-up efforts would be a good investment, particularly with respect to our other etiologic goals of tracking behavior changes during adolescence and into early adulthood. Accordingly, in close consultation with the study sponsor, we opted to limit future follow-up efforts to our panel samples from the eighth-grade classes of 1991 to 1993.

By 2001, we had collected four follow-up surveys from these cohorts (through modal age 22), and these data are of primary interest in this book. (Subsequently, we obtained a fifth follow-up survey at modal age 24, but this book uses those later-arriving data only for a limited number of confirmatory analyses included in the appendix.)

To sum up this brief history, the adolescent panel used in this book consists of several thousand young men and women first surveyed in 1991, 1992, or 1993 as part of the eighth-grade cross-sectional MTF surveys and then tracked using mail follow-up surveys at 2-year intervals. Our respondents have provided self-report data at modal ages 14, 16, 18, 20, and 22. As detailed later, these data include family background, educational experiences, delinquent behaviors, and substance use; also, of particular importance, the data include academic attainment at age 22—a point 4 years after most graduated from high school. Thus, we have been able to examine a nationally representative sample—from age 14 (when most had not yet become seriously involved with any sort of substance use) tracked through age 22 (by which time some were high school dropouts, others were college graduates, and the rest were arrayed across the intermediate levels of academic attainment).

SAMPLE CHARACTERISTICS AND REPRESENTATIVENESS

The analyses reported in this book are intended primarily to examine relationships among factors in the lives of adolescents and young adults, and a minimum requirement for such analyses is a sample that includes a wide variety of individuals and characteristics. But an important additional purpose of the book is to provide accurate descriptive data; to meet that objective, we need an accurately representative sample. Some of the more technical aspects of the sampling and survey procedures are described in the appendix; the present section provides an overview of the most important of those procedures.

Survey Methods

The MTF surveys of eighth-grade students were conducted in public and private schools, selected by a multistage probability sampling procedure so as to be representative of students throughout the 48 contiguous United States. The numbers of participating schools were 162 in 1991, 159 in 1992, and 156 in 1993; the numbers of eighth-grade students surveyed were 17,844, 19,015, and 18,820, respectively. This large base has been useful for the MTF epidemiological reporting, and the in-school survey administration procedures permitted the data to be gathered in a cost-effective fashion. The more expensive mail procedures used to generate panel data required us to limit follow-up sample sizes; fortunately, the obtained panel samples are of adequate size for our purposes, particularly given that we had oversampled those at greatest risk of becoming high school dropouts. This oversampling, of course, requires the use of corrective weights in analysis, with lower weights assigned to the (originally oversampled) high-risk individuals; otherwise, the samples would be distorted and show disproportionately large numbers of individuals with low grades and poor school experiences.

The primary purpose of oversampling high-risk students was to increase the (unweighted) numbers of dropouts in later follow-ups. Another purpose was to increase the (again unweighted) numbers of respondents involved in problem behaviors such as delinquency and substance use, both of which occur more frequently among students at high academic risk. Of course, the advantage of these greater raw numbers of cases is an improved degree of precision in examining relatively rare behaviors. A further advantage of our oversampling of individuals at high academic risk is that it provided some counterbalancing against the higher than average panel losses (panel attrition) among the high-risk individuals.[2]

Response Rates

As just mentioned, follow-up response rates were poorer than average among those at highest academic risk. Even after extensive efforts to track down respondents and encourage them to complete the questionnaires, response rates at the first follow-up (modal age 16) differed sharply; 91% of those in the lowest risk stratum completed this initial follow-up questionnaire, contrasted with only 60% of those in the highest risk stratum. These differences continued throughout the later follow-ups, as detailed in the appendix (see Table A.3.1).

Although total response rates can be calculated in several ways, it seems most appropriate and accurate to present response rates after inclusion of weights to compensate for the initial stratification, as shown in Table 3.1. When this is done, overall response rates are about 81% for the first follow-up, 67% for the second (Wave 3, modal age 18), 63% for the third (Wave 4, modal age 20), and 57% for the fourth (Wave 5, modal age 22). Table 3.1 also shows that response rates dropped more steeply for males than females.

Not only were panel losses disproportionately high among individuals at high academic risk, losses were also disproportionately high among individuals who had been involved with cigarette use and/or other substance use by the end of eighth grade. (Of course, these often were the same individuals.) So the problem for analyses such as those presented here is that panel attrition can distort the samples, making them less representative. Specifically, panel attrition could lead us to underestimate dropping out, delinquency, and substance use.

---

[2]The stratification by Academic Risk Score was the primary factor in developing the follow-up target samples. Additional selection procedures were employed to make the target samples (within each of the four risk strata) as accurately representative as possible with respect to geographical region, gender, ethnicity, and drug use. Further, individuals who reported frequent absence during the preceding 4 weeks (due to illness, truancy, or other reasons) were proportionately oversampled to correct for the bias introduced by not including those who were absent on the day of the survey. These additional selection procedures had relatively minor impacts on the samples; details are included in the appendix.

TABLE 3.1
Response Rates by Gender*

| | Wave 1, Modal Age 14 |
	Wtd. N^*
Males	2885
Females	3050
Total	5936

| | Wave 2, Modal Age 16 | |
	Wtd. N^*	% of Age-14 Target
Males	2252	78
Females	2567	84
Total	4820	81

| | Wave 3, Modal Age 18 | |
	Wtd. N^*	% of Age-14 Target
Males	1715	59
Females	2239	73
Total	3955	67

| | Wave 4, Modal Age 20 | |
	Wtd. N^*	% of Age-14 Target
Males	1586	55
Females	2141	70
Total	3726	63

| | Wave 5, Modal Age 22 | |
	Wtd. N^*	% of Age-14 Target
Males	1420	49
Females	1975	65
Total	3395	57

*Ns in this table have been weighted to compensate for the initial selection stratification (see text).

There are various ways of dealing with the problems of attrition when analyzing panel data (Allison, 2003; Kalton, 1983; McGuigan, Ellickson, Hays, & Bell, 1997). One way is to limit analyses to only those who provide complete follow-up data; that avoids problems of missing data, but distorts the sample as just noted. The other extreme is to exclude no one, but try to fill in the gaps for many respondents by imputing the missing data (a process discussed briefly in the following section). In the present analyses, we follow a middle ground. We have been cautious about imputation, particularly when it comes to academic attainment. Accordingly, we have included in these analyses only those who participated in at least one of the follow-ups occurring *after* high school—that is, the third (modal age 20) or the fourth (modal age 22). This provided us with complete age-22 academic attainment data for the great majority of included respondents, and for the rest it gave us attainment information (including dropout status) through age 20. That also left us with most of our original target sample (70%, weighted, which we consider to be a decent level of retention for large-scale panel studies of adolescents and young adults).

Nevertheless, two problems remain. First, by *excluding* from the panel analyses those who did not participate in either the age-20 or age-22 follow-ups, we introduced certain distortions, including underestimates of early substance use. Second, by *including* in the panel analyses some individuals who missed whole data collections or skipped certain questionnaire items, we were left with a certain amount of missing data— holes in the panel data that needed to be filled in order to carry out some of our more complex analyses. We addressed these two problems with two different techniques that work well in combination. We used an imputation technique to fill in any missing data for those individuals who were included in the panel. To take account of the roughly 30% (weighted) who were excluded, we employed poststratification reweighting to recreate the original eighth-grade distributions for a number of key variables.

Imputation

As just noted, some of those who participated in the age-20 and/or age-22 follow-ups missed one or more of the earlier follow-ups, and thus were missing all of the data collected in those surveys. Others participated in all follow-ups, but still missed some of the questions for one reason or another. All of these instances of missing data needed to be taken into account. The approach we chose was to use a computer program called

IVEware (Raghunathan, Lepkowski, Van Hoewyk, & Solenberger, 2001) that, in effect, estimates what the missing data should be based on all other responses of the individual in question, as well as how variables are interrelated among other respondents (see also Raghunathan, Solenberger, & Van Hoewyk, 2002).

Poststratification

Even after using the imputation program to fill in the missing data on those included in the adolescent panel, we still had the problem of dealing with the roughly 30% who had been targeted for the panel but did not participate long enough to be included (i.e., those whose panel participation ended before age 20). Because we had age-14 data for everyone, we could ascertain how much distortion resulted from the loss of these individuals; most notably, we could see that substance use at age 14 had been lower among those who would continue participating as panel members, compared with those who would not.

To deal with this problem, at least in part, we used poststratification to reweight the retained panel sample so as to reproduce as nearly as practicable the original age-14 distributions along a number of key dimensions. The details are spelled out in the appendix. In brief, we separated respondents into categories according to substance use (smoking, drinking, marijuana use, and cocaine use), a measure of academic success (consisting of the Academic Risk Score mentioned earlier, with extra weight given to grade point average in eighth grade), and a race/ethnicity dimension that captured major differences in panel attrition (African-Americans and Hispanics showed lower than average rates of panel participation).

The revised weighting reproduced the original age-14 total sample distributions very closely, especially in measures of substance use. To take just one example, this poststratification approach means that panel participants who had smoked at age 14 were given somewhat increased sample weights to compensate for the fact that early smokers were less likely than average to participate in the panel surveys through at least age 20. We are under no illusion that age-14 smokers who continued in the study are identical to age-14 smokers who did not, but we believe they are at least somewhat similar, particularly when matched on academic success and race/ethnicity. The practical effect of this particular reweighting is not only a recapturing of the total sample proportions of smokers at age 14; it also yields higher estimated proportions of smokers at later ages than if the reweighting were not done. Moreover, those higher estimates are very consistent with data from the MTF surveys of

12th-grade students and young adults (with dropouts excluded from the comparisons; see Bachman, Johnston et al., 2006).

Further Weighting of the Sample

One further problem arises because of the several kinds of weighting involved in developing the adolescent panel used for analyses in this book. Recall that in selecting target follow-up samples from among the participants in our initial eighth-grade samples, we overselected those at high risk for dropping out and underselected those most likely to be educationally successful. That meant that in later analyses we needed to downweight the former and upweight the latter. The differences in actual response rates among these initial selection strata were such that, when our poststratification step was applied, the downweighting versus upweighting distinctions were reduced. Nevertheless, it remained the case that some categories of respondents had fewer real observations than their numbers of weighted cases. As an example, among women who completed 3 or more years of college, we would have had 900 weighted cases based on an actual 690 observations. Our solution to this problem was to further adjust *all* weights by a factor of .75 to generate an "Effective N."[3] Thus, in the example just noted, our weighted number of cases (i.e., the Effective N) is now 675, or just slightly lower than the 690 observations on which they were based.

The overall downweighting of the sample by a factor of .75 has no effect on means, correlations, or other coefficients, except that standard errors are increased by 15% (the calculation was 1.0 divided by the square root of .75, which equals 1.15). This slightly conservative approach is also intended to take account of any other design effects involved in our multistage stratified sample.

MEASURES USED

A complete listing of the measures used in our analyses, along with means and standard deviations, is provided in Table 3.2. Question wordings, including response categories, are provided in Table A.3.2 in the appendix.

---

[3]For more on the "Effective N" concept, see the appendix section on "N—or what's in a number?"

TABLE 3.2
Descriptive Statistics

	Scale Range		Males Effective *N* = 1361		Females Effective *N* = 1739	
	Min.	Max.	Mean	Standard Deviation	Mean	Standard Deviation
African-American	0	1	0.13	0.33	0.14	0.34
Hispanic	0	1	0.09	0.29	0.10	0.30
Other race	0	1	0.16	0.37	0.15	0.36
White	0	1	0.62	0.49	0.61	0.49
Large MSA	0	1	0.27	0.45	0.27	0.44
Other MSA	0	1	0.45	0.50	0.48	0.50
Non-MSA	0	1	0.27	0.45	0.25	0.43
Parents' education level	1	11	6.82	2.40	6.53	2.44
Number of parents Wave 1	0	2	1.75	0.52	1.74	0.50
Number of parents Wave 2	0	2	1.74	0.52	1.68	0.56
Number of parents Wave 3	0	2	1.63	0.67	1.52	0.73
Lived with 2 parents Waves 1–3	0	1	0.65	0.48	0.59	0.49
Parent involvement index Wave 1	4	16	11.52	2.87	11.41	2.66
Parent involvement index Wave 2	4	16	10.54	2.71	10.17	2.67
Parent involvement index Wave 3	4	16	8.96	2.88	8.94	2.69
Held back grade 8 or earlier	1	3	1.28	0.53	1.18	0.42
Suspended/expelled grade 8 or earlier	1	3	1.45	0.75	1.22	0.55
GPA (self-reported) Wave 1	1	6	3.59	1.33	3.84	1.30
GPA (self-reported) Wave 2	1	6	3.44	1.22	3.69	1.26
GPA (self-reported) Wave 3	1	6	3.61	1.21	3.94	1.18
Mean secondary school GPA	1	6	3.55	1.08	3.83	1.10
College plans Wave 1	1	4	3.25	0.92	3.45	0.78
College plans Wave 2	1	4	3.18	0.90	3.34	0.86
College plans Wave 3	1	4	3.05	1.03	3.28	0.95
Mean secondary school college plans	1	4	3.18	0.84	3.38	0.74
Held back Wave 1 to Wave 2	0	1	0.08	0.27	0.05	0.23
Held back Wave 2 to Wave 3	0	1	0.10	0.30	0.07	0.25
Suspended/expelled W1 to W2	0	1	0.15	0.36	0.11	0.32
Suspended/expelled W2 to W3	0	1	0.16	0.37	0.10	0.30
Serious scholastic setbacks W1 to W2	0	2	0.23	0.46	0.17	0.41
Serious scholastic setbacks W2 to W3	0	2	0.26	0.50	0.17	0.41
High school dropout by Wave 3	0	1	0.16	0.36	0.14	0.35
Sent to the office Wave 1	1	5	2.02	1.16	1.53	0.92
Sent to the office Wave 2	1	5	1.79	1.01	1.46	0.87
Sent to the office Wave 3	1	5	1.76	1.06	1.34	0.77
Days cut school Wave 1	1	7	1.40	1.11	1.40	1.09
Days cut school Wave 2	1	8	1.83	1.68	1.71	1.46
Days cut school Wave 3	1	8	2.87	2.27	2.39	2.02
Skipped classes Wave 1	1	6	1.28	0.83	1.30	0.82
Skipped classes Wave 2	1	6	1.50	0.98	1.56	1.07
Skipped classes Wave 3	1	6	2.06	1.38	1.68	1.11

TABLE 3.2
Descriptive Statistics (*continued*)

	Scale Range Min.	Max.	Males Effective *N* = 1361 Mean	Standard Deviation	Females Effective *N* = 1739 Mean	Standard Deviation
Delinquency index Wave 1[1]	0	7	1.84	1.86	1.20	1.47
Delinquency index Wave 2	0	7	1.62	1.79	1.01	1.38
Delinquency index Wave 3	0	7	1.47	1.66	0.75	1.14
Evenings out Wave 1	1	6	3.31	1.69	3.00	1.49
Evenings out Wave 2	1	6	3.53	1.50	3.19	1.40
Evenings out Wave 3	1	6	3.73	1.37	3.31	1.41
Hours worked Wave 1	0	7	0.91	1.53	0.65	1.13
Hours worked Wave 2	0	11	1.96	2.72	1.39	2.24
Hours worked Wave 3	0	11	3.75	3.23	3.15	2.88
Preferred hours of work Wave 1[2]	0	7	3.21	1.95	3.02	1.70
Preferred hours of work Wave 2	0	11	5.26	2.66	4.60	2.52
Preferred hours of work Wave 3	0	11	6.18	2.76	5.41	2.48
Religious attendance Wave 1	1	4	2.90	1.11	2.99	1.06
Religious attendance Wave 2	1	4	2.73	1.09	2.83	1.07
Religious attendance Wave 3	1	4	2.51	1.08	2.60	1.04
Religious importance Wave 1	1	4	2.72	1.02	2.85	0.98
Religious importance Wave 2	1	4	2.71	1.04	2.81	0.99
Religious importance Wave 3	1	4	2.66	1.06	2.83	1.00
Self-esteem index Wave 1[1]	0	8	5.89	2.10	5.55	2.27
Self-esteem index Wave 2	0	8	6.40	2.05	5.94	2.38
Self-esteem index Wave 3	0	8	6.45	2.12	6.27	2.21
30-day cigarette use Wave 1	0	6	0.32	0.88	0.29	0.78
30-day cigarette use Wave 2	0	6	0.56	1.24	0.61	1.26
30-day cigarette use Wave 3	0	6	0.98	1.56	0.86	1.42
30-day marijuana use Wave 1	0	6	0.11	0.59	0.09	0.51
30-day marijuana use Wave 2	0	6	0.34	1.06	0.28	0.92
30-day marijuana use Wave 3	0	6	0.75	1.62	0.45	1.22
Annual cocaine use Wave 1	0	6	0.04	0.36	0.03	0.33
Annual cocaine use Wave 2	0	6	0.03	0.32	0.04	0.34
Annual cocaine use Wave 3	0	6	0.16	0.77	0.09	0.53
30-day alcohol use Wave 1	0	6	0.55	1.16	0.47	0.97
30-day alcohol use Wave 2	0	6	0.72	1.26	0.66	1.27
30-day alcohol use Wave 3	0	6	1.10	1.41	0.79	1.14
Heavy drinking in the last 2 weeks W1	0	5	0.33	0.93	0.29	0.85
Heavy drinking in the last 2 weeks W2	0	5	0.52	1.12	0.36	0.92
Heavy drinking in the last 2 weeks W3	0	5	0.82	1.31	0.55	1.13
Academic attainment at age 22	1	8	4.33	1.88	4.66	1.96

Note: W1 = Wave 1 data collection (grade 8, modal age 14), W2 = Wave 2 data collection (modal age 16), W3 = Wave 3 data collection (modal age 18)

[1] The items in this index appeared in only one of two forms randomly distributed to respondents in their schools. Effective *N* is thus only half of that shown.

[2] This item appeared in only one of two forms randomly distributed to respondents in their schools. Its first appearance was in 1992. Effective *N* is thus only one third of that shown.

Product–moment correlations among all of the measures, computed separately for males and females, are presented in Tables A.3.3a and b in the appendix.

A large subset of the measures was used in more intensive analyses (multiple classification analyses and structural equation models). Table 3.3 lists these measures, and shows frequency distributions separately for males and females (both Effective Ns and percentages).

TABLE 3.3
Frequency Distributions of Selected Key Variables

Variable	Males Effective N = 1361		Females Effective N = 1739	
	Wtd. N	Percent	Wtd. N	Percent
Race/ethnicity				
African-American	175	12.9	237	13.6
Hispanic	125	9.2	173	9.9
Other race	219	16.1	263	15.1
White	842	61.9	1065	61.2
Population density				
Large MSA	371	27.3	471	27.1
Other MSA	619	45.5	828	47.6
Non-MSA	372	27.3	439	25.2
Parents' education level[1]				
1 (Low)	204	15.0	337	19.4
2	262	19.3	351	20.2
3	358	26.3	448	25.8
4	351	25.8	391	22.5
5 (High)	187	13.7	211	12.1
Lived with 2 parents Waves 1–3				
Yes	885	65.0	1034	59.5
No	476	35.0	705	40.5
Parent involvement index Wave 1				
1 (Low)	137	10.1	156	9.0
2	319	23.4	432	24.8
3	538	39.5	759	43.6
4 (High)	367	27.0	391	22.5
Held back grade 8 or earlier				
Never	1034	76.0	1455	83.7
Once	271	19.9	258	14.8
More than once	56	4.1	26	1.5
Suspended/expelled grade 8 or earlier				
Never	967	71.1	1476	84.9
Once	182	13.4	151	8.7
More than once	213	15.7	112	6.4

TABLE 3.3

Frequency Distributions of Selected Key Variables (*continued*)

Variable	Males Effective *N* = 1361		Females Effective *N* = 1739	
	Wtd. *N*	Percent	Wtd. *N*	Percent
Mean secondary school GPA				
D or below	24	1.8	11	0.6
C- or C	196	14.4	168	9.7
C+ or B-	447	32.8	512	29.4
B or B+	462	33.9	587	33.8
A-	167	12.3	327	18.8
A	65	4.8	132	7.6
Mean secondary school college plans				
Definitely won't	53	3.9	30	1.7
Probably won't	221	16.2	185	10.6
Probably will	515	37.8	612	35.2
Definitely will	573	42.1	911	52.4
Serious scholastic setback W1 to W2				
None	1078	79.2	1476	84.9
One	258	19.0	237	13.6
Two	25	1.8	26	1.5
Serious scholastic setback W2 to W3				
None	1043	76.6	1464	84.2
One	281	20.6	249	14.3
Two	37	2.7	25	1.4
Delinquency index (W2-3 combined)				
No incidents	293	21.5	626	36.0
1 or 2 incidents	423	31.1	643	37.0
3 or 4 incidents	285	20.9	275	15.8
5 or 6 incidents	170	12.5	122	7.0
7 or 8 incidents	101	7.4	51	2.9
9 to 14 incidents	88	6.5	22	1.3
High school dropout by Wave 3				
Yes	213	15.7	251	14.4
No	1148	84.3	1488	85.6

Note: W1 = Wave 1 data collection (grade 8, modal age 14), W2 = Wave 2 data collection (modal age 16), W3 = Wave 3 data collection (modal age 18)

[1] For MCA analyses and related figures, the 11-category measure was bracketed to a 5-category measure to provide sufficient cases in all categories. The 11-category measure was bracketed in the following manner: 1–4 = 1, 5 = 2, 6–7 = 3, 8–9 = 4, 10–11 = 5.

ANALYSIS METHODS AND RATIONALE

In an earlier book, we introduced what we called "Carson's dictum." Because it seems at least equally relevant here, we repeat it now—with apologies to any who may have thought once was enough:

> "You buy the premise, you buy the sketch!"—Johnny Carson, the *Tonight Show*.

> During the many years that Johnny Carson hosted the *Tonight Show*, a frequent occurrence was a sketch performed by the "Mighty Carson Art Players." The sketch was usually based on a very far-fetched premise, which was then followed to its bizarre conclusion. More often than not, when the drama reached a particularly outlandish point, the audience would groan loudly. That was Carson's cue to step out of character for a moment in order to look offended and address the audience thus: "Hey, look folks, you buy the premise, you buy the sketch!"

> Carson's dictum often comes to mind (well, to the mind of at least one of the authors) when considering structural equation modeling. Guided by some theory, or at least some theorizing, the structural equation modeler connects a set of variables by drawing arrows showing the hypothesized directions of causation. Then some very complicated equation solving takes place in order for the modeler to be able to attach numbers to the arrows and to assess the degree of fit—that is, how consistent the data are with the hypothesized structure. What the model's numbers do not tell us, however, is whether the arrows really do run in only one direction, whether the direction specified is the "true" direction, or indeed whether there are variables left out that should be included. Rather, the reader is often left to decide whether to "buy the premise ..." We should add that Carson's dictum is by no means limited to structural equation modeling. Rather, it seems applicable to a great deal of social science analyses carried out using real data from real people in real (i.e., nonexperimental) circumstances.

> We mention Carson's dictum at the start of this section on analysis strategy not to suggest that we have solved the problem of deriving causal conclusions from correlational data, but rather to acknowledge (once again) that we have not. At points during our analyses, we impose assumptions that we ourselves recognize are not entirely plausible, because such oversimplifying assumptions are sometimes necessary to advance the analyses. We try at such points to acknowledge our assumptions, sometimes by referring again to Carson's dictum. (Bachman et al., 2002, pp. 27–28)

All of those cautions noted in our earlier book are equally applicable in the present volume. The availability of panel data provides the opportunity to sort out chronology to some degree, but having panel data does not provide any guarantees that our causal interpretations are correct and complete. One response to this fundamental uncertainty is to make use of more than one form of data analysis.

Analysis Strategy

We begin each chapter with descriptive bivariate analyses showing the overall shape of relationships, we next examine multivariate relationships using relatively neutral regression analysis approaches (which do not make many causal assumptions), and only then do we turn to structural equation modeling (which does). In addition, the structural equation modeling effort entails testing various alternative assumptions about causal ordering.

The details of our analysis approach are presented simultaneously with the analyses themselves beginning in chapter 4. We provide here a few more general observations about analysis strategy. Because it can be difficult to model multiple constructs across five waves of measurement, it was necessary for us to be selective concerning which variables and how many data points to include in analyses.

Selectivity

One form of selectivity is the choice of which variables to include in analyses. A considerable number of variables were considered for inclusion and subjected to some exploratory analyses. Among the smaller number of variables selected, we made further distinctions about whether to include them in all stages of analyses. For example, although we document how measures of self-esteem, work preferences, and work experiences during high school are related to other variables, including substance use and academic attainment, we chose not to include those dimensions in our structural equation models, because they seemed to add little above and beyond the other more central measures of educational successes and failures. This reduction in variables helped keep the already large and complex structural models from becoming unmanageable.

A different kind of selectivity was our decision to focus on substance use during the first three survey waves (modal ages 14, 16, and 18) in most of our analyses, including the structural equation modeling. We do provide some descriptive findings on substance use spanning the full period from ages 14 to 22, as illustrated in chapter 1, but our primary focus in this book is on adolescent substance use. Thus, for the majority of our analyses, we include three waves of measures of educational experiences, delinquency, and substance use, along with earlier background factors and academic attainment at age 22.

Finally, we were selective in deciding which causal paths to include in the structural models. Many of these decisions, along with their underlying rationales, are discussed in the following chapters (with further details available in the appendix). But we understand that other scientists would not necessarily make all of the same decisions. With that in mind, electronic versions of covariance matrices sufficient to permit others to experiment with different models, should they wish to do so, are available on request from the authors.[4]

Separate Analyses for Males and Females

All of the analyses in this book were conducted and are reported separately for men and women. Although this obviously doubles the numbers of tables and figures to be examined, it has several important advantages. First, it provides convenient opportunities to examine and comment on gender differences. Second, it fully controls for gender differences that otherwise might be confounded—particularly given that females report somewhat lower levels of some kinds of substance use and have higher average levels of educational aspirations and successes as shown in Table 3.2. Third, to the extent that findings are similar or parallel across genders—and that turns out to be the case, to a large extent—we have a kind of replication that adds to our confidence in the generality of our findings. Finally, the dual presentation of results seems not unduly burdensome, because in fact the two sets of findings are generally closely parallel, usually allowing for a single description of findings for both males and females.

Separate Reporting for Different Forms of Substance Use

We have chosen to organize our presentation of findings into separate chapters for different categories of substance use. We precede the substance-use chapters with chapter 4, devoted to examining and modeling educational attainment, and with chapter 5, focusing on delinquent behavior. To the extent that we consider factors relating to or predicting the different behaviors, this separation seems to work well. When it comes to structural modeling, however, things become more complicated.

Our structural modeling approach begins in chapter 4 with a preliminary model of academic attainment, a model that does not take account of delinquency or substance use. In chapter 5 we expand the model, first to include delinquency, and then again at the end of the chapter to include

---

[4]The electronic matrices can be requested by e-mail addressed to MTFinfo@isr.umich.edu. The message should request covariance matrices from this volume.

the substance-use dimensions. We include the full set of substance-use dimensions in this expansion, modeling their interrelationships with each other. (The one exception is that we were unsuccessful in including current alcohol use and instances of heavy drinking as separate dimensions in a single model; accordingly, separate and parallel models are used to deal with this limitation, as noted in chap. 9.)

Although we use what is essentially just one model (estimated separately for males and females) treating all substance-use dimensions simultaneously, our explication of the findings proceeds in a chapter-by-chapter fashion. Specifically, we discuss findings for cigarette use in chapter 6, marijuana use in chapter 7, cocaine use in chapter 8, and alcohol use in chapter 9. Because much of the structural model material is identical across chapters 6–9, we have placed tabular summaries including factor loadings, fit indices, variance explained, and key effects in the appendix (in Tables A.3.4–9). An extensive tabular summary of the full model findings, incorporating all substances, is provided in the appendix (in Table A.3.10).

A Focus on Consistent Findings, Well Documented

Given the variety of analysis approaches we used, as well as the range of focal behaviors (educational attainment, delinquency, and the use of four different substances), there is some risk of getting lost in the details. In our reporting in the following chapters, we seek to focus on findings that appear consistently and coherently across analysis methods. Although our primary focus in this book is on relational analyses, we also try to include descriptive accuracy as a part of our reporting.

As for documenting our analyses, we attempt to strike a reasonable balance between reporting too little or too much. There is a fair amount of detail in the individual chapters that follow, and a good deal more in the appendix. Still further details are available in supplementary publications that we cite. Because we have reached clear conclusions about the causal relationships linking educational success and substance use, and because some of these conclusions may be controversial, we consider it especially important to make a great deal of the supporting evidence available.

Readers should have little trouble discerning our overall conclusions from this wealth of data—we announced them at the start of chapter 1 and repeated them later in that chapter. In the chapters that follow, we try to organize and present the supporting evidence in ways that are clear and readily approachable.

Chapter 4

Educational Success and Failure: Causes and Correlates

Nearly three decades ago, a chapter on predictors of academic attainment began by outlining some basic questions:

> Why do some individuals extend their educations through college and into graduate school whereas others drop out of high school? What are the factors of background, ability, earlier educational experience, plans, values, attitudes, and behaviors that predict—and perhaps help to determine—later levels of educational attainment? To what extent do such basic factors as family background and ability show a direct or continuing effect on educational attainment, and to what extent do they appear to have an 'indirect' impact via their influence on other factors such as educational success in the pre-high school years? (Bachman, O'Malley, & Johnston, 1978, p. 19)

At the end of that chapter the following conclusion was reached:

> ... the determinants of educational attainment are well-known by tenth grade. Those determinants are ... successful experiences in, and a positive attitude toward, schooling. Background and ability continue to have moderate direct effects, but their impact is primarily through the schooling variables. This is not a particularly profound finding, but it certainly underscores the importance of educational behaviors and experiences during the pre-high school years. (Bachman et al., 1978, p. 54)

The present chapter reexamines those questions and relationships. This time we begin earlier (eighth grade), and we use far more extensive samples, more recent cohorts, and somewhat more sophisticated and comprehensive methods of analysis. Despite these improvements, we did not expect to reach fundamentally different conclusions about the determinants of academic attainment; nevertheless, we considered it useful to replicate and

49

extend the earlier findings. More important, the new findings reported in this chapter lay the groundwork for the later chapters (6–9) exploring how substance use among American adolescents in the late 20th century (and the early 21st century) relates to adolescent educational successes and failures, problem behavior in general, and adult academic attainment.

PLAN FOR THIS CHAPTER

Our analyses in this chapter focus exclusively on educational success and failure and include a number of important indicators. Grade point average (GPA) in school can be a clear indicator of success. Plans to complete college can indicate present levels of school success, as well as the possibility of future academic attainment. A clear indicator of scholastic failure is having been held back a year or more. Other indicators of failure to adjust well in school are suspension, expulsion, truancy, and the like. These and other factors are interrelated; moreover, all of them contribute—in varying degrees, some positively and some negatively—to longer term educational and occupational attainment.

We also examine a number of other possible correlates and predictors of educational attainment as well as substance use. These include delinquency, frequency of evenings out for fun and recreation, actual and preferred hours of work during the school year, religious attendance and importance, and self-esteem.

Focusing on Academic Attainment as a Long-Term Outcome

We focus special attention on one indicator of longer term educational success: the amount (primarily number of years) of schooling an individual has completed by modal age 22. This is a powerful indicator, although it does have some important limitations. For example, simply knowing that someone has a 4-year college degree does not tell us the area of study, the quality of the school, the extent to which the student excelled in the work, or the amount of skills and knowledge that will be retained during the years that follow. Nevertheless, knowing that someone has a bachelor's degree tells us quite a bit about an individual's experiences thus far, and it also tells us that the individual is likely to do relatively well in contemporary society. Society places high value on the talents and motivations (i.e., input characteristics) necessary to obtain a college degree, as well as the skills and abilities learned or enhanced in the process of getting the degree (i.e., the value added by higher education). Above and beyond the talents, motivations, skills, and abilities needed to obtain a college degree, another form of value added is the sheer credential value of the degree in the job market. (The same is true, albeit to a lesser extent, for an associate's degree compared with a high school degree, or for a high school diploma compared with the lack of any diploma.) Although it certainly does not capture all of what may be connoted by *educational success*, the number of years of schooling completed can be considered a valuable dimension in its own right, as well as a fairly good proxy for many other aspects of educational success—as is illustrated throughout this chapter.

Using Multiple Analysis Methods and Perspectives

To make full use of our data to inform our major research questions, we employ multiple analytic approaches. Rather than spell out these analysis approaches in advance and in the abstract, we explain the analysis techniques and their rationale as we go so that readers can have concrete examples of how the techniques are applied and what we can learn from them. We begin this chapter by defining and describing academic attainment in our sample of young men and women. Next, we provide a brief overview of predictors, showing how they correlate with academic attainment and how they contribute jointly in multivariate analyses. We include zero-order correlations showing how strongly each factor is connected with academic attainment, along with multivariate coefficients indicating the extent to which the contributions to prediction are independent or overlapping. We also use additional data from the large-scale Monitoring the Future (MTF) cross-sectional samples to examine how closely our particular survey panel corresponds with later cohorts of adolescents. Finally, we employ structural equation modeling in an effort to impose a causal structure interpreting how background factors, grades, and college plans during the high school years relate to each other and contribute to longer term (i.e., age-22) academic attainment.

ACADEMIC ATTAINMENT AT AGE 22: A SNAPSHOT OF A MOVING TARGET

This book covers a crucial interval in the educational life course of young people in the United States. At the start of the interval, nearly all are in school; by the end, many have finished their schooling or soon will. Our primary panel analyses began with eighth grade, when most respondents were age 14; the endpoint was 8 years later, when most were age 22.[1]

---

[1] We also undertook a limited set of analyses focused on the subset of respondents who remained in the panel study through age 24, which showed that our primary findings and conclusions remain unchanged.

During that interval, these young people were sorted—by their own actions as well as factors outside their control—into what we can treat as a continuum of academic attainment. That continuum is captured reasonably well by the following eight categories[2]:

1. School dropout, no general education diploma (GED), no years of college completed
2. GED only, no years of college
3. High school diploma only, no years of college
4. One year of college completed
5. Two years of college completed
6. Three years of college completed
7. Four years of college completed, no bachelor's degree
8. Bachelor's degree (or higher, although virtually none reached a higher level by age 22)

There are, of course, many reasons for valuing higher education, not the least of which is that each increase along this continuum is worth a considerable amount in lifetime earnings, on average. Recent research shows that each step on this eight-category continuum was worth roughly $5,000 per year (in year 2000 dollars). Over a 40-year working career, that would amount to roughly a $1 million advantage for someone with a bachelor's degree (Category 8 on the scale) versus someone with only a high school diploma (Category 3).[3]

---

[2]This scale was developed from two measures—one asking about highest degree/ diploma attained, and the other asking about number of years of schooling completed. Details appear in Table A.3.2 in the appendix. Variations on this eight-point scale were examined, collapsing some categories, but such variations yielded no appreciable differences in correlations; based on these and other analyses, we are satisfied that the eight-category scale used here does a good job of capturing the continuum of academic attainment. For some figures and tables, however, abbreviated (collapsed) versions of the scale are used for clarity (see e.g., chapter 1 figures).

[3]These generalizations are based on U.S. Census Current Population Reports across the years 1990 to 2000, converted to year 2000 dollars, based on males ages 25 and older who were employed full time. Among workers 25 years old and older, median annual incomes for men with some high school education but no completion were about $25,000 to $26,000; for those with high school completion (including equivalency), about $33,000 to $34,000; and for those with a bachelor's or higher degree, about $57,000 to $60,000. Women's earnings were lower; however, it seems likely that generational changes will reduce such discrepancies. Accordingly, we offer the rough estimate of an additional $5,000 per year in full-time earnings for each additional point on the academic attainment scale as a guideline when considering the pay-off value (in year 2000 dollars) of education. For a much more rigorous attempt to quantify the dollar value of education, see Day and Newburger (2002).

Academic Attainment as a Moving Target

"Life-long learning" has become a sort of mantra in secondary education in the United States. The realities of a rapidly changing labor market put a premium on workers who are willing and able to acquire new skills and master the latest technologies. In this volume, we focus on academic attainment at age 22 primarily as an outcome of other prior causal factors.[4] We do so knowing full well that age-22 educational attainment is a snapshot of a formal educational process that begins much earlier and may, for some, not reach a conclusion until many years later. As a snapshot of the educational process, age-22 educational attainment has the virtue of capturing much of the socially expected course of formal educational development. By age 22, the large majority of young people have attained their high school diploma, and many of those high school graduates who moved on immediately to college have received an associate's degree or are making progress toward a bachelor's degree. Indeed, as we see later, some have already completed a bachelor's degree.

That said, it is worth emphasizing that a snapshot of attainment at age 22 (or any age, for that matter) does not capture all of the steps along the way. For example, if a young woman at age 22 reports a high school diploma as the highest level she attained, we may not know whether she dropped out of high school for some period before returning to complete work for her diploma. Other analyses (reported in Table A.4.1 in the appendix) show that, among those who were in the high school graduates category at age 22 (Category 3), about 14% had, just 2 years earlier, reported being a dropout (i.e., out of school without having obtained a diploma). Viewing it the opposite way, those same analyses also reveal that, among those who had been dropouts at age 20, the majority had moved up to a higher point on our academic attainment scale 2 years later: Specifically, fewer than one third remained in the dropout category (Category 1), nearly half had attained a GED (Category 2), most of the rest had obtained a high school diploma (Category 3), and a few (roughly 1 in 10) had completed 1 or more years of college by age 22.

Nor does a snapshot at age 22 predict all the steps that follow. Our limited analyses of age-24 follow-up data (see Table A.4.1 in the appendix) reveal that about one third of those who had remained dropouts

---

[4]Other studies of MTF data, using young adult follow-up surveys based on samples originally surveyed in 12th grade, have shown that different educational experiences and their associated lifestyles have important implications for substance use (Bachman, Wadsworth, O'Malley, Johnston, & Schulenberg, 1997; Bachman et al., 2002; Schulenberg et al., 1994; Schulenberg, Merline et al., 2005; Schulenberg, O'Malley et al., 2005).

through age 22 had, 2 years later, moved up—some to a GED and some to a regular high school diploma or even more. A more important finding involves those who at age 22 reported having completed 3 or 4 years of college; 2 years later, nearly two thirds of them reported that they had completed a bachelor's degree.

Before leaving the topic of academic attainment as a moving target, we should note another form of movement: differences across cohorts. High school dropout rates declined substantially during much of the 20th century, and during the same period the proportions of high school graduates entering college increased dramatically (Johnston et al., 2005b). Also, proportions of female college aspirants and actual entrants have increased; they now exceed the proportions of men (Johnston et al., 2005b). Although we consider our panel findings to be quite accurate for those who were in eighth grade in 1991 to 1993 (corresponding to the high school graduating classes of 1995–1997), it should be kept in mind that overall academic attainment was somewhat lower for earlier cohorts and may differ also (either higher or lower) for later cohorts. Nevertheless, we believe that the *relationships* among factors that we report here have a good deal of generality—in part because similar relationships were observed and reported three decades earlier (e.g., Bachman, 1970; Bachman et al., 1978).

In sum, we recognize that academic attainment is a dynamic process; the older the respondents at time of measurement, the more who will have attained a high school diploma or a bachelor's degree or, for that matter, an advanced degree. Nevertheless, it is also true that age 22 is a good point at which to pin down this moving target. Although further changes will occur with increased age, and although we cannot predict exactly which individuals will move on to a higher level of attainment after a few years, the fact remains that attainment by age 22 is strongly correlated with attainment at later ages, and thus can serve as a good proxy for longer term academic attainment.[5] As the remainder of this chapter illustrates, the eight-point continuum of academic attainment at age 22 is strongly related to many other factors, ranging from family background to high school grades and college plans. Subsequent chapters, along with chapter 1, illustrate meaningful links between academic attainment and substance use.

---

[5]Consistent with this assertion are the high product–moment correlations between age-22 academic attainment and age-24 attainment measured on the same scale: $r = .87$ for males and .88 for females. (The correlations just discussed exclude those whose age-22 data were imputed; if the imputed cases are included, the correlations drop slightly, to $r = .80$ and .83, respectively.)

How Many Go How Far?

Figure 4.1 shows, for our panel of eighth graders originally surveyed in 1991 to 1993, the academic levels they attained in 1999 to 2001 when they were at modal age 22. The figure shows that the majority had completed at least 1 year of college, and many were within a year or two of a bachelor's degree. The figure also shows the slightly higher average levels of attainment for young women compared with young men, a finding consistent with other recent studies (summarized by Powers & Wojtkiewicz, 2004). Specifically, by age 22, about 30% of men versus 39% of women had completed 3 or more years of college, whereas 43% of men compared with 36% of women had no years of college completed.

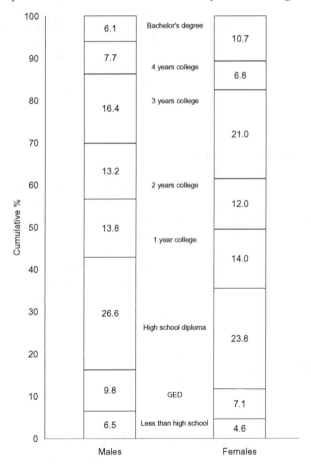

Figure 4.1. Academic attainment at age 22 (1999–2001): males and females.

Relatively few men or women at age 22 reported having completed a 4-year degree—not surprising given that the surveys were mailed out in the spring of their fourth year after high school. Some of those in Category 7 would complete their degrees only a few months later, and most individuals in Category 6 as well as Category 7 would do so within 2 years.[6] Thus, we view those in all three of the top categories as having done extensive college work and more likely than not to complete a bachelor's degree within a year or two.

MAJOR CORRELATES/PREDICTORS OF ACADEMIC ATTAINMENT

In this section, we introduce several possible correlates of longer term (i.e., age-22) academic attainment. All of these variables were measured at least 4 years prior to age 22, and most were measured 8 years prior, when respondents were in eighth grade (i.e., modal age 14). Thus, on the basis of chronology alone, these correlates can all be considered predictors of academic attainment. Whether these predictors are also *causes* of academic attainment is a far more complex matter, and chronology is only one kind of evidence required to support that claim. Another kind of evidence involves the overlap among variables in their prediction of academic attainment. Multiple regression analysis is one method for examining overlap among predictors, and we use it in this section to provide an overview of which variables appear to make some independent (i.e., nonoverlapping) contribution to the prediction of academic attainment. (Actually, we use two versions of multiple regression, in Tables 4.1 and 4.2, as outlined later. We use both versions because they are complementary.)

Table 4.1 presents product–moment correlations and standardized multiple regression findings for this chapter. This and similar multiple regression tables in subsequent chapters are large and contain a considerable amount of detail. The regression tables for later chapters are often placed in the appendix; however, Table 4.1 is central for much that follows, so we include it in the text.

We begin by noting a few features of Table 4.1, along with some summary findings. The table includes a long list of variables (predictors), which

---

[6]As noted previously, further follow-up data show that the majority of those who were in Categories 6 and 7 at modal age 22 had moved to Category 8 by age 24, as shown in Table A.4.1 in the appendix.

are discussed in the following sections. Column 1 presents zero-order product–moment correlations; these show the strength (and direction—positive or negative) of the linear relationship between each predictor variable and academic attainment at age 22 (treated as the dependent variable). Note that Column 1 includes some measures that do not appear in the regression analyses, but are of interest for other reasons.[7] Columns 2 and 3 consist of standardized multiple regression coefficients showing each variable's contribution to prediction of academic attainment when all other variables in that column are included in the prediction. Column 2 shows results when only what we consider the most important predictors are included in the equation; the adjusted R-squared value at the bottom of Column 2 indicates that nearly half of the variance in academic attainment can be explained by the partial set of predictors (.43 among men and .49 among women). Column 3 shows the results when a large number of additional predictors are included in the equation. A comparison of the R-squared values in Columns 2 and 3 shows that the predictors in the upper portion of the table provide nearly as much explanatory power as the much larger set of predictors. We note that Table A.4.2 in the appendix adds dropout status at modal age 18 (third wave of data collection) to the predictors in Column 2 of Table 4.1. Adding dropout status contributes to explained variance, although less than 3%. (This column in the appendix table is useful for comparisons with later structural equation models because the later models include age-18 dropout status as a predictor.)

A second set of regression analyses in this section focuses on only the key predictors, showing in richer detail how they are related to academic attainment at age 22. In contrast to the summary information provided in Table 4.1, Table 4.2 presents data for each category of a predictor. The table reports results from multiple classification analysis (MCA), a form of dummy variable regression analysis (Andrews, Morgan, & Sonquist, 1967). The dependent variable in the table is a dichotomy indicating whether the respondent had (by age 22) completed at least 1 year of college. Showing information by separate predictor categories is especially useful for dimensions involving small categories that, because of their limited size, cannot generate large correlations or regression coefficients, but that nevertheless may show levels of attainment that depart sharply from average. Column 1 in Table 4.2 shows actual percentages of respondents

---

[7]There are alternative versions of some predictors included in Column 1 (e.g., GPA reported at 8th, 10th, and 12th grades, as well as the mean of all three), and only one version was included in the regressions.

TABLE 4.1a

OLS Regressions Predicting Academic Attainment at Age 22 (8 Levels)[1]
Eighth-Grade Class Years 1991–1993: Males

Effective *N* = 1361	Column 1 Zero-Order Correlation	Column 2 Standardized Regression Coefficient	Column 3 Standardized Regression Coefficient
African-American	**-.077**	-.017	-.021
Hispanic	**-.109**	**-.050**	**-.048**
Other race	**-.070**	-.013	-.006
White	**.171**		
Large MSA	**.082**	.035	.038
Other MSA	.032		
Non-MSA	**-.118**	-.034	-.033
Parents' education level	**.336**	**.095**	**.085**
Number of parents Wave 1	**.182**		
Number of parents Wave 2	**.172**		
Number of parents Wave 3	**.232**		
Lived with 2 parents Waves 1–3	**.237**	**.076**	**.067**
Parent involvement index Wave 1	**.152**	-.010	-.023
Parent involvement index Wave 2	**.097**		
Parent involvement index Wave 3	**.071**		
Held back grade 8 or earlier	**-.287**	**-.058**	**-.055**
Suspended/expelled grade 8 or earlier	**-.291**	**-.087**	**-.066**
GPA Wave 1	**.438**	**.082**	**.072**
GPA Wave 2	**.465**	**.138**	**.139**
GPA Wave 3	**.421**	**.081**	**.064**
Mean secondary school GPA	**.527**		
College plans Wave 1	**.321**	-.008	-.004
College plans Wave 2	**.411**	**.063**	**.054**
College plans Wave 3	**.515**	**.262**	**.239**
Mean secondary school college plans	**.523**		
Held back Wave 1 to Wave 2	**-.141**		
Held back Wave 2 to Wave 3	**-.190**		
Suspended/expelled Wave 1 to Wave 2	**-.169**		
Suspended/expelled Wave 2 to Wave 3	**-.125**		
Serious scholastic setback W1 to W2	**-.213**	**-.082**	**-.065**
Serious scholastic setback W2 to W3	**-.208**	**-.080**	**-.054**
High school dropout by Wave 3	**-.455**		

[1] These OLS (ordinary least squares) regressions were run with SAS statistical analyses software. A covariance matrix constructed with pairwise deletion served as the input data, because of missing values on the variables described in Notes 2 and 3 below. Coefficients that are p<.05 (two-tailed) are shown in **bold**.

TABLE 4.1a

OLS Regressions Predicting Academic Attainment at Age 22 (8 Levels)[1]
Eighth-Grade Class Years 1991–1993: Males (*continued*)

Effective N = 1361	Column 1 Zero-Order Correlation	Column 2 Standardized Regression Coefficient	Column 3 Standardized Regression Coefficient
Sent to the office Wave 1	**-.222**		.027
Sent to the office Wave 2	**-.218**		.028
Sent to the office Wave 3	**-.259**		-.040
Days cut school Wave 1	**-.136**		.000
Days cut school Wave 2	**-.197**		-.013
Days cut school Wave 3	**-.168**		-.011
Skipped classes Wave 1	**-.078**		.031
Skipped classes Wave 2	**-.190**		-.011
Skipped classes Wave 3	**-.138**		-.031
Delinquency index Wave 1[2]	**-.209**		-.016
Delinquency index Wave 2	**-.159**		-.035
Delinquency index Wave 3	**-.123**		.004
Evenings out Wave 1	-.055		-.018
Evenings out Wave 2	**-.081**		.005
Evenings out Wave 3	.006		.015
Hours worked Wave 1	**-.101**		-.011
Hours worked Wave 2	**-.079**		.017
Hours worked Wave 3	**-.142**		-.012
Preferred hours of work Wave 1[3]	**-.095**		-.005
Preferred hours of work Wave 2	**-.201**		-.022
Preferred hours of work Wave 3	**-.259**		**-.047**
Religious attendance Wave 1	**.231**		.048
Religious attendance Wave 2	**.251**		.021
Religious attendance Wave 3	**.212**		.004
Religious importance Wave 1	**.134**		.003
Religious importance Wave 2	**.153**		.039
Religious importance Wave 3	**.115**		-.043
Self-esteem index Wave 1[2]	**.171**		.025
Self-esteem index Wave 2	**.105**		-.029
Self-esteem index Wave 3	**.141**		.042
Multiple R		.657	.671
R Squared		.432	.450
R Squared, adjusted		.431	.448

[2] The items in this index appeared in only one of two forms randomly distributed to respondents in their schools. Effective N is thus only half of that shown.

[3] This item appeared in only one of two forms randomly distributed to respondents in their schools. Its first appearance was in 1992. Effective N is thus only one third of that shown.

Note: W1 = Wave 1 data collection (grade 8, modal age 14), W2 = Wave 2 data collection (modal age 16), W3 = Wave 3 data collection (modal age 18)

TABLE 4.1b

OLS Regressions Predicting Academic Attainment at Age 22 (8 Levels)[1]
Eighth-Grade Class Years 1991–1993: Females

Effective *N* = 1739	Column 1	Column 2	Column 3
	Zero-Order Correlation	Standardized Regression Coefficient	Standardized Regression Coefficient
African-American	**-.114**	-.025	-.022
Hispanic	**-.112**	-.045	-.037
Other race	-.014	.010	.012
White	**.160**		
Large MSA	**.090**	**.057**	**.053**
Other MSA	-.023		
Non-MSA	**-.065**	-.007	-.001
Parents' education level	**.370**	**.167**	**.143**
Number of parents Wave 1	**.152**		
Number of parents Wave 2	**.190**		
Number of parents Wave 3	**.295**		
Lived with 2 parents Waves 1–3	**.272**	**.108**	**.087**
Parent involvement index Wave 1	**.126**	-.007	-.020
Parent involvement index Wave 2	**.099**		
Parent involvement index Wave 3	.025		
Held back grade 8 or earlier	**-.244**	**-.046**	-.039
Suspended/expelled grade 8 or earlier	**-.233**	**-.054**	-.038
GPA Wave 1	**.409**	**.088**	**.088**
GPA Wave 2	**.413**	**.109**	**.093**
GPA Wave 3	**.379**	**.093**	**.088**
Mean secondary school GPA	**.469**		
College plans Wave 1	**.303**	.004	.004
College plans Wave 2	**.385**	**.084**	**.078**
College plans Wave 3	**.480**	**.289**	**.277**
Mean secondary school college plans	**.500**		
Held back Wave 1 to Wave 2	**-.158**		
Held back Wave 2 to Wave 3	**-.153**		
Suspended/expelled W1 to W2	**-.162**		
Suspended/expelled W2 to W3	**-.133**		
Serious scholastic setback W1 to W2	**-.212**	**-.046**	-.029
Serious scholastic setback W2 to W3	**-.191**	**-.060**	**-.045**
High school dropout by Wave 3	**-.425**		

[1] These OLS (ordinary least squares) regressions were run with SAS statistical analyses software. A covariance matrix constructed with pairwise deletion served as the input data, because of missing values on the variables described in Notes 2 and 3 below. Coefficients that are p<.05 (two-tailed) are shown in **bold**.

TABLE 4.1b

OLS Regressions Predicting Academic Attainment at Age 22 (8 Levels)[1]
Eighth-Grade Class Years 1991–1993: Females (*continued*)

Effective N = 1739	Column 1 Zero-Order Correlation	Column 2 Standardized Regression Coefficient	Column 3 Standardized Regression Coefficient
Sent to the office Wave 1	**-.202**		-.005
Sent to the office Wave 2	**-.213**		.024
Sent to the office Wave 3	**-.195**		-.014
Days cut school Wave 1	**-.125**		.004
Days cut school Wave 2	**-.203**		-.040
Days cut school Wave 3	**-.180**		-.025
Skipped classes Wave 1	**-.120**		.004
Skipped classes Wave 2	**-.147**		-.030
Skipped classes Wave 3	-.029		.014
Delinquency index Wave 1[2]	**-.163**		.012
Delinquency index Wave 2	**-.137**		-.016
Delinquency index Wave 3	**-.079**		.033
Evenings out Wave 1	**-.055**		.005
Evenings out Wave 2	-.022		-.006
Evenings out Wave 3	**.058**		-.005
Hours worked Wave 1	.015		.007
Hours worked Wave 2	-.038		.003
Hours worked Wave 3	**-.083**		-.022
Preferred hours of work Wave 1[3]	-.044		.005
Preferred hours of work Wave 2	**-.229**		-.029
Preferred hours of work Wave 3	**-.283**		**-.068**
Religious attendance Wave 1	**.162**		.022
Religious attendance Wave 2	**.167**		.018
Religious attendance Wave 3	**.172**		**.066**
Religious importance Wave 1	.038		-.011
Religious importance Wave 2	.045		-.010
Religious importance Wave 3	.013		**-.064**
Self-esteem index Wave 1[2]	**.145**		.028
Self-esteem index Wave 2	**.084**		-.006
Self-esteem index Wave 3	**.093**		-.022
Multiple R		.697	.711
R Squared		.485	.505
R Squared, adjusted		.485	.504

[2] The items in this index appeared in only one of two forms randomly distributed to respondents in their schools. Effective N is thus only half of that shown.

[3] This item appeared in only one of two forms randomly distributed to respondents in their schools. Its first appearance was in 1992. Effective N is thus only one third of that shown.

Note: W1 = Wave 1 data collection (grade 8, modal age 14), W2 = Wave 2 data collection (modal age 16), W3 = Wave 3 data collection (modal age 18)

TABLE 4.2a

Multiple Classification Analyses Predicting Percentage
Who Have Completed at Least One Year of College by Age 22
Age 14 in 1991–1993: Males

Grand Mean = 58.7
Effective *N* = 1361

	Percentage Who Have Completed at Least One Year of College by Age 22					
	Col. 1	Col. 2	Col. 3	Col. 4	Col. 5	Col. 6
Variable	Bivariate	Multivariate				
Race/ethnicity						
African-American	51.9	56.6	60.3	58.0	57.9	58.2
Hispanic	47.5	54.2	55.7	56.9	56.9	57.3
Other race	51.7	53.1	54.1	58.5	58.5	58.5
White	63.6	61.3	60.0	59.2	59.2	59.1
Population density						
Large MSA	63.9	63.5	63.6	61.2	61.2	60.9
Other MSA	60.7	59.3	59.3	58.8	58.8	59.0
Non-MSA	50.2	52.9	52.9	56.1	56.1	56.0
Parents' education level						
1 (Low)	37.2	42.0	45.9	52.6	52.6	52.2
2	42.6	44.5	45.6	51.2	51.1	51.2
3	61.5	61.1	60.7	61.3	61.2	61.5
4	69.9	68.0	66.7	63.2	63.2	63.0
5 (High)	78.6	75.1	72.3	62.7	62.7	63.1
Lived with 2 parents Waves 1–3						
Yes	65.6	63.7	62.4	60.8	60.8	60.1
No	45.8	49.4	51.8	54.9	54.9	56.1
Parent involvement index Wave 1						
1 (Low)	44.4	51.4	55.1	60.4	60.4	61.0
2	55.9	58.6	59.0	60.7	60.7	60.5
3	59.9	59.2	59.1	58.7	58.7	58.6
4 (High)	64.8	60.8	59.3	56.4	56.4	56.5
Held back grade 8 or earlier						
Never	65.9		62.7	60.7	60.7	60.0
Once	37.7		46.1	52.5	52.4	54.0
More than once	27.9		46.0	53.1	53.1	57.8
Suspended/expelled grade 8 or earlier						
Never	65.9		62.9	60.6	60.5	59.7
Once	46.8		51.6	56.0	56.2	56.9
More than once	36.1		45.6	52.4	52.7	55.8
Mean secondary school GPA						
D or below	13.1			45.9	46.2	51.8
C- or C	28.5			48.1	48.1	50.1
C+ or B-	47.0			53.1	53.1	52.8
B or B+	70.6			63.7	63.7	62.9
A-	85.2			68.5	68.4	68.3
A	94.7			73.9	73.6	73.2
Mean secondary school college plans						
Definitely won't	10.5			28.8	28.8	31.6
Probably won't	24.3			37.6	37.6	40.0
Probably will	51.6			54.3	54.4	54.5
Definitely will	82.8			73.5	73.5	72.2

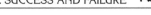

TABLE 4.2a
Multiple Classification Analyses Predicting Percentage Who Have Completed at Least One Year of College by Age 22 Age 14 in 1991–1993: Males (*continued*)

Grand Mean = 58.7
Effective *N* = 1361

Variable	Col. 1 Bivariate	Col. 2	Col. 3	Col. 4	Col. 5	Col. 6
		Multivariate				
Serious scholastic setback W1 to W2						
None	63.1			60.4	60.4	59.9
One	43.5			53.3	53.4	54.6
Two	28.9			41.9	42.1	49.5
Serious scholastic setback W2 to W3						
None	63.6			60.9	60.8	60.7
One	43.7			51.9	52.0	52.3
Two	35.6			50.3	50.5	52.9
Delinquency index (W2–3 combined)						
No incidents	65.6				59.3	59.2
1 or 2 incidents	61.6				59.3	59.1
3 or 4 incidents	58.6				58.4	58.6
5 or 6 incidents	54.2				58.2	58.4
7 or 8 incidents	46.2				56.1	56.2
9 to 14 incidents	45.4				58.8	59.1
High school dropout by Wave 3						
Yes	16.1					39.4
No	66.6					62.3
Multiple *R*		0.347	0.406	0.552	0.552	0.570
R Squared		0.120	0.165	0.304	0.305	0.325

Factor Summary*

	eta	beta	beta	beta	beta	beta
Race/ethnicity	**.129**	.069	.049	.015	.015	.011
Population density	**.110**	**.080**	**.080**	.038	.039	.037
Parents' education level	**.293**	**.242**	**.204**	**.103**	**.103**	**.105**
Lived with 2 parents Waves 1–3	**.192**	**.139**	**.103**	**.057**	**.057**	.039
Parent involvement index	**.117**	.053	.024	.033	.033	.033
Held back grade 8 or earlier	**.262**		**.144**	**.070**	**.071**	.048
Suspended/expelled grade 8 or earlier	**.237**		**.138**	**.063**	.060	.032
Mean secondary school GPA	**.411**			**.158**	**.157**	**.144**
Mean secondary school college plans	**.474**			**.292**	**.291**	**.263**
Serious scholastic setback W1 to W2	**.176**			**.073**	**.072**	.049
Serious scholastic setback W2 to W3	**.180**			**.079**	**.078**	**.071**
Delinquency index (W2–3 combined)	**.126**				.017	.016
High school dropout by Wave 3	**.373**					**.169**

*All eta and beta statistics p<.05 are shown in **bold**.

See Table 3.3 for frequency distributions of predictor variables.

Note: W1 = Wave 1 data collection (grade 8, modal age 14), W2 = Wave 2 data collection (modal age 16), W3 = Wave 3 data collection (modal age 18)

TABLE 4.2b

Multiple Classification Analyses Predicting Percentage
Who Have Completed at Least One Year of College by Age 22
Age 14 in 1991–1993: Females

Grand Mean = 61.7
Effective *N* = 1739

Percentage Who Have Completed
at Least One Year of College by Age 22

Variable	Col. 1 Bivariate	Col. 2	Col. 3	Col. 4	Col. 5	Col. 6
		Multivariate				
Race/ethnicity						
African-American	55.8	63.4	68.0	66.1	66.3	64.6
Hispanic	53.9	62.2	63.8	64.7	64.8	64.4
Other race	62.2	63.1	63.4	65.7	65.6	65.5
White	69.5	66.2	64.9	64.6	64.5	65.0
Population density						
Large MSA	71.8	70.1	70.0	68.8	68.7	68.5
Other MSA	64.6	63.4	63.9	64.3	64.2	64.3
Non-MSA	58.3	62.3	61.5	62.2	62.3	62.3
Parents' education level						
1 (Low)	38.4	41.8	44.3	53.8	53.8	55.1
2	54.9	55.7	56.5	61.5	61.5	61.1
3	68.8	68.8	68.2	67.5	67.4	67.4
4	79.0	77.6	76.5	70.2	70.3	69.5
5 (High)	89.7	85.8	83.5	73.5	73.4	73.5
Lived with 2 parents Waves 1–3						
Yes	74.3	72.2	70.9	68.2	68.2	67.1
No	51.3	54.3	56.3	60.2	60.2	61.9
Parent involvement index Wave 1						
1 (Low)	52.9	61.6	64.0	68.3	68.3	68.2
2	59.4	62.1	63.1	63.5	63.5	63.7
3	67.4	66.7	66.2	65.4	65.5	65.3
4 (High)	71.1	66.0	65.0	64.3	64.3	64.3
Held back grade 8 or earlier						
Never	70.1		67.9	66.4	66.4	66.2
Once	39.6		50.3	57.4	57.6	58.5
More than once	27.5		46.8	56.6	56.7	59.6
Suspended/expelled grade 8 or earlier						
Never	69.6		67.5	66.1	66.1	65.7
Once	41.8		52.8	60.9	60.6	61.8
More than once	35.5		48.3	56.1	55.6	59.2
Mean secondary school GPA						
D or below	15.6			58.5	58.1	66.0
C- or C	28.2			52.6	52.3	54.9
C+ or B-	51.5			60.2	60.1	60.5
B or B+	69.3			64.9	64.9	64.2
A-	87.6			74.7	74.8	74.0
A	93.2			76.1	76.2	75.6
Mean secondary school college plans						
Definitely won't	4.1			23.1	23.1	28.6
Probably won't	18.6			34.0	33.9	38.4
Probably will	51.2			56.7	56.6	56.5
Definitely will	85.6			78.2	78.3	77.2

TABLE 4.2b

Multiple Classification Analyses Predicting Percentage
Who Have Completed at Least One Year of College by Age 22
Age 14 in 1991–1993: Females (*continued*)

Grand Mean = 61.7 Effective *N* = 1739	Percentage Who Have Completed at Least One Year of College by Age 22					
	Col. 1	Col. 2	Col. 3	Col. 4	Col. 5	Col. 6
Variable	Bivariate	Multivariate				
Serious scholastic setback W1 to W2						
None	69.0			65.7	65.8	65.3
One	42.6			61.0	60.6	63.2
Two	38.2			56.9	56.7	61.7
Serious scholastic setback W2 to W3						
None	68.4			66.0	66.0	65.7
One	47.5			60.3	60.1	61.7
Two	37.3			52.3	52.4	56.0
Delinquency index (W2–3 combined)						
No incidents	68.4				64.4	64.4
1 or 2 incidents	67.6				64.8	64.7
3 or 4 incidents	59.8				65.0	65.0
5 or 6 incidents	52.4				65.8	65.9
7 or 8 incidents	54.1				69.9	70.1
9 to 14 incidents	47.1				69.5	70.3
High school dropout by Wave 3						
Yes	17.7					44.8
No	72.9					68.4
Multiple *R*		0.407	0.450	0.585	0.585	0.603
R Squared		0.166	0.203	0.342	0.343	0.363

Factor Summary*

	eta	beta	beta	beta	beta	beta
Race/ethnicity	**.128**	.034	.028	.013	.013	.006
Population density	**.102**	**.066**	**.067**	**.052**	**.050**	.049
Parents' education level	**.350**	**.306**	**.275**	**.138**	**.138**	**.127**
Lived with 2 parents Waves 1–3	**.236**	**.184**	**.150**	**.082**	**.082**	**.054**
Parent involvement index	**.118**	.045	.027	.028	.028	.025
Held back grade 8 or earlier	**.246**		**.139**	**.070**	**.069**	**.059**
Suspended/expelled grade 8 or earlier	**.230**		**.126**	**.058**	**.061**	.039
Mean secondary school GPA	**.400**			**.147**	**.149**	**.132**
Mean secondary school college plans	**.506**			**.331**	**.332**	**.298**
Serious scholastic setback W1 to W2	**.202**			.040	.043	**.017**
Serious scholastic setback W2 to W3	**.169**			.053	.054	.037
Delinquency index (W2–3 combined)	**.114**				.022	.024
High school dropout by Wave 3	**.407**					**.174**

*All eta and beta statistics p<.05 are shown in **bold**.

See Table 3.3 for frequency distributions of predictor variables.

Note: W1 = Wave 1 data collection (grade 8, modal age 14), W2 = Wave 2 data collection (modal age 16), W3 = Wave 3 data collection (modal age 18)

in each category completing at least 1 year of college, with no adjustment for other factors (i.e., it shows the bivariate relationship). At the bottom of Column 1 are eta statistics; etas are analogous to product–moment correlations except that etas (a) capture any nonlinear relationships in addition to linear ones, and (b) are never negative—their values can range from 0 to 1.0. All of the remaining columns in Table 4.2 report multivariate analyses, showing estimated relationships when other factors in the column are controlled (i.e., included in the equation). At the bottom of these columns are beta coefficients, analogous to multiple regression coefficients (but including linear plus nonlinear relationships, again with values ranging from 0 to 1.0).

There are five different sets of predictors shown in Columns 2 to 6, with each column expanding on the previous set. We made use of all of these data in examining findings and reporting results; for that reason, we include all of the columns here, although most of the time readers can focus on only certain columns or simply rely on the descriptions in the text. The different columns correspond fairly closely to our treatment in the text, as well as to the structural equation model introduced later in this chapter, so we provide the following listing and brief rationale for each of the columns in Table 4.2.

Column 1, as noted previously, shows for each category the actual percentages of respondents in that category completing at least 1 year of college. This is useful descriptive information, but it takes no account of the extent to which the relationship may overlap with—and perhaps be caused by—other factors.

Column 2 shows shared effects of demographic and family background factors, and thus indicates how much of the dependent variable (academic attainment, in this chapter) is explainable from these early influences.

Column 3 adds important early educational background experiences prior to the end of eighth grade: having been held back a grade, and having been suspended or expelled. Comparing Columns 2 and 3 thus indicates how much *additional* variance is explained by these two factors, and it also shows to what extent and in what ways the patterns of prediction from the Column 2 factors are influenced by the inclusion of the additional predictors.

Column 4 adds dimensions of adolescent educational experiences: GPA averaged across the first three surveys (modal ages 14–18), college plans (expectations) also averaged across the first three surveys, experiences of scholastic setbacks (grade retention, suspension, and/or expulsion) between ages 14 and 16, and scholastic setbacks between ages 16 and 18. Comparing this column with the previous ones shows the marginal explanatory contribution of these additional factors to the adolescent educational experience.

Column 5 adds delinquent behaviors (averaged across the age 16 and 18 measures—for which we have full information for all respondents) to the set of predictors. It can be seen that it makes no appreciable addition to the prediction of long-term academic attainment (compare Columns 4 and 5), but in chapters 6 to 9 we see that it adds considerably to the prediction of various forms of substance use—and that is the reason for including it in all tables of this type.

Column 6 adds dropping out of high school by age 18 to the set of predictors. A comparison with Column 5 indicates that this is an important factor in later academic attainment. This is hardly surprising given that dropouts at modal age 22 constitute the bottom category in our scale of academic attainment. Nevertheless, as discussed later in this chapter, we considered it important to include this dimension in our structural equation model, and for sake of comparability we include it also in Column 6 of Table 4.2.

Race/Ethnicity

There are racial/ethnic differences in academic attainment, as indicated by dummy variables in the first rows of Table 4.1. Table 4.2 (Column 1) shows substantial differences in college attendance among racial/ethnic groups. About 64% of White men in our sample completed 1 or more years of college by age 22, compared with 52% of African-American men, 48% of Hispanic men, and 52% of men in the "Other race" category. Among women, the corresponding figures are 70% for Whites, 56% for African Americans, 54% for Hispanics, and 62% for those in the "Other race" category. When controls are introduced for population density and parental characteristics (Column 2), the percentage point difference in college attendance rates between Whites and African Americans drops from 12 to 5 for men and from 14 to 3 for women. The percentage difference between Whites and Hispanics drops from 16 to 7 for men and from 16 to 4 for women. As additional factors are controlled (see Columns 3 and 4 in Table 4.2), the racial/ethnic differences become even smaller.

What are the background factors that contribute most heavily to academic attainment and thus might account for much of the racial/ethnic differences in attainment? As shown by the beta statistics in the lower portion of Table 4.2, the strongest background contributors are parental education and the presence of both parents in the home; of lesser importance are urban density and parental involvement with the student in eighth grade. The finding that racial/ethnic differences overlap with socioeconomic and other background factors is hardly new; nevertheless, it remains exceedingly important. For those who hold that racial inequality in the United States is largely a socioeconomic matter, these data surely provide some support—at least when it comes to college attendance by young adults at the end of the 20th century and the start of the 21st. Parental education is a good indicator of overall socioeconomic level, although it also represents other factors that contribute positively to children's academic success. Similarly, the presence of both parents has a great deal to do with family economic circumstance, although here again it also represents much more.

Race and ethnicity differences are complex and deserving of special attention. Accordingly, we devote separate analyses to that topic in later publications. For now, it is sufficient to note that overall differences are controlled to some extent by our inclusion of the dummy variables in regression analyses and later in structural equation models. We note that such efforts do not fully capture interactive (i.e., nonadditive) racial/ethnic differences, some of which we expect to report elsewhere; however, we have conducted additional analyses sufficient to ensure that the full-sample findings reported here have not been substantially distorted by such interactions.

Population Density

Students who live in large metropolitan statistical areas (MSAs) in eighth grade (and thus most often throughout high school) are most likely to go to college, whereas those in nonurban areas are least likely to do so. The bivariate differences between these two groups are just below 14 percentage points for both men and women in terms of likelihood of completing at least 1 year of college (see Column 1 in Table 4.2). Controls for other background factors (see Column 2) reduce this differential somewhat, and further controls for educational success factors (see Column 4) reduce the differential to about 5 to 7 percentage points. The multiple regression analyses in Table 4.1 also reveal that, even after controlling for a full range of other predictors (including grades and college plans), academic attainment is slightly higher among those who grew up in large cities (or suburbs thereof), compared with those who grew up in nonmetropolitan areas.

Parental Education

Parental education is a widely used proxy for family socioeconomic level, but it is also a likely indicator of the educational modeling and expectations in the home environment. For these and other reasons, parental education (reported by respondents when they were in eighth grade) is among the strongest correlates of academic attainment at age 22. The regression coefficients in Table 4.1 indicate that, although the contribution from parental education overlaps with other predictors, a substantial contribution is nonoverlapping. As can be seen in Table 4.2 and Figure 4.2, children of the most highly educated parents are more than twice as likely to complete a year or more of college, compared with children of the least educated parents.[8] Moreover, even when other background factors are controlled (see Column 2 in Table 4.2), the ratio remains high at fully two to one for females and nearly two to one for males (see also the notations for adjusted percentages in Fig. 4.2). There are multiple and overlapping reasons for the positive relationship between parental education and children's academic attainment. These include the myriad things that more highly educated parents are likely to do, starting early in their children's lives, to prepare them for academic success in elementary school, secondary school, and eventually college.

When the equations include students' own grades, college plans, and any serious scholastic setbacks, the differences linked to parental education are substantially reduced (see Column 4 in Table 4.2, also notations in Fig. 4.2). This does not diminish the importance of parental education as a factor influencing children's academic attainment; rather, it indicates that a good portion of the impact is indirect via the children's educational successes and aspirations (as we illustrate later in the section featuring structural equation modeling). That said, it must be added that, even with all of these other factors controlled, there are still percentage-point spreads of about 10 for men and 20 for women in rates of completing a year or more of college when we contrast those having the most versus the least educated parents. Certainly one likely reason for this residual

---

[8]The five-level scale of parental education, shown in the MCA tables and figures, is a bracketed version of the 11-category scale used in the regression analyses (see notes to Table 3.3 for details). Table 4.2 and Figure 4.2 indicate the numbers or proportions of respondents in each predictor category. They show that there are only about half as many respondents whose parents' educational levels rank at the top of the scale (Level 5), compared with those whose parents are next highest (Level 4). This is indicated by the weighted numbers of cases in the table (left-hand column). The figure also clearly shows this through the widths of the bars, which are set proportionate to the weighted numbers of cases in each category. The procedure of varying bar width, which is used in subsequent figures, has the further advantage of depicting the total proportion of respondents within the total area under the bars. Thus, for example, Figure 4.2 shows that a higher *total proportion* of college students come from families with parental education at Level 4 versus Level 5, although the *rate* of college entrance is higher for the latter category.

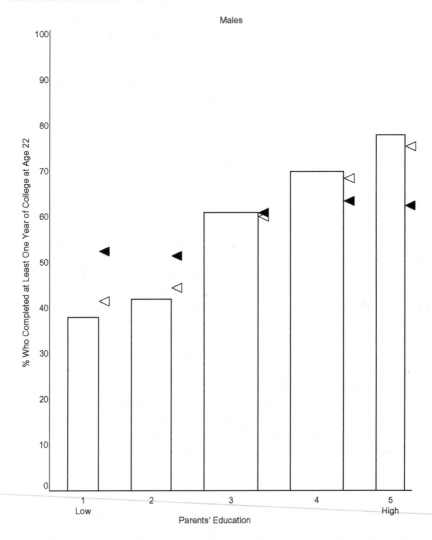

The main bars are unadjusted estimates. The bar width is proportionate to the weighted number of cases in the category.

◁ Percentage adjusted for race/ethnicity, population density, number of parents, and parental involvement (Column 2 in Table 4.2a)

◀ Percentage adjusted for race/ethnicity, population density, number of parents, parental involvement, having been held back, suspension/expulsion, GPA, college plans, and serious scholastic setbacks between Waves 1 and 2 and Waves 2 and 3 (Column 4 in Table 4.2a)

Figure 4.2a.   Percentage of young adults who have completed at least 1 year of college at age 22 (1999–2001) by level of parents' education (1 = low, 5 = high): males.

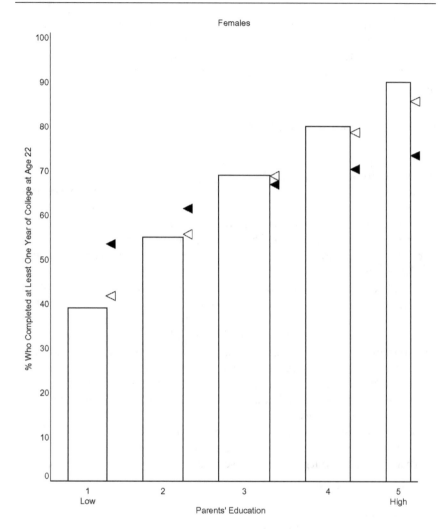

The main bars are unadjusted estimates. The bar width is proportionate to the weighted number of cases in the category.

◁ Percentage adjusted for race/ethnicity, population density, number of parents, and parental involvement (Column 2 in Table 4.2b)

◀ Percentage adjusted for race/ethnicity, population density, number of parents, parental involvement, having been held back, suspension/expulsion, GPA, college plans, and serious scholastic setbacks between Waves 1 and 2 and Waves 2 and 3 (Column 4 in Table 4.2b)

Figure 4.2b. Percentage of young adults who have completed at least 1 year of college at age 22 (1999–2001) by level of parents' education (1 = low, 5 = high): females.

direct (i.e., nonoverlapping) impact is that parents with higher levels of education are better able to provide the financial resources needed for college, and this financial advantage occurs above and beyond impacts of parental education on adolescents' earlier educational successes and aspirations.

Presence of Both Parents in Home

Another aspect of family/parental background is reflected by a measure of family intactness—specifically, the number of parents living in the same home as the respondent. This was measured at each of the first three data collections (i.e., modal ages 14, 16, and 18), and Table 4.1 indicates that each of these measurements is correlated with educational attainment, although the correlations grow stronger with increasing age. Moreover, a single indicator of whether two parents were present in the home at all three surveys is also correlated with attainment.[9] The multiple regression coefficients show that a considerable portion of the prediction from this measure overlaps with other predictors; nevertheless, an important nonoverlapping contribution also remains. For reasons of parsimony, we have opted to employ the single measure of two-parent presence throughout high school as a background measure in subsequent analyses. A further reason for using the single measure is our belief that a family *about to be disrupted* by the departure of a parent within a few years may already be an environment less conducive to a son or daughter's educational success.[10]

Further details are provided in Table 4.2 and Figure 4.3, showing that students from two-parent families are about half again as likely to complete at least 1 year of college as are those from families without both parents

---

[9]We recognize, of course, that just because a student reports two parents living in the home at all three data collections, it does not necessarily follow that they are *the same parents* or that they were present on an uninterrupted basis. Nevertheless, we believe that these two conditions held true for the great majority of those students who at all three surveys reported that they were living with two parents.

[10]As evidence of this assertion, we note that GPAs in 8th grade were a bit more strongly correlated with number of parents present at 12th grade ($r = .20$, males and females combined) than with number of parents present at eighth grade ($r = .15$). We are loath to attribute family disruptions to poor student performance several years earlier. The much more plausible interpretation is that families headed for separation and/or divorce are already disrupted and thus make a poorer-than-average contribution to their children's academic performance in eighth grade (as well as to their longer term academic attainment).

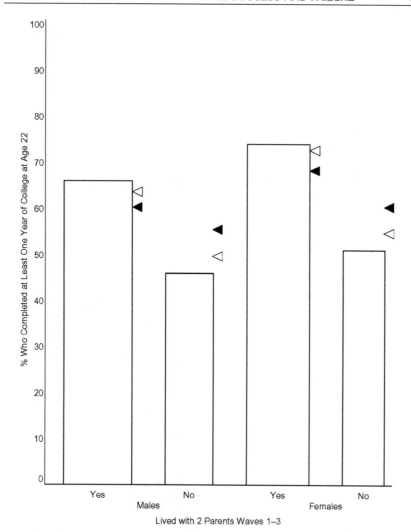

The main bars are unadjusted estimates. The bar width is proportionate to the weighted number of cases in the category.

◁ Percentage adjusted for race/ethnicity, population density, number of parents, and parental involvement (Column 2 in Table 4.2a & b)
◀ Percentage adjusted for race/ethnicity, population density, number of parents, parental involvement, having been held back, suspension/expulsion, GPA, college plans, and serious scholastic setbacks between Waves 1 and 2 and Waves 2 and 3 (Column 4 in Table 4.2a & b)

Figure 4.3. Percentage of young adults who have completed at least 1 year of college at age 22 (1999–2001) by presence of two parents in the home at ages 14, 16, and 18: males and females.

present. Among males the difference is 66% versus 46%, and among females it is 74% versus 51%. With other *background* factors controlled (see Column 2 in Table 4.2, also notations in Fig. 4.3), these percentage differences are reduced only modestly. When the students' GPA, college plans, and any serious scholastic setbacks are included in the equations, the percentage differences are further reduced. Yet even with all of these factors controlled, students with both parents in the home are 6% to 8% more likely to complete at least 1 year of college (see Column 4 in Table 4.2).

Of interest, a slightly higher proportion of males (65%) than females (59%) reported living with two parents at all of the three data collections (calculated from the weighted *N* column in Table 4.2). This is consistent with MTF cross-sectional surveys of 8th-, 10th-, and 12th-grade respondents in recent years. There is a slight but consistent tendency for higher proportions of males than females (3%–4%, on average) to report their father living in the same home with them; in contrast, there is no consistent gender difference in reports of living with their mother—high rates are reported by both males and females. It may be that fathers of teenage sons are somewhat more hesitant to separate and leave home than are fathers of teenage daughters (Mott, 1994)—perhaps reflecting a view that sons are especially likely to need "a father's presence."

As noted earlier, we treat the presence or absence of two parents throughout high school as a background factor, even if the departure of one parent occurs as late as age 18, because a family on the brink of parental separation may already be a less-than-optimal environment for children's educational development (although it is likely that a two-parent family with strained marital relations is worse than a more harmonious single-parent family) (Amato & Keith, 1991b; Hetherington & Stanley-Hagan, 1999). It is also the case, of course, that parental separation generally reduces financial resources available to the children, including funds for college (Amato & Keith, 1991a; McLanahan & Sandefur, 1994). Consistent with this observation is the finding, noted previously and detailed in the structural equation modeling that follows, that an important portion of the impact of parental presence or absence on academic attainment is direct, above and beyond impacts on GPA and other indicators of success in school.

Parental Involvement in Students' Lives

A measure of parental involvement in students' lives was developed based on four aspects of parental oversight and participation: checking on homework, helping with homework, requiring chores, and limiting TV viewing. For the correlations and regression analyses, equally weighted means across these four aspects were used as indexes of parental involvement at each of the three grades.[11] As Table 4.1 (Column 1) shows, parental involvement in early years (i.e., at least as early as eighth grade) was more important than later parental involvement as a predictor of long-term academic attainment. The multivariate regression coefficients in Tables 4.1 and 4.2 indicate that any effects of early parental involvement on academic attainment overlap with other factors (primarily college plans, judging from the structural equation models reported later in the chapter).

Summarizing our findings on family background, we see that both parental education and family intactness retain some independent positive contribution to academic attainment, even after GPA, college plans, and a variety of other factors are included in the multivariate analyses. This is fully consistent with the notion that there are economic advantages to having highly educated parents and an intact (i.e., two-parent) family, and that such advantages make some direct contribution to a young person's ability to enter and complete college above and beyond the indirect contributions via good grades and college plans (Wallerstein & Lewis, 1998).

Scholastic Setbacks

Most students reach eighth grade without ever having experienced grade retention (having been held back) or suspension or expulsion from school. For those who do, such experiences are likely to be memorable—indeed, momentous—events in their lives as well as their parents' lives. Each of these scholastic setbacks usually indicates that a student has not adjusted well to the requirements of school. A student's grade retention is an indicator of poor academic performance or, in rare cases, a major health problem. A student's suspension or expulsion is an indicator of an unwillingness or inability to follow school rules and requirements. These are more than just symptoms or indicators, however; they are also fairly dramatic and public events in their own right, carrying further consequences. Among the consequences can be the feeling of being labeled by friends, classmates, and significant adults as someone who has failed to do well in school.

---

[11]In the structural equation modeling reported later in this chapter, the four aspects were treated as four indicators; the resulting (optimized) weights are nearly equal.

Grade Retention (Ever Held Back)

The large majority of students in our sample were never held back a grade in school. Among boys, about one in four had ever been held back (as of the end of eighth grade); 20% of the total sample had been held back just once, and 4% had been held back more than once. Among girls, the rates were lower. It is worth noting that during the 1990s, the rates of grade retention declined to levels a bit lower than those for our panel mentioned previously—specifically, to totals of about 15% for males and 10% for females (see Table A.4.3 in the appendix). Although relatively rare, grade retention is still a fairly strong predictor of low academic attainment (see Table 4.1). As shown in Table 4.2 and Figure 4.4, those held back were only about half as likely to complete at least 1 year of college, compared with classmates never held back. The table and figure also show that this differential is cut roughly in half when background factors (including suspension or expulsion) are controlled, and it is cut in half again (to about one quarter of the original size—see beta coefficients at the bottom of Table 4.2) when grades and college plans throughout high school also are controlled. It thus appears that some of the effects associated with being held back operate indirectly through grades and/or college plans during secondary school (as shown later in the section on structural equation modeling).

We caution against interpreting the relationships described previously as necessarily showing effects or impacts of the actual grade-retention experience. Although the experience and aftermath of grade retention (including identification by many classmates and teachers as someone who *flunked*) may be traumatic (Pierson & Connell, 1992), it must also be recognized that grade retention does not ordinarily happen capriciously or at random. In most cases, this scholastic setback is a symptom of prior educational difficulties, and it would be difficult (short of a rather unlikely controlled experiment) to establish just how much, if any, of the low achievement should be credited to grade retention per se.

Suspension or Expulsion

Another serious scholastic setback is being suspended or expelled from school. Fully 29% of boys reported having been suspended or expelled, and more than half of these (16% of the total) indicated that it happened more than once (prior to the end of eighth grade). The rates are much lower among girls, with 9% reporting just one suspension or expulsion and 6% reporting more than one. It appears that rates of suspension or

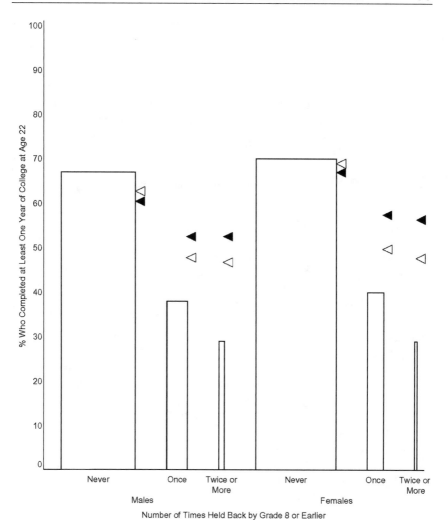

Figure 4.4.   Percentage of young adults who have completed at least 1 year of college at age 22 (1999–2001) by ever held back a whole grade as of Grade 8: males and females.

expulsion have not changed much in recent years (see Table A.4.4 in the appendix). As shown in Table 4.2 and illustrated in Figure 4.5, only 36% of males and females who experienced two or more suspensions or expulsions (by the end of eighth grade) had completed at least a year of college by age 22, in contrast to 66% of males and 70% of females who had not experienced this form of scholastic setback at all, and 47% and 42%, respectively, who experienced it only once. As was true for grade retention, the shared relationships when controlling for other background factors are smaller than the bivariate ones, and controls for grades and college plans reduce coefficients further (see Tables 4.1 and 4.2), again suggesting that some effects are indirect.

Grades and College Plans

As shown in the first column of Table 4.1, the most powerful predictors of academic attainment at age 22 are grades—specifically, self-reported GPA during the past year—and college plans. Table 4.1 shows correlations and regression coefficients separately for self-reported GPA at the end of 8th, 10th, and 12th grades (as well as for means across all three grades). The table reveals an important difference between GPA and college plans in terms of patterns of correlations across age. Whereas GPA values at any of the three grades are about equally good as predictors of eventual academic attainment, college plans become increasingly better predictors as students move from 8th to 10th to 12th grade. It is also noteworthy that the zero-order correlations for *mean* GPA and *mean* college plans are roughly .50, indicating that either of these dimensions alone can account for about one quarter of the variance in attainment. Clearly, these dimensions are central to our exploration of academic attainment; they deserve key roles in our structural equation modeling efforts. First, let us provide a bit more detail on each.

As shown in Table 4.2 and illustrated in Figure 4.6, *mean* GPA is an excellent predictor of the level of education attained by age 22. Entering college (and completing at least 1 year) was seven times as likely among males with a GPA of A versus males with a GPA of D or lower (95% vs. 13%); for females, the ratio was nearly as large (93% vs. 16%).

The product–moment correlations in Table 4.1 indicate that 8th-grade GPA predicts later academic attainment almost as well as do 10th- and 12th-grade GPA; in fact, 12th-grade GPA is actually a slightly weaker correlate of long-term attainment, and we discuss the possible reasons for this later. For now, the point to remember is that, by the end of eighth grade, much of what contributes to academic attainment or nonattainment is firmly in place.

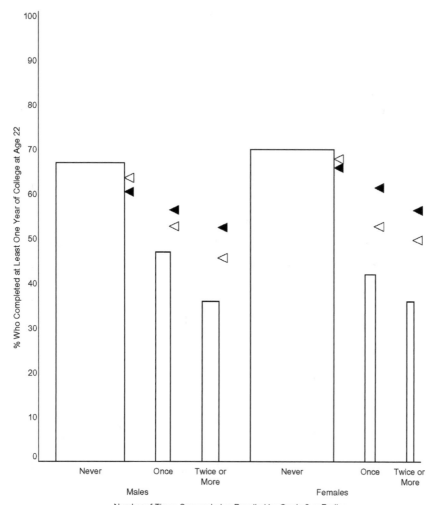

The main bars are unadjusted estimates. The bar width is proportionate to the weighted number of cases in the category.

◁ Percentage adjusted for race/ethnicity, population density, number of parents, parental involvement, and having been held back (Column 3 in Table 4.2a & b)
◀ Percentage adjusted for race/ethnicity, population density, number of parents, parental involvement, having been held back, suspension/expulsion, GPA, college plans, and serious scholastic setbacks between Waves 1 and 2 and Waves 2 and 3 (Column 4 in Table 4.2a & b)

Figure 4.5. Percentage of young adults who have completed at least 1 year of college at age 22 (1999–2001) by ever suspended or expelled Grade 8 or earlier: males and females.

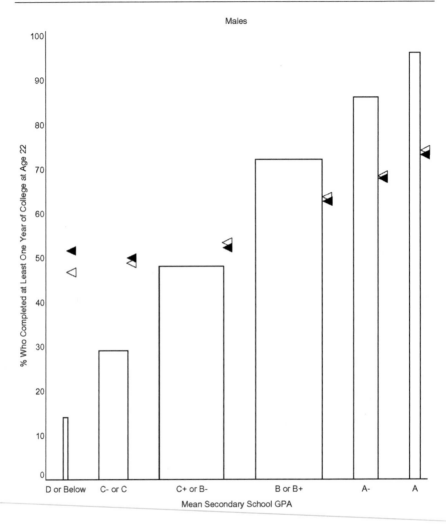

The main bars are unadjusted estimates. The bar width is proportionate to the weighted number of cases in the category.

◁ Percentage adjusted for race/ethnicity, population density, parents' education, number of parents, parental involvement, ever having been held back, college plans, and serious scholastic setbacks between Waves 1 and 2 and Waves 2 and 3 (Column 4 in Table 4.2a)

◀ Percentage adjusted for race/ethnicity, population density, parents' education, number of parents, parental involvement, ever having been held back, GPA, college plans, serious scholastic setbacks between Waves 1 and 2 and Waves 2 and 3, delinquency index (Waves 2 and 3 combined), and high school dropout by Wave 3 (Column 6 in Table 4.2a)

Figure 4.6a. Percentage of young adults who have completed at least 1 year of college at age 22 (1999–2001) by mean secondary school GPA Grades 8, 10, and 12 combined: males.

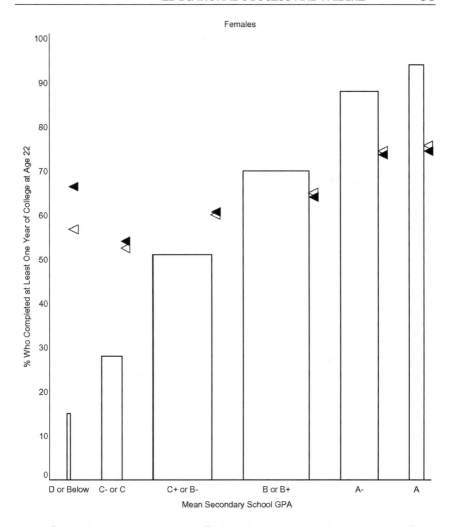

The main bars are unadjusted estimates. The bar width is proportionate to the weighted number of cases in the category.

◁ Percentage adjusted for race/ethnicity, population density, parents' education, number of parents, parental involvement, ever having been held back, college plans, and serious scholastic setbacks between Waves 1 and 2 and Waves 2 and 3 (Column 4 in Table 4.2b)
◀ Percentage adjusted for race/ethnicity, population density, parents' education, number of parents, parental involvement, ever having been held back, GPA, college plans, serious scholastic setbacks between Waves 1 and 2 and Waves 2 and 3, delinquency index (Waves 2 and 3 combined), and high school dropout by Wave 3 (Column 6 in Table 4.2b)

Figure 4.6b. Percentage of young adults who have completed at least 1 year of college at age 22 (1999–2001) by mean secondary school GPA Grades 8, 10, and 12 combined: females.

One factor that does change considerably in its predictive power after eighth grade is college plans. College expectations decline somewhat between 8th and 12th grades (shown in Table 3.2), but also become more accurate in forecasting actual college attainment. Among males, the zero-order correlations between college plans and academic attainment (at age 22) rise from 0.32 to 0.41 to 0.52 as adolescents move from modal ages 14 to 16 to 18 (corresponding to 8th, 10th, and 12th grades for most); among females, the upward progression is nearly identical, from 0.30 to 0.39 to 0.48 (see Table 4.1). It is not surprising that expectations of going to college become more accurate as most young people progress through high school; for most of our panel respondents, the Wave 3 survey occurred late in their senior year, by which time many students have already received notice of acceptance by one or more colleges and have confronted questions about whether and how they can afford the financial costs.

Perhaps more surprising is the fact that, even as early as eighth grade, plans and expectations about college closely foreshadow the later outcomes. Among eighth graders in our panel who expected they "definitely would" complete a 4-year college program, fully 67% of males and 73% of females did complete at least 1 year (and most completed more) by modal age 22; among eighth graders expecting they "definitely would not" complete a 4-year program, only 26% of males and 21% of females completed a year or more of college.[12] This is further evidence that, before adolescents even enter high school, the factors that determine their later academic attainment are already largely in place.

Serious Scholastic Setbacks During High School

We showed earlier in this chapter that being held back a grade or suspended/expelled during the first eight grades of school can have important negative implications for later academic attainment. What about such setbacks when they occur during the high school years? We should first note that the large majority of students experience no such setbacks during high school. For the 2-year interval between late 8th grade and late 10th grade, only 14% of boys and 11% of girls in our panel reported either of these setbacks, and only about 1% of boys and girls reported both. For the next 2-year interval, reports were even fewer: 11% and 1% for boys,

---

[12]These findings are based on separate analyses. The Table 4.2 MCA findings, showing even larger differences, are based on *mean* college plans calculated across three surveys (i.e., combining data from modal ages 14, 16, and 18).

8% and less than 0.5% for girls. Less than one third of these setbacks involved being held back; most involved suspension or expulsion. Although they are infrequent during high school, each of the two types of setbacks is important, and preliminary examination revealed that each is linked to academic attainment as well as other dimensions of interest. Accordingly, we include them in our analyses.

Those who experienced either of these serious scholastic setbacks during high school were only about two thirds as likely as their high school classmates to complete at least 1 year of college, and the handful who experienced *both* kinds of setbacks within a 2-year interval were far less likely to go to college (see Column 1 in Table 4.2). When other factors such as GPA and college plans are controlled, these differences are substantially diminished, but not reduced to zero. Later in this chapter, using structural equation modeling, we can see some of the ways in which these serious setbacks are linked with GPA and college plans.

ADDITIONAL CORRELATES/PREDICTORS OF ACADEMIC ATTAINMENT

We now touch more briefly on several other variables considered in our analyses of contributors to academic attainment. In considering dimensions for inclusion, we were mindful of possible connections not only with academic attainment, but also with substance use.

Delinquency and Other Problem Behaviors

A number of other behaviors measured at each grade fall within the category often treated as problem behaviors (Donovan, Jessor, & Costa, 1988; Jessor & Jessor, 1977) and serve as strong and consistent correlates of substance use (Ellickson et al., 2004; Hawkins, Catalano, & Miller, 1992; Tubman, Gil, & Wagner, 2004). These include misbehaving in school (leading to being sent to the office), cutting days of school, skipping classes, as well as a more general (i.e., not specific to school) index of delinquent behaviors. Consistent with earlier research (Osgood, Johnston, O'Malley, & Bachman, 1988; Osgood, Wilson, O'Malley, Bachman, & Johnston, 1996), all of these behaviors correlate positively with each other and with substance use (data shown in Table A.3.3 in the appendix, and in later chapters). Column 1 in Table 4.1 shows that all of these behaviors also correlate negatively with academic attainment, but Column 2 indicates that none makes any appreciable unique contribution to prediction once other variables (including background factors, grades, and college plans) are included in the equation. The measure of delinquency, as we show later, is particularly likely to be associated with various forms of substance use. Accordingly, we return to this measure in greater detail in the next chapter.

Evenings Out for Fun and Recreation

Another correlate of substance use among students is their frequency of evenings out for fun and recreation, but Table 4.1 shows that on average this measure does not have any strong or consistent relationship with longer term academic attainment. Perhaps some students stay home on school nights to work on their homework because they want to (to maintain their good scholastic performance), whereas others may do so because they have to (to bring up their lower levels of performance). Conversely, among students who go out frequently, it may be that some do so because they do not care about homework, but others do so because they quickly and efficiently manage their homework. It could also be the case that successful students are more likely than average to be part of peer networks involved in fun activities during evenings. Although we suspect that spending evenings out for fun and recreation can influence academic performance, and vice versa, it appears that the patterns of causation are multiple and not easy to disentangle.

Actual and Preferred Hours of Work

Other analyses of MTF data have shown that number of hours of part-time work during the school year, as well as students' *preferences* for such work, are positively correlated with substance use (Bachman et al., 2003; Safron, Schulenberg, & Bachman, 2001). Table 4.1 shows that these dimensions, particularly in 12th grade, are negative predictors of academic attainment at age 22, although the multivariate coefficients indicate large overlaps with other predictors.

Religious Attendance and Importance

Numerous analyses of MTF data (Wallace, Brown, Bachman, & LaVeist, 2003; Wallace & Forman, 1998; Wallace & Muroff, 2002; Wallace & Williams, 1997) and other research (Nonnemaker, McNeely, & Blum, 2003; Wills, Yaeger, & Sandy, 2003) have shown that students who frequently attend religious services and/or rate religion to be important in their lives are less likely to use cigarettes, alcohol, and illicit drugs. Table 4.1 shows that religious attendance is also positively correlated with long-term academic attainment (Column 1), although there is little evidence of any contribution that is not explained by, or mediated through, other variables (Column 2). The findings for ratings of importance of religion are less clear and consistent.

Self-Esteem

Self-esteem shows modest positive correlations with long-term academic attainment (as well as somewhat stronger correlations with eighth-grade GPA, as shown in Table A.3.3 in the appendix). The multivariate coefficients show virtually no unique contribution to the prediction of attainment.

We Focus on the "Short List" of Predictors

As noted earlier, a comparison of Columns 2 and 3 in Table 4.1 shows that the additional correlates reported in this section contribute rather little to the prediction of academic attainment, above and beyond the prediction provided by grades, college plans, and background factors. Our structural equation modeling, presented later in this chapter, is thus limited to the short list of predictors. We do not consider these other dimensions to be unimportant, but in this instance we find that the need for parsimony in modeling outweighs the tendency to be inclusive. The one exception we make, starting in the next chapter, is to include the delinquency measure as a key indicator of tendencies toward problem behaviors—tendencies that may moderate relationships between educational experiences and substance use.

A STRUCTURAL EQUATION MODEL OF ACADEMIC ATTAINMENT

In the previous sections, we examined a variety of important predictors and how they relate to academic attainment. We also noted some of the ways in which the predictors appear to overlap. We now take a much closer look at interrelationships among predictors, attempting to discern how background factors and earlier educational experiences combine with grades and college plans during the high school years to contribute to academic attainment by age 22.

It is of interest in its own right to examine the dynamic relationships among background factors, GPA, and college plans throughout secondary school as they contribute to eventual academic attainment. But examining these relationships also provides the background for our efforts in later chapters to understand the dynamics of how substance use is related to educational success—both short and longer term. If we want to see how smoking, drinking, and illicit drug use may result from and/or contribute to scholastic performance (or nonperformance), then it should help if we can begin with a fairly clear view of how other factors combine to shape academic accomplishments.

The method employed in the remainder of this chapter, and included in chapters to follow, is structural equation modeling (SEM). SEM presents analysts with an array of options and choices, resulting in numerous decisions to be made as the analyses progress. Although some details of the structural models have been placed in the appendix, the rationale for our decisions about the broad shape of the model is included here. The model is displayed in Figure 4.7. Path coefficients are included in the figure, but we defer discussion of those values until after we have outlined our rationale for the model. Figure 4.7 continues our practice of reporting findings separately for the two genders. There are some gender differences, but we are far more impressed with gender similarities than differences. This consistency across genders adds to our confidence in the SEM findings. Summary listings of the model fit statistics, variance explained for each of the endogenous factors in the model (*R* Squares), and relationships and impacts (direct and total) of all predictors in the model on academic attainment are shown in Tables A.4.5 to A.4.7 in the appendix.

Background Measures as Exogenous Factors

All background measures discussed earlier are treated as exogenous factors in our model. These include three race/ethnicity dummy variables (excluding the fourth category, White, as the comparison), two urban density dummy variables (excluding the middle category as the comparison), parental education, presence of both parents in the home, parental involvement in students' lives (with four indicators, as noted earlier and detailed in the appendix), and two aspects of educational background prior to the end of eighth grade—grade retention and suspension/expulsion.

These exogenous factors are allowed to correlate (with each other) and are treated as potential causes of all other variables in the model (with

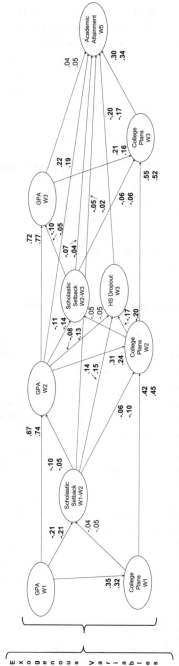

Coefficients for male sample shown above coefficients for female sample. Coefficients that are p<.05 (two-tailed) are shown in **bold**.

Note: W1 = Wave 1 data collection (grade 8, modal age 14), W2 = Wave 2 data collection (modal age 16), W3 = Wave 3 data collection (modal age 18), W5 = Wave 5 data collection (modal age 22)

Model Fit Statistics

	Males	Females
Comparative Fit Index (CFI)	.992	.991
Root Mean-Square Error of Approximation (RMSEA)	.040	.044
Chi-Square	309	427
Degrees of Freedom	97	97

Figure 4.7. Basic structural equation model of academic attainment.

one exception).[13] We recognize that this approach of fully controlling the exogenous factors is less parsimonious than if we required impacts on later endogenous factors to be only indirect via eighth-grade factors; however, the full control approach has several advantages. First, model fit is considerably improved, indicating that we have not distorted the findings to fit the model. Second, we are able to observe at all points whether the controls for the exogenous factors make important differences; most of the time they do not, but there are some interesting exceptions noted later. Third, and particularly important, by retaining the potential for the exogenous control factors to impact virtually any endogenous factor in the model, we establish a practice that may prove useful when substance-use measures are included in models used in later chapters. For example, we are consistent in taking into account differences in race/ethnicity and urban density throughout our analyses. By doing so, we document any racial/ethnic differences in the substance-use measures (in the listings of direct and total effects that accompany the figures), as well as in the factors that pertain directly to educational success or failure.

Interconnecting GPA, College Plans, and Academic Attainment

As can be seen in Figure 4.7, we model GPA in 8th grade as causing GPA in 10th grade, which in turn causes GPA in 12th grade. Actually, the term *GPA* may be a bit of a misnomer at this stage of our analysis (albeit a convenient one because it makes easier the match with the analyses in the earlier portion of the chapter). Our model assumes a latent factor that might be termed *scholastic success*, which we view as determined by a constellation of student abilities and motivations to perform well in school. We view this latent factor of scholastic success as relatively stable across time, but still subject to (mostly gradual) change. This underlies our decision to model the factor at 8th grade as a primary cause of the factor at 10th grade, and so on. Our one available indicator, self-reported GPA, does a reasonably good job of capturing the effects of these student characteristics as reflected in the grades assigned by teachers based on performance in various classes.

However, GPA is not a perfect indicator, even of grade-getting ability, particularly because in our study GPA is measured (i.e., "sampled") at

---

[13]The sole exception is that early experiences of grade retention or suspension/expulsion are treated as potential causes only of eighth-grade endogenous factors, plus age-22 academic attainment. The rationale is that impacts on 10th- and 12th-grade endogenous factors operate indirectly, whereas later serious scholastic setbacks are captured by the change measures.

only three points during the secondary school years (the ends of 8th, 10th, and 12th grades). Consider the fluctuations occurring from one semester to another in selection/assignment of courses and teachers; some are more demanding than others, and equal levels of student ability and motivation can lead to different grades depending on these and other influences. Although our use of GPA across whole years helps to reduce the effects of such perturbations, the fact remains that some students may have a tough year in 8th grade, others in 10th grade, still others in 9th or 11th grades; of course, some students may not experience any particularly difficult or atypical years. We thus consider our GPA measures to have some modest degree of error, including sampling error as well as any reporting error (all factor loadings are set at 0.90, as shown in Table A.3.4 in the appendix).

College plans are modeled in a fashion analogous to GPA, and for much the same reasons. We view college plans as relatively stable but evolving during high school. Unlike GPA, the measure of college plans does not depend on correct recall, because respondents are asked simply to indicate their expectations of completing a 4-year college program (using a four-point scale: "definitely won't," "probably won't," "probably will," "definitely will"). Although this short scale limits accuracy of measurement (particularly given that large proportions of respondents choose the top category: "definitely will"), the college plans measure yielded reliability and stability estimates fairly similar to those for GPA. Accordingly, the error estimates were set to produce factor loadings of .90 (see Table A.3.4 in the appendix).

How are GPA and college plans to be connected in a model of academic attainment? We explored a number of possibilities, including cross-lagged paths (allowing each to predict the other 2 years later, and including all of the exogenous factors as predictors, as illustrated in Fig. A.4.1 in the appendix). After trying various combinations, we found that the simplest and best-fitting model treats GPA as a cause of college plans at the same measurement point (i.e., 8th-grade GPA predicting 8th-grade college plans, and the same at 10th and 12th grades, as shown in Fig. 4.7—see also Fig. A.4.1 in the appendix). It should be noted that the GPA measure covers all of the academic year, whereas the college plans measure asks about expectations at the time of the survey. Thus, the causal linkage chosen for our model is consistent with the chronology of the survey: GPA during the past year influences current college expectations.

We did consider the possibility that college expectations at one point influence GPA at a later point, but although this seems plausible enough, we found no evidence to support it. Specifically, we tried adding lagged predictions from 8th-grade college plans to 10th-grade GPA, and similarly from 10th-grade college plans to 12th-grade GPA; the paths were all close to zero, thus confirming that the one-way causal interpretations shown in the model are consistent with the data and a lagged reciprocal causation is not needed.

How should the GPA and college plans factors be linked to academic attainment at age 22? Initially, we modeled the third point (corresponding to modal age 18, when most were nearing the end of 12th grade) as the direct cause, through which any effects of earlier GPA and college plans should have indirect impacts. That proved fully workable for college plans, which grow increasingly accurate throughout high school. For GPA, however, it was inconsistent with the finding that 10th-grade GPA is a slightly better predictor of academic attainment than is 12th-grade GPA (see Table 4.1), for reasons discussed later in this chapter. Accordingly, we added a direct path from 10th-grade GPA to academic attainment at age 22, as shown in Figure 4.7, thereby improving the fit of the model.

Incorporating Serious Scholastic Setbacks Into the Model

One of the final steps in model building was to incorporate the experiences of serious scholastic setbacks—being held back a grade and/or being suspended or expelled—that occurred during the final years of secondary school. As noted earlier, these events are relatively infrequent (and thus cannot account for much variance in eventual academic attainment, simply because too few students are affected); however, for those involved, the differences in attainment are substantial. By including these measures in the model, we are able to explore to what extent the events may be directly causal and to what extent they are merely symptoms of more fundamental problems (as captured by the other elements in the model).

An additional reason for including these scholastic setbacks in the model is that they may be related to substance use. In subsequent chapters, we incorporate various forms of substance use into the model in an effort to determine their relationships with educational successes and failures. Our inclusion of scholastic setbacks in the model makes it possible to consider whether such experiences contribute to substance use, or vice versa.

The serious scholastic setbacks occurred between the surveys and are modeled accordingly, as shown in Figure 4.7. We considered it likely that they could be influenced by prior GPA and college plans, and also could contribute to later GPA and college plans; therefore, all of these paths are included in the model. We also considered it plausible that scholastic

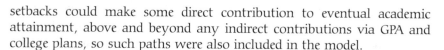

setbacks could make some direct contribution to eventual academic attainment, above and beyond any indirect contributions via GPA and college plans, so such paths were also included in the model.

Incorporating Age-18 Dropout Status Into the Model

Another kind of scholastic setback, even more serious than those discussed earlier, is dropping out of school within 4 years after eighth grade (i.e., modal age 18). At first glance, it may seem strange to include this dimension as a predictor of educational attainment at age 22 because the lack of a high school diploma actually defines the bottom position on our attainment scale. Nevertheless, we concluded that a dynamic model of academic attainment should take account of the fact that a portion of young people have already taken actions by age 18 that do much to shape their attainment by age 22. First, those who stay in school and are about to receive their high school diploma have effectively ruled out dropout or GED-only status; that is, they already have moved beyond the bottom two categories on the attainment scale. Second, although those who are in dropout status at the third (modal age 18) data collection are by no means doomed to remain dropouts, it is nevertheless true that dropout status at modal age 18 does have important effects on longer term academic attainment. Thus, we considered it important to include this dimension in the model.

College aspirations and expectations are likely to be among the factors contributing to staying in school. Accordingly, our model treats college plans measured at 10th grade (modal age 16) as a factor affecting dropout status at age 18. Because most dropping out occurs between modal ages 16 and 18, this set of causal assumptions seems consistent with chronology.

Another potentially important cause of dropping out is GPA. We opted not to include age-18 GPA among the causes, given that dropping out may occur at an earlier age. Instead we include GPA at age 16 as a direct cause (age-14 GPA is not included as a direct cause, but contributes to dropping out indirectly via age-16 GPA and other intervening factors).

STRUCTURAL MODEL FINDINGS: BACKGROUND (EXOGENOUS) FACTORS

Our examination of structural model findings makes use of Figure 4.7, which details causal paths among endogenous factors. Additional model findings appear in Tables A.4.5 to A.4.7 in the appendix. In earlier sections of this chapter, we have shown overall (bivariate) correlations between each of the factors and academic attainment, and we have taken a first look at how some of the factors may overlap in these relationships. Now we have another perspective, this one provided by the (causal) model described previously. We are well aware of the danger that one can get back from models merely what one builds in. (Recall Carson's Dictum: "You buy the premise, you buy the sketch.") With that in mind, we have tried to be cautious in specifying the model and in interpreting the results.

We begin with some general observations based on the results shown in Figure 4.7. First, the overall fit of the model to the data is reasonably good for both males and females. The Comparative Fit Index (CFI) is .992 for males and .991 for females, and the Root Mean Square Error of Approximation (RMSEA) is .040 for males and .044 for females. The R-squared values for prediction of academic attainment at age 22 are .474 for males and .524 for females. The similarity of these R-squared values to those shown in Column 4 of Table 4.1 may be viewed as further evidence that the model fits the data well and does not seriously distort any important relationships.[14]

The Importance of Parents

It is often observed that one key to a long and healthy life is to choose the right parents; in other words, genetic inheritance plays a central role in health and longevity. Having the right parents is also an important key to academic attainment. For good academic health, one wants to have parents who are well educated; in general, it also helps if they are not separated, divorced, or on the verge of either separation or divorce. The educational environment that parents provide, both in the home and in their choices of elementary and secondary schools for their children, has an impact on academic attainment. So also do the resources that educated

---

[14]The model R-squared values differ slightly from those in Table 4.1 (Column 4) using nearly all of the same predictors in simple multiple regression analyses. Two causes for such differences are worth noting. On one hand, assuming other things equal, R-squared values in the model would be higher because several of the relationships in the model (primarily those involving GPA and college plans) have been adjusted upward slightly (i.e., disattenuated) by corrections for error. On the other hand, constraints imposed by the model could have acted to lower R-squared values, although in fact it appears that little of this occurred.

and intact families (i.e., those enjoying better economic circumstances, on average) are able to provide when it comes time to pay for college. Although none of these characteristics is absolutely necessary or sufficient for academic success, the fact remains that parents are central to the educational experiences and outcomes of children.

Among all of the exogenous factors in our model, parental education shows the largest effects on academic attainment—total effects of 0.23 for males and 0.32 for females, some of which are indirect via GPA and college plans (for details, see Table A.4.7 in the appendix). As noted earlier in this chapter, the direct effects of parental education on academic attainment, above and beyond any contributions to earlier scholastic success and aspirations, may reflect the impact of family socioeconomic level on the average student's ability to pay for college. Indeed, even the impacts of parental education on college plans, a strong relationship that is evident as early as eighth grade, may arise in part because students of better educated parents are taught not only that college is important but also that it is affordable (Lareau, 2003).

The presence of both parents in the home throughout high school shows the next largest effects among the exogenous factors in the model—total effects on academic attainment of 0.14 for males and 0.21 for females. Some of these effects are indirect; children from two-parent families have higher GPAs in eighth grade (and later), are less likely to experience serious scholastic setbacks (grade retention, suspension, or expulsion), and are substantially less likely to drop out of high school by age 18. An appreciable portion of the effects is direct, again suggesting that parental ability to contribute to the costs of college has an additional positive impact on academic attainment.

It is of interest that parental education and parental presence in the home matter a bit more for academic attainment among females than males. Both of these factors, as noted previously, may have a good deal to do with the affordability of college. It is possible that parental financial resources matter somewhat less for males than for females when it comes to college attendance; however, it is beyond our present scope to resolve that issue. In a meta-analysis, Amato and Keith (1991a) state:

> ... the univariate and multivariate analyses indicate that parental divorce is linked to low educational attainment more strongly among women than men. This result is consistent with previous literature showing that non-custodial fathers are more likely to maintain contact with sons than with daughters and more likely to provide child support payments to sons than to daughters (Hetherington, Cox, & Cox, 1982). (p. 56)

Peters (1991) reported that Canadian adolescent girls expect to receive a greater percentage of their college tuition and other expenses (i.e., not food, lodging, or clothing) from their parents than do adolescent boys. Powell and Steelman (1989) found that having brothers decreased the odds of receiving parental assistance for college, but having sisters did not (suggesting that parents will give more of their limited income to sons).

Parental involvement in homework, as well as parental supervision of TV watching and chores, correlates positively with academic attainment, but appears to make little contribution (either direct or indirect). GPA and college expectations in eighth grade are somewhat higher among students whose parents show higher levels of involvement; nevertheless, the total effects of the parental involvement factor on long-term academic attainment are small and fall short of being statistically significant.

Other Background Factors

As can be seen in Table A.4.7 in the appendix, three out of the six total effects for the race/ethnicity measures fall short of statistical significance. This should not be taken to indicate that no important academic attainment differences are linked to race/ethnicity (indeed, the bivariate factor correlations are all significant). Rather, it suggests to us that such differences are largely overlapping with other factors in the model, particularly the other exogenous factors such as parental education. An examination of the path coefficients for the race/ethnicity factors (data not shown) generally revealed small effects. One exception worth noting is that, among both males and females, it appears that those in the "Other race" category (i.e., neither White nor African-American nor Hispanic) are somewhat below average in eighth-grade GPA when other background factors are controlled in the model. Another exception is that dropping out as of age 18 is less likely than average among African-American females (with other factors controlled), whereas that is not the case for African-American males. In subsequent publications, we look more closely at differences linked to race/ethnicity. For the present, it is sufficient to note that such differences are controlled in the model, and they do not confound the findings reported here.

The differences linked to population density yield several statistically significant total effects on academic attainment at age 22, as shown in Table A.4.7. Those from large metropolitan statistical areas (MSAs) show slightly higher levels of academic attainment than the comparison group (those from smaller MSAs). Additionally, males (but not females) from more rural areas (i.e., non-MSAs) may be somewhat lower than average in academic attainment. These effects appear to be more direct than indirect, suggesting that there may be differences in availability of higher education opportunities linked to urban density. Such matters lie outside our scope of inquiry here, but it is important to note that our model controls for such differences.

We reported earlier in this chapter that early experiences of having been held back a grade in school, or having been suspended or expelled, are generally clear indicators of important scholastic difficulties. Moreover, such scholastic setbacks can be traumatic in their own right and thus cause additional difficulties. These problems can be expected to overlap with poor grades and low college aspirations, and the findings in Table A.4.7 show that they do; there are significant indirect effects on academic attainment, which occur most notably via eighth-grade GPA. There are also some significant direct effects, indicating that even after grades and college plans throughout high school are taken into account, there remain some additional negative impacts of these early setbacks. (Later scholastic setbacks show further negative impacts, as reported later in this chapter.)

STRUCTURAL MODEL FINDINGS: HIGH SCHOOL (ENDOGENOUS) FACTORS

Grade Point Average

Grade point average is a strongly positive predictor of later academic attainment, as shown throughout this chapter. As modeled in Figure 4.7, GPA is highly stable throughout high school; stability estimates range from .67 to .77. Table A.4.7 shows that GPA as early as the end of eighth grade has strong effects on age-22 academic attainment. Because no direct effect was found to be necessary, these effects of 8th-grade GPA are entirely indirect, primarily via GPA in later years (mostly 10th grade), to a lesser extent via college plans, and to a slight extent via serious scholastic setbacks occurring after 8th grade.

GPA at the end of 10th grade has strong direct effects on academic attainment (recall that the direct path was a necessary addition to the model to improve fit). The model also allows for indirect effects of 10th-grade GPA, primarily via college plans and 12th-grade GPA. Incidentally, if our data collections had included GPA measures for every year, we might have found the strongest connections between 11th-grade GPA and academic attainment because that year's GPA is the one most likely to affect college admission decisions—a fact that is not lost on high school students, parents, teachers, and counselors. GPA at the end of 12th grade, although strongly *correlated* with academic attainment, does not show large direct or indirect effects on attainment as modeled. In other words, once 10th-grade GPA is taken into account, the GPA at the end of 12th grade makes relatively little additional impact on later academic attainment. (As suggested above, we suspect it would show even less impact if 11th-grade GPA data were available for inclusion in the model.) The limited contribution of 12th-grade GPA in the model is not especially surprising; senior-year GPAs are probably a bit less representative of student abilities than GPAs in earlier years because some students perceive their senior-year grades as less crucial for college admission. In addition, some students are completing less important graduation requirements, whereas others are actually taking more difficult advanced placement (AP) courses (which may be graded according to fairly demanding standards). Our data do not permit us to distinguish these various influences, but the findings do indicate clearly that 12th-grade GPA is less strongly *predictive* of attainment than 10th-grade GPA (see Table 4.1, Column 1) and (according to the model) a lot less important in terms of added *influence* on attainment.

GPA is an important predictor of age-18 dropout status, as shown in Figure 4.7. For reasons of clarity and parsimony, we modeled the causal path from 10th-grade GPA to dropping out; however, the zero-order correlations with dropping out are nearly identical whether we focus on 8th- or 10th-grade GPA (and also GPA measured at 12th grade, for that matter; see Table A.3.3 in the appendix). Thus, it appears that the general tendency to do well in school is quite consistent across time, and it is somewhat arbitrary which of the several sampling points is chosen as causal—at least when it comes to predicting dropping out of high school.

College Plans

In contrast to GPA, which at all three time points is strongly predictive of academic attainment, college expectations become increasingly more accurate predictors of attainment as students move from modal age 14 (end of 8th grade) to modal age 18 (end of 12th grade, for most). As noted earlier, expectations by the end of 12th grade often reflect firm commitments between students and colleges. Consistent with our expectations, college plans in 10th grade also show negative effects on dropping out of high school. The model treats college plans/expectations as a gradually evolving characteristic of students, and the fairly high-stability coefficients (.42–.55) seem consistent with this assumption. It is worth repeating that college plans are substantially influenced by GPA; although both GPA and college plans show a good deal of cross-time stability, there continue to be contributions from GPA to college plans throughout high school.

Serious Scholastic Setbacks After Eighth Grade

We reported earlier that relatively few individuals have experienced being held back a grade or suspended or expelled during the final 4 years of high school, but those who have show distinctly lower than average levels of academic attainment by age 22. Figure 4.7 indicates that scholastic setbacks at both time intervals (corresponding roughly to Grades 9–10 and Grades 11–12) show significant negative total effects for males, whereas for females the only significant effects are those at the first time interval. The standardized coefficients are not especially large, reflecting the relatively small proportions of respondents involved; however, the unstandardized coefficients (data not shown) are substantial, indicating that for the particular individuals involved the impact is considerable. Our model treats only the first 2-year interval as a cause of dropping out of high school, and that effect is substantial for both males and females.

The model allows serious scholastic setbacks to be influenced by earlier GPA and college plans, and in turn to affect later GPA and college plans. As shown in Figure 4.7, all such links are negative (as expected), but some are quite small. In general, the links involving GPA are stronger (among both males and females, all eight links are statistically significant; see Table A.4.7), compared with those involving college plans (four out of eight are significant). In particular, low GPA at the end of eighth grade increases the likelihood of being held back, suspended, or expelled sometime during the next 2 years. This is further evidence that early educational successes and failures, as reflected in eighth-grade GPA, can have long-term effects on academic attainment; these impacts occur not just via later GPA, but also via later scholastic setbacks as well as college plans.

Dropout Status at Age 18

As noted earlier, dropout status at the time of the third wave of data collection (modal age 18) has a strong influence on academic attainment at age 22. Although it is possible to move beyond dropout status in subsequent years, few of the dropouts in our panel moved very far. It is perhaps worth a reminder that many of the other factors in our model have indirect effects on attainment via the age-18 dropout factor. Nevertheless, the dropout factor makes an important separate contribution to the prediction of academic attainment at age 22; indeed, the unique contribution amounts to about 3% of variance.[15]

SUMMARY AND CONCLUSIONS

In this chapter, we explored factors that contribute to long-term academic attainment, following a nationally representative sample of young people from modal age 14 to modal age 22. This is a crucial interval in the educational life course, a period during which goals and prospects become realities—or fall short of realization. At age 14, virtually all youth in the United States are enrolled in school; 8 years later, some have dropped out before completing high school, some have ended their education with a high school diploma, and some are nearing the end of a 4-year college program. The present findings show that factors predicting these different levels of academic attainment are, to a large extent, firmly in place before the end of eighth grade.

Parental background is an important contributor to academic attainment. Young people go further in school if their parents are well educated (see Fig. 4.2) and if two parents are present in the home throughout high school (see Fig. 4.3). The impacts of these parental background factors are both indirect and direct, according to our model of academic attainment (see Table A.4.7 in the appendix and Fig. 4.7). High parental education levels and an intact family tend to increase students' grades and college aspirations by the time they are in eighth grade, thereby making indirect contributions to later academic attainment. An intact family (both parents present in the home) is particularly important as a protective factor against dropping out of high school. Parental background factors also show direct impacts on academic attainment at age 22, above and beyond the contributions to earlier scholastic success, and these direct impacts likely include socioeconomic factors. Not only are highly educated parents more likely to want college for their children and socialize them to value education, they also are more likely to be able to help with the expenses.

---

[15]This calculation is based on a comparison of R-squared values when the dropout factor is omitted from the model (data not shown). Fairly similar increments in R-squared values (2.0% to 2.9% of explained variance) appear also in Table 4.2 (contrasting Columns 5 and 6) and in Table A.4.2 in the appendix (contrasting Columns 2 and 3).

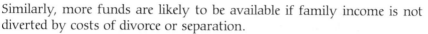

Similarly, more funds are likely to be available if family income is not diverted by costs of divorce or separation.

Racial/ethnic differences in academic attainment are of great importance as well as great complexity. We intend to focus on these in future publications. For now it should be noted that such differences are at least mostly controlled in our analyses; they appear to overlap largely with other factors in the model, such as parental background (see Table A.4.7 in the appendix).

Population density shows some small impacts on academic attainment, even after other factors are controlled. Students from larger metropolitan areas show slightly higher than average attainment. Those from more rural areas show slightly lower than average attainment, although for females this relationship overlaps other factors entirely.

Students' own educational backgrounds, up to the end of eighth grade, are important determinants of longer term academic attainment. These include past scholastic setbacks such as grade retention (see Fig. 4.4) and suspension or expulsion (see Fig. 4.5), as well as recent (i.e., end of eighth grade) educational performance and aspirations reflected in GPAs (see Fig. 4.6) and college plans.

Events occurring after eighth grade also matter a great deal, although they are largely predictable from what comes before. The most important information from the high school years (shown in Fig. 4.7) is GPA at the end of 10th grade, college expectations 2 years later (when many have already made firm plans and commitments), and dropout status at age 18. In addition, although serious scholastic setbacks—being held back, suspended, or expelled—affect relatively few students during the high school years, those who are involved experience substantial negative impacts on long-term academic attainment (see Fig. 4.7).

As shown in our structural model, these educational experiences during the high school years largely *mediate* the effects of earlier factors in place before the end of eighth grade, and they are thus crucial to longer term academic attainment. Events during high school that impact students' grades, their college plans, or their likelihood of experiencing serious scholastic setbacks can change the course of their academic development, causing that course to deviate from what would be projected based on the students' background and earlier accomplishments. Such changes, especially if dramatic, are likely to be negative rather than positive—if only because it is easier and more common to underachieve than to overachieve. Few students who have failed to establish patterns of good school performance and high grades can suddenly acquire such behaviors late during high school, but school performance can drop sharply given an abrupt loss of interest and motivation.

What kinds of events might have adverse impacts on the course of academic development during high school and afterward? Among the usual suspects are smoking, drinking, and illicit drug use, along with other problem behaviors. To the degree that such behaviors cause students to pay less attention to their grades, be less interested in pursuing a college education, have impaired ability to learn or retain information, cut classes or whole days of school, or get suspended or expelled from school, our findings in this chapter suggest that there should be long-term consequences reflected in lowered academic attainment. To what extent does this actually occur in connection with cigarette use, alcohol use, illicit drug use, or delinquency in general? These are issues we explore in the chapters that follow.

Chapter 5

Delinquency and Other Problem Behaviors Linked With Educational Success and Failure

Researchers interested in adolescent substance use often place it in a larger context of problem behaviors (Brook & Newcomb, 1995; Cooper, Wood, Orcutt, & Albino, 2003; Donovan & Jessor, 1985; Jessor, Donovan, & Costa, 1991; Jessor & Jessor, 1977; Kandel, 1988; Osgood, Anderson, & Shaffer, 2005). Earlier research using Monitoring the Future (MTF) data has shown positive correlations between delinquent behavior and substance use (Osgood et al., 1988; Schulenberg, Merline et al., 2005; Schulenberg, Wadsworth, O'Malley, Bachman, & Johnston, 1996), and we see similar correlations in later chapters based on our present panel data. So before turning our attention to substance use, we focus on a set of delinquent behaviors that tend to emerge relatively early in adolescence, diminish during high school, and then diminish further as high school ends and the experiences of emerging adulthood begin (Arnett, 2001).

We address two broad and interrelated questions in this chapter. First, to what extent do academic successes and failures and their prior causes contribute to adolescent delinquency? Second, to what extent does adolescent delinquency influence academic outcomes during adolescence and into young adulthood?

PLAN FOR THIS CHAPTER

Most of the measures and methods employed in this chapter were introduced in chapter 4. But whereas in that chapter we had a single long-term

101

outcome of interest—academic attainment at age 22—in this chapter we extend our interests to include problem behaviors and focus primarily on delinquent behaviors during much of adolescence (measured at modal ages 14, 16, and 18). We seek to understand the relationship between adolescent delinquency and academic success, and to do so we also need to examine their prior causes. In the previous chapter we explored predictors of academic attainment; in this chapter we take a similar approach, examining how those predictors of academic attainment may also relate to adolescent delinquency.

We begin with a description of delinquent behaviors based on data from our longitudinal panel. Then we consider the extent to which the predictors of academic attainment, as shown in Tables 4.1 and 4.2, are also predictors of an index of adolescent delinquency. We complete our analysis in this chapter by expanding the chapter 4 model of academic attainment to include delinquency measured at modal ages 14, 16, and 18. At the end of the chapter we expand the model further to include various forms of substance use, also measured at modal ages 14, 16, and 18. Portions of this expanded model are discussed in each of the next four chapters.

DELINQUENCY IN ADOLESCENCE AND YOUNG ADULTHOOD

The measure of delinquency used in these analyses is based on seven questionnaire items, asking respondents whether and how often they had done the following things during the last 12 months:

1. Gotten into a serious fight in school or at work.
2. Taken part in a fight where a group of your friends were against another group.
3. Hurt someone badly enough to need bandages or a doctor.
4. Taken something not belonging to you worth under $50.
5. Taken something not belonging to you worth over $50.
6. Gone into some house or building when you weren't supposed to be there.
7. Damaged school property on purpose.

Each item has a 5-point response scale ranging from "not at all" to "five or more times." Because the majority response to each item is "not at all" and the next most likely response is "once," we dichotomized responses for analysis purposes, distinguishing zero instances versus one or more. This dichotomization captures most of the information and also facilitates interpretation.

Figure 5.1 shows percentages of males and females in our panel sample reporting each of the delinquent behaviors for the 12-month period prior to each survey, covering all survey waves.[1] All of the behaviors tend to decline with age; generally the proportions reporting having engaged in a behavior drop by more than half between modal ages 14 and 22. Interpersonal aggression (Items 1–3 listed at the beginning of this section) drops steadily with age. Theft of items worth less than $50 (Item 4) is the most widely reported of the delinquent behaviors, engaged in by more than one third of the males and more than one fifth of the females during each of the adolescent years sampled (in Waves 1–3). Theft of items worth more than $50 (Item 5) is much less frequent; however, it shows smaller declines with age. Trespassing (Item 6) drops steadily and substantially with age—by two thirds among males and four fifths among females. Intentional damage of school property (Item 7) declines during adolescence and drops sharply once most respondents leave high school.

In general, males are more likely than females to report each of the behaviors—often two or three times as likely. The one exception is that, at the end of eighth grade (modal age 14), girls are equally as likely as boys to report that during the last 12 months they had "taken part in a fight where a group of your friends were against another group." Two years later, the rate is lower among females than males, and by 4 years later (modal age 18) the rate is nearly twice as high among males. This finding of relatively high rates of gang fighting reported by eighth-grade girls is not a random error in our panel data; the MTF cross-sectional surveys of eighth graders replicate the pattern of findings shown here. It is possible, of course, that eighth-grade girls and boys attach different interpretations to "a fight where a group of your friends were against another group," particularly given that the other two items about interpersonal and physical aggression ("a serious fight in school or at work" and "hurt someone badly enough to need bandages or a doctor") are reported more often by the boys than the girls.

The MTF cross-sectional surveys of high school students in 8th, 10th, and 12th grades have not revealed any important historical trends downward (or upward) in these delinquent behaviors (data not shown). We therefore interpret the declines shown in Figure 5.1 as age related or maturational. These age-related declines that continue into emerging adulthood

---

[1]The delinquent behavior items were included on only a random one half of the Wave 1 (eighth-grade) survey forms, so delinquency data from that initial survey are based on only half of the total respondents. That random half sample of respondents did not differ from the other half any more than would be expected by chance (and none of those differences was judged to be of any importance). Accordingly, we are comfortable extrapolating from the Wave 1 half sample to the total sample with respect to delinquency at modal age 14.

Males

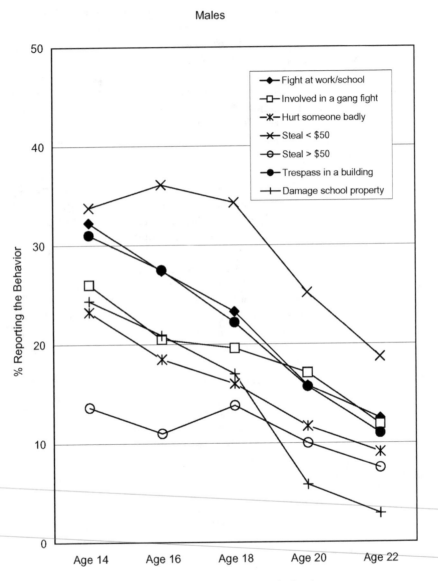

Figure 5.1a. Percentage involved in delinquent behavior (panel respondents age 14 in 1991–1993): males.

Females

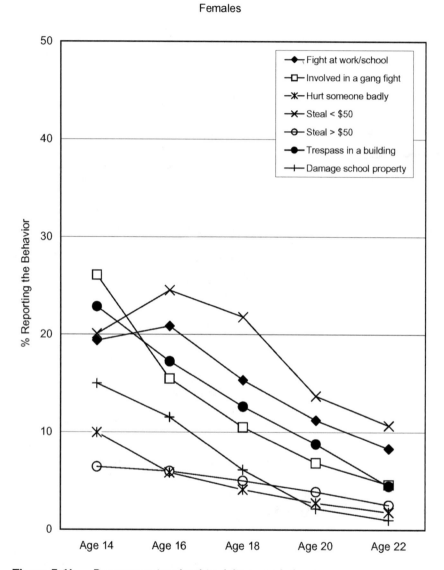

Figure 5.1b. Percentage involved in delinquent behavior (panel respondents age 14 in 1991–1993): females.

are welcomed, of course, but hardly surprising (e.g., Schulenberg & Zarrett, 2006). As adolescents grow older, the consequences of interpersonal aggression, theft, and vandalism become more severe. With increased age, most such behaviors are also likely to be seen as "kids' stuff," discouraged and disapproved of by peers.

Constructing a Seven-Category Measure of Delinquent Behavior

The seven aspects of delinquent behavior listed previously and shown in Figure 5.1 are certainly not an exhaustive list; rather, we view them as a sampling of the more common delinquent behaviors that occur during adolescence. Responses to each of the seven items are all positively correlated with the rest of the items in the list, within survey waves and across waves, among both males and females. Treating the seven items as a scale, we can also distinguish two subscales; the first three items indicate interpersonal aggression, and the next four indicate theft and vandalism. Correlations among items are somewhat higher within the subscales; however, preliminary analyses confirmed that it was not necessary to analyze the subscales separately.[2] We also explored whether there was much to be gained by developing separate weights for each of the seven items, after which we concluded that equal weights work quite well. Our delinquency measure is thus a simple count (0–7) of how many kinds of delinquent behavior were reported for the 12 months preceding the survey.

MAJOR CORRELATES/PREDICTORS
OF ADOLESCENT DELINQUENCY

In this section, we return to the predictors or correlates that were examined in chapter 4 as they related to academic attainment at age 22. Now, however, we consider their relationship with adolescent delinquency. As in chapter 4, we employ multivariate linear regression analysis as well as multiple classification analysis (MCA), a form of dummy variable

---

[2]Specifically, we examined how the full delinquency measure and the two subscales correlated with each of the substance-use measures. Across the first three survey waves (modal ages 14, 16, and 18), we found that the full scale consistently showed the strongest correlations with each form of substance use. The four-item theft and vandalism subscale generally showed the next strongest correlations, slightly stronger than the three-item interpersonal aggression subscale, as would be expected simply on the basis of scale reliability. We discovered no patterns indicating that separate treatment of the two subscales in our analyses would be worth the considerable additional complications (and computations) that would be involved.

regression analysis. Specifically, the regression analyses predict delinquency reported at modal ages 14, 16, and 18, in each case covering behaviors during the preceding year, whereas the MCA focuses on delinquency reported at modal age 18. (The formats used in these tables were chosen so as to be consistent with tables in subsequent chapters dealing with substance use.)

Table 5.1 presents the multiple linear regression analyses. These analyses employ the same set of predictors used in chapter 4; the means and standard deviations for those predictors are shown in Table 3.2. We continue the practice of reporting findings separately for males and females (see Table 5.1). There are three sets of columns in each table, focusing on delinquency reported at modal ages 14 (Columns 1–3), 16 (Columns 4–6), and 18 (Columns 7–9). Columns 1, 4, and 7 present zero-order product–moment correlations showing the strength of the bivariate linear relationships between the "predictor" or "independent variable" shown in the row and the "criterion" or "dependent variable" shown in the column. The remaining columns present standardized multiple regression coefficients showing each variable's contribution to "prediction" when all variables in that column are included in the equation; in addition, the multiple R and R-squared values at the bottom of the column show how much variance is "explained" by the predictors.[3]

A comparison of the three sets of columns in Table 5.1 (particularly the multiple R and R-squared values at the bottom) shows that the predictability of delinquency, especially predictability from most background and academic success or failure measures, declines with age. This is not altogether surprising, given that the amounts of delinquency (as well as variance) decline with age. But closer inspection of the table reveals some shifts with age that seem particularly noteworthy. For example, although GPA and college plans relate negatively to delinquency at all time points, the links are stronger at modal age 14 than at later ages (this can be seen especially clearly when focusing on the high school mean scores for GPA and college plans). We note several other age-related differences later in the chapter.

Table 5.2 presents multiple classification analyses; these provide additional detail, showing for respondents in each predictor category the

---

[3]We sometimes use terms such as "predictor" or "independent variable" and "dependent variable" simply because they are conventions often used in reporting regression analyses. They imply causal assumptions that are not always appropriate for these analyses; indeed, they can be quite inappropriate, as for example when we include a Wave 3 "predictor" of a Wave 1 "outcome." Accordingly, we often place such terms in quotation marks as reminders that we are not necessarily making assertions about causation, or even about chronology.

TABLE 5.1a
OLS Regressions Predicting Number of Types of Delinquency (Index)[1]
Reported at Ages 14, 16, and 18: Males

	Age 14[3]		
	Column 1	Column 2	Column 3
Effective N = 1361	Zero-Order Correlation	Standardized Regression Coefficient	Standardized Regression Coefficient
African-American	.011	**-.054**	-.026
Hispanic	.082	.023	.021
Other race	.009	-.031	-.027
White	-.063		
Large MSA	.063	.046	.040
Other MSA	-.020		
Non-MSA	-.040	-.036	-.015
Parents' education level	-.112	.020	-.017
Number of parents Wave 1	-.095		
Number of parents Wave 2	-.060		
Number of parents Wave 3	-.092		
Lived with 2 parents Waves 1–3	-.112	.004	.010
Parent involvement index Wave 1	-.199	-.108	-.065
Parent involvement index Wave 2	-.121		
Parent involvement index Wave 3	-.097		
Held back grade 8 or earlier	.190	.035	.023
Suspended/expelled grade 8 or earlier	.373	**.295**	**.186**
GPA Wave 1	-.249	**-.084**	**-.073**
GPA Wave 2	-.193	-.013	.013
GPA Wave 3	-.158	.013	.038
Mean secondary school GPA	-.241		
College plans Wave 1	-.187	-.026	-.003
College plans Wave 2	-.194	-.051	-.029
College plans Wave 3	-.165	.015	.013
Mean secondary school college plans	-.226		
Held back Wave 1 to Wave 2	.054		
Held back Wave 2 to Wave 3	.104		
Suspended/expelled Wave 1 to Wave 2	.062		
Suspended/expelled Wave 2 to Wave 3	.075		
Serious scholastic setback W1 to W2	.079	.058	.022
Serious scholastic setback W2 to W3	.118	.063	.041
High school dropout by Wave 3	.218	.044	.036
Sent to the office Wave 1	.342		**.115**
Sent to the office Wave 2	.260		.027
Sent to the office Wave 3	.219		.027
Days cut school Wave 1	.260		.054
Days cut school Wave 2	.170		.010
Days cut school Wave 3	.124		.006
Skipped classes Wave 1	.283		**.119**
Skipped classes Wave 2	.239		.062
Skipped classes Wave 3	.132		.033
Evenings out Wave 1	.133		.025
Evenings out Wave 2	.146		**.055**
Evenings out Wave 3	.059		.014
Hours worked Wave 1	.088		.001
Hours worked Wave 2	.062		.015
Hours worked Wave 3	.061		.008
Preferred hours of work Wave 1[2]	.061		.008
Preferred hours of work Wave 2	.087		-.017
Preferred hours of work Wave 3	.061		-.028
Religious attendance Wave 1	-.139		.008
Religious attendance Wave 2	-.170		-.009
Religious attendance Wave 3	-.149		.001
Religious importance Wave 1	-.123		-.012
Religious importance Wave 2	-.139		-.069
Religious importance Wave 3	-.109		.020
Self-esteem index Wave 1[1]	-.130		-.027
Self-esteem index Wave 2	-.082		.008
Self-esteem index Wave 3	-.079		-.027
Multiple R		.416	.523
R Squared		.173	.273
R Squared, adjusted		.164	.254

[1] These OLS (ordinary least squares) regressions were run with SAS statistical analyses software. A covariance matrix constructed with pairwise deletion served as the input data, because of missing values on the variables described in Notes 2 and 3 below. Coefficients that are p<.05 (two-tailed) are shown in **bold**.

TABLE 5.1a

OLS Regressions Predicting Number of Types of Delinquency (Index)[1]
Reported at Ages 14, 16, and 18: Males (*continued*)

	Age 16			Age 18	
Column 4	Column 5	Column 6	Column 7	Column 8	Column 9
Zero-Order Correlation	Standardized Regression Coefficient	Standardized Regression Coefficient	Zero-Order Correlation	Standardized Regression Coefficient	Standardized Regression Coefficient
-.019	-.071	-.027	-.020	-.044	.007
.030	-.005	-.009	.031	.011	.017
.010	-.025	-.013	.046	.021	.034
-.012			-.039		
.054	.023	.027	.045	.023	.023
.014			.000		
-.069	-.053	-.023	-.045	-.029	.006
-.011	.082	.024	-.026	.033	-.021
-.055			-.015		
-.030			-.008		
-.068			-.034		
-.071	-.002	-.003	-.044	.002	-.001
-.125	-.074	-.038	-.057	-.023	.015
-.130			-.067		
-.081			-.078		
.077	-.019	-.011	.010	-.051	-.037
.260	.234	.116	.155	.154	.073
-.148	.004	-.001	-.095	.025	.015
-.170	-.050	.045	-.124	-.015	.039
-.162	-.065	-.038	-.152	-.093	-.037
-.191			-.147		
-.091	.012	.018	-.048	.023	.022
-.151	-.082	-.027	-.105	-.053	-.022
-.096	.056	.060	-.087	.017	.042
-.140			-.100		
.056			.077		
.063			.066		
.129			.113		
.070			.137		
.132	.118	.050	.132	.122	.063
.090	.050	.022	.141	.111	.068
.160	.046	.021	.086	-.001	-.009
.296		.075	.187		.008
.401		.220	.270		.106
.240		.019	.276		.121
.128		-.037	.074		-.034
.232		.084	.132		.030
.145		.002	.163		.027
.160		.036	.116		.039
.317		.152	.198		.062
.185		.066	.225		.138
.108		-.001	.066		-.013
.172		.060	.127		.040
.116		.035	.179		.105
.065		.012	.089		.058
.029		-.007	.030		.010
.052		.019	.065		.045
.057		.007	.033		-.011
.061		-.027	.039		-.018
.054		.005	.020		-.037
-.044		.074	-.068		.037
-.106		.011	-.099		.047
-.100		.016	-.133		-.044
-.079		-.002	-.108		-.045
-.130		-.077	-.119		-.016
-.099		.004	-.132		-.041
-.086		.000	-.060		.001
-.202		-.134	-.119		-.030
-.101		.000	-.173		-.105
	.356	.546		.268	.472
	.127	.298		.072	.223
	.117	.279		.062	.202

[2] This item appeared in only one of two forms randomly distributed to respondents in their schools. Its first appearance was in 1992. Effective *N* is thus only one third of that shown.

[3] The age-14 delinquency items appeared in only one of two forms randomly distributed to respondents in their schools. Effective *N* is thus only half of that shown.

Note: W1 = Wave 1 data collection (grade 8, modal age 14), W2 = Wave 2 data collection (modal age 16), W3 = Wave 3 data collection (modal age 18)

TABLE 5.1b

OLS Regressions Predicting Number of Types of Delinquency (Index)[1]
Reported at Ages 14, 16, and 18: Females

Age 14[3]

Effective *N* = 1739	Column 1 Zero-Order Correlation	Column 2 Standardized Regression Coefficient	Column 3 Standardized Regression Coefficient
African-American	.031	-.035	-.015
Hispanic	.056	.022	.012
Other race	.064	.042	.040
White	-.104		
Large MSA	.031	.007	-.002
Other MSA	.039		
Non-MSA	-.077	-.059	-.038
Parents' education level	-.124	.004	.012
Number of parents Wave 1	-.101		
Number of parents Wave 2	-.104		
Number of parents Wave 3	-.139		
Lived with 2 parents Waves 1–3	-.144	-.024	-.019
Parent involvement index Wave 1	-.174	-.095	-.041
Parent involvement index Wave 2	-.119		
Parent involvement index Wave 3	-.054		
Held back grade 8 or earlier	.096	-.031	-.009
Suspended/expelled grade 8 or earlier	.305	.226	.057
GPA Wave 1	-.234	-.053	.001
GPA Wave 2	-.213	-.051	.003
GPA Wave 3	-.184	-.012	-.004
Mean secondary school GPA	-.247		
College plans Wave 1	-.196	-.067	-.033
College plans Wave 2	-.174	-.026	-.019
College plans Wave 3	-.127	.029	.009
Mean secondary school college plans	-.207		
Held back Wave 1 to Wave 2	.106		
Held back Wave 2 to Wave 3	.055		
Suspended/expelled Wave 1 to Wave 2	.117		
Suspended/expelled Wave 2 to Wave 3	.089		
Serious scholastic setback W1 to W2	.149	.062	.010
Serious scholastic setback W2 to W3	.099	.026	-.009
High school dropout by Wave 3	.225	.080	.048
Sent to the office Wave 1	.432		.252
Sent to the office Wave 2	.303		.088
Sent to the office Wave 3	.212		.012
Days cut school Wave 1	.269		.111
Days cut school Wave 2	.205		.026
Days cut school Wave 3	.138		.000
Skipped classes Wave 1	.271		.089
Skipped classes Wave 2	.215		.042
Skipped classes Wave 3	.116		.012
Evenings out Wave 1	.145		.055
Evenings out Wave 2	.071		-.003
Evenings out Wave 3	.018		-.010
Hours worked Wave 1	.042		.031
Hours worked Wave 2	.031		-.005
Hours worked Wave 3	.060		.004
Preferred hours of work Wave 1[2]	.046		.013
Preferred hours of work Wave 2	.106		-.004
Preferred hours of work Wave 3	.124		.019
Religious attendance Wave 1	-.109		.022
Religious attendance Wave 2	-.136		-.040
Religious attendance Wave 3	-.115		.031
Religious importance Wave 1	-.107		-.026
Religious importance Wave 2	-.094		.013
Religious importance Wave 3	-.087		-.026
Self-esteem index Wave 1	-.154		-.045
Self-esteem index Wave 2	-.110		-.016
Self-esteem index Wave 3	-.087		-.012
Multiple *R*		.413	.558
R Squared		.170	.311
R Squared, adjusted		.163	.295

[1] These OLS (ordinary least squares) regressions were run with SAS statistical analyses software. A covariance matrix constructed with pairwise deletion served as the input data, because of missing values on the variables described in Notes 2 and 3 below. Coefficients that are p<.05 (two-tailed) are shown in **bold**.

TABLE 5.1b

OLS Regressions Predicting Number of Types of Delinquency (Index)[1]
Reported at Ages 14, 16, and 18: Females (*continued*)

	Age 16				Age 18	
Column 4	Column 5	Column 6		Column 7	Column 8	Column 9
Zero-Order Correlation	Standardized Regression Coefficient	Standardized Regression Coefficient		Zero-Order Correlation	Standardized Regression Coefficient	Standardized Regression Coefficient
.010	-.052	.001		.026	-.032	.010
.000	-.035	-.016		.002	-.024	-.001
.054	.022	.039		.010	-.012	-.001
-.047				-.027		
.075	.056	.026		.111	.093	.068
.001				-.030		
-.078	-.038	-.029		-.079	-.024	-.016
-.068	.035	.018		-.026	.034	.023
-.073				-.050		
-.087				-.055		
-.095				-.063		
-.106	-.010	-.008		-.065	.000	.002
-.126	-.066	-.011		-.064	-.034	-.001
-.148				-.083		
-.071				-.041		
.052	-.037	-.014		.013	-.053	-.035
.211	.155	.048		.153	.119	.042
-.193	.000	.005		-.137	-.007	-.005
-.246	-.171	-.027		-.171	-.077	-.024
-.166	.017	.036		-.177	-.083	-.008
-.237				-.189		
-.148	-.041	-.024		-.055	.019	.033
-.173	-.064	-.027		-.100	-.032	-.019
-.081	.067	.051		-.092	-.030	-.029
-.166				-.106		
.107				.045		
.043				.033		
.210				.098		
.064				.140		
.220	.153	.054		.100	.056	.004
.073	.016	-.032		.123	.082	.026
.179	.048	-.007		.082	-.025	-.056
.255		.010		.177		.008
.485		.308		.259		.083
.282		.044		.338		.221
.159		.023		.104		.008
.315		.066		.196		.057
.161		.013		.155		.024
.173		.027		.136		.039
.358		.172		.207		.041
.158		.035		.212		.114
.117		.025		.096		.023
.162		.066		.099		.012
.078		.019		.132		.065
.029		.009		.029		.008
.039		.008		.029		.001
.046		-.002		.049		.009
.027		.010		.017		.007
.094		.023		.052		.002
.087		-.002		.077		.016
-.094		.017		-.042		.029
-.140		-.019		-.088		-.029
-.141		.010		-.116		-.022
-.089		.019		-.050		.008
-.172		-.075		-.075		.040
-.132		-.008		-.111		-.051
-.112		-.004		-.086		-.018
-.212		-.087		-.093		.017
-.139		-.030		-.162		-.094
	.371	.586			.295	.479
	.138	.344			.087	.229
	.130	.329			.079	.211

[2] This item appeared in only one of two forms randomly distributed to respondents in their schools. Its first appearance was in 1992. Effective *N* is thus only one third of that shown.

[3] The age-14 delinquency items appeared in only one of two forms randomly distributed to respondents in their schools. Effective *N* is thus only half of that shown.

Note: W1 = Wave 1 data collection (grade 8, modal age 14), W2 = Wave 2 data collection (modal age 16), W3 = Wave 3 data collection (modal age 18)

TABLE 5.2a
Multiple Classification Analyses Predicting Mean Number of Types of
Delinquency (Index) Reported at Age 18: Males

Grand Mean = 1.47
Effective *N* = 1361

Variable	Col. 1 Bivariate	Col. 2	Col. 3	Col. 4	Col. 5
		Multivariate			
Race/ethnicity					
African-American	1.38	1.34	1.28	1.26	-0.09
Hispanic	1.62	1.55	1.55	1.50	0.16
Other race	1.64	1.63	1.62	1.56	0.18
White	1.41	1.44	1.45	1.48	-0.05
Urban density					
Large MSA	1.59	1.57	1.55	1.55	0.12
Other MSA	1.46	1.47	1.47	1.47	0.00
Non-MSA	1.34	1.34	1.37	1.37	-0.12
Parents' education level					
1 (Low)	1.57	1.52	1.48	1.41	1.41
2	1.48	1.47	1.46	1.40	1.40
3	1.50	1.51	1.51	1.49	1.49
4	1.34	1.38	1.38	1.43	1.43
5 (High)	1.50	1.49	1.52	1.63	1.63
Lived with 2 parents Waves 1–3					
Yes	1.41	1.42	1.44	1.47	-0.05
No	1.56	1.55	1.51	1.45	0.10
Parent involvement index					
1 (Low)	1.74	1.69	1.63	1.58	1.58
2	1.49	1.48	1.47	1.45	1.45
3	1.43	1.44	1.45	1.45	1.45
4 (High)	1.38	1.40	1.42	1.46	1.46
Held back grade 8 or earlier					
Never	1.46		1.51	1.51	1.51
Once	1.49		1.36	1.32	1.32
More than once	1.51		1.21	1.24	1.24
Suspended/expelled grade 8 or earlier					
Never	1.30		1.29	1.31	1.31
Once	1.78		1.79	1.70	1.70
More than once	1.95		1.97	1.98	1.98
Mean secondary school GPA					
D or below	1.77			1.43	1.43
C- or C	1.84			1.63	1.63
C+ or B-	1.53			1.46	1.46
B or B+	1.43			1.51	1.51
A-	1.20			1.35	1.35
A	0.72			0.97	0.97

TABLE 5.2a
Multiple Classification Analyses Predicting Mean Number of Types of
Delinquency (Index) Reported at Age 18: Males (*continued*)

Grand Mean = 1.47
Effective *N* = 1361

Variable	Col. 1 Bivariate	Col. 2	Col. 3	Col. 4	Col. 5
		Multivariate			
Mean secondary school college plans					
Definitely won't	1.66			1.46	1.46
Probably won't	1.65			1.46	1.46
Probably will	1.61			1.56	1.56
Definitely will	1.25			1.38	1.38
Serious scholastic setback W1 to W2					
None	1.36			1.37	1.37
One	1.81			1.78	1.78
Two	2.41			2.42	2.42
Serious scholastic setback W2 to W3					
None	1.34			1.37	1.37
One	1.83			1.74	1.74
Two	2.20			2.10	2.10
High school dropout by Wave 3					
Yes	1.80				1.46
No	1.40				1.47
Multiple *R*		0.109	0.187	0.277	0.277
R Squared		0.012	0.035	0.077	0.077

The header row above reads: Estimated Mean Number of Types of Delinquency.

Factor Summary*

	eta	beta	beta	beta	beta
Race/ethnicity	**.060**	.052	.058	.051	.051
Urban density	**.054**	.052	.040	.041	.041
Parents' education level	.047	.033	.032	.045	.045
Lived with 2 parents Waves 1–3	.044	.037	.020	.007	.007
Parent involvement index	**.061**	.048	.036	.024	.024
Held back grade 8 or earlier	.010		**.048**	.054	.054
Suspended/expelled grade 8 or earlier	**.158**		**.164**	**.155**	**.155**
Mean secondary school GPA	**.147**			.081	.081
Mean secondary school college plans	**.112**			.046	.046
Serious scholastic setback W1 to W2	**.132**			**.126**	**.126**
Serious scholastic setback W2 to W3	**.141**			**.111**	**.111**
High school dropout by Wave 3	**.086**				.001

*All eta and beta statistics p<.05 are shown in **bold**.

See Table 3.3 for frequency distributions of predictor variables.

Note: W1 = Wave 1 data collection (grade 8, modal age 14), W2 = Wave 2 data
collection (modal age 16), W3 = Wave 3 data collection (modal age 18)

TABLE 5.2b
Multiple Classification Analyses Predicting Mean Number of Types of Delinquency (Index) Reported at Age 18: Females

		Estimated Mean Number of Types of Delinquency			
Grand Mean = 0.75 **Effective N = 1739**					
	Col. 1	Col. 2	Col. 3	Col. 4	Col. 5
Variable	Bivariate	Multivariate			
Race/ethnicity					
African-American	0.83	0.77	0.70	0.68	0.68
Hispanic	0.76	0.71	0.70	0.68	0.68
Other race	0.78	0.78	0.77	0.75	0.75
White	0.73	0.75	0.77	0.78	0.79
Urban density					
Large MSA	0.96	0.96	0.95	0.94	0.94
Other MSA	0.72	0.73	0.72	0.71	0.71
Non-MSA	0.60	0.59	0.61	0.63	0.63
Parents' education level					
1 (Low)	0.79	0.79	0.77	0.68	0.69
2	0.84	0.84	0.83	0.79	0.78
3	0.74	0.75	0.75	0.75	0.75
4	0.63	0.63	0.64	0.70	0.70
5 (High)	0.82	0.80	0.82	0.92	0.92
Lived with 2 parents Waves 1–3					
Yes	0.69	0.70	0.72	0.75	0.75
No	0.84	0.83	0.81	0.76	0.76
Parent involvement index					
1 (Low)	0.86	0.82	0.79	0.78	0.78
2	0.83	0.81	0.80	0.79	0.79
3	0.73	0.74	0.74	0.76	0.76
4 (High)	0.67	0.70	0.71	0.70	0.70
Held back grade 8 or earlier					
Never	0.75		0.77	0.78	0.78
Once	0.77		0.68	0.60	0.61
More than once	0.92		0.71	0.65	0.66
Suspended/expelled grade 8 or earlier					
Never	0.68		0.68	0.70	0.70
Once	1.14		1.13	1.01	1.02
More than once	1.23		1.20	1.12	1.14
Mean secondary school GPA					
D or below	1.53			1.20	1.22
C- or C	1.13			1.00	1.01
C+ or B-	0.88			0.83	0.83
B or B+	0.72			0.75	0.75
A-	0.52			0.57	0.56
A	0.46			0.59	0.59

TABLE 5.2b

Multiple Classification Analyses Predicting Mean Number of Types of
Delinquency (Index) Reported at Age 18: Females *(continued)*

Grand Mean = 0.75
Effective *N* = 1739

Variable	Col. 1	Col. 2	Col. 3	Col. 4	Col. 5
	Bivariate		Multivariate		
Mean secondary school college plans					
Definitely won't	0.80			0.61	0.63
Probably won't	1.00			0.86	0.88
Probably will	0.85			0.80	0.80
Definitely will	0.64			0.71	0.70
Serious scholastic setback W1 to W2					
None	0.70			0.72	0.72
One	1.10			0.96	0.97
Two	0.75			0.62	0.63
Serious scholastic setback W2 to W3					
None	0.69			0.71	0.71
One	1.11			1.01	1.01
Two	1.01			0.86	0.88
High school dropout by Wave 3					
Yes	0.98				0.69
No	0.72				0.77
Multiple *R*		0.158	0.211	0.282	0.282
R Squared		0.025	0.044	0.079	0.080

Factor Summary*

	eta	beta	beta	beta	beta
Race/ethnicity	.031	.017	.027	.037	.039
Urban density	**.118**	**.121**	**.113**	**.105**	**.105**
Parents' education level	**.068**	.065	.058	.064	.063
Lived with 2 parents Waves 1–3	**.065**	**.057**	.039	.003	.005
Parent involvement index	**.056**	.041	.032	.028	.028
Held back grade 8 or earlier	.018		.029	.057	.056
Suspended/expelled grade 8 or earlier	**.158**		**.150**	**.115**	**.118**
Mean secondary school GPA	**.175**			**.116**	**.119**
Mean secondary school college plans	**.114**			.053	.056
Serious scholastic setback W1 to W2	**.120**			**.073**	**.076**
Serious scholastic setback W2 to W3	**.131**			**.092**	**.094**
High school dropout by Wave 3	**.082**				.024

*All eta and beta statistics p<.05 are shown in **bold**.

See Table 3.3 for frequency distributions of predictor variables.

Note: W1 = Wave 1 data collection (grade 8, modal age 14), W2 = Wave 2 data
collection (modal age 16), W3 = Wave 3 data collection (modal age 18)

mean numbers of delinquent behaviors reported at modal age 18. The means are based on the 1-year time sample preceding the survey and are thus a reasonably good indicator of the number of different delinquent behaviors engaged in during late adolescence (the range of possible scores is 0–7). The table format is closely comparable to that used in the previous chapter (Table 4.2).[4] The MCA approach captures both linear and nonlinear relationships and thus has the potential to explain more variance—that is, produce higher multiple-R values. In fact, however, the values in the final column in Table 5.2 are very similar to those in Column 8 of Table 5.1; because these are based on virtually identical sets of predictors, we can conclude that the relationships treated as continuous variables show nearly linear relationships with delinquency.[5]

Race/Ethnicity and Population Density

Racial/ethnic differences in reports of delinquency are neither large nor consistent across time, as can be seen in Table 5.1. The one exception is that White females reported less delinquency than other females at modal age 14, but such differences mostly disappeared by modal age 18.

As for population density, it is perhaps not surprising that reports of delinquency tended to be slightly above average among those from large metropolitan areas, and slightly below average among those from nonmetropolitan areas (based on the bivariate correlations). As can be seen in the tables, these differences are reduced somewhat, but not eliminated, when other factors are included in the equations.

---

[4]Specifically, Column 1 (Bivariate Coefficient) shows actual mean scores for respondents in each category, with no adjustment for other factors (i.e., the bivariate relationships). At the bottom of Column 1 are eta statistics, analogous to product–moment correlations with two exceptions: They capture any nonlinear relationships in addition to linear ones, and they are never negative—their values can range from 0 to 1.0. The remaining columns report multivariate analyses, showing relationships when other factors in the column are controlled (i.e., included in the equation). At the bottom of these columns are beta coefficients, analogous to multiple regression coefficients (but again including linear plus nonlinear relationships).

[5]The only differences in the sets of predictors are that in the MCAs we use means across all three ages for GPA and college plans. Our examination of Table 5.1 led us to conclude that this makes little difference—except, of course, for simplifying the MCA presentations.

Parental Education

As shown in Table 5.1, parental education has a modestly negative bivariate relationship with delinquency reported at modal age 14, but that disappears when other factors are included in the equation. At later ages there is rather little relationship. So the findings with respect to delinquency are quite different from the findings with respect to academic attainment, for which parental education has a considerable positive effect.

Presence of Both Parents at Home

Having two parents present throughout adolescence is associated with lower delinquency, especially delinquency reported at modal age 14, as shown by the bivariate correlations in Table 5.1. Once other factors are included in multivariate regressions, however, little or no contribution remains. This suggests that if having both parents present in the home tends to reduce delinquency during early adolescence, the effect is largely indirect via educational experiences—an interpretation given some support by the structural equation modeling reported later in this chapter. Here again the impacts on delinquency are far less impressive than the impacts on academic attainment noted in chapter 4.

Parental Involvement in Students' Lives

Parental oversight and participation in homework, requiring chores, and limiting television viewing at modal age 14 are negatively related to delinquency in early adolescence, and to a lesser extent to delinquency several years later (see Table 5.1). These relationships are cut nearly in half when educational successes and failures are included in the equation (comparing Table 5.1 Column 1 vs. Column 2, Column 4 vs. Column 5, and Column 7 vs. Column 8). So it appears that much of the effects of parental involvement, especially on later delinquency, are also indirect via educational experiences.

Grade Retention, and Suspension or Expulsion, by End of Eighth Grade

Table 5.1 shows that young men who were held back one or more times before the end of eighth grade also reported greater than average delinquency during the prior year, but the relationship was much weaker for delinquency in the year prior to age 16 and was essentially zero for delinquency in the year prior to age 18. A similar pattern appears for young women, although it is weaker. Once other factors (including suspension or expulsion, truancy, and being sent to the office) are controlled, these relationships between grade retention and delinquency go to zero or actually turn slightly negative. It thus appears that being held back makes no direct contribution to delinquency.

As might be expected, the story is quite different for suspension or expulsion, penalties that usually result from misbehavior. Table 5.1 shows that suspension or expulsion prior to the end of eighth grade is moderately correlated with early delinquency (correlations of .37 for males and .31 for females), less strongly with delinquency prior to age 16 (correlations of .26 and .21), and still less strongly with delinquency prior to age 18 (correlations of .16 and .15). Controls for background and measures of educational success and aspirations (see Columns 2, 5, and 8) reduce these relationships only modestly. So it would seem that individuals who misbehave in school to the point that they are suspended or expelled tend to be the same individuals who engage in other disapproved behaviors—that is, delinquent acts. Figure 5.2 and Table 5.2 show that even for delinquency years later (i.e., delinquency reported for the year prior to modal age 18), young men who had been suspended more than once prior to the end of eighth grade report more than half again as many delinquent behaviors (a mean of 2.0) compared with those never suspended (a mean of 1.3). The rates are lower for young women, but the ratio is similar (means of 1.2 vs. 0.7). Controls for other factors reduce these differences only slightly for females and not at all for males.

Grade Point Average

Students who do well in school are less likely to engage in delinquent behaviors. This negative relationship is shown in Tables 5.1 and 5.2. The greater detail in Table 5.2 shows that delinquency rates during the year before modal age 18 are two to three times greater among those with GPAs of C or lower compared with the straight-A students. The tables also show that even with background and other indicators of educational success or failure controlled, delinquency rates remain lower than average among students with the best grades.

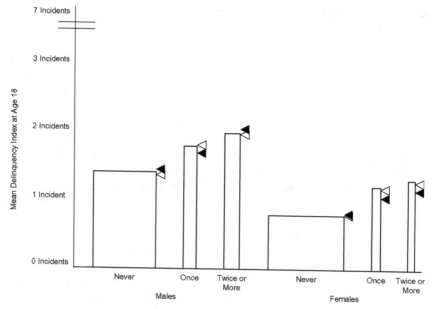

The main bars are unadjusted estimates. The bar width is proportionate to the weighted number of cases in the category.

◁ Number of incidents adjusted for race/ethnicity, population density, parents' education, number of parents, parental involvement, and ever having been held back (Column 3 in Table 5.2a & b)

◀ Number of incidents adjusted for race/ethnicity, population density, parents' education, number of parents, parental involvement, ever having been held back, GPA, college plans, and serious scholastic setbacks between Waves 1 and 2 and Waves 2 and 3 (Column 4 in Table 5.2a & b)

Figure 5.2. Mean delinquency index at age 18 by Grade 8 or earlier suspension or expulsion: males and females.

College Plans

Those who definitely expect to complete a 4-year college program report lower than average rates of delinquency. Here again the links are stronger with earlier versus later delinquency. But in the multivariate analyses controlling for other factors—especially suspensions or expulsions—the links grow much weaker or disappear. It thus appears that if college plans play some role in protecting against a problem behavior syndrome, it is a less important role than that played by good grades.

Serious Scholastic Setbacks During High School (After Eighth Grade)

We have just seen that suspension or expulsion *prior to the end of eighth grade* is linked with delinquency—most strongly with delinquency reported at modal age 14, but also with delinquency reported later. Now we turn to instances of suspension or expulsion, and also instances of grade retention (being held back a grade), that occur *after* eighth grade—that is, in the intervals between surveys at modal ages 14–16 or 16–18. At either interval such setbacks occurred for just over one in five males in our panel sample, and smaller proportions of females; nevertheless, they show positive correlations with delinquency (as documented in Table 5.1).

Table 5.1 provides further detail showing that setbacks at both intervals (i.e., between Waves 1 and 2, or between Waves 2 and 3) are positively correlated with delinquency reported at modal ages 14, 16, and 18. The table also shows correlation coefficients separately for the two types of setbacks—instances of grade retention and instances of suspension or expulsion—and all of these correlations are positive, although most are not very large. The pattern of relationships across time is consistent with an interpretation of mutual causation; we think it likely that prior delinquency may contribute to scholastic setbacks, and that setbacks also contribute to subsequent delinquency. Accordingly, as shown later in this chapter, we incorporate both paths of causation in our structural equation model, and the model findings provide support for this interpretation of reciprocal causation.

Dropping Out of High School by Age 18

As indicated by the bivariate correlations in Table 5.1, adolescents with a history of delinquency were more likely to become high school dropouts before age 18. The table also shows that delinquency during the year prior to the initial (modal age 14) survey is a better predictor of dropping out (product–moment correlations of .21 and .23) than is later delinquency (correlations of .16 and .18 for the age-16 measure, .09 and .08 for the age-18 measure). This might suggest that early involvement in problem behaviors contributes to dropping out; however, the regression analyses in Table 5.1 indicate that most of the relationships between delinquency and dropping out overlap with background and other indicators of educational success or failure, so it does not appear that delinquency is a particularly important direct contributor to dropping out.

The findings in Table 5.2 are consistent with these interpretations, as are the structural equation model findings reported later in this chapter.

ADDITIONAL CORRELATES/PREDICTORS OF ADOLESCENT DELINQUENCY

A number of additional dimensions were explored in chapter 4 as possible predictors of educational attainment. After examining those relationships, as reported in Table 4.1, we opted to focus in that chapter on the short list of predictors reviewed previously. However, for analyses predicting delinquency, as well as those predicting substance use in later chapters, some of the additional measures turn out to be important and are thus worth reviewing briefly here.

Various Problem Behaviors

Table 5.1 shows that our measure of delinquency is positively correlated with the two measures of truancy (cutting classes and skipping whole days of school) and particularly strongly correlated with whatever misbehaviors in school earn a trip to the office. All of these correlations are strongest among variables measured at the same survey wave, but there are substantial correlations even when the measurement periods differ by as much as 4 years. The multivariate regression coefficients show that the links between delinquency and being sent to the office remain strong even when truancy and other factors are controlled. None of these findings is surprising; all are consistent with our focus on a broad syndrome of problem behaviors that is linked with early school experiences.

Evenings Out for Fun and Recreation

Adolescents who spend frequent evenings out for fun and recreation also report above-average rates of delinquent behaviors—many of which may be performed during those evenings out. Table 5.1 shows again that the correlations are generally strongest when the measurement periods match. The table also shows that some relationship remains even when other factors are controlled. It is beyond our present scope to try to demonstrate which causal directions contribute most to these positive links; obviously, frequent evenings out may make it easier to engage in delinquent behaviors, but it may also be that those intending to engage in such behaviors make a point to be out often. Still, it is worth noting that evenings out for fun and recreation happened with *far* greater frequency than any of the delinquent behaviors. In other words, the overwhelming majority of evenings out involved no delinquent behaviors. This suggests that adolescents who are more frequently out in the evenings are simply more often exposed (albeit at low frequencies, and no doubt somewhat randomly) to opportunities for delinquency. If the alternative causal direction dominated, and evenings out were substantially driven by the desire to engage in delinquency, we should expect rather larger rates of delinquency than we observe.

Actual and Preferred Hours of Work

Delinquency shows consistently positive bivariate correlations with both preferred and actual hours of work (shown in Table 5.1). These correlations are generally small, and the multivariate regression coefficients are near zero. It thus appears that work preferences and behaviors do not have much direct impact on delinquency, nor does delinquency appear to impact preferred or actual work hours.

Religious Attendance and Importance

Adolescents who frequently attend religious services and/or rate religion as important in their lives are less likely to engage in delinquent behaviors. As can be seen in Table 5.1, these negative correlations appear consistently across time, ranging (when matched for survey wave) from −.11 to −.17. For the most part, the multivariate coefficients are rather small, with some positive and some negative values, suggesting that any impacts of religiosity on delinquency are largely indirect.

Self-Esteem

Table 5.1 shows consistently negative correlations between measures of self-esteem and delinquency, and the links are strongest for measures in the same survey wave. The links are reduced, sometimes to zero, in the multivariate analyses. Whether and to what extent self-esteem deters delinquency or delinquency lowers self-esteem is a highly complex topic far beyond the scope of this investigation (but see Bynner, O'Malley, & Bachman, 1981; Jang & Thornberry, 1998; Kaplan, 2001; Vermeiren, Bogaerts, Ruchkin, Deboutte, & Schwab-Stone, 2004). For present purposes, it is sufficient to note that a negative relationship exists, but it is modest enough (especially with other factors controlled) that we do not feel compelled to include it in our structural equation models.

ADDING DELINQUENCY TO THE STRUCTURAL EQUATION MODEL OF ACADEMIC ATTAINMENT

The structural model of academic attainment, developed in chapter 4 and shown in Figure 4.7, was designed so that it could be expanded to include adolescent problem behaviors, especially various forms of substance use. The first stage of expansion incorporates delinquent behavior, as shown in Figure 5.3. The figure includes path values and other findings; however, we defer discussion of the findings until after we outline our rationale for treatment of delinquency in the newly expanded model.

Locating Delinquency in the Causal Network

First of all, we treat delinquency measured at each of the first three survey waves as potentially caused by all of the exogenous factors in the model (shown in Fig. 4.7). Second, we treat delinquency at each wave as one of the causes—indeed, it turns out to be the primary "cause"—of delinquency at the next wave. This simply takes account of the stability of delinquent behaviors (and the findings indicate that the stability is fairly high).[6]

The third and most important causal assumption, as illustrated in Figure 5.3, is that we model delinquency at modal age 14 (end of eighth grade) as being caused by GPA and college plans measured at age 14, and we impose the same causal ordering at modal ages 16 and 18. Our reasons for choosing this causal ordering are primarily conceptual. We view early academic successes and failures (as reflected in GPA), as well as early academic adjustment and commitment (as reflected in college plans), as contributors to adolescents' acceptance or rejection of adult norms—including adult norms against delinquent behaviors (and, in later chapters, norms against substance use). This is the primary reason for modeling GPA and college plans

---

[6]Consistent with our treatment of GPA and college plans, we view our delinquency measures at several time points as indicators of an underlying tendency that has much consistency across time. Viewed this way, our 7-item scale contains measurement error—not only due to inaccuracies in reporting, whether intentional or accidental, but also due to limitations in the sampling of particular delinquent behaviors and the sampling of particular 12-month intervals. Accordingly, all factor loadings were set at 0.90, as shown in Table A.3.4 in the appendix.

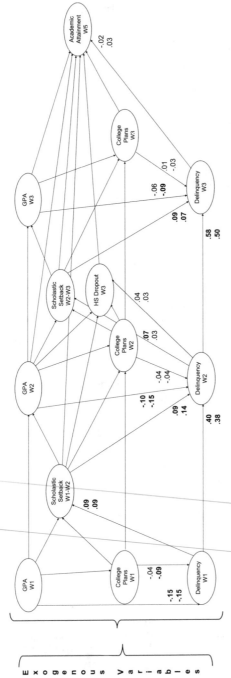

Path coefficients are displayed in pairs. The coefficient for the males is above the coefficient for the females. Coefficients that are p<.05 (two-tailed) are shown in **bold**. Path coefficients for the upper portion of the model differ only slightly from those shown in Figure 4.7 and are thus not included here.

Note: W1 = Wave 1 data collection (grade 8, modal age 14), W2 = Wave 2 data collection (modal age 16), W3 = Wave 3 data collection (modal age 18), W5 = Wave 5 data collection (modal age 22)

	Males	**Females**
Comparative Fit Index (CFI)	.994	.993
Root Mean-Square Error of Approximation (RMSEA)	.038	.040
Chi-Square	377	489
Degrees of Freedom	129	129

Figure 5.3. Structural equation model of academic attainment (including delinquency).

at each survey point as among the causes of delinquency measured at the same point. We explored treating delinquency at each of the first two waves as causes of later GPA and college plans; however, such lagged causal links would introduce unnecessary complications and produce no improvement in the model (based on fit indicators and measures of strain).[7]

The fourth causal assumption in the model is that delinquency contributes to subsequent serious scholastic setbacks, which in turn contribute to subsequent delinquent behaviors. Thus, as shown in Figure 5.3, delinquency reported at the first survey wave (modal age 14) is a potential contributor to scholastic setbacks (grade retention or suspension/expulsion) between modal ages 14 and 16; these setbacks in turn are potential contributors to delinquency reported at modal age 16. The figure also shows that similar causal connections are included between the second and third waves (modal ages 16–18).[8]

The fifth causal assumption is that delinquency may be among the causes of dropping out of high school before age 18. As shown in Figure 5.3, we treat delinquency measured at modal age 16 as a potential direct cause, whereas earlier delinquency can have indirect causal effects.

The final causal assumption shown in the model is that delinquency at age 18 is allowed to have direct effects on academic attainment at age 22, and earlier delinquency is allowed to have indirect effects. We considered it important to include such possible effects so as to estimate to what extent delinquency actually contributes to academic outcomes, in contrast to simply showing a correlation because of its links with earlier academic successes and failures.

---

[7]We also computed simple cross-lagged models allowing GPA and delinquency each to predict the other 2 years later (but with no prediction in either direction at the same survey point). Results, shown in Figure A.5.1 in the appendix (middle panel), indicate no meaningful lagged prediction from delinquency to later GPA among females and slight negative prediction among males. However, a model predicting just from GPA to delinquency measured at the same time point (bottom panel in Fig. A.5.1) provided equal or better fit.

[8]We recognize that measurement chronology does not fit perfectly with these causal assumptions. The scholastic setbacks are fairly neatly contained in the interval between surveys; however, the delinquency measurement refers to the prior 12 months. Thus, for example, delinquency reported at the second wave could refer to events that took place prior to an instance of suspension occurring (fairly late) between the first and second waves. (Indeed, the delinquency could even have triggered the suspension.) Accordingly, the estimates for these causal paths should be treated with even more than the usual degree of caution.

TABLE 5.3
Direct and Total Effects of Predictors on Delinquency Index at Wave 1, Wave 2, and Wave 3*

Predictors	Delinquency Wave 1 Males Direct	Males Total	Females Direct	Females Total	Delinquency Wave 2 Males Direct	Males Total	Females Direct	Females Total	Delinquency Wave 3 Males Direct	Males Total	Females Direct	Females Total
African-American	**-.060**	-.054	-.035	-.039	-.042	-.056	-.032	-.039	-.011	-.037	.001	-.010
Hispanic	.027	.028	.026	.027	-.013	.001	-.046	-.029	.013	.017	-.009	-.019
Other race	-.032	-.016	.042	**.055**	-.014	-.008	.007	.042	.034	.041	-.024	.004
Large MSA	.050	.041	.015	.008	.013	.028	**.065**	**.068**	.015	.029	**.073**	**.108**
Non-MSA	-.036	-.031	**-.062**	**-.069**	-.054	**-.065**	-.018	**-.059**	-.001	-.040	-.006	-.046
Parents' education level	.029	-.008	.006	-.052	**.092**	.048	.047	-.034	-.009	.007	.037	-.011
Lived with 2 parents Waves 1–3	-.001	-.015	-.041	**-.067**	-.012	-.033	.003	**-.064**	.007	-.022	.019	-.039
Parent involvement index	**-.163**	**-.178**	**-.146**	**-.167**	-.052	**-.140**	-.055	**-.136**	.035	-.053	.007	-.065
Held back grade 8 or earlier	.026	**.062**	-.045	-.006		**.041**		.021		**.030**		.025
Suspended/expelled grade 8 or earlier	**.325**	**.366**	**.255**	**.294**		**.155**		**.134**		**.098**		**.081**
GPA Wave 1	**-.150**	**-.163**	**-.149**	**-.177**		**-.171**		**-.221**		**-.134**		**-.182**
GPA Wave 2					**-.101**	**-.113**	**-.149**	**-.157**		**-.115**		**-.169**
GPA Wave 3									**-.057**	**-.056**	**-.092**	**-.097**
College plans Wave 1	-.036	-.036	**-.088**	**-.088**		-.035		-.057		-.021		-.038
College plans Wave 2					-.037	-.037	-.036	-.036		-.022		-.031
College plans Wave 3									.006	.006	-.031	-.031
Serious scholastic setback W1 to W2					**.094**	**.109**	**.135**	**.147**		**.068**		.081
Serious scholastic setback W2 to W3									**.085**	**.090**	**.073**	**.081**
Delinquency Wave 1					**.400**	**.409**	**.382**	**.395**		**.239**		**.200**
Delinquency Wave 2									**.576**	**.582**	**.502**	**.504**
Delinquency Wave 3												

Direct and Total Effects of Delinquency at Wave 1, Wave 2, and Wave 3 on Education Factors*

Predictors	GPA Wave 2 Total	College Plans Wave 2 Total	Serious Scholastic Setback W1 to W2 Direct	Total	GPA Wave 3 Total	College Plans Wave 3 Total	Serious Scholastic Setback W2 to W3 Direct	Total	High School Dropout Wave 3 Direct	Total	Academic Attainment Wave 5 Direct	Total
Delinquency Wave 1												
Males	**-.009**	**-.008**	**.086**	**.086**	**-.009**	-.008				.028		**-.021**
Females	**-.005**	**-.010**	**.092**	**.092**	-.004	-.007				.028		-.005
Delinquency Wave 2												
Males					-.007	-.006	**.067**	**.067**	.036	.036		-.025
Females					-.001	-.002	.027	.027	.030	.030		.007
Delinquency Wave 3												
Males											-.019	-.019
Females											.026	.026

*Coefficients that are p<.05 (two-tailed) are shown in **bold**.

Note: W1 = Wave 1 data collection (grade 8, modal age 14), W2 = Wave 2 data collection (modal age 16), W3 = Wave 3 data collection (modal age 18)

Structural Model Findings

Many results of incorporating delinquency into the structural equation model of academic attainment can be seen in Figure 5.3 and the accompanying tabular data in Table 5.3. We begin by noting that adding three measures of delinquency to the model makes no meaningful difference in our overall ability to predict academic attainment at age 22; R-squared values increase by only .001 for males and even less for females. A careful comparison of findings from the present chapter with those in chapter 4 reveals that most path coefficients shown in Figure 4.7 were not appreciably changed by our inclusion of delinquency in the model.[9] One exception is that with delinquency included, the paths from GPA to serious scholastic setbacks are slightly smaller (by about .01), and those from college plans to serious scholastic setbacks are at most *very* slightly smaller. Paths from serious scholastic setbacks to later GPA and college plans are virtually unchanged. Paths contributing to academic attainment at age 22 are totally unchanged. In sum, adding delinquency to the model produces no important changes in the findings about academic attainment reported in chapter 4.

We turn next to the paths relating to delinquency, beginning with GPA and college plans as possible causes. Figure 5.3 shows that for both boys and girls there are direct negative paths from GPA to delinquency at each of the three waves. The Wave 1 paths are both $-.15$ (statistically significant); at Waves 2 and 3 the direct effects of GPA on delinquency are mostly smaller, but early GPA also has indirect effects on later delinquency (via delinquency at earlier waves). The findings thus suggest that early success in school (as indicated by high GPA in eighth grade) may be a protective factor against delinquent behavior, whereas doing poorly in school may increase the likelihood of delinquency. College plans at Wave 1 show no significant direct effects among males, but among females there is a significant negative effect; at later waves the effects are small, inconsistent, and nonsignificant. These findings suggest that once we take account of scholastic success as reflected by GPA, college aspirations make little additional contribution as a deterrent to delinquency.

---

[9]Accordingly, we do not duplicate those coefficients in Figure 5.3, but rather focus on the new coefficients involving delinquency. Tables A.5.1 through A.5.3 in the appendix provide model fit statistics, variance explained (R Square) for all endogenous factors in the model, and summary listings of direct and total effects of each predictor in the model on academic attainment. Comparing the tabular material regarding direct and total effects on academic attainment, included in Tables A.4.7 and A.5.3, provides one indication of just how little the chapter 4 model findings are changed by the inclusion of delinquency. Indeed, when the model is expanded further to include substance use (as described at the end of this chapter), there is still little change in the coefficients shown in Figure 4.7, as can be seen in Table A.5.4 in the appendix.

What about the links involving serious scholastic setbacks? Figure 5.3 shows that all four direct causal paths between delinquency and serious scholastic setbacks are almost all significant, ranging from .07 to .09 among boys and from .03 to .14 among girls. So, on the whole, it appears that delinquent behaviors may contribute to subsequent scholastic setbacks, and vice versa. The figure also shows small positive (but nonsignificant) direct effects of Wave 2 delinquency on dropping out of high school by age eighteen: .04 for boys and .03 for girls.

The tabular material related to Figure 5.3 includes several findings worth noting here. First, we can see in Table A.5.2 that prior causal factors in the model explain a good deal of variance in Wave 1 delinquency (R-squared values of .25 for boys and .20 for girls). The values are appreciably higher by Wave 3, but this is primarily because of the stability of delinquency (stability paths ranging from .38 to .58). We have already noted that GPA is the more important endogenous factor contributing to Wave 1 delinquency. Among the exogenous factors, two contributors to Wave 1 delinquency stand out (see Table 5.3): delinquency is substantially higher among those suspended or expelled prior to eighth grade (total effects of .37 for boys and .29 for girls); and delinquency is lower among those whose parents are closely involved in homework, require chores, and limit television time (total effects of −.18 for boys and −.17 for girls). So it seems clear that some of the factors involved in educational success and failure also influence delinquency.

Based on those relationships alone, we could expect just the kinds of links between educational factors and delinquency that were reported earlier in this chapter. The model findings, which include adjustments designed to remove the effects of measurement error, show overall bivariate factor correlations with academic attainment that are fairly substantial for Wave 1 delinquency (−.20 for males, −.19 for females; see Table A.5.3) and weaker but still significant for delinquency at later waves.

But does delinquency *add* anything to the story of educational success? Specifically, does it make any lasting contribution to academic attainment at age 22? One answer provided by the model is that the direct effects of delinquency measured at Wave 3 on age-22 academic attainment are nonsignificant and essentially zero (−.02 for males, .03 for females). But perhaps earlier delinquency makes contributions that are indirect, via scholastic setbacks or dropping out. The answer to that question involves *total effects* of delinquency within the model constraints (see Table A.5.3). The effects are all very small, ranging from −.03 to .03, and five out of the six fall short of statistical significance. In addition, as noted earlier, including all of the delinquency measures in the model adds only .001 or less to the explained variance in academic attainment. We therefore conclude that adolescent delinquency, although *correlated* with eventual academic attainment, has rather little *impact* on it one way or the other.

SUMMARY AND CONCLUSIONS CONCERNING DELINQUENCY

Delinquent behaviors such as getting into fights, stealing, trespassing, and vandalism occur with decreasing frequency over the course of adolescence. Nearly all of these behaviors have reached their peak by or before modal age 14, the time covered by our first survey (see Fig. 5.1). Compared with substance-using behaviors—smoking, drinking, and the use of marijuana or cocaine—these delinquent acts tend to be earlier-emerging forms of deviancy or problem behavior. For that reason, the chapters that follow include delinquency among the potential causes or precursors of substance-using behaviors.

Among background factors that relate to adolescent delinquency, the most important is parental involvement in students' lives. Age-14 students whose parents participate in homework, require chores, and limit TV viewing are less likely to engage in delinquent behaviors then or later. Delinquency is also lower when both parents are present in the home throughout adolescence; however, any effects are largely indirect via educational experiences.

One of the educational experiences most strongly associated with delinquent behavior is suspension or expulsion, and that holds true for such setbacks occurring both before and after the end of eighth grade. The structural equation model findings (Fig. 5.3) suggest a reciprocal causal relationship between delinquent behaviors and scholastic setbacks after eighth grade, with each contributing to the other. In contrast, students who are successful in school, as indicated by their good grades, are relatively unlikely to engage in delinquent behavior.

Given these links between delinquency and measures of educational success and failure, it is no surprise that academic attainment at age 22 is predicted (negatively) by delinquency, as indicated by the bivariate factor correlations (BFCs) in Table A.5.3. These correlations are strongest from delinquency early in adolescence, when such behaviors are most frequent. But correlation (or prediction) is not necessarily causation, and our structural equation model indicates that delinquency itself does not do very much to impair academic attainment. Rather, it appears that

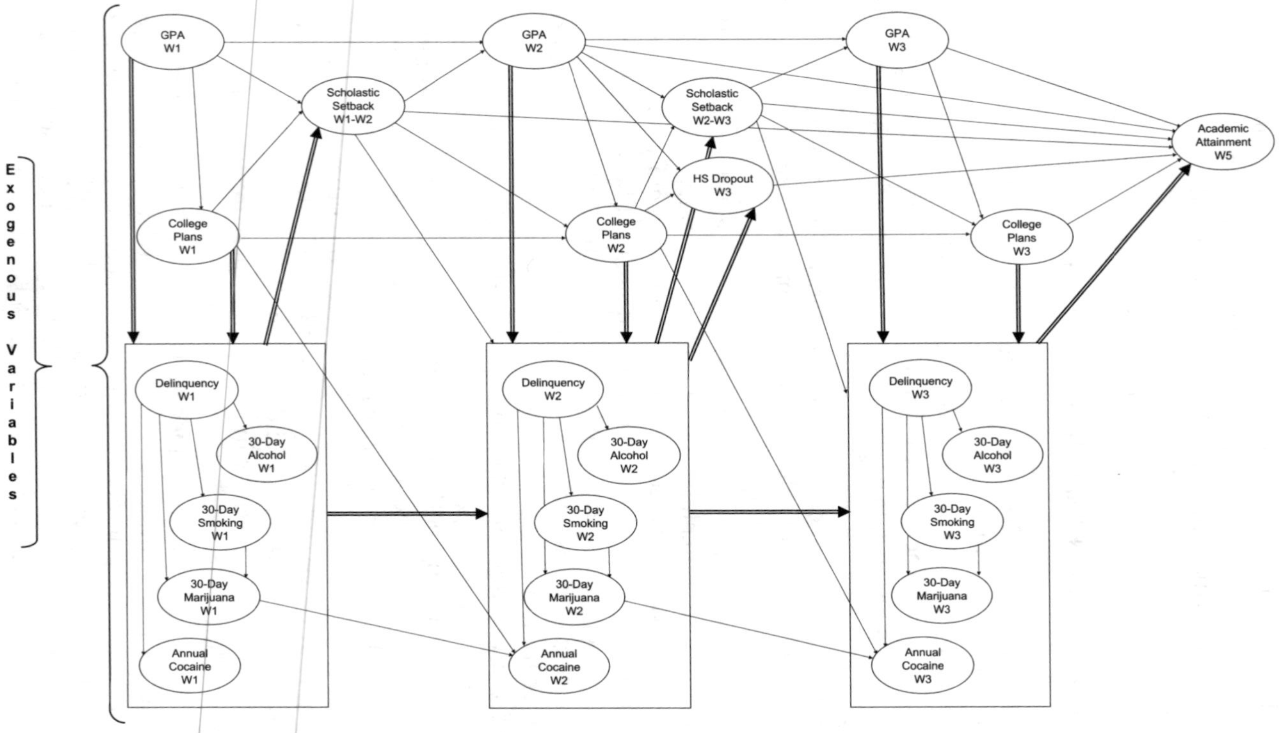

Figure 5.4. Schematic overview of structural equation model of academic attainment and substance use.

Note: W1 = Wave 1 data collection (grade 8, modal age 14), W2 = Wave 2 data collection (modal age 16), W3 = Wave 3 data collection (modal age 18), W5 = Wave 5 data collection (modal age 22) those same factors that contribute to academic success—both short and longer term—also provide some protection against adolescent delinquency. It also appears that early educational successes themselves provide some further protection against delinquency.

EXPANDING THE STRUCTURAL EQUATION MODEL TO INCLUDE SUBSTANCE USE

We have just shown how the structural equation model of academic attainment could be expanded to include delinquent behaviors. That effort points the way to further expansions so as to include various types of substance use. Figure 5.4 provides a schematic overview of the model used in all subsequent chapters. Because several forms of substance use are treated as causally connected, as outlined later in this chapter, our full model includes all of the substances. After careful comparisons, we concluded that the findings for delinquency were not importantly affected by the inclusion of the new substance-use factors in the model—just as the findings in chapter 4 were not importantly affected by the addition of delinquency to the model. Table A.5.4 in the appendix compares direct effects and total effects of all predictors on academic attainment based on the educational attainment model in chapter 4 versus the full model shown in Figure 5.4. This provides further evidence that the inclusion of delinquency and the substance-use factors does not substantially affect the basic findings in chapter 4.

Figure 5.4 illustrates several features of our full model. We note the features briefly here and expand as necessary in later chapters. First, each of the substance-use dimensions is treated in much the same way that we treat delinquency. Specifically, (a) each form of substance use is treated as caused by GPA, college plans, and serious scholastic setbacks, as well as all the exogenous factors shown in Figure 4.7; (b) each form of substance use is treated as a potential cause of later scholastic setbacks (including dropping out of high school); (c) each form of substance use measured at age 18 is treated as a potential cause of academic attainment at age 22; and (d) each form of substance use is treated as a cause of later use of the same substance, thus taking account of stability. (Rather than be overwhelmed by a thicket of arrows, we have placed delinquency and the substance-use measures for each survey wave in a box, and have used heavy arrows to signify linkages that are common to all factors in the box.)

Second, we treat delinquency at each survey wave as one of the causes of substance use at that wave. Our primary rationale is that delinquency is an early-emerging form of problem behavior, and that being involved in delinquent behaviors may contribute to substance use both directly (e.g., via theft of cigarettes or alcohol) and indirectly (e.g., via friendship groups that share deviant behaviors). A secondary rationale is that the measures of delinquent behaviors span events during the prior 12 months, whereas most of the substance-use measures cover a span of just 30 days or less.

Third, we posit a limited set of causal links among forms of substance use. Cigarette use is treated as a contributor to marijuana use reported at the same survey wave, for reasons discussed in chapter 7. Marijuana use is treated as one of the causes of cocaine use; however, because cocaine use is reported for the preceding 12 months whereas marijuana use covers just the preceding 30 days, and for other reasons discussed in chapter 8, we opted to treat prediction of cocaine use as lagged. That is, cocaine use reported at Wave 2 is treated as caused by marijuana use reported at Wave 1, and Wave 3 cocaine use is treated as caused by marijuana use reported at Wave 2. (The prediction from college plans to cocaine use is also lagged because of similar concerns about measurement chronicity.)

When we incorporated dimensions of substance use into the model, we followed the same strategy as when we incorporated delinquency; we explored various alternatives to satisfy ourselves that no important causal paths were omitted, that the results were interpretable, and that the model showed acceptable levels of fit. We imposed causal connections between substances only when the justification seemed clear; otherwise, we took what we considered to be a more conservative approach and simply allowed disturbances to correlate while not imposing a causal ordering. We discuss some of these decisions in greater detail as needed in subsequent chapters. For now it is sufficient to note that imposing certain causal connections among substances (from smoking to marijuana use to cocaine use) does not appreciably change the bottom line in any of our analyses or conclusions concerning how educational successes and failures are linked with substance use. The full details of the expanded model are too extensive to be included in a form similar to that used in Figure 5.3; instead, we provide such details in appendix tables. In each of the next four chapters, we focus our attention on one dimension of substance use, and we report the most relevant portions of the model findings for that substance. We turn first to the findings for cigarette use, detailed in chapter 6.

Chapter 6

How Smoking Is Linked With Educational Success and Failure

In chapter 1, we presented initial findings from the present research, and in chapter 2, we summarized evidence from earlier research, all indicating that adolescent smoking is negatively associated with educational success and positively associated with educational failures. In this chapter, we examine those associations more closely, using Monitoring the Future (MTF) cross-sectional data as well as data from our adolescent longitudinal panel. We see that a strong negative connection between educational success and smoking has remained consistent despite upward and downward shifts in adolescent smoking rates during recent decades.

But more than simply documenting the correlations between educational success and smoking, in this chapter we attempt to untangle the causal connections involved. We ask, in effect, these questions: Does smoking stunt one's educational growth? Does poor educational performance increase the likelihood that a youth will become a smoker? Is the association the result of other prior causes? Is it a mixture of these several dynamics—that is, all of the above?

These are high-stakes questions involving life-altering consequences. It is more than a matter of "your money *or* your life"—it is *both*. Clearly, educational success during adolescence and early adulthood affects opportunities and rewards throughout a lifetime (Cagney & Lauderdale, 2002; Caspi, Wright, Moffitt, & Silva, 1998; Clausen, 1991; Jaffee, 2002; Miech & Shanahan, 2000; Murrell & Meeks, 2002; Schoon, Parsons, & Sacker, 2004; Zhan & Pandey, 2002). So if it were found that smoking interferes with academic attainment, then long-term loss of earnings would be yet another reason to discourage adolescent smoking. (In addition, there is a more immediate financial cost: the price of cigarettes can easily exceed $1,000 per year among smokers who consume more than a half pack a day.) Most important, of course, the smoking habit can be exceedingly difficult to break, and the consequences of chronic smoking include a variety of health problems and a considerable shortening of life expectancy (U.S. Department of Health and Human Services, 2004). So if educational failures contribute to the onset of adolescent smoking (and thus to subsequent adult dependency on cigarettes), that would represent a substantial additional cost to educational failures—a cost that often is easily overlooked, but should not be.

PLAN FOR THIS CHAPTER

In this chapter, we continue to use the measures and methods introduced in chapter 4 and used again in chapter 5. In chapter 5, we sought to understand the relationship between academic success and adolescent delinquency. In this chapter, we seek to understand the relationship between academic success and cigarette use, while also taking account of how delinquency fits into the picture.

We begin with a brief look at smoking rates based on data from cross-sectional MTF samples and from our longitudinal panel of adolescents. Then using the panel data and following the path taken in chapter 5, we consider the extent to which the predictors of academic attainment, as shown in Tables 4.1 and 4.2, are also predictors of smoking. These findings show that, in general, factors that relate positively to academic attainment relate negatively to smoking; however, the correspondence is far from perfect—some factors that predict strongly to one predict only weakly or not at all to the other. As in the previous two chapters, we examine certain of the relationships in greater detail using tables and figures based on multiple classification analysis. In the final stage of analysis, we employ the structural equation model of academic attainment, now expanded to include smoking (as well as delinquency and other substance use), with the goal of addressing the questions of causal influence outlined previously.

ADOLESCENT SMOKING RATES IN RECENT DECADES

We offer several perspectives on adolescent smoking among recent cohorts. First, we consider cross-sectional findings showing how smoking rates differ by age, and we note secular trends (historic shifts) as well as stable cohort differences in smoking during recent years. Then we focus on our adolescent panel data to learn more about individual patterns of change in smoking. One theme that emerges consistently from this descriptive look at smoking is its high degree of stability; once individuals begin to smoke on a regular basis, most of them continue to do so. That stability goes a long way toward accounting for the fact that the links with educational success and failure, once established, remain impressively strong into adulthood.

Evidence Based on Cross-Sectional Data

Smoking rates for our adolescent panel respondents (shown later in this section) are generally quite consistent with corresponding cross-sectional MTF findings at the same points in time. The eighth-grade cross-sectional data for 1991 to 1993 are directly comparable to our panel sample at modal age 14. The 10th-grade cross-sectional data for 1993 to 1995 are largely comparable to the panel data for modal age 16, except that the panel includes a small number of respondents who dropped out of school prior to the end of 10th grade. The 12th-grade cross-sectional data for 1995 to 1997 are only somewhat comparable to the panel data for modal age 18 because high school dropouts are included in the panel sample, whereas they are not part of the 12th-grade samples.[1] Let us consider briefly the smoking findings from the MTF cross-sectional surveys because they provide an important context for the panel findings detailed here.

Figure 6.1, adapted from Johnston, O'Malley et al. (2005b), shows 30-day and daily prevalence rates for cigarette smoking for 12th graders starting in 1975 and for 8th and 10th graders starting in 1991 (data for males and females are combined in this figure). It is clear that prevalence rates of monthly and daily smoking increase with age (i.e., grade in school). It is also clear that smoking rates increased during the early and mid-1990s, and subsequently declined. The pattern shown in the figure is largely consistent with a secular trend interpretation, in that the increases and decreases in all three grade levels occurred at approximately the same times. Johnston and colleagues note several historical correlates, all of which may have contributed to the increase from 1991 to 1996: Cigarette prices dropped on

---

[1]A further difference between our present panel data and the published cross-sectional findings from MTF is that our panel data are adjusted (weighted) to compensate for absenteeism at the time of the initial (i.e., base-year) eighth-grade survey. Such an adjustment is not routinely part of the annual data reported from the MTF cross-sections; the differences are not large enough to concern us here.

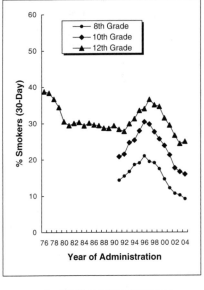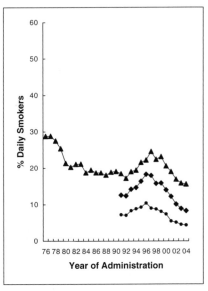

Any Smoking in the Last 30 Days   Daily Smoking in the Last 30 Days

Data collected from annual national in-school surveys by Monitoring the Future.

Figure 6.1.   Trends in 30-day prevalence of any smoking and 30-day prevalence of daily use of cigarettes for 8th, 10th, and 12th graders.

average due to increased price competition between brands, cigarette advertising and promotion had grown more effective at reaching youth, and smoking was increasingly portrayed in the entertainment media. The authors suggest that the subsequent across-the-board decline in youth smoking, starting in 1997, may have been influenced by adverse publicity surrounding the tobacco companies' legal settlement with the state attorneys general, price increases, and vigorous antismoking advertising and other prevention efforts. They also note that this decline coincided with increases in perceived harmfulness of smoking (after 1995) and disapproval of smoking (after 1996).

Johnston, Bachman, and O'Malley's (2005) report of MTF cross-sectional findings includes a number of cross-tabulations that are relevant to the present work. Briefly, the cross-sectional data show only modest gender differences in smoking and large differences related to race/ethnicity (with Whites more likely to smoke than African Americans or Hispanics). Smoking is inversely related to parental education, as well as to the students'

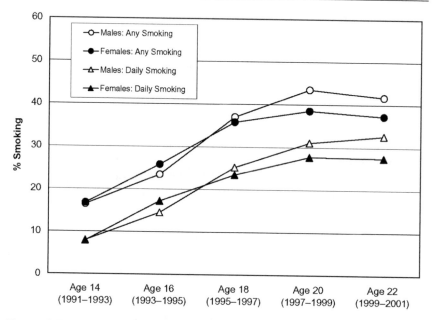

Figure 6.2. Percentage of panel respondents smoking in the last 30 days: males and females.

own college plans. Each of these patterns in the cross-sectional surveys is entirely consistent with findings reported later in this chapter based on our adolescent panel.

The age progression in smoking for our panel respondents is shown in Figure 6.2. The figure shows that rates of monthly and daily smoking were low and nearly identical for males and females in eighth grade (modal age 14). Proportions of smokers at both monthly and daily levels rose by modal age 16 and again by modal age 18, at which point proportions of male smokers were slightly higher than proportions of female smokers. Over the next 2 years (to modal age 20), proportions of smokers increased a little more, with the gender gap widening slightly; by modal age 22, there were no further increases in proportions of monthly and daily smokers. The rise in smoking rates from age 14 to age 18 occurred in 1991 to 1997 and thus may have been influenced by the secular rise during that period (see Fig. 6.1). It seems clear, however, that most of the increase is associated with age-related differences in opportunities and temptations to smoke, rather than period effects. A comparison of the data in Figures 6.1 and 6.2 indicates a close overlap between the two; thus, with respect to smoking reports, our adolescent panel appears closely representative of the larger population, as reflected in the MTF cross-sectional surveys.

Patterns or "Trajectories" of 30-Day Smoking Based on Panel Data

The descriptions provided previously, based on cross-sectional survey data, show quite clearly that smoking increases with age, from modal ages 14 through 20. But such data taken alone are not adequate to describe individual-level changes in smoking. For example, it would be theoretically possible to have one set of individuals smoking on a daily basis at age 14, a randomly different (but larger) set of individuals smoking daily at age 16, yet another (still larger) set of individuals smoking at age 18, and so on. That is not, of course, what happens; most individuals who are daily smokers at one age continue to be daily smokers 2 years later and beyond. The great advantage of our present panel data is that we can look at a variety of patterns or trajectories of change (or nonchange) across time, subject only to the constraints that our smoking measure covers frequency of cigarette use in the past 30 days (distinguishing between none at all, less than one cigarette per day, one to five per day, about a half pack per day, about one pack per day, about one and one-half packs per day, and two packs or more per day), and smoking is assessed only every 2 years. Although those constraints can contribute to measurement error, we see that they are not a severe handicap when studying something as stable as cigarette use.

The richness of opportunity provided by five waves of panel data comes at the cost of complexity. A seven-category measure across five waves permits a huge number of possible combinations: seven to the fifth power (which equals 16,807). But suppose we consider just a simple, albeit important, dichotomy: Let us distinguish between those who reported that in the past 30 days they smoked one or more cigarettes a day and those who reported smoking less than that (usually not at all). With just five waves of data, and with just this simple dichotomy distinguishing daily smokers versus nondaily smokers, the number of possible combinations is still fairly large: two to the fifth power equals 32. These 32 patterns are displayed in Table A.6.1 in the appendix. From the standpoint of simplifying analysis, the table contains both good and bad news. The bad news is that there are no empty cells; there is at least one of our panel respondents in each of the 32 categories. The good news is that most of those cell frequencies are quite small, and we can actually account for 94% of the total sample by focusing on half of the categories organized into just three groups. The largest group consists of a single category—those who did not report daily smoking at any of the five surveys (covering modal ages 14–22). The next largest group consists of five categories, all having in common that once the individuals reported smoking on a daily basis they continued to report daily smoking at each survey thereafter (through age 22). The third largest group consists of ten categories, all having the commonality that the individuals at one or more times reported daily smoking, but then stopped and did not start again (at least not by modal age 22).

Let us now take a closer look at the three major groupings outlined previously. First, most individuals in our sample—57% of the total (55% of males and 59% of females)—appear in just 1 of the 32 possible categories: those who did not report daily smoking (during the preceding 30 days) at any of the five data collections. Of course, a few among this 57% may have experienced a month or more of daily smoking at one or more other (i.e., nonsampled) times during the period from age 14 through age 22; however, it is clear that the large majority of them did not. Indeed, among the 18-year-olds in our panel sample who had not smoked daily at any of the first three data collections, only about 6% reported that they had ever smoked regularly in the past, about half said they had never smoked, and most of the rest reported having smoked only once or twice. In our annual surveys of high school seniors, we consistently find large majorities reporting that never in their lifetime did they smoke on a regular basis (Bachman et al., 2005; Johnston, Bachman et al., 2005; and earlier volumes in the same series). Our findings are also consistent with Chassin, Presson, Pitts, and Sherman (2000), who reported that approximately 60% of the youth in their longitudinal sample were nonsmokers.

Out of the remaining 31 categories, the five largest all involve individuals who at some time began smoking on a daily basis and then continued to do so consistently (at least when consistency is assessed at 2-year intervals). In other words, these individuals began daily smoking at various points in time and then continued to report daily smoking through age 22. Those who reported daily smoking only at the last wave (age 22) comprise 4.6% of the total sample, another 5.7% made the transition to daily smoking by the fourth wave (age 20), 6.5% did so by the third wave (age 18), and another 5.4% did so by the second wave (age 16). Only 3.0% reported daily smoking at all five of the surveys (i.e., starting before modal age 14). So among the 43% of the total sample who did not abstain from daily smoking at all five sample points, the majority (comprising 25% of the total sample) crossed the threshold into daily smoking only once and then remained daily smokers (again, based on our 2-year intervals of surveys).

We have thus far accounted for 82% of the total panel sample using only 6 of the 32 possible transition patterns for daily smoking. This descriptive analysis of smoking transitions was made easy by one fundamental property of tobacco: Once adolescents (or adults, for that matter) begin smoking it on a daily basis, most find it difficult to quit.

TABLE 6.1

Selected Patterns of Daily Smoking Over Five Waves

Patterns of Daily Smoking[a]	"Age of Initiation" Continuum[b]	Percent of Total[c]		
		Sample	Males	Females
Never a daily smoker	NNNNN	(1)	57.0	54.5	59.0
Initiated and then	NNNNY	(2)	4.6	6.0	3.5
continued daily smoking	NNNYY	(3)	5.7	6.5	5.1
	NNYYY	(4)	6.5	7.8	5.6
	NYYYY	(5)	5.4	5.2	5.5
	YYYYY	(6)	3.0	2.9	3.1
			82.2	82.9	81.8

[a] N = No daily smoking, Y = Daily smoking in the last 30 days. Wave 1 is represented in the first (left-most) entry in the sequence. Wave 5 is represented in the last (right-most) entry in the sequence.

[b] A new variable was created utilizing the patterns of daily smoking shown in Table 6.1. Those who never reported daily smoking (NNNNN) were coded as 1. Those who reported daily smoking in all five waves (YYYYY) were coded as 6.

[c] These percentages do not add to 100% because those with more complex patterns are not included (see text).

This stability, while good news from an analysis standpoint, is of course very bad news from a public health standpoint.

It is possible to array these largest six categories in an orderly fashion along a rough continuum representing age of initiation into "permanent" daily smoking, as shown in Table 6.1. For the 82% of the sample included in this ordering, it is a simple matter to explore how strongly this "age of initiation into permanent daily smoking" is correlated with the extent of smoking at any of the ages examined. We expected that the earlier the age of initiation, the higher would be the average amount of smoking, whether that smoking was reported at age 14, 16, 18, 20, or 22. As shown in Table 6.2, the associations are indeed positive and strong, especially by late adolescence or early adulthood; from age 18 onward, all Pearson product–moment correlations equal or exceed .83, and eta coefficients are even higher. From this we conclude that, although the *transition patterns* are quite interesting from a descriptive standpoint, we can now be fairly confident that individual differences in *amounts* of smoking, measured at various times, are closely linked to individual differences in age of initiation into permanent daily smoking. Thus, our analyses focusing on specific

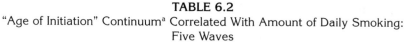

TABLE 6.2
"Age of Initiation" Continuum[a] Correlated With Amount of Daily Smoking:
Five Waves

	Total Sample	Males	Females
Smoking in the last 30 days at Wave 1 (age 14)			
Pearson's r	.534	.502	.563
eta*	.573	.536	.599
eta**	.849	.853	.848
Smoking in the last 30 days at Wave 2 (age 16)			
Pearson's r	.746	.719	.760
eta*	.796	.765	.817
eta**	.907	.908	.901
Smoking in the last 30 days at Wave 3 (age 18)			
Pearson's r	.876	.855	.872
eta*	.920	.904	.925
eta**	.924	.921	.915
Smoking in the last 30 days at Wave 4 (age 20)			
Pearson's r	.895	.888	.880
eta*	.937	.928	.936
eta**	.926	.925	.914
Smoking in the last 30 days at Wave 5 (age 22)			
Pearson's r	.872	.848	.826
eta*	.902	.877	.902
eta**	.927	.937	.905

[a] A new variable was created utilizing the patterns
of daily smoking shown in Table 6.1. Those who
never reported daily smoking (NNNNN) were
coded as 1. Those who reported daily smoking
in all five waves (YYYYY) were coded as 6.
Correlations were based on only those who were
included in the "age of initiation" continuum.

* with "Age of Initiation" as the dependent variable

** with "Age of Initiation" as the independent variable

time samples (at modal ages 14, 16, and 18) capture a good deal of the total story on adolescent smoking.[2]

Now (using Table A.6.1 in the appendix) we turn to the 18% of our panel sample who did not fall neatly into the six largest categories. Most of them (12.3% of the total sample) showed some pattern of permanently quitting, by which we mean that they stopped daily smoking and did not return to it (within the limits of our 2-year sequence of time samples). Of these, let us first consider the 7.9% of our total panel sample who were precocious in their cigarette use, already smoking on a daily basis by the time of the first data collection (modal age 14). The prognosis is not good for such individuals; most remained daily smokers 8 years later. Only about one quarter of them (2.4% of the total sample) moved into the nondaily smoker category and remained there; half of those who did quit (1.2% of the total sample) stopped daily smoking by age 16, with fewer stopping at age 18 (.3%), age 20 (.3%), and age 22 (.6%). The most common form of permanent quitting involved those who were not yet daily smokers at age 14, but then rose above the daily smoking threshold at one of the follow-up surveys, only to return to nondaily smoker status by the next survey; some of these individuals had their one report of daily smoking at age 16 (1.4% of the total sample), and more did so at ages 18 (2.7%) and 20 (2.6%). A few other individuals rose above the daily smoking threshold and stayed there for more than one wave: .8% of the total sample reported daily smoking at age 16 and again at age 18, 1.3% at ages 18 and 20, and 1.0% at ages 16, 18, and 20.

The remaining 4.7% of the sample are scattered across 16 different categories showing on-again off-again patterns of daily smoking, and their numbers are too few to try to examine systematically. But because the great majority of our panel members fit into just a few groupings, and because their transitions in daily smoking are strongly correlated with their rates of smoking at various points during adolescence and young adulthood, we can make use of linear regression analyses and structural equation modeling without having to deal with a complicated set of pattern variables. As we see next, these rates of smoking during adolescence are predictable by a number of factors, including key indicators of educational success and failure.

---

[2]As further evidence that the continuum of initiation into permanent daily smoking closely parallels the measure of amount of smoking at age 18, we note that multiple classification analyses of the sort presented later in this chapter were conducted with both measures and produced nearly identical results.

MAJOR CORRELATES/PREDICTORS
OF ADOLESCENT SMOKING

Early in chapter 4, we used regression analyses to provide an overview of factors likely to predict academic attainment. Now we apply the same approach as one way of considering whether and to what extent those same factors are correlates and predictors of adolescent smoking. The findings are summarized in Table A.6.2, which closely parallels Table 5.1. Here again we present zero-order correlations and then multiple regression coefficients predicting smoking at modal ages 14, 16, and 18. We use the term "predict" to be consistent with usual nomenclature for regression analyses, but clearly for certain measures this should not be taken literally (e.g., age-16 GPA *correlates* with age-14 smoking, but cannot *predict* it). We opted to include the same sets of predictors for all ages of smoking to facilitate comparisons; the structural equation model presented later in the chapter takes account of causal, or at least temporal, ordering.

We also make use of multiple classification analysis (MCA) to look more closely at how the key predictors of academic attainment predict cigarette use. The MCAs focus on predicting daily cigarette use at age 18; we chose the age-18 measure because it occurs later in the chronological sequence than nearly all of the predictors.[3] At the third data collection, modal age 18, daily smoking was reported by 25% of the males and 23% of the females in our panel. As we noted earlier, a few 18-year-olds smoked cigarettes less frequently, but the great majority of those who did not smoke daily simply did not smoke at all. The MCA results, presented in Table 6.3, focus on only a small portion of the material included in Table A.6.2; however, the MCAs provide greater detail, showing results for each predictor category.[4] Moreover, our decision to focus on daily smoking permits a straightforward discussion of percentages; fortunately, using this dichotomy, rather than the seven-point scale, imposes only a small penalty in terms of lost information.[5]

---

[3]We conducted parallel MCAs predicting smoking at age 22. The results are quite similar, albeit slightly weaker, compared with those for smoking at age 18.

[4]There are a few other differences between Table A.6.2 and Table 6.3. To simplify presentation, the analyses in Table 6.3 use mean scores across three waves of data collection (ages 14, 16, and 18) for the measures of GPA and college plans, rather than the separate measures from each of the three surveys. Another difference is that the analyses in Table 6.3 involve prediction of the dichotomous daily smoking measure, whereas the analyses in Table A.6.2 use the seven-point measure of smoking during the last 30 days. Finally, of course, the MCA analyses in Table 6.3 capture nonlinear as well as linear relationships, whereas the regression analyses in Table A.6.2 capture only linear relationships (except where we used dummy variables for race/ethnicity and urban density). However, because the relationships shown in Table 6.3 are largely linear, this latter distinction matters relatively little in this case.

[5]Multiple R values are approximately .02 higher using the full seven-point scale.

TABLE 6.3a

Multiple Classification Analyses Predicting Percentage Who Report
Any Daily Smoking in the Last 30 Days at Age 18: Males

Grand Mean = 25.2
Effective *N* = 1361

Variable	Percentage Reporting Any Daily Smoking in the Last 30 Days					
	Col. 1	Col. 2	Col. 3	Col. 4	Col. 5	Col. 6
	Bivariate	Multivariate				
Race/ethnicity						
African-American	13.5	11.9	9.0	9.2	10.5	10.4
Hispanic	17.4	16.1	15.3	14.2	14.0	13.8
Other race	28.9	28.6	28.0	25.3	25.3	25.3
White	27.8	28.4	29.3	30.1	29.9	29.9
Urban density						
Large MSA	21.5	22.6	22.1	23.2	22.6	22.8
Other MSA	26.5	26.6	26.6	26.6	26.5	26.4
Non-MSA	26.7	25.6	26.0	24.9	25.6	25.7
Parents' education level						
1 (Low)	26.6	26.4	23.7	19.9	20.4	20.6
2	28.3	28.0	27.3	23.9	24.5	24.5
3	27.7	27.6	28.0	27.5	27.6	27.5
4	21.8	22.3	23.0	25.2	24.8	24.9
5 (High)	21.0	20.9	22.8	28.4	27.6	27.4
Lived with 2 parents Waves 1–3						
Yes	23.7	23.6	24.5	25.7	25.7	26.1
No	28.1	28.2	26.5	24.2	24.2	23.6
Parent involvement						
1 (Low)	35.0	34.6	31.6	28.5	27.8	27.5
2	28.9	28.4	28.0	27.4	27.1	27.2
3	24.5	24.4	24.6	24.8	24.9	24.9
4 (High)	19.4	20.1	21.3	22.7	23.1	23.1
Held back grade 8 or earlier						
Never	22.7		23.7	24.7	24.6	24.9
Once	32.8		30.4	27.1	27.8	27.0
More than once	35.3		27.8	24.3	24.1	21.8
Suspended/expelled grade 8 or earlier						
Never	20.6		20.7	22.0	23.1	23.5
Once	30.6		30.5	26.9	25.8	25.4
More than once	41.3		41.0	38.2	34.4	32.8
Mean secondary school GPA						
D or below	61.6			46.9	44.7	41.9
C- or C	41.8			33.9	32.8	31.8
C+ or B-	30.2			28.5	28.6	28.7
B or B+	19.6			22.8	22.8	23.1
A-	9.9			14.7	15.4	15.5
A	6.0			12.3	14.5	14.7

TABLE 6.3a

Multiple Classification Analyses Predicting Percentage Who Report
Any Daily Smoking in the Last 30 Days at Age 18: Males (*continued*)

Grand Mean = 25.2

	Percentage Reporting Any Daily Smoking in the Last 30 Days					
Effective *N* = 1361	Col. 1	Col. 2	Col. 3	Col. 4	Col. 5	Col. 6
Variable	Bivariate			Multivariate		
Mean secondary school college plans						
Definitely won't	48.9			35.9	35.3	33.9
Probably won't	40.5			32.1	32.1	30.8
Probably will	28.3			26.7	26.2	26.1
Definitely will	14.4			20.2	20.7	21.4
Serious scholastic setback W1 to W2						
None	22.0			22.6	23.2	23.4
One	36.1			34.0	32.0	31.5
Two	51.3			45.4	40.5	36.8
Serious scholastic setback W2 to W3						
None	21.8			23.0	23.4	23.5
One	36.0			32.3	31.2	31.1
Two	38.3			32.9	30.6	29.4
Delinquency (W2–3 combined)						
No incidents	14.8				18.5	18.5
1 or 2 incidents	17.3				19.0	19.1
3 or 4 incidents	27.4				27.7	27.6
5 or 6 incidents	32.7				30.2	30.1
7 or 8 incidents	42.9				36.9	36.9
9 to 14 incidents	56.3				46.4	46.3
High school dropout by Wave 3						
Yes	47.3					34.9
No	21.1					23.4
Multiple *R*		.194	.270	.387	.425	.432
R Squared		.038	.073	.150	.180	.187

Factor Summary*

	eta	beta	beta	beta	beta	beta
Race/ethnicity	**.125**	**.143**	**.170**	**.177**	**.168**	**.169**
Urban density	.052	.039	.043	.033	.038	.035
Parents' education level	**.070**	.065	.053	.063	.056	.053
Lived with 2 parents Waves 1–3	.049	.051	.021	.017	.016	.027
Parent involvement	**.108**	**.099**	.074	.046	.038	.038
Held back grade 8 or earlier	**.104**		**.062**	.022	.030	.025
Suspended/expelled grade 8 or earlier	**.178**		**.174**	**.134**	**.093**	**.077**
Mean secondary school GPA	**.261**			**.156**	**.142**	**.133**
Mean secondary school college plans	**.244**			**.111**	**.104**	.088
Serious scholastic setback W1 to W2	**.152**			**.121**	**.093**	**.081**
Serious scholastic setback W2 to W3	**.141**			**.091**	**.076**	**.073**
Delinquency (W2–3 combined)	**.270**				**.186**	**.184**
High school dropout by Wave 3	**.220**					**.096**

*All eta and beta statistics p<.05 are shown in **bold**.

See Table 3.3 for frequency distributions of predictor variables.

Note: W1 = Wave 1 data collection (grade 8, modal age 14), W2 = Wave 2 data collection
(modal age 16), W3 = Wave 3 data collection (modal age 18)

TABLE 6.3b

Multiple Classification Analyses Predicting Percentage Who Report Any Daily Smoking in the Last 30 Days at Age 18: Females

Grand Mean = 23.4
Effective *N* = 1739

	Col. 1	Col. 2	Col. 3	Col. 4	Col. 5	Col. 6
Variable	Bivariate			Multivariate		
Race/ethnicity						
African-American	10.9	6.1	3.1	2.6	3.5	4.4
Hispanic	13.3	10.1	9.6	9.1	9.7	9.9
Other race	22.7	22.4	22.1	20.9	20.9	20.9
White	28.0	29.7	30.5	31.0	30.7	30.5
Urban density						
Large MSA	23.2	24.7	24.5	24.2	23.1	23.2
Other MSA	23.7	23.7	23.4	23.1	23.3	23.2
Non-MSA	23.2	21.5	22.2	23.3	24.1	24.1
Parents' education level						
1 (Low)	28.6	29.5	28.4	24.3	24.9	24.1
2	27.6	28.3	27.8	26.0	26.0	26.2
3	22.9	22.6	22.9	23.1	22.9	22.9
4	18.1	17.2	17.8	20.4	20.7	21.2
5 (High)	19.1	18.8	19.8	24.1	23.0	22.9
Lived with 2 parents Waves 1–3						
Yes	18.7	17.9	18.7	20.2	20.4	21.1
No	30.3	31.5	30.4	28.1	27.8	26.9
Parent involvement						
1 (Low)	31.2	27.8	26.3	25.3	24.9	24.9
2	27.8	26.9	26.5	26.0	25.5	25.4
3	22.5	22.5	22.8	23.2	23.4	23.4
4 (High)	17.3	19.6	20.1	20.1	20.7	20.7
Held back grade 8 or earlier						
Never	22.5		23.1	23.7	23.5	23.6
Once	28.4		25.5	22.3	23.3	22.7
More than once	26.6		22.3	19.2	19.3	17.6
Suspended/expelled grade 8 or earlier						
Never	21.2		21.1	21.9	22.3	22.5
Once	32.8		32.7	27.7	25.8	25.1
More than once	40.1		41.4	38.3	35.2	33.1
Mean secondary school GPA						
D or below	78.0			57.7	55.7	51.2
C- or C	38.7			31.2	29.6	28.1
C+ or B-	30.3			28.7	27.9	27.7
B or B+	20.4			22.1	22.3	22.7
A-	14.0			16.5	17.9	18.3
A	9.5			12.9	14.1	14.5

TABLE 6.3b
Multiple Classification Analyses Predicting Percentage Who Report Any Daily Smoking in the Last 30 Days at Age 18: Females (*continued*)

Grand Mean = 23.4
Effective *N* = 1739

	Percentage Reporting Any Daily Smoking in the Last 30 Days					
	Col. 1	Col. 2	Col. 3	Col. 4	Col. 5	Col. 6
Variable	Bivariate	Multivariate				
Mean secondary school college plans						
Definitely won't	41.6			26.8	28.0	24.8
Probably won't	38.9			28.7	28.0	25.4
Probably will	27.0			24.5	24.1	24.2
Definitely will	17.3			21.5	21.9	22.5
Serious scholastic setback W1 to W2						
None	21.0			22.0	22.5	22.8
One	37.4			31.5	29.0	27.5
Two	34.2			29.1	27.1	24.3
Serious scholastic setback W2 to W3						
None	21.1			21.9	22.1	22.2
One	35.2			31.4	30.2	29.3
Two	40.4			35.7	35.5	33.4
Delinquency (W2–3 combined)						
No incidents	12.9				15.7	15.7
1 or 2 incidents	23.1				23.8	23.9
3 or 4 incidents	34.2				31.3	31.3
5 or 6 incidents	39.4				33.2	33.1
7 or 8 incidents	43.7				36.3	36.2
9 to 14 incidents	63.5				50.2	49.8
High school dropout by Wave 3						
Yes	47.7					35.1
No	19.3					21.5
Multiple *R*		.271	.301	.370	.403	.413
R Squared		.073	.090	.137	.162	.171

Factor Summary*

	eta	beta	beta	beta	beta	beta
Race/ethnicity	.158	.215	.243	.254	.244	.235
Urban density	.006	.028	.019	.011	.009	.009
Parents' education level	.099	.115	.099	.045	.044	.040
Lived with 2 parents Waves 1–3	.135	.157	.135	.091	.086	.068
Parent involvement	.103	.069	.057	.050	.041	.040
Held back grade 8 or earlier	.050		.021	.017	.012	.018
Suspended/expelled grade 8 or earlier	.129		.135	.100	.077	.062
Mean secondary school GPA	.225			.149	.128	.115
Mean secondary school college plans	.175			.055	.047	.025
Serious scholastic setback W1 to W2	.136			.078	.054	.038
Serious scholastic setback W2 to W3	.126			.086	.076	.065
Delinquency (W2–3 combined)	.246				.170	.170
High school dropout by Wave 3	.235					.113

*All eta and beta statistics p<.05 are shown in **bold.**

See Table 3.3 for frequency distributions of predictor variables.

Note: W1 = Wave 1 data collection (grade 8, modal age 14), W2 = Wave 2 data collection (modal age 16), W3 = Wave 3 data collection (modal age 18)

Race/Ethnicity and Population Density

MTF surveys in high schools have consistently shown sharply lower rates of cigarette use reported by African-American and Hispanic students, compared with White students (Bachman, Johnston, & O'Malley, 1991; Johnston et al., 2005b; Wallace et al., 2003). Our present panel data also show large differences in smoking. Table 6.3 (Column 1) shows that, prior to controls for any other predictors, African-American males are only about half as likely as White males to be daily smokers, and among females the ratio is about one third. Hispanic rates of daily smoking are nearly as low as those for African Americans. Column 2 of the table suggests that if the groups did not differ in certain parental factors discussed later in the chapter, the differences in smoking rates would be even more striking—especially among females. Further controls for academic success actually heighten these differences in smoking rates, albeit only slightly.

Population density appears unrelated to the likelihood of daily smoking among the females in our panel sample (see Table 6.3). Among males, those not living in large cities have slightly higher daily smoking rates, and that is not substantially changed by controls for background or other factors. Data from the MTF cross-sectional samples of 10th- and 12th-grade students show daily smoking proportions that are highest in nonmetropolitan areas and lowest in large urban areas among both males and females, but such differentials are smaller when analyses are limited to White students only. Because the large cross-sectional samples do not show consistent gender differences in the patterns of smoking linked with urban density, we discount the small gender differences shown in Table 6.3 and treat urban density primarily as something to be controlled while we focus attention on the links between educational success and substance use.

Parental Education

Adolescents whose parents have the highest levels of education are somewhat less likely than average to be daily smokers (rates of about 20% at age 18), whereas those with the least educated parents are slightly more likely than average to be daily smokers (about 28%), based on the bivariate coefficients shown in the first column of Table 6.3. The multivariate findings show little change in this pattern when other background factors are included as predictors (Column 2) or even when further controls are introduced for early grade retention or suspension/expulsion (Column 3). However, that negative relationship does not remain once GPA, college plans, and scholastic setbacks later than Grade 8 are included in the equation (Column 4). It thus appears that parents' education has only modest impacts on their children's likelihood of smoking, and these impacts are primarily indirect via educational success—a conclusion consistent with the structural equation findings presented later. As we see next, other aspects of family life may make more of a difference in adolescent smoking than parental education.

Presence of Both Parents at Home

Having both parents present in the home throughout the high school years appears to be a protective factor against adolescent smoking. Table 6.3 shows that, among 18-year-old males who lived with both parents at home during the past 4 years, only 24% were daily smokers, compared with 28% among those who did not have both parents present throughout that period of their lives. The females in our panel showed larger differences: 19% versus 30%. Chassin et al. (2005) also report less adolescent smoking in two- versus one-parent families. The multivariate analyses indicate that these differences in rates of daily smoking linked to parental presence in the home are undiminished by controls for differences in parental involvement (discussed in the next section), race/ethnicity, urban density, or parental educational level (see Column 2 in Table 6.3). Adding grade retention and suspension/expulsion (by eighth grade) to the equation reduces the modest difference among males, but scarcely affects the larger difference among females (see Column 3). When further controls for GPA, college plans, and more recent scholastic setbacks are added to the equations, no (nonoverlapping) relationship remains for males, and the difference for females is reduced (from 12% to 8%; see Column 4), thus suggesting that effects are largely indirect—especially among males.

Based on the findings summarized previously, we conclude that having both parents present at home during the high school years is advantageous—not only in terms of long-term academic attainment (as shown in chap. 4), but also in terms of protection from the onset of regular cigarette use. Our panel data suggested there might be gender differences in the extent of this effect; however, we failed to replicate such differences with our large cross-sectional samples, leading us to conclude that there probably are not important gender differences.[6]

Parental Involvement in Students' Lives

Another more potent protective factor against smoking seems to be parental involvement with their early adolescents. Table A.6.2 shows that parents' involvement (monitoring and participating in homework, requiring chores, and limiting TV viewing) with their children at age 14 is negatively linked with smoking throughout high school and beyond; moreover, the earlier (age-14) involvement and monitoring seems somewhat more important than that which occurs 2 or 4 years later. Although the links with later smoking are not as strong as the links with precocious (i.e., age-14) smoking, the data in Table 6.3 (Column 1) show that, by age 18, those whose parents were least involved 4 years earlier are nearly twice as likely to be daily smokers (about 31%–35%), compared with those whose parents were most involved (only about 17%–19% smoke daily).

The multivariate coefficients in Table 6.3 show that these protective effects of parental involvement overlap only modestly with parental education and presence in the home (Column 2); they also overlap with early grade retention or suspension/expulsion (Column 3) and with educational success during secondary school (Column 4). Yet even with all such factors controlled, rates of daily smoking are still about five to six percentage points lower among those whose parents had been most involved, compared with those whose parents had been least involved. These differences (shown in Column 4) fall short of statistical significance; nevertheless, they are consistent across males and females. In any case, the total effects attributed to parental involvement in our structural model (shown later) are important and significant. This is certainly consistent with the frequently aired public service announcement, "Parents: the anti-drug."

---

[6]We examined MTF cross-sectional data from 10th and 12th graders combined across two 6-year intervals (1992–1997 and 1998–2003). We found that 12th graders living with both parents were about two percentage points less likely to be daily smokers, on average, compared with those not living with both parents (a statistically significant difference given the large sample sizes). Among 10th graders, the difference was significantly larger— about four percentage points. (We suspect that the difference between grades arises because relatively few adolescents drop out of school before the end of 10th grade, whereas by 12th grade, many of the individuals who are most likely to be smokers have already dropped out and are thus not included in our 12th-grade cross-sectional surveys.) Most important, gender differences were neither large nor consistent; on average, male and female effects of an intact family on smoking were virtually identical in the large cross-sectional samples.

Grade Retention, and Suspension or Expulsion, by End of Eighth Grade

Students held back a grade prior to the end of eighth grade are more likely than others to be daily smokers at age 14, and somewhat more likely to be daily smokers at later ages also (see Table A.6.2 in the appendix). Table 6.3 (Column 1) shows that, by age 18, females are about 6 percentage points more likely to be daily smokers if they had been held back prior to eighth grade, whereas among males the difference is about 10 percentage points. With other factors controlled, including more recent indicators of educational success (see Column 4), early grade retention shows no clear separate effect on smoking. It thus appears that any effects of these early grade failures operate indirectly via other factors.

In contrast, academic misbehaviors reflected in suspension or expulsion prior to the end of eighth grade show large and long-lasting links with smoking. Figure 6.3 shows that, compared with those never suspended or expelled, those who had that experience once before the end of eighth grade are half again as likely to be smokers by age 18, and those suspended or expelled two or more times are about twice as likely to be or become daily smokers. As the figure indicates, these large differences are reduced only modestly by controls for other factors. It thus appears that young adolescents (age 14 or younger) who misbehave sufficiently in school to warrant suspension or expulsion are also likely to misbehave in the form of initiating smoking—a habit that tends to persist years later, as evidenced by the age-18 data shown in the figure. Whether these early suspensions and expulsions contribute to early smoking more than vice versa is not readily discernable from the available data; however, in the final portion of this chapter, we are able to explore likely causal directions involving scholastic setbacks that occur later than age 14.

Grade Point Average

We illustrated in chapter 1 that there is a strong inverse relationship between grade point average (GPA) and likelihood of smoking. The data in Table 6.3 (Column 1) show again the dramatic differences; for example, fewer than 10% of students who averaged A throughout high school were daily smokers at modal age 18, contrasted with about 40% of those who averaged C or C-. Only a handful of students averaged D or below, but their likelihood of daily smoking was even higher—nearly two thirds for the males and more than three quarters for the females (Column 1 in Table 6.3). The relationship between grades and smoking overlaps to

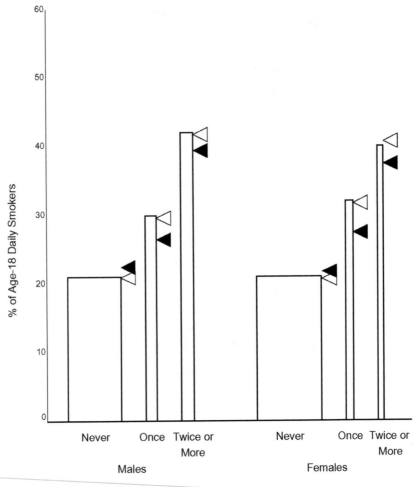

The main bars are unadjusted estimates. The bar width is proportionate to the weighted number of cases in the category.

◁ Percentage adjusted for race/ethnicity, population density, parents' education, number of parents, parental involvement, and ever having been held back (Column 3 in Table 6.3a & b)

◀ Percentage adjusted for race/ethnicity, population density, parents' education, number of parents, parental involvement, ever having been held back, GPA, college plans, and serious scholastic setbacks between Waves 1 and 2 and Waves 2 and 3 (Column 4 in Table 6.3a & b)

Figure 6.3. Percentage of age-18 daily smokers by number of times suspended or expelled Grade 8 or earlier: males and females.

some extent with relationships involving other indicators of scholastic success or failure, as indicated by the multivariate findings. Nevertheless, even after controls for these other factors, GPA remains among the strongest predictors of daily smoking; compared with students whose grades averaged A, those with grades of C or C- were about three times as likely to be daily smokers, and those with grades of D or below were about four times as likely to be daily smokers (Column 4 in Table 6.3).

College Plans

College plans are another strong negative correlate of daily smoking by age 18, as shown in Table 6.3 and illustrated in Figure 6.4. Those who say they "probably" or "definitely" will not complete a 4-year college program (averaged across college plans at ages 14, 16, and 18) are roughly three times more likely to be daily smokers at age 18, compared with those expecting they "definitely will" complete college (Column 1). After controls for other indicators of scholastic success or failure (see Column 4), the differences in daily smoking rates remain substantial among males, but drop to nonsignificance among females.

Serious Scholastic Setbacks During High School (After Eighth Grade)

Students held back a grade, or suspended or expelled, during the years following eighth grade are almost twice as likely to be daily smokers at age 18, compared with those experiencing no such setbacks (see Column 1 of Table 6.3). When other factors are controlled (see Column 4), the positive connections between such setbacks and smoking remain, albeit somewhat reduced in size. Clearly, the connections between scholastic setbacks and cigarette use can reflect more than one possible direction of causation. As we have stressed at several points in this book, doing poorly in school appears to be part of a syndrome of problem behaviors that often includes smoking cigarettes. Moreover, we have suggested that lack of success in school may contribute to an adolescent's involvement in such a syndrome and thus may contribute fairly directly to smoking. Finally, the reverse causation may operate also—as, for example, when smoking on school property is the grounds for a student's suspension or expulsion. In the next section, using structural equation modeling, we attempt to deal with several causal pathways by treating smoking as a possible outcome of earlier scholastic setbacks, but also as a possible cause of later setbacks.

Dropping Out of High School by Age 18

One of the most dramatic scholastic setbacks, of course, occurs when a student drops out of high school. Table 6.3 shows that among dropouts (about 15% of our sample as of age 18), nearly half are daily cigarette smokers—more than twice the rate among nondropouts (see Table 6.3, Column 1). The multivariate analyses (Column 6) show that even with other measures of educational success and failure (and also delinquency) controlled, the link between dropping out and smoking remains large.

ADDITIONAL CORRELATES/PREDICTORS OF ADOLESCENT SMOKING

We turn now to those additional dimensions that are not especially strong predictors of academic attainment (see chap. 4), but that do show some links with delinquency (see chap. 5). These correlates of delinquency also tend to be correlates of smoking; moreover, when these dimensions are included in regression analyses, the contributions of GPA and college plans are sharply reduced (see Table A.6.2 in the appendix). So now we review how these additional dimensions are linked with adolescent smoking.

Various Problem Behaviors

Smoking is more likely than average among adolescents involved in skipping whole days of school, cutting classes, or other misbehaviors that result in being sent to the office. Even stronger correlations appear between smoking and the general index of delinquent behavior, which was the focus of our analyses in chapter 5. There is considerable overlap among these predictors, especially among the several measures of school-related misbehavior. The delinquency measure remains important; however, some of the other measures (particularly those for the matching time period) also retain considerable predictive value—most notably being sent to the office because of misbehaviors in school. (Of course, it is also true that smoking is among the behaviors that merit a trip to the office.)

As for the correlation between adolescent smoking and the general measure of delinquency, one perspective is that smoking, at least at ages 14 and 16, is a specific form of delinquent behavior, and that both smoking and delinquency can fall under the category of deviant behaviors.

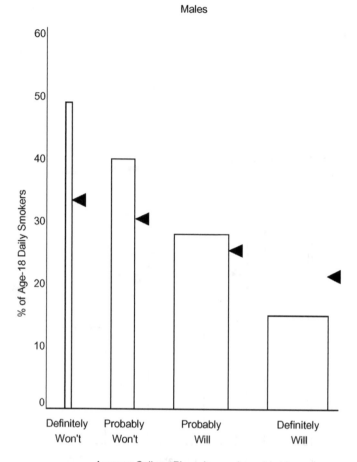

Males

% of Age-18 Daily Smokers

Average College Plans Across Ages 14–18

The main bars are unadjusted estimates. The bar width is proportionate to the weighted number of cases in the category.

 Percentage adjusted for race/ethnicity, population density, parents' education, number of parents, parental involvement, GPA, ever having been held back, ever having been suspended/expelled, serious scholastic setback between Waves 1 and 2 and Waves 2 and 3, delinquency, and dropout by Wave 3 (Column 6 in Table 6.3a)

Figure 6.4a. Percentage of age-18 daily smokers by average college plans across ages 14–18: males.

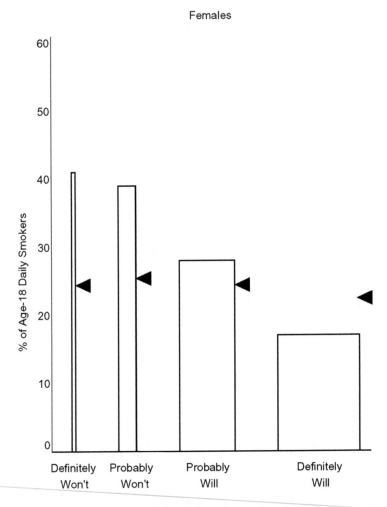

Females

% of Age-18 Daily Smokers

Average College Plans Across Ages 14–18

The main bars are unadjusted estimates. The bar width is proportionate to the weighted number of cases in the category.

◄ Percentage adjusted for race/ethnicity, population density, parents' education, number of parents, parental involvement, GPA, ever having been held back, ever having been suspended/expelled, serious scholastic setback between Waves 1 and 2 and Waves 2 and 3, delinquency, and dropout by Wave 3 (Column 6 in Table 6.3b)

Figure 6.4b. Percentage of age-18 daily smokers by average college plans across ages 14–18: females.

Indeed, even tobacco companies have taken to publicly disapproving teen smoking—although some critics have been so unkind as to question their sincerity! In any case, our regression analyses indicate a considerable overlap between smoking and (other) delinquent behavior, so we return to that overlap later in the chapter.

Evenings Out for Fun and Recreation

We mentioned in chapter 4 that adolescents who frequently spend evenings out for fun and recreation are also more likely than average to be substance users, and the correlation coefficients in Table A.6.2 show this to be true of smoking. The regression coefficients in the table reveal that the links with smoking are largely, but not entirely, overlapping with other predictors. Again, causal interpretation is difficult: Does being out for fun and recreation make it easier to smoke? Do adolescent smokers choose to be out more often (to smoke, among other things)? We believe the answer is "yes" to both questions; although the problem of sorting out causation remains, it is worthwhile to document the overlap.

Actual and Preferred Hours of Work

Table A.6.2 shows consistently positive zero-order correlations between hours of part-time work during the school year and cigarette smoking. The correlations with smoking are also positive, and generally higher, for adolescents' *preferences* for part-time work during school. We have reported elsewhere (Bachman et al., 2003) that the desire for (long) hours of part-time work during the school year generally emerges earlier among adolescents than the actual work; here is additional evidence that the desire, perhaps more so than the work, appears to be involved with substance use—in this case, cigarette use. The coefficients for actual and preferred work remain mostly positive when treated as multivariate predictors of smoking; however, these multivariate coefficients are generally quite small, indicating considerable overlap with other predictors.[7]

---

[7]Some of this overlap, of course, involves the other measures of work hours and preferences. Given six overlapping measures (both actual and preferred hours at all three waves) included simultaneously as predictors, there is bound to be a substantial reduction in coefficient size.

Religious Attendance and Importance

Adolescents who attend religious services frequently, as well as those who rate religion as important in their lives (often the same individuals), are less likely than average to be cigarette smokers. The correlation coefficients in Table A.6.2 show that this negative association is present for both males and females throughout adolescence. Indeed, the correlations with smoking are much the same no matter whether religious attendance and importance are measured at age 14, 16, or 18. This is consistent with the high stability of religiosity, and it suggests that religious involvement may have protective effects relatively early. The multivariate regression coefficients in the table are small, suggesting that some of the protective effects of religion may be indirect via other factors that influence smoking.[8]

Self-Esteem

Students with low self-esteem at the end of eighth grade were more likely to be smokers at eighth grade and also 2 and 4 years later. Self-esteem in later years is also associated negatively with smoking, but in general the earlier self-esteem scores are equally strong—or stronger—predictors of smoking throughout adolescence. The regression coefficients in Table A.6.2 indicate that these relationships are largely, but not entirely, overlapping with other predictors of smoking.

A STRUCTURAL EQUATION MODEL INCLUDING ACADEMIC ATTAINMENT AND SMOKING

The structural equation model of academic attainment, developed in chapter 4 (see Fig. 4.7), was expanded at the end of chapter 5 to include delinquent behaviors and the use of various substances during adolescence (see Fig. 5.3). The broad rationale for the expansion was presented in chapter 5 and need not be repeated here; however, it may be useful to offer a brief rationale specific to smoking and its causal relationships with academic success and failure.

As shown earlier in this chapter, although smoking clearly emerges in the behaviors of some adolescents at modal age 14 (eighth grade), it

---

[8]But here again regression coefficients are reduced in size because all six measures of religiosity are included simultaneously as predictors.

becomes more widespread and frequent as adolescents grow older. In contrast, patterns of scholastic success, as reflected in GPA, are established well before age 14 and show a high degree of stability thereafter (as shown in Fig. 4.7). We view these differences in stability as evidence in favor of the causal priority of GPA. (For college plans, in contrast, stabilities between modal ages 14 and 16 are roughly equal to those for smoking.)

Our most important considerations in locating smoking within the causal framework are conceptual. We view smoking as a relatively late-emerging aspect of a problem behavior syndrome. We consider poor scholastic performance (in many cases) to be an earlier emerging aspect of the syndrome, and poor performance may then contribute to adolescents' rejection of, or rebellion against, adult norms—including the norm against adolescent smoking. Measures of the possible mediating mechanisms through which such effects may occur prior to age 14 are not available to be included in our model, so we show the effects as direct from GPA to smoking. As for college plans, a similar argument could be made that rejecting the norm of college aspiration may make it easier to also reject the norm against smoking. We recognize that a reverse argument could be made. Moreover, we consider it plausible that smoking leads adolescents to associate with other smokers, who tend to be lower than average in academic aspirations and achievements; as a result of these peer influences, smoking really could stunt intellectual growth.

The previous discussion is far from unambiguous as to how smoking should be located in our causal model, especially in the case of college plans; fortunately, the empirical evidence provides some additional confirmation of our choices. Bryant et al. (2000) found that eighth-grade smoking did not show significant effects on academic achievement or school misbehavior 2 years later, whereas achievements and misbehaviors at eighth grade did show effects on cigarette smoking 2 years later. Our own preliminary analyses, prior to adopting our model, also showed that smoking did not have consistent 2-year lagged effects on GPA or college plans.[9]

Although we did not find it necessary to treat smoking as a direct cause of GPA or college plans in our model, we considered it important that the model examine the extent to which smoking might contribute to serious scholastic setbacks (grade retention, suspension, or expulsion). Indeed

---

[9]For example, we employed simple structural equation models linking GPA and smoking, allowing cross-lagged influences (each on the other) from ages 14 to 16, and again from 16 to 18 as illustrated in Figure A.6.1 in the appendix (middle panel). All cross-lags were negative in sign, but the impacts of smoking on later GPA were all small, whereas all impacts of GPA on later smoking were larger (−.11 to −.21).

smoking on school property can be grounds for suspension in most schools and even expulsion in some.[10] We also considered it important to examine whether smoking seemed to contribute to dropping out of high school by age 18, although the causal mechanisms there seemed less clear.

Among the most important causal paths specified in the model are those linking smoking to academic attainment at age 22. Smoking at age 18 is given a direct causal path to academic attainment; smoking at earlier ages has indirect paths, most notably via age-18 smoking and dropout status at age 18. These paths are important because they examine the possibility that smoking may be more than just a symptom of dysfunctional or problem behavior, and that it may make its own contributions to academic difficulties.

Structural Equation Model Findings

Figure 6.5 and Table 6.4 highlight certain structural equation model findings specific to adolescent smoking; the findings shown are a subset of those included in the "Total Structural Model" portion of the appendix (Table A.3.10). The fit indexes (Fig. 6.5; see also Table A.3.4 in the appendix for a more complete list of fit indicators) show that this model provides an acceptable—indeed excellent—fit to the data. As expected, eighth-grade smoking is influenced by several of the exogenous factors. In particular, early (i.e., age-14) smoking occurs more frequently among those suspended or expelled prior to the end of eighth grade and among those with less parental involvement. As modeled, these effects are partially indirect via delinquency. Interestingly, parental education makes little direct contribution to smoking, although it does have some indirect effects via GPA and college plans in inhibiting smoking among females. The model results again confirm that smoking is less likely among African Americans and Hispanics than among Whites (the comparison group). (All of the exogenous variable effects on smoking, direct and total, are listed in Table 6.4.)

Turning now to the endogenous variables, we observe first that smoking shows high levels of stability from ages 14 to 16 and even higher levels during later adolescence. This is true among both males and females, although females consistently show higher levels of stability. So those smoking at age 14 are more likely to smoke also at age 16, those smoking at age 16 are much more likely than average to be smokers also at age 18, and so on.

---

[10]A recent survey of schools showed that violation of school tobacco policies is grounds for suspension in up to 80% of schools, and in some of them (up to 20% of the total) it can be grounds for expulsion (Johnston, O'Malley, Delva, Bachman, & Schulenberg, 2005).

TABLE 6.4
Direct and Total Effects of Predictors on 30-Day Cigarette Smoking at Wave 1, Wave 2, and Wave 3*

Predictors	Smoking Wave 1 Males Direct	Total	Females Direct	Total	Smoking Wave 2 Males Direct	Total	Females Direct	Total	Smoking Wave 3 Males Direct	Total	Females Direct	Total
African-American	-.125	-.139	-.203	-.217	-.095	-.165	-.147	-.253	-.083	-.168	-.112	-.252
Hispanic	-.084	-.077	-.095	-.085	-.045	-.077	-.099	-.140	-.084	-.122	-.100	-.178
Other race	-.011	-.005	-.049	-.021	-.025	-.015	-.091	-.083	-.028	-.014	-.037	-.078
Large MSA	-.029	-.022	-.004	-.007	.003	-.003	.003	.011	-.038	-.043	-.003	.017
Non-MSA	-.012	-.010	.000	-.029	.008	.000	.020	-.011	-.017	-.018	.027	.000
Parents' education level	.013	-.016	-.024	-.076	.020	-.030	.030	-.069	.021	-.034	-.024	-.096
Lived with 2 parents Waves 1–3	.005	-.006	-.054	-.094	-.043	-.070	-.056	-.147	.022	-.034	-.039	-.153
Parent involvement index	-.139	-.202	-.147	-.213	.021	-.121	.017	-.124	-.045	-.133	-.006	-.088
Held back grade 8 or earlier	.076	.117	.036	.059		.082		.051		.066		.048
Suspended/expelled grade 8 or earlier	.120	.229	.151	.276		.146		.172		.110		.125
GPA Wave 1	-.058	-.125	-.109	-.180		-.217		-.246		-.220		-.244
GPA Wave 2					-.098	-.160	-.093	-.141		-.216		-.206
GPA Wave 3									-.124	-.145	-.125	-.138
College plans Wave 1	-.078	-.087	-.033	-.065		-.096		-.084		-.071		-.057
College plans Wave 2					-.116	-.124	-.084	-.090		-.108		-.064
College plans Wave 3									-.067	-.066	-.009	-.012
Serious scholastic setback W1 to W2					.071	.116	.108	.149		.086		.103
Serious scholastic setback W2 to W3									.037	.067	.043	.060
Delinquency index Wave 1	.239	.239	.339	.339		.198		.240		.140		.165
Delinquency index Wave 2					.223	.223	.180	.180		.198		.165
Delinquency index Wave 3									.132	.132	.119	.119
30-day cigarette smoking Wave 1					.407	.410	.465	.472		.218		.278
30-day cigarette smoking Wave 2									.527	.530	.582	.588
30-day cigarette smoking Wave 3												

Direct and Total Effects of 30-Day Cigarette Smoking at Wave 1, Wave 2, and Wave 3 on Education Factors*

Predictors		GPA Wave 2 Total	College Plans Wave 2 Total	Serious Scholastic Setback W1 to W2 Direct	Total	GPA Wave 3 Total	College Plans Wave 3 Total	Serious Scholastic Setback W2 to W3 Direct	Total	High School Dropout Wave 3 Direct	Total	Academic Attainment Wave 5 Direct	Total
30-day cigarette Wave 1	Males	-.003	-.003	.042	.029	-.004	-.003		.018		.075		-.034
	Females	-.002	-.005	.001	.046	-.004	-.006		.045		.103		-.049
30-day cigarette Wave 2	Males					-.005	-.004	.035	.048	.144	.152		-.071
	Females					-.005	-.006	.072	.095	.200	.204		-.094
30-day cigarette Wave 3	Males											-.045	-.057
	Females											-.074	-.085

*Coefficients that are p<.05 (two-tailed) are shown in **bold**.

Note: W1 = Wave 1 data collection (grade 8, modal age 14), W2 = Wave 2 data collection (modal age 16), W3 = Wave 3 data collection (modal age 18)

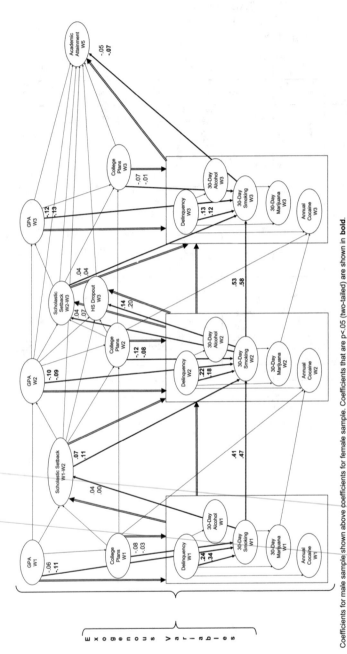

Coefficients for male sample shown above coefficients for female sample. Coefficients that are p<.05 (two-tailed) are shown in **bold**.

Note: W1 = Wave 1 data collection (grade 8, modal age 14), W2 = Wave 2 data collection (modal age 16), W3 = Wave 3 data collection (modal age 18), W5 = Wave 5 data collection (modal age 22)

Model Fit Statistics

	Males	Females
Comparative Fit Index (CFI)	.996	.995
Root Mean-Square Error of Approximation (RMSEA)	.023	.027
Chi-Square	549	712
Degrees of Freedom	316	316

Figure 6.5. Structural equation model of academic attainment and substance use, focusing on cigarette use.

The next general observation is that delinquency influences smoking to a considerable extent at age 14 (path coefficients of .24 for males, .34 for females), to a lesser extent at age 16 (coefficients of .22 for males, .18 for females), and to a still smaller extent at age 18 (coefficients of .13 for males, .12 for females).[11]

The model further shows that educational matters have important impacts on smoking, and in the early years these impacts occur largely via delinquency. GPA consistently shows negative effects on smoking; the better a student performs in school, the less likely he or she is to smoke. Students expecting to go to college are also less likely to be smokers, although there seem to be no further effects of college plans on smoking by age 18. This general pattern of protective effects of educational success holds in much the same fashion for males and females. Serious scholastic setbacks (suspension, expulsion, or being held back a grade) increase the chances of smoking, both directly and indirectly via delinquency. In sum, the findings in Figure 6.5 generally indicate that educational success decreases the likelihood of smoking, whereas scholastic setbacks increase that likelihood.

But what do the findings tell us about whether smoking plays a causal role as well, inhibiting educational success or increasing the likelihood of setbacks? Does smoking really stunt one's educational growth? As already noted, we found no clear indication of direct negative effects of smoking on subsequent GPA or college plans, so such paths are not included in the model. Moreover, the model provides little evidence that smoking increases the likelihood of serious scholastic setbacks. However, smoking at age 16 does show significant positive effects on the likelihood of being a high school dropout by age 18, about equally strong among males and females (path coefficients of .14 and .20, respectively). Finally, smoking at age 18 shows negative direct effects on academic attainment at age 22 (path coefficients of −.05 for males[12] and −.07 for females), and smoking at earlier ages shows significant indirect effects on academic attainment (coefficients of −.03 and −.05 for age-14 smoking; −.07 and −.09 for age-16 smoking;

---

[11]Here, as at other points in the development of the model, we carried out exploratory modeling using cross-lagged prediction from age 14 to age 16, and age 16 to age 18. Figure A.6.2 in the appendix shows relationships between delinquency and smoking, and indicates that lagged impacts of delinquency on smoking 2 years later are substantial, whereas the reverse impacts (of smoking on later delinquency) are quite small. This is consistent with the view that general patterns of delinquency emerge earlier than most smoking behavior.

[12]The direct effect for males falls short of statistical significance, but the total effect (−.06) is significant.

all are significant). One reason that these coefficients are rather small is because—fortunately—the proportions of regular smokers among adolescents are relatively small. So we undertook some further analyses to show more clearly how smokers and nonsmokers differ in educational attainment.

We turned again to MCA, this time illustrating how smoking at modal age 16 predicts dropping out by modal age 18. The results are displayed in Figure 6.6. The bar widths in the figure remind us that the large majority of our panel members did not smoke at all at age 16, and the height of the bars shows that by age 18 relatively few of these nonsmokers had dropped out of high school (about 11% of males and 9% of females). Among the smokers, however, rates of dropping out were much higher. Roughly speaking, compared with the nonsmokers, the odds of dropping out by age 18 were two-and-a-half times greater among those who (at age 16) smoked only one to five cigarettes per day, three to four times greater among those who smoked about a half pack per day, and five to six times greater among those who smoked a pack a day or more. Fewer than 5% of the 16-year-olds in our panel were pack-a-day smokers; of this 5%, more than half of them had dropped out by age 18. The figure shows that after controls for background factors, as well as grades, college plans, and delinquency at age 16, the differences in dropout rates were reduced; but even with these factors controlled, pack-a-day smoking was associated with a tripled risk of dropping out.

FURTHER ANALYSES INCLUDING FRIENDS' SMOKING

How is it that smoking may contribute to lowered academic attainment? One possible mechanism involves peer influence. Smokers tend to associate with other smokers, and smokers in general have lower than average academic performance and aspirations (as documented earlier in this chapter). Accordingly, a student who smokes is less likely than average to have educationally ambitious friends. This notion can be viewed as a rough analogy to the health impacts of secondhand smoke. Smokers inhale additional smoke just because they tend to associate with other smokers; similarly, it might be the case that smokers incorporate additional adverse feelings about education just because of their friends' negative feelings.

It is indeed the case that adolescent smokers in our sample reported greater than average proportions of friends who smoke. Product–moment correlations between self-reported smoking and friends' smoking are about .43 to .45 at ages 14 through 22. (When we focus on means of reports computed across three time samples—ages 14, 16, and 18—the correlation

Males

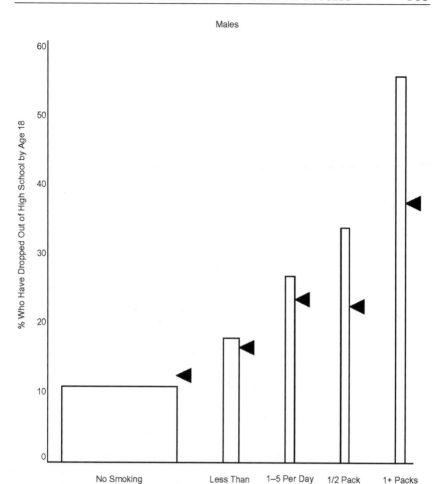

Cigarette Smoking in Last 30 Days at Age 16

The main bars are unadjusted estimates. The bar width is proportionate to the weighted number of cases in the category.

◀ Percentage adjusted for held back by 8th grade, suspended/expelled by 8th grade, race/ethnicity, population density, parents' education level, number of parents in the home, parental involvement, 10th-grade GPA, 10th-grade college plans, and 10th-grade delinquency

Figure 6.6a. Percentage of students who have dropped out of high school by age 18 (1995–1997) by frequency of cigarette smoking in the last 30 days at age 16: males.

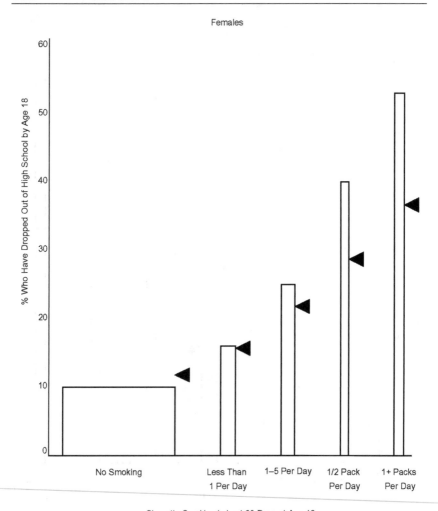

Females

The main bars are unadjusted estimates. The bar width is proportionate to the weighted number of cases in the category.

◀ Percentage adjusted for held back by 8th grade, suspended/expelled by 8th grade, race/ethnicity, population density, parents' education level, number of parents in the home, parental involvement, 10th-grade GPA, 10th-grade college plans, and 10th-grade delinquency

Figure 6.6b. Percentage of students who have dropped out of high school by age 18 (1995–1997) by frequency of cigarette smoking in the last 30 days at age 16: females.

rises to .59, no doubt because combining the three reports reduces measurement error.) So the survey data confirm street-corner observation: Smokers hang out with other smokers. But these high correlations do not help us much with a fundamental chicken-and-egg problem: which comes first, the adolescent's smoking or the association with friends who smoke? It seems likely that causation runs both ways and is largely inextricable.

Without trying to resolve the questions about causal direction, we conducted some relatively simple analyses to see whether friends' use of cigarettes contributed to the prediction of academic attainment. First, using regression analyses (not shown here), we considered own use and friends' use separately as predictors. Compared with the variance explained in chapter 4, the modest additional contribution from respondents' own smoking is more than twice as large as that from friends' use. Further, it is clear that *adding* friends' use to adolescents' own smoking produces virtually no increase in adjusted R squares.

We also substituted friends' smoking for respondents' own smoking in earlier structural equation models to see whether it made any difference. The answer is that the fit measures were largely unchanged, whereas prediction of academic attainment was trivially reduced compared with the model using respondents' smoking behaviors. In particular, the links with dropping out (by age 18) were weaker for friends' smoking than for self-reported smoking. Thus, from an analysis standpoint, friends' use appears to be little more than a proxy for own use. That does not rule out the possibility that among the reasons for smokers' higher dropout rates and lower longer term academic attainment is the fact that they hang out with other smokers (who are below average in academic achievement and aspiration); however, it suggests that friends' use is at most only part of the story.

SUMMARY AND CONCLUSIONS

We introduced this chapter with a multiple-choice question: What accounts for the substantial negative correlation between smoking and academic attainment? Does A cause B, does B cause A, or does C (other common factors) cause both A and B? The correct answer, of course, is "all of the above." But the research in this chapter does provide some basis for concluding that smoking has at most a small negative impact on academic attainment, whereas earlier educational successes and failures have quite a lot to do with whether an adolescent becomes a smoker. Moreover, the prior causes of educational success and failure have important impacts on smoking as well.

We began by noting that rates of smoking among secondary school students have shifted several times during recent decades, reaching one peak at about 1976 to 1977, then declining throughout the 1980s, only to rise again during much of the 1990s, and then decline after 1997 (see Fig. 6.1). Despite these secular shifts in proportions of student smokers, the correlates of smoking have remained largely the same; most notably, daily smoking has consistently been far below average among students who get good grades and plan to complete a 4-year college program (Johnston et al., 2005b).

Our panel data correspond closely with the cross-sectional findings summarized previously, and that leaves us confident in generalizing from our current findings based on the adolescent panel. The panel data have the great advantage of showing various trajectories of smoking—patterns of change or nonchange—across the age range 14 to 22 years. What emerges from that analysis of trajectories, as well as our more complex structural equation modeling, is a picture of great stability. The majority of our panel respondents were not daily smokers at any of the five survey points; indeed, most of this group did not smoke at all. Among those who did report daily smoking at any point in the study, most continued to report daily smoking at all subsequent survey points, a smaller number managed to stop and not resume at later surveys, and still fewer (less than 6% of the total sample) showed on-again off-again patterns of daily smoking across the five survey points. Our cross-sectional findings show that by the end of high school, many smokers say they would like to quit, and the majority of smokers say they expect not to be smoking 5 years hence (Bachman et al., 2005). Nevertheless, the present data and other MTF panel analyses (Bachman et al., 1997, 2002; Schulenberg et al., 1994) indicate that most who were smoking at age 18 will continue to smoke. This stability of smoking behavior, in the face of a widespread desire to quit, is strong evidence of the addictive properties of tobacco.

The multivariate analyses show large racial and ethnic differences, with smoking rates lower among African-American and Hispanic youth compared with White youth. These analyses also show that parental education and having both parents present in the home are negatively correlated with smoking, but have little impact independent of other predictors. Parental involvement in their children's lives at age 14 shows modest protective effects, inhibiting smoking at least at younger ages. It was not feasible to include measures of parent–child or parent–parent relations in our data collections, but it seems likely to us that at least some of the effects linked with number of parents in the home reflect the quality of interpersonal relationships in the family.

Students' educational backgrounds prior to the end of eighth grade are important predictors of smoking—not just smoking at the end of eighth grade, but also at ages 16, 18, and even 22. Those who have experienced grade retention, suspension, expulsion, poor GPAs, and low college aspirations are more likely than average to be or become smokers. Smoking is also more likely than average among adolescents who skip school, cut classes, and get sent to the office for misbehaving.

A number of other correlates of smoking appear in our analyses. Smoking is more likely among those who report engaging in delinquent behavior, who spend frequent evenings out for fun and recreation (and perhaps smoking), who prefer to (and later do) work long hours at part-time jobs during the school year, who have low self-esteem, and who are low in religiosity. These correlates of smoking show a good deal of overlap with each other and with some of the other predictors noted previously.

Earlier findings and our own preliminary findings, as well as our conceptual perspective, all support our treatment of GPA and college plans at eighth grade as causally prior to smoking at the end of eighth grade, with similar causal orderings at ages 16 and 18. Our structural equation model, an expansion of that introduced in chapter 4, incorporates those premises. The model analyses suggest that educational successes are protective factors that decrease the likelihood of smoking, whereas scholastic setbacks are risk factors that increase that likelihood. It seems clear from these analyses that educational successes and failures do have long-lasting impacts on smoking behaviors.

What about reverse causal impacts? Here the findings are not as strong, but they suggest that smoking plays at least a modest causal role in influencing academic attainment. We considered smoking to be a potential cause of dropping out of high school by age 18, and it does appear to have such an impact. We also found small but significant impacts of smoking at age 18 on academic attainment at age 22.

We conducted further explorations in an effort to understand mechanisms whereby smoking might have direct and/or indirect impacts on academic attainment. We found that delinquency and smoking have partly overlapping impacts on academic attainment. These impacts are modest in size, with the delinquency impacts smaller than those for smoking. Overall, our findings are consistent with the general notion that both smoking and delinquency are components/indicators of a problem behavior syndrome, with delinquency emerging somewhat earlier than smoking. We also explored whether friends' smoking might contribute (negatively) to academic attainment. There are strong correlations between reports of own smoking and friends' smoking, confirming that smokers pick other smokers as friends (and, of course, vice versa). However, friends' smoking makes no additional contribution to predicting academic attainment, so it may be little more than a proxy for the respondents' own smoking.

We conclude that early educational successes and failures play an important role in influencing whether an adolescent becomes a smoker, whereas smoking plays at most a minor role among the determinants of academic success. It appears to us that the strong negative association between smoking and academic attainment—lasting to age 40 and probably beyond, as shown in chapter 1—occurs primarily via the following process: Those who are poorly adjusted to schooling by the time they reach adolescence are less willing to follow the rules and more willing to act in ways that are generally socially disapproved. To what extent this willingness to rebel is a direct result of their educational failures remains difficult to document, although our attempt to model one form of rebellion—cigarette smoking—suggests that educational failure contributes substantially. In any case, if the youthful pattern of rebelling does include cigarette smoking, that habit can be very difficult to break. Because smoking and educational attainment are both such stable forms of behavior, the connections forged during adolescence tend to be long lasting—extending well into adulthood. Smoking can therefore be viewed as another consequence—indeed, a serious consequence—of educational failure.

Chapter 7

How Marijuana Use Is Linked With Educational Success and Failure

We concluded in the previous chapter that educational successes and failures contribute to adolescent cigarette use, most likely because those who have made a poor adjustment to schooling are more willing to act in ways that are socially disapproved (at least by more conventional segments of society). If that is correct, then it also seems likely that early educational failures would contribute to use of another socially disapproved substance: marijuana. Marijuana has been the most widely used illicit drug in recent decades, and use begins at earlier ages than most other illicit drugs (Johnston et al., 2005b). Moreover, the most common mode of administration for marijuana matches that for cigarettes. So, given the strong links between early educational experiences and cigarette use, we expect similar linkages with marijuana use to be evident as well.

In contrast to these similarities between cigarette and marijuana use, there is one particularly important distinction: Regular cigarette use among adolescents often—indeed, usually—progresses to the point of habituation. Among high school seniors, about two thirds of current cigarette users (those reporting any use in the past 30 days) smoke daily—many at the rate of a half pack or more, whereas only about one quarter of current marijuana users report use at a daily or near daily level (Bachman et al., 2005; Johnston, O'Malley et al., 2005a, and earlier volumes in the same series). Moreover, marijuana use is a less stable behavior than cigarette use, particularly between ages 14 and 16, as we see later in the chapter.

PLAN FOR THIS CHAPTER

We follow much the same strategy in this chapter as we used in chapter 6. We examine marijuana use rates based on cross-sectional Monitoring the Future (MTF) samples as well as our longitudinal panel of adolescents. Because of the potential close link with cigarette use, we also examine the correlations between cigarette and marijuana use. We then consider whether the predictors of academic attainment shown in chapter 4, as well as the predictors of smoking shown in chapter 6, are also predictors of marijuana use; this analysis relies primarily on regression and multiple classification analysis. Finally, we examine findings from our structural equation model in order to explore possible paths of causal influence between educational factors and marijuana use.

MARIJUANA USE IN RECENT DECADES

During the peak of marijuana use at the end of the 1970s, about 60% of high school seniors had used marijuana sometime during their lifetimes, and about 37% were current users (i.e., had used at least once during the last 30 days). Rates of use gradually declined during the 1980s and early 1990s, so that by 1992 only 33% of high school seniors reported use during their lifetimes. Lifetime use reported by seniors then rose to about 50% in the late 1990s and declined slightly thereafter (Johnston et al., 2005b). Similarly, Figure 7.1 shows that annual and 30-day prevalence rates among high school seniors reached their peak in the late 1970s, then dropped fairly steadily until 1992, after which they rose for the next 5 years. The upward shift from 1992 through 1997 (or 1996) is also evident in MTF data from 8th- and 10th-grade students, included in Figure 7.1. Finally, the figure shows some modest declines in prevalence of marijuana use after 1997. This pattern of findings clearly fits a secular trend interpretation because the shifts appear in parallel fashion across age groups at just about exactly the same time points. In other analyses, we have shown that such period shifts correspond with, and can be attributed to, shifts in perceived risks and disapproval associated with marijuana use (Bachman, Johnston, & O'Malley, 1990, 1998; Bachman, Johnston, O'Malley, & Humphrey, 1988).

What is important for present purposes is the fact that overall rates of marijuana use doubled during the period in which our panel respondents went from modal ages 14 (in 1991–1993) to 18 (in 1995–1997). It may be worth noting that during that same period, college aspirations continued their historic rise (Wirt et al., 2004). That combination of findings does

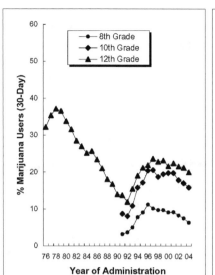
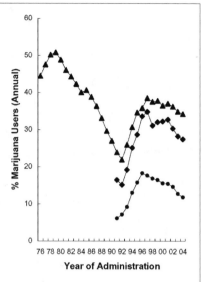

Any Marijuana Use in the Last 30 Days   Any Marijuana Use in the Last Year

Data collected from annual national in-school surveys by Monitoring the Future.

Figure 7.1. Trends in 30-day prevalence and annual prevalence of marijuana use for 8th, 10th, and 12th graders.

not provide any evidence that, for the population as a whole, marijuana use among adolescents had any overall negative impact on their academic aspirations during the 1990s.

The MTF cross-sectional findings comparing subgroups (Johnston et al., 2005b) show that marijuana use is more prevalent among males than females, especially by the time they reach 12th grade. Prevalence levels are also distinctly lower among students with plans to complete college, although here the differences are more pronounced at earlier grades. Among 8th-grade students, marijuana use in recent years has been more than twice as likely for those reporting the lowest versus the highest levels of parental education; however, that difference is smaller among 10th graders, and there is little or no relationship among 12th graders. (In a later chapter, we note somewhat similar patterns of grade differences for alcohol use.) These results from the large-scale cross-sectional surveys of high school students are consistent with our present findings based on the panel survey of adolescents.

Racial/ethnic differences in the cross-sectional data vary across grades, perhaps because of differential dropout rates: "In 8th grade, Hispanics have the highest rate of use, while Whites and African Americans are similar and have a considerably lower rate. By 10th grade, Whites have rates of use similar to Hispanics ... and African Americans have lower rates than either Whites or Hispanics. By 12th grade, Whites quite consistently have had the highest rates, Hispanics slightly lower ones, and African Americans the lowest" (Johnston et al., 2005b, p. 183). We examine racial/ethnic differences in our panel data later in the chapter.

The age progression in marijuana use for our panel respondents is shown in Figure 7.2. Annual prevalence (any use in the previous 12 months) was lower than 10% at modal age 14 (eighth grade), then rose to above 20% at age 16, and at ages 18 to 22 exceeded 30% among females and reached about 40% among males (showing the same sort of gender difference as noted previously for the larger MTF cross-sectional surveys). Monthly prevalence rates (any use during the past 30 days) were a little more than half as large, with the same emerging pattern of gender differences. Thus, by age 18, a substantial minority of our panel sample (about one in three) had used marijuana in the past year, but fewer (about one in five) had used it as recently as the past month. Recall that these panel sample members grew from ages 14 to 18 during a pronounced upward secular trend in marijuana use among adolescents (1992–1997); accordingly, it would be a mistake to conclude that these changes shown in Figure 7.2 were due entirely to aging or maturation. Rather, the data in Figure 7.1 remind us that age differences *within any given year* during that period were smaller than the total age-related changes reflected in our panel data. So for the particular individuals we are studying in our adolescent panel, the changes in marijuana use between ages 14 and 18 involve not only typical maturation, but also a widespread upward trend in marijuana use among youth and young adults in general.

THE CLOSE LINK BETWEEN CIGARETTE AND MARIJUANA USE IN ADOLESCENCE

We noted at the outset of this chapter that cigarettes and marijuana typically involve the same mode of administration—that is, both are smoked. They also have in common that their use is socially disapproved and therefore likely to appeal to youth wishing to rebel. For these reasons, we expected substantial overlaps between the two behaviors: Those who

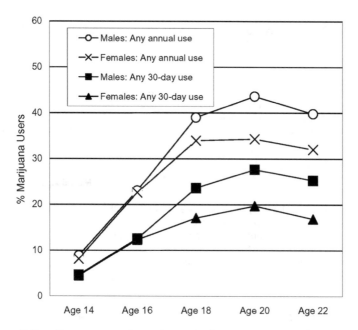

Figure 7.2. Percentage of panel respondents using marijuana in the last year or last 30 days: males and females.

use cigarettes should be more likely to use marijuana and vice versa, and the amounts of use should correlate as well. Table 7.1 confirms these expectations, showing product–moment correlations between cigarette use (30-day) and marijuana use (both 30-day and 12-month) at each of the five survey points for our panel sample. The table also shows the high correlations between 30-day and 12-month marijuana-use measures (most greater than .8). We note in passing that the 12-month marijuana-use measure yields correlations that are consistently a bit larger than those for the 30-day marijuana measure, reflecting the fact that marijuana use is relatively infrequent for many adolescents, and thus the 12-month measure involves less in the way of unreliability due to time-sampling error (even though a longer recall period is involved).[1] The correlations between cigarette and marijuana use are strongest at modal

---

[1]Despite that, we focus primarily on the 30-day measure because we can better pin down chronology and sequence. Moreover, our structural equation models include adjustments for measurement reliability, making it less of a problem. Nevertheless, we repeated a number of analyses with the 12-month measure and found results that closely parallel those for the 30-day measure.

TABLE 7.1
Pearson Correlations Between Cigarette Smoking and Marijuana Use

Males

	Modal Age				
	14	16	18	20	22
30-day cigarette use and 30-day marijuana use	.366	.389	.371	.333	.276
30-day cigarette use and annual marijuana use	.452	.470	.456	.364	.330
30-day marijuana use and annual marijuana use	.803	.807	.783	.831	.812

Females

	Modal Age				
	14	16	18	20	22
30-day cigarette use and 30-day marijuana use	.359	.387	.333	.309	.235
30-day cigarette use and annual marijuana use	.451	.443	.391	.358	.277
30-day marijuana use and annual marijuana use	.802	.813	.782	.832	.812

All correlations in this table are p<.05 (two-tailed).

ages 14, 16, and 18 (for the 12-month marijuana-use measure, product–moment correlations range from .39–.47); the correlations then decline slightly by age 20 (r = .36 for both males and females) and again by age 22 (r = .33 for males, .28 for females). This decline in strength of correlation after age 18 is consistent with our observation at the start of the chapter: Cigarette users tend to become locked into that behavior, whereas most marijuana users engage in the behavior much less frequently and are less likely to become habituated.

The correlations in Table 7.1 are drawn from the large matrix in the appendix (Table A.3.3) showing correlations among all the measures, including autocorrelations reflecting stability across time. The cross-time correlations for marijuana are substantially lower than those for cigarette use, consistent with less stability and higher measurement error for marijuana use.

MAJOR CORRELATES/PREDICTORS OF
ADOLESCENT MARIJUANA USE

Here, as in the previous chapter, we make use of multivariate linear regression analyses predicting current (last 30 days) marijuana use at each of three waves (modal ages 14, 16, and 18 shown in Table A.7.1 in the appendix), as well as multiple classification analyses (MCA) predicting prevalence of current marijuana use at modal age 18 (shown in Table 7.2). We are interested in factors that correlate with marijuana use, both bivariately and when other factors are included in the equation. Again, we follow usual nomenclature for regression analyses and refer to these correlates as "predictors" while recognizing that causal ordering (and, in some cases, even chronological sequence) may not run from "predictor" to outcome or "dependent variable." For ease of interpretation, we focus primarily on the MCA results, but also note important additional findings from the linear regression results.[2]

The sets of predictors used in this chapter are identical to those used in chapter 6 predicting current cigarette use. We are thus able to consider whether the patterns of relationships involving cigarette use are also evident for marijuana use (comparing Table A.6.2 with Table A.7.1, and Table 6.3 with Table 7.2). We expected a good deal of similarity given our observations that the two forms of substance use are correlated, and that both are socially disapproved and thus may represent forms of adolescent rebellion. Our findings, summarized in the following section, do indeed show many similarities in patterns of prediction for the two forms of substance use, along with several important differences. One broad difference is linked to the fact that marijuana use tends to emerge at somewhat later ages than cigarette use, so at age 14 most correlations are lower for marijuana use. At later ages, it is still the case that indicators of educational success and failure tend to correlate more strongly with cigarette use than marijuana use; however, when it comes to certain problem behaviors, the links are sometimes stronger with marijuana use rather than cigarette use.

Race/Ethnicity

African-American females at modal age 18 are distinctly less likely than average to report marijuana use during the past 30 days (Column 1 in Table 7.2), and after taking account of other predictors, this difference is

---

[2]Readers closely comparing results in Tables 7.2 and A.7.1 may note small differences in *R*-squared values indicating variance explained. One reason for these differences is that the MCA analyses in Table 7.2 capture nonlinear as well as linear relationships, thus potentially increasing variance explained. However, the MCA analyses predict a dichotomous *prevalence* measure of marijuana use in the past 30 days (any use vs. none), and this restriction to a dichotomy tends to lower estimates of variance explained when compared with the linear regressions in Table A.7.1 predicting the *amount* of marijuana use in the past 30 days. We thus have two differences potentially working in opposite directions. Nevertheless, the results of these two multivariate analysis approaches correspond quite closely on the whole.

TABLE 7.2a

Multiple Classification Analyses Predicting Percentage Who Report Any Marijuana Use in the Last 30 Days at Age 18: Males

Grand Mean = 23.6
Effective _N_ = 1361

Variable	Col. 1 Bivariate	Col. 2	Col. 3	Col. 4	Col. 5	Col. 6
		Percentage Reporting Any Marijuana Use in the Last 30 Days		Multivariate		
Race/ethnicity						
African-American	21.5	19.5	17.9	18.0	19.8	19.7
Hispanic	26.0	23.6	23.5	22.3	21.7	21.6
Other race	25.7	25.4	25.2	23.5	23.5	23.5
White	23.1	24.0	24.4	25.0	24.7	24.7
Urban density						
Large MSA	26.5	26.5	26.0	26.6	25.9	26.0
Other MSA	24.3	24.5	24.5	24.4	24.2	24.1
Non-MSA	19.6	19.1	19.7	19.2	20.2	20.2
Parents' education level						
1 (Low)	26.4	24.7	23.5	21.1	21.7	21.8
2	24.9	24.3	24.1	21.9	22.7	22.7
3	24.4	24.3	24.5	24.0	24.1	24.0
4	20.0	21.4	21.6	23.3	22.8	22.9
5 (High)	24.0	24.1	25.0	28.7	27.3	27.2
Lived with 2 parents Waves 1–3						
Yes	20.7	20.9	21.4	22.3	22.3	22.4
No	29.0	28.6	27.7	26.0	26.1	25.7
Parent involvement						
1 (Low)	30.9	29.0	27.4	25.1	24.1	24.0
2	29.0	28.5	28.2	27.8	27.3	27.4
3	22.7	23.1	23.3	23.4	23.6	23.6
4 (High)	17.4	18.0	18.6	19.6	20.1	20.1
Held back grade 8 or earlier						
Never	22.6		23.8	24.3	24.1	24.2
Once	26.9		23.8	22.0	23.0	22.5
More than once	26.4		19.4	18.1	18.1	16.9
Suspended/expelled grade 8 or earlier						
Never	20.2		20.6	21.3	22.8	23.1
Once	25.9		25.4	23.0	21.3	21.1
More than once	37.2		35.8	34.4	29.0	28.2
Mean secondary school GPA						
D or below	49.9		42.3	39.2	37.6	
C- or C	37.6		32.8	31.2	30.7	
C+ or B-	25.3		24.1	24.1	24.2	
B or B+	20.0		21.6	21.6	21.8	
A-	15.1		18.4	19.4	19.4	
A	7.6		13.0	16.7	16.8	

TABLE 7.2a
Multiple Classification Analyses Predicting Percentage Who Report Any Marijuana Use in the Last 30 Days at Age 18: Males (*continued*)

Grand Mean = 23.6
Effective *N* = 1361

	Percentage Reporting Any Marijuana Use in the Last 30 Days					
	Col. 1	Col. 2	Col. 3	Col. 4	Col. 5	Col. 6
Variable	Bivariate			Multivariate		
Mean secondary school college plans						
Definitely won't	32.1			23.8	23.2	22.4
Probably won't	31.8			25.3	25.3	24.7
Probably will	27.2			26.1	25.4	25.3
Definitely will	16.4			20.6	21.4	21.7
Serious scholastic setback W1 to W2						
None	20.9			21.4	22.3	22.4
One	32.3			30.4	27.7	27.3
Two	51.0			45.5	39.1	37.1
Serious scholastic setback W2 to W3						
None	21.2			22.1	22.6	22.7
One	30.5			27.7	26.1	26.0
Two	38.7			34.5	31.5	30.8
Delinquency (W2–3 combined)						
No incidents	9.0				12.1	12.1
1 or 2 incidents	15.9				17.0	17.0
3 or 4 incidents	24.9				24.6	24.6
5 or 6 incidents	34.4				32.5	32.5
7 or 8 incidents	47.6				44.0	44.0
9 to 14 incidents	56.4				49.8	49.7
High school dropout by Wave 3						
Yes	38.8					28.8
No	20.8					22.6
Multiple *R*		.160	.201	.290	.383	.385
R Squared		.026	.041	.084	.146	.148

Factor Summary*

	eta	beta	beta	beta	beta	beta
Race/ethnicity	.033	.039	.053	.055	.040	.041
Urban density	**.062**	.067	.058	**.067**	.051	.052
Parent education level	**.053**	.030	.029	.053	.040	.038
Lived with 2 parents Waves 1–3	**.094**	**.086**	**.071**	.042	.043	.037
Parent involvement	**.113**	**.098**	**.085**	.069	.060	.061
Held back grade 8 or earlier	.043		.020	.035	.029	.037
Suspended/expelled grade 8 or earlier	**.145**		**.130**	.110	.056	.049
Mean secondary school GPA	**.192**			.125	.101	.095
Mean secondary school college plans	**.150**			.061	.046	.040
Serious scholastic setback W1 to W2	**.138**			.109	.071	.063
Serious scholastic setback W2 to W3	**.106**			.068	.045	.042
Delinquency (W2–3 combined)	**.326**				**.266**	**.265**
High school dropout by Wave 3	**.155**					.053

*All eta and beta statistics p<.05 are shown in **bold**.

See Table 3.3 for frequency distributions of predictor variables.

Note: W1 = Wave 1 data collection (grade 8, modal age 14), W2 = Wave 2 data collection (modal age 16), W3 = Wave 3 data collection (modal age 18)

TABLE 7.2b

Multiple Classification Analyses Predicting Percentage Who Report Any
Marijuana Use in the Last 30 Days at Age 18: Females

Grand Mean = 17.1
Effective *N* = 1739

	Percentage Reporting Any Marijuana Use in the Last 30 Days					
	Col. 1	Col. 2	Col. 3	Col. 4	Col. 5	Col. 6
Variable	Bivariate	Multivariate				
Race/ethnicity						
African-American	10.0	8.1	6.6	6.3	7.4	7.6
Hispanic	16.0	15.9	16.0	15.6	16.3	16.3
Other race	19.0	19.2	18.9	18.1	17.9	17.9
White	18.3	18.8	19.1	19.5	19.2	19.1
Urban density						
Large MSA	19.7	19.7	19.5	19.3	18.0	18.1
Other MSA	17.6	17.5	17.4	17.1	17.3	17.3
Non-MSA	13.2	13.4	13.9	14.6	15.6	15.6
Parents' education level						
1 (Low)	14.8	14.4	14.0	12.0	12.6	12.4
2	17.0	17.4	17.1	16.1	16.2	16.2
3	18.4	18.3	18.4	18.4	18.0	18.0
4	14.7	14.8	15.1	16.3	16.9	17.0
5 (High)	22.3	22.4	22.6	25.2	24.0	24.0
Lived with 2 parents Waves 1–3						
Yes	14.6	13.9	14.2	14.9	15.1	15.3
No	20.7	21.7	21.3	20.2	19.9	19.7
Parent involvement						
1 (Low)	20.3	19.2	18.6	18.4	18.0	18.0
2	20.7	20.4	20.2	20.1	19.5	19.5
3	16.6	16.8	16.9	17.1	17.2	17.3
4 (High)	12.7	13.2	13.2	13.2	13.7	13.7
Held back grade 8 or earlier						
Never	17.4		17.7	18.0	17.8	17.9
Once	15.5		14.2	12.3	13.4	13.3
More than once	13.0		11.3	9.9	10.1	9.7
Suspended/expelled grade 8 or earlier						
Never	15.9		15.6	16.0	16.5	16.6
Once	21.1		22.2	19.9	17.9	17.7
More than once	27.6		29.2	27.2	23.4	22.9
Mean secondary school GPA						
D or below	45.2			38.1	35.4	34.4
C- or C	21.7			19.9	17.7	17.4
C+ or B-	19.8			19.6	18.7	18.7
B or B+	18.3			18.8	19.1	19.2
A-	10.4			10.3	11.9	12.0
A	9.3			10.8	12.2	12.3

TABLE 7.2b
Multiple Classification Analyses Predicting Percentage Who Report Any
Marijuana Use in the Last 30 Days at Age 18: Females (*continued*)

Grand Mean = 17.1

Effective N = 1739

Variable	Col. 1 Bivariate	Col. 2	Col. 3	Col. 4	Col. 5	Col. 6
			Multivariate			
Mean secondary school college plans						
Definitely won't	15.9			13.0	14.1	13.4
Probably won't	23.9			21.4	20.6	20.1
Probably will	18.4			17.7	17.3	17.3
Definitely will	14.8			15.9	16.3	16.4
Serious scholastic setback W1 to W2						
None	16.4			16.9	17.4	17.4
One	21.0			18.6	15.7	15.3
Two	18.2			14.7	12.5	11.8
Serious scholastic setback W2 to W3						
None	15.7			16.0	16.2	16.3
One	24.6			22.9	21.6	21.4
Two	23.1			21.4	21.5	21.1
Delinquency (W2–3 combined)						
No incidents	7.3				8.7	8.7
1 or 2 incidents	16.8				17.1	17.1
3 or 4 incidents	26.1				24.5	24.5
5 or 6 incidents	30.7				27.9	27.9
7 or 8 incidents	43.8				41.5	41.5
9 to 14 incidents	51.8				46.9	46.9
High school dropout by Wave 3						
Yes	25.2					19.6
No	15.7					16.6
Multiple R		.171	.195	.244	.321	.322
R Squared		.029	.038	.059	.103	.104

Factor Summary*

	eta	beta	beta	beta	beta	beta
Race/ethnicity	**.078**	**.098**	**.113**	**.118**	**.105**	**.103**
Urban density	**.064**	**.062**	.055	.046	.024	.025
Parent education level	**.065**	**.068**	**.070**	**.069**	**.085**	**.086**
Lived with 2 parents Waves 1–3	**.079**	**.101**	**.092**	**.098**	**.063**	**.058**
Parent involvement	**.078**	**.069**	.065	.064	.054	.054
Held back grade 8 or earlier	.022		.038	.059	.048	.050
Suspended/expelled grade 8 or earlier	**.083**	**.098**	**.076**	.045	.042	
Mean secondary school GPA	**.127**		**.113**	**.089**	**.087**	
Mean secondary school college plans	**.076**		.047	.036	.032	
Serious scholastic setback W1 to W2	.042		.017	.022	.026	
Serious scholastic setback W2 to W3	**.086**		**.066**	**.052**	.049	
Delinquency (W2–3 combined)	**.260**			**.224**	**.224**	
High school dropout by Wave 3	**.089**				.028	

*All eta and beta statistics p<.05 are shown in **bold**.

See Table 3.3 for frequency distributions of predictor variables.

Note: W1 = Wave 1 data collection (grade 8, modal age 14), W2 = Wave 2 data collection
(modal age 16), W3 = Wave 3 data collection (modal age 18)

somewhat increased (unmasked). African-American males show mostly small differences from White males. Other racial/ethnic groups differ rather little from each other in marijuana use in these analyses. Overall, racial/ethnic differences in marijuana use are not nearly as large as those for cigarette use. Again, we note that a further exploration of racial/ethnic differences is reserved for a separate publication.

Urban Density

Adolescents in our panel who (at age 14) lived in nonmetropolitan areas were somewhat less likely than average to use marijuana. Some small differences remained for both males and females after controls for background and educational factors (see Tables A.7.1 and 7.2); however, by age 22, there were no clear differences in marijuana use linked to urban density of age-14 residence (based on additional regression analyses not shown).

Parental Education

Table A.7.1 shows modest negative correlations between parental education and marijuana use at age 14, but the correlations at age 16 are low and nonsignificant, and by age 18 the linear relationships are essentially zero. In the presence of the other predictors, a small positive relationship emerges by age 18 (significant only in the MCA for females), and Table 7.2 shows that it involves mostly the extremes: Young women with the most educated parents were somewhat more likely than average to use marijuana, and those with the least educated parents were a bit less likely to do so. But it should be kept in mind that this pattern appears only when the other factors noted in the following sections are held constant—that is, when other things associated with parental education are controlled.

Presence of Both Parents in the Home

Living in a home with two parents throughout adolescence substantially decreases the likelihood of marijuana use. Those without two parents consistently present were almost half again as likely to be current marijuana users—29% versus 21% among males at age 18, and 21% versus 15% among females at age 18 (see Table 7.2, Column 1). This relationship is virtually unchanged when other parental factors are controlled (see

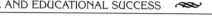

Column 2). However, it is reduced to some extent when additional predictors are included (see remaining columns), suggesting that some of the effects of parental presence are indirect.

Parental Involvement in Students' Lives

Another important parental factor is involvement in their children's lives (monitoring and participating in doing homework, requiring chores, and limiting TV viewing). As can be seen in Table 7.2 (Column 1), marijuana use at age 18 was almost twice as likely among those whose parents had been least involved (4 years earlier) compared with those whose parents had been most involved. The relationship is reduced but not eliminated by controls for other background factors (see Column 2), but when still other factors are included (remaining columns) the coefficients are further reduced and fall below the significance threshold. Here again the pattern of findings suggests some of the effects of parental involvement are indirect via educational experiences.

Grade Retention, and Suspension or Expulsion, by End of Eighth Grade

We saw in chapter 6 that having been held back a grade prior to the end of eighth grade showed little effect on cigarette use once other factors were controlled. The same appears to be true for marijuana use. Although we found a zero-order relationship showing slightly higher marijuana use at age 14 among those (especially males) who had been held back, there was no such relationship between early grade retention and marijuana use at age 18; moreover, in the presence of controls for other factors, there was no appreciable multivariate relationship between early grade retention and marijuana use at any age (based on Table A.7.1). Thus, our conclusion regarding cigarettes applies to marijuana as well: Any effects of these early grade failures apparently operate indirectly via other factors.

Also parallel to our findings for cigarette use, Table A.7.1 shows that suspension or expulsion prior to the end of eighth grade is an important predictor of marijuana use—not only at the end of eighth grade, but also throughout adolescence. As shown in Table 7.2 and illustrated in Figure 7.3, those who had been suspended or expelled two or more times prior to the end of eighth grade were nearly twice as likely to be current marijuana users, compared with those not suspended or expelled at all.

Controls for background factors show little effect (based on regression analyses not shown); however, most of the relationships between suspension or expulsion and marijuana use are quite low (and nonsignificant) when delinquency is included in the equation (see Table A.7.1). This is consistent with our view that early misbehaviors in school are part of a larger syndrome of deviant or problem behaviors, activities that can have lasting effects in the form of substance use—marijuana as well as cigarettes.

Delinquent Behavior

Delinquent behavior reported at age 14 is clearly predictive of marijuana use, and this early delinquency predicts marijuana use not only at age 14, but also at subsequent ages; indeed, early delinquency predicts later marijuana use more strongly than it predicts later cigarette use. Moreover, delinquent behavior during later adolescence (reported at modal ages 16 and 18, combined) is strongly correlated with marijuana use at age 18, as illustrated in Figure 7.4 and detailed in Table 7.2. Those who reported 9 or more (out of a possible 14) delinquent behaviors during the two 12-month periods prior to the surveys, compared with those who reported none, were six to eight times as likely to be current marijuana users at age 18 (56% vs. 9% for males; 52% vs. 7% for females). With all other predictors included in the equation, the ratio remains nearly as large (50% vs. 12% for males; 47% vs. 9% for females). It thus seems clear that involvement in problem behaviors can substantially increase the likelihood of marijuana use.

The bivariate correlations included in Table A.7.1 provide some additional perspectives on the relationship between delinquency and marijuana use, and we highlight these particular correlations in Table 7.3. Comparing correlations with marijuana use at three time points (modal ages 14, 16, and 18), we note first that the correlations are generally strongest within survey waves. For example, delinquency for the year prior to age 18 is correlated fairly strongly with marijuana use for the 30 days prior to the age-18 survey ($r = .28$ for males, .23 for females) and less strongly with earlier marijuana use (e.g., correlations between delinquency reported at age 18 and marijuana use reported at age 14 are only .04 for males and .07 for females). However, when we look at how early delinquency relates to both early and later marijuana use, the differences across waves are much smaller. Specifically, delinquency reported at

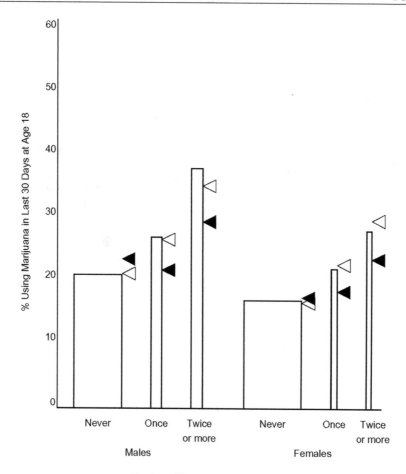

The main bars are unadjusted estimates. The bar width is proportionate to the
weighted number of cases in the category.

◁ Percentage adjusted for race/ethnicity, population density, parents' education,
number of parents, parental involvement, and held back (Column 3 in Table 7.2a & b)
◀ Percentage adjusted for race/ethnicity, population density, parents' education, number of
parents, parental involvement, GPA, college plans, held back, suspension/expulsion,
serious scholastic setback between grade 8 and 10 and 10 and 12, delinquency, and
dropout by grade 12 (Column 6 in Table 7.2a & b)

Figure 7.3. Any marijuana use in the last 30 days reported at age 18 by
suspension or expulsion in Grade 8 or earlier: males and females.

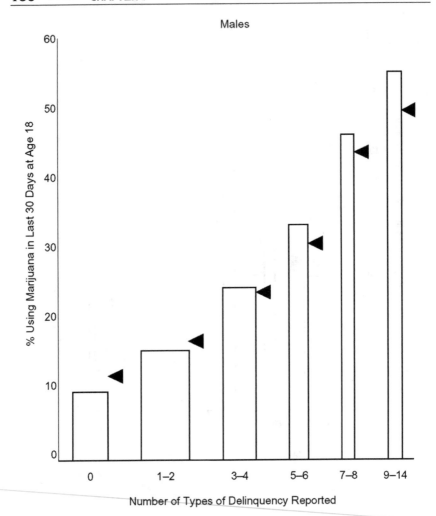

The main bars are unadjusted estimates. The bar width is proportionate to the weighted number of cases in the category.

◀ Percentage adjusted for race/ethnicity, population density, parents' education, number of parents, parental involvement, GPA, college plans, held back, suspension/expulsion, serious scholastic setback between grade 8 and 10 and 10 and 12, and dropout by grade 12 (Column 6 in Table 7.2a)

Figure 7.4a. Marijuana use in the last 30 days at age 18 by delinquency index for ages 16 and 18 combined: males.

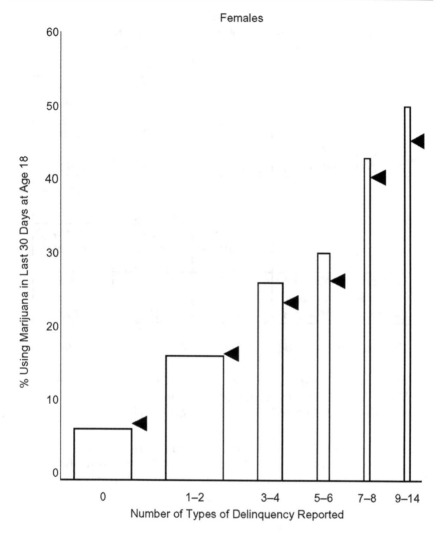

The main bars are unadjusted estimates. The bar width is proportionate to the weighted number of cases in the category.

◀ Percentage adjusted for race/ethnicity, population density, parents' education, number of parents, parental involvement, GPA, college plans, held back, suspension/expulsion, serious scholastic setback between grade 8 and 10 and 10 and 12, and dropout by grade 12 (Column 6 in Table 7.2b)

Figure 7.4b. Marijuana use in the last 30 days at age 18 by delinquency index for ages 16 and 18 combined: females.

TABLE 7.3

Bivariate Correlations Between Delinquency and 30-Day
Marijuana Use at Wave 1, Wave 2, and Wave 3

	Males		
	30-Day Marijuana Wave 1	30-Day Marijuana Wave 2	30-Day Marijuana Wave 3
Delinquency Wave 1	**.219**	**.270**	**.249**
Delinquency Wave 2	**.118**	**.339**	**.281**
Delinquency Wave 3	.041	**.245**	**.282**

	Females		
	30-Day Marijuana Wave 1	30-Day Marijuana Wave 2	30-Day Marijuana Wave 3
Delinquency Wave 1	**.235**	**.239**	**.163**
Delinquency Wave 2	**.117**	**.338**	**.200**
Delinquency Wave 3	.070	**.184**	**.232**

Correlations that are $p<.05$ (two-tailed) are shown in **bold**.

Note: W1 = Wave 1 data collection (grade 8, modal age 14),
W2 = Wave 2 data collection (modal age 16),
W3 = Wave 3 data collection (modal age 18)

age 14 correlates fairly strongly with marijuana use reported at all three ages (correlations of .22, .27, .25 for males; .24, .24, .16 for females). It thus appears that early involvement in delinquent behaviors has rather long-lasting effects on marijuana use.

Grade Point Average

Just as grade point average (GPA) is a strong predictor of cigarette use, so also is it a strong predictor of marijuana use. As shown in Table 7.2 and illustrated in Figure 7.5, very few students (only about 2% of males and fewer than 1% of females) had D or below averages throughout secondary school, but among those who did, half of the males and nearly half of the females were current marijuana users at age 18; in contrast, fewer than 1 in 10 of the straight-A students were current users.

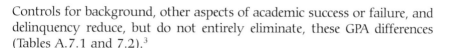

Controls for background, other aspects of academic success or failure, and delinquency reduce, but do not entirely eliminate, these GPA differences (Tables A.7.1 and 7.2).[3]

College Plans

As we found for cigarette use in chapter 6, marijuana use is negatively correlated with college plans; however, the correlations involving marijuana are weaker (shown in Table A.7.1).

Serious Scholastic Setbacks During High School (After Eighth Grade)

Just as we found for daily smoking in chapter 6, current marijuana use at modal age 18 is roughly half again as likely among those who were held back a grade, or suspended or expelled, during the years following eighth grade. As can be seen in Table 7.2 (see also Table A.7.1), controls for other factors reduce the relationships somewhat. The zero–order correlations in Table A.7.1 show a pattern that seems relevant to our notions about causal ordering; new scholastic setbacks occurring between modal ages 14 and 16 (Wave 1 to Wave 2) are more strongly linked with marijuana use at age 16 than use at age 14, and similarly setbacks between ages 16 and 18 (Wave 2 to Wave 3) are more strongly linked with marijuana use at age 18 than use at age 16 (for males only; for females there is no difference). In other words, there tends to be a slightly stronger link with marijuana use occurring (primarily) *after* the scholastic setback rather than before, at least for males. That seems consistent with the argument that educational failures and school misbehavior contribute to marijuana use more than the reverse, which is the causal ordering imposed in our structural equation model.

---

[3]Figure 7.5 and Table 7.2 show the negative relationship between GPA and current marijuana prevalence as roughly linear among males, but less linear among females. We discount this departure from linearity in our female panel sample as most likely due to random sampling fluctuations. An examination of the large-scale cross-sectional samples from the MTF surveys of high school seniors in 1995 to 1997 (the years when our panel sample was at modal age 18) shows relationships for both males and females that are quite linear. (The large-scale samples also show higher proportions of male than female seniors as current marijuana users, entirely consistent with our panel data.)

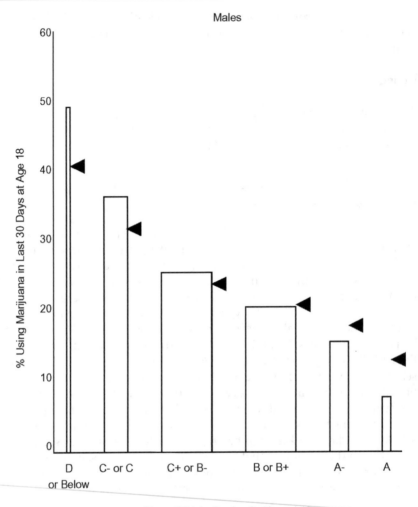

Males

% Using Marijuana in Last 30 Days at Age 18

Mean GPA in Grades 8, 10, and 12

The main bars are unadjusted estimates. The bar width is proportionate to the weighted number of cases in the category.

◀ Percentage adjusted for race/ethnicity, population density, parents' education, number of parents, parental involvement, college plans, held back, suspension/ expulsion, college plans, and serious scholastic setbacks Wave 1 to Wave 2 and Wave 2 to Wave 3 (Column 4 in Table 7.2a)

Figure 7.5a.   Marijuana use in the last 30 days at age 18 by mean secondary school GPA (Grades 8, 10, and 12 combined): males.

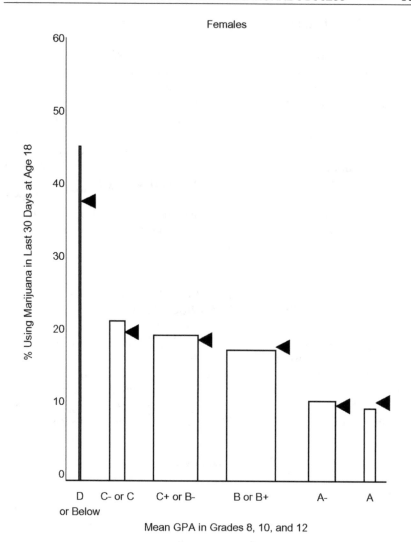

Females

% Using Marijuana in Last 30 Days at Age 18

D or Below   C- or C   C+ or B-   B or B+   A-   A

Mean GPA in Grades 8, 10, and 12

The main bars are unadjusted estimates. The bar width is
proportionate to the weighted number of cases in the category.

◀ Percentage adjusted for race/ethnicity, population density, parents'
education, number of parents, parental involvement, college plans,
held back, suspension/expulsion, college plans, and serious scholastic
setbacks Wave 1 to Wave 2 and Wave 2 to Wave 3 (Column 4 in Table
7.2b)

Figure 7.5b. Marijuana use in the last 30 days at age 18 by mean
secondary school GPA (Grades 8, 10, and 12 combined): females.

Dropping Out of High School by Age 18

Those who dropped out of school by age 18 were more likely to be current marijuana users at age 18 (see Table 7.2, Column 1). The connection is not as large as that between cigarette use and dropping out, and much of it overlaps with other factors (as shown in the right-hand column of Table 7.2; see also Table A.7.1). Dropping out prior to age 18 would have generally occurred prior to the 30-day marijuana use reported at age 18; however, marijuana use at earlier ages is predictive of dropping out, as shown by the correlations in Table A.7.1 (Column 1 for age 14 and Column 4 for age 16). Also, dropping out is more strongly correlated with marijuana use at age 16 than with marijuana use at age 18 (see Table A.7.1, Column 4 vs. Column 7). It thus appears that marijuana use and dropping out are complexly connected. It also seems likely that cigarette use is implicated in those connections—a point to which we return later.

ADDITIONAL CORRELATES/PREDICTORS OF ADOLESCENT MARIJUANA USE

It is of interest to note the similarities and differences between cigarette use and marijuana use as they relate to a number of additional correlates/predictors. In this section, we compare correlation and regression coefficients in Tables A.6.2 and A.7.1, focusing especially on the data for ages 16 and 18, the ages at which marijuana use has emerged to a considerable extent, but is still strongly correlated with cigarette use.

Delinquency and Other Problem Behaviors

As we found for cigarette use, marijuana use among adolescents is more likely than average among those who engage in cutting classes, skipping days of school, or other behaviors that are cause for being sent to the office. At ages 16 and 18, skipping classes is correlated more strongly with marijuana use than with cigarette use, and the same is true of our measure of general delinquency.

Evenings Out for Fun and Recreation

By the time adolescents reach modal age 16, marijuana use is more likely among those who spend frequent evenings out for fun and recreation. The regression coefficients show that here, as with cigarette use, there is a good deal of overlap with other predictors; however, evenings out retain some contribution, even with all other factors controlled. Once again causation is likely to run in both directions: Being out for fun and recreation provides opportunities and temptations for marijuana use, but it also seems likely that those intending to use marijuana choose to be away from home in order to do so.

Actual and Preferred Work Hours

We saw in chapter 6 that adolescent cigarette smokers were more likely than average to prefer long hours of part-time work during the school year, and (particularly by ages 16 and 18) they were also more likely to actually be working those longer hours. Preferred and actual work hours (during the school year) are also correlated positively with marijuana use; however, the linkages are distinctly weaker than those for cigarette use (most are nonsignificant), and the multivariate regression coefficients are near zero. It thus appears that part-time work wishes and behaviors make relatively little contribution to marijuana use, or vice versa.

Religious Attendance and Importance

Much the same as we found for cigarette use, marijuana use correlates negatively with frequency of attendance at religious services and with ratings of importance of religion. Here again the multivariate regression coefficients are mostly small (and not always negative), indicating that any impacts of religious involvement overlap with other predictors. A close look at Table A.7.1 reveals that in general the measures of religiosity correlate most strongly with marijuana use at modal age 18 and least strongly with use at modal age 14. This is consistent with the fact that marijuana use does not emerge among many adolescents until age 16 or later. The other finding of interest in Table A.7.1 is that, even at age 14, religious attendance and importance are at least somewhat predictive of later marijuana use, especially among females. This is consistent with the high stability of religiosity; also, it suggests that religious involvement has its protective effects relatively early and often indirectly via other factors.

Self-Esteem

Our measure of self-esteem consistently shows small but significant negative correlations with marijuana use (in 16 out of 18 correlations). The multivariate regression coefficients, however, are all near zero. We thus have little evidence that marijuana use has much impact on self-esteem or that self-esteem is a strong protective factor against use of this substance (except, possibly, some indirect effects via educational successes or failures).

STRUCTURAL EQUATION MODEL: ACADEMIC ATTAINMENT AND MARIJUANA USE

The structural equation model of academic attainment, developed in chapter 4 (see Fig. 4.7), was expanded in chapter 5 to include delinquency (Fig. 5.3) and then substance use (Fig. 5.4). Following our approach for cigarette use, we model current (30-day) marijuana use at modal age 14 (late in eighth grade) as being caused in part by GPA and also by college plans, both measured at age 14 but reflecting fairly stable ongoing tendencies.[4] The same causal ordering is imposed at ages 16 and 18. We also model current marijuana use as a potential direct cause of scholastic setbacks, dropping out (by age 18), and academic attainment (by age 22). Finally, and particularly important, we also model marijuana use as being caused in part by cigarette use (at the same survey wave).

Much of our general rationale for selecting this causal sequence was spelled out earlier with respect to cigarette use, and that rationale applies equally well to marijuana use. However, our treatment of marijuana use took the additional step of treating smoking as causally prior for the following reasons. First, cigarette use tends to emerge earlier; adolescents who have tried marijuana have almost always at least tried cigarettes first, and thus many learned how to inhale smoke. Second, cigarette use tends to show stronger correlations with educational factors than does marijuana use, as just documented, and that seems consistent with the notion that educational successes and failures may contribute to marijuana use *via* their

---

[4]We chose to focus on marijuana use during the past 30 days, rather than use during the past 12 months, even though the 12-month measure involved more respondents as users, showed greater variance, and thus tended to yield (slightly) higher correlations. We prefer the current use (30-day) measure because it is more consistent with the chronology implied by our causal modeling choices, and also because it is consistent with the 30-day smoking measure reported in chapter 6. Nevertheless, as a safeguard, we conducted parallel structural equation model analyses using the 12-month marijuana-use measure; we found that the 12-month measure produced slightly larger estimates (as expected, given the larger variance in that measure), but we also found the results for the two measures to be similar (also as expected because at most survey points the 30-day and 12-month marijuana-use measures correlate above .80).

impacts on cigarette use (whereas the reverse explanation—that educational impacts on cigarette use occur via marijuana use—seems less plausible). Third, when we tried models involving cross-lagged causation across 2-year intervals, the lags from cigarette use to later marijuana use tended to be stronger than those from marijuana use to later cigarette use (but we also found that the 2-year lags showed distinctly weaker coefficients than those linking cigarette use and marijuana use at the same survey wave). So for these reasons, both conceptual and empirical, we treat cigarette use as among the causes of marijuana use rather than the reverse.[5]

Structural Model Findings

The structural model findings for marijuana, highlighted in Figure 7.6 and Table 7.4, are largely consistent with our expectations based on the regression and MCA findings reported earlier in this chapter.[6] With respect to the exogenous factors, having been held back a grade prior to the end of eighth grade makes small but significant indirect contributions to marijuana use at ages 16 and 18. Much the same can be said for having been suspended or expelled prior to the end of eighth grade, except that here the effects are distinctly larger and include marijuana use at age 14. Parental involvement at age 14 continues to appear as a protective factor against marijuana use; here again the effects are mostly indirect, largely via delinquency and cigarette use. Having both parents present in the home throughout adolescence shows mostly small and inconsistent negative direct effects on early marijuana use; however, total effects reach significance for male use at age 16 and for both male and female use at age 18. Parental education overlaps with other predictors to such an extent that it has little in the way of direct or indirect effects. Most racial/ethnic differences are neither large nor consistent across ages and

---

[5]We recognize, however, that not everyone may agree with our decision to assign causal priority to cigarette use. With that in mind, we note that we tried rerunning the model, replacing the causal connections between cigarette use and marijuana use with the more neutral approach of correlated disturbances; the model fit was unchanged and the remaining coefficients were not appreciably changed. Most important, all paths from marijuana use to educational factors were virtually identical to those reported here. So we conclude that our modeling of the causal direction between cigarette use and marijuana use does not distort or bias results concerning educational impacts.

[6]The results presented in this chapter are a subset of a much larger set of results. Summary listings of model fit statistics, variance explained (R Square) in endogenous factors, bivariate factor correlations, direct and total effects of each predictor on academic attainment, and a tabular summary of all direct and total effects in the model are available in Tables A.3.4 through A.3.10 in the appendix.

TABLE 7.4
Direct and Total Effects of Predictors on Marijuana Use at Wave 1, Wave 2, and Wave 3*

| Predictors | 30-Day Marijuana Wave 1 | | | | 30-Day Marijuana Wave 2 | | | | 30-Day Marijuana Wave 3 | | | |
| | Males | | Females | | Males | | Females | | Males | | Females | |
	Direct	Total	Direct	Total	Direct	Total	Direct	Total	Direct	Total	Direct	Total
African-American	.045	-.018	.044	-.064	.001	-.082	-.051	**-.166**	-.010	-.080	.016	**-.141**
Hispanic	.032	.003	**.070**	.033	.002	-.026	.000	-.056	.011	-.022	.020	-.065
Other race	.018	.015	.029	.025	.010	.006	-.042	-.054	-.004	.011	.032	-.018
Large MSA	-.034	-.041	-.047	-.050	.016	.018	.029	.045	.004	.006	-.019	.023
Non-MSA	-.026	-.037	-.041	-.060	-.034	-.052	-.023	-.056	-.024	-.060	-.016	-.051
Parents' education level	-.013	-.022	.025	-.025	.020	.010	.024	.024	.056	.039	.053	.021
Lived with 2 parents Waves 1–3	.025	.018	.014	-.039	-.033	-.071	.037	-.045	-.038	**-.086**	-.019	**-.088**
Parent involvement index	-.073	**-.177**	-.027	**-.148**	-.034	**-.152**	-.053	**-.159**	-.033	**-.142**	-.041	**-.146**
Held back grade 8 or earlier	.008	.067	-.012	.018		.056		.034		.051		.032
Suspended/expelled grade 8 or earlier	.018	**.164**	.038	**.199**		.123		.138		.105		.111
GPA Wave 1	-.031	-.096	-.002	-.112		**-.164**		**-.199**		**-.185**		**-.183**
GPA Wave 2					.006	**-.103**	-.034	**-.136**		**-.174**		**-.143**
GPA Wave 3									-.090	**-.127**	-.009	-.059
College plans Wave 1	.022	-.019	-.026	-.066		-.072		-.063		-.048		-.040
College plans Wave 2					-.057	**-.112**	-.011	-.056		-.069		-.025
College plans Wave 3									.016	.003	.049	.041
Serious scholastic setback W1 to W2					.021	**.101**	-.015	.087		.081		.080
Serious scholastic setback W2 to W3									.021	.058	-.006	.021
Delinquency Wave 1	**.115**	**.218**	**.094**	**.254**		**.231**		**.242**		**.175**		**.187**
Delinquency Wave 2					**.315**	**.394**	**.301**	**.368**		**.317**		**.281**
Delinquency Wave 3									**.169**	**.197**	**.125**	**.164**
30-day cigarette smoking Wave 1	**.428**	**.428**	**.472**	**.472**		**.199**		**.241**		**.136**		**.200**
30-day cigarette smoking Wave 2					**.353**	**.353**	**.366**	**.366**		**.271**		**.357**
30-day cigarette smoking Wave 3									**.214**	**.214**	**.330**	**.330**
30-day marijuana Wave 1					**.123**	**.120**	**.142**	**.150**		.052		.071
30-day marijuana Wave 2									**.441**	**.443**	**.447**	**.448**
30-day marijuana Wave 3												

Direct and Total Effects of 30-Day Marijuana Use at Wave 1, Wave 2, and Wave 3 on Education Factors*

| Predictors | | GPA Wave 2 Total | College Plans Wave 2 Total | Serious Scholastic Setback W1 to W2 | | GPA Wave 3 Total | College Plans Wave 3 Total | Serious Scholastic Setback W2 to W3 | | High School Dropout Wave 3 | | Academic Attainment Wave 5 | |
				Direct	Total			Direct	Total	Direct	Total	Direct	Total
30-day marijuana Wave 1	Males	.003	.003	-.031	-.031	.003	.002		-.005		.016		-.001
	Females	-.005	-.010	.094	.094	-.004	-.006		.002		.016		-.011
30-day marijuana Wave 2	Males					-.004	-.003	.037	.037	.023	.023		-.030
	Females					-.003	-.004	.062	.062	.011	.011		-.023
30-day marijuana Wave 3	Males											-.056	-.056
	Females											-.032	-.032

*Coefficients that are p<.05 (two-tailed) are shown in **bold**.

Note: W1 = Wave 1 data collection (grade 8, modal age 14), W2 = Wave 2 data collection (modal age 16), W3 = Wave 3 data collection (modal age 18)

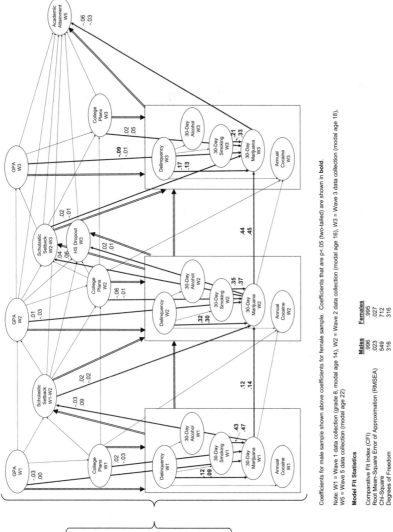

Coefficients for male sample shown above coefficients for female sample. Coefficients that are p<.05 (two-tailed) are shown in **bold**.

Note: W1 = Wave 1 data collection (grade 8, modal age 14), W2 = Wave 2 data collection (modal age 16), W3 = Wave 3 data collection (modal age 18), W5 = Wave 5 data collection (modal age 22)

Model Fit Statistics

	Males	Females
Comparative Fit Index (CFI)	.996	.995
Root Mean-Square Error of Approximation (RMSEA)	.023	.027
Chi-Square	549	712
Degrees of Freedom	316	316

Figure 7.6. Structural equation model of academic attainment and substance use, focusing on marijuana use.

genders; still, African Americans show significantly lower marijuana use than Whites, with the differences larger for females than for males. Effects linked to urban density are all quite small and nonsignificant.

Early delinquency (reported for the year prior to the end of eighth grade—i.e., the period from modal ages 13–14) shows strong links with both cigarette use and marijuana use. The direct effects of delinquency on cigarette use are strongest at age 14 and drop off sharply thereafter. For marijuana use, however, the effects of delinquency are much stronger at modal age 16, consistent with the fact that on average marijuana use emerges later than cigarette use. In addition to the direct effects of early delinquency on early marijuana use, early delinquency has substantial indirect effects on marijuana use at all ages, primarily via cigarette use. This is all quite consistent with the notion that some delinquent behaviors emerge quite early in adolescence, often followed by cigarette use and then marijuana use. We have modeled the causal directions in that order, although we recognize that a variety of interpretations are possible.

Turning now to relationships among substance-use measures, the first thing to note is that current (i.e., 30-day) marijuana use shows little stability between ages 14 and 16, but stability increases dramatically for the interval between ages 16 and 18. The stability coefficients for the later interval are nearly as large as those for cigarette use, whereas for the earlier interval the marijuana use coefficients are only about one third the size of those for cigarette use.[7] This emergent stability is consistent with the fact that prevalence of monthly marijuana use tends to emerge somewhat later than prevalence of monthly cigarette use; specifically, between modal ages 14 and 16, the proportion of adolescents who use marijuana monthly nearly triples for males and more than doubles for females (see Fig. 7.2), whereas monthly cigarette users increase by a much smaller proportion (see Fig. 6.2).

The next thing to note is how cigarette use affects marijuana use. The impacts are quite strong at the first wave, indicating that 14-year-olds who smoke cigarettes are much more likely than others to use marijuana

---

[7]It should be kept in mind that these stability coefficients include adjustments to correct for measurement unreliability—adjustments that are much larger for marijuana use than for cigarette use. The unadjusted product–moment correlations across time intervals (i.e., autocorrelations) are distinctly higher for cigarette use than for marijuana use at all time intervals because the cigarette-use measures contain much less error. Cigarette use is frequent enough so that most adolescents will give much the same answer about their use during the last 30 days whether they are asked the question in one month or another. In contrast, marijuana use is far less frequent, on average, and that means that simple "time-sampling" measurement error tends to lower the autocorrelations for the 30-day marijuana-use measure (compared with autocorrelations for the 12-month marijuana-use measure). The adjustments in the structural equation models are designed to correct measurement errors, and thus yield a truer representation of cross-time stability of the *general tendency* to use each substance.

also. By ages 16 and 18, the direct links are weaker but still statistically significant. The strong initial *correlation* between cigarette use and marijuana use is echoed in later years to a considerable extent simply because of high stability, especially for cigarette use.

The connections between marijuana use and factors related to educational success show patterns mostly consistent with those for cigarette use. Although the direct effects of educational factors on marijuana use are generally weaker than those on cigarette use, there are also indirect effects on marijuana use via cigarette use (see Table 7.4). GPAs show negative effects on marijuana use, mostly indirect, with early GPA showing consistently negative impacts on marijuana use reported at all three ages. The coefficients for college plans are mostly negative, but only some reach statistical significance. So here, as we found for cigarettes, academic success and involvement seem to provide at least modest protection against substance use. In contrast, serious scholastic setbacks (suspension, expulsion, or being held back a grade) occurring between ages 14 and 16 appear to be risk factors, increasing the likelihood of subsequent marijuana use (much of the effect is indirect via delinquency and cigarette use).

Does marijuana use play any causal role, contributing to subsequent educational setbacks? Our findings suggest that it does little; none of the coefficients showing impacts of marijuana use on educational outcomes reaches statistical significance (see Fig. 7.6). For example, marijuana use is positively correlated with dropping out; however, when other relevant factors are taken into account, the path coefficients in the structural equation model are small and nonsignificant. As for academic attainment at age 22, marijuana use at all three ages shows negative coefficients; here again, however, all are small and nonsignificant.

Another perspective on the impacts of marijuana use is provided in Figure 7.7, based on a multiple classification analysis (MCA) showing how marijuana use reported at age 16 predicts dropping out by age 18. A similar analysis reported in chapter 6 (Fig. 6.6) showed that the small subset of 16-year-olds who smoked a pack or more of cigarettes daily were much more likely than average to have dropped out within 2 years. Much the same can now be said for the small subset of our panel respondents who at age 16 used marijuana 10 or more times during the past month—compared with their classmates who used no marijuana, these frequent users were at least three times as likely to have dropped out by 2 years later. Was this increased risk the consequence of their marijuana use? The likely answer is: mostly no. Figure 7.7 shows that after controlling for background factors, age-16 grades, college plans, and delinquency, frequent marijuana use is associated with a doubled risk of dropping out. However, once age-16 cigarette use is also controlled, consistent with our structural model and the

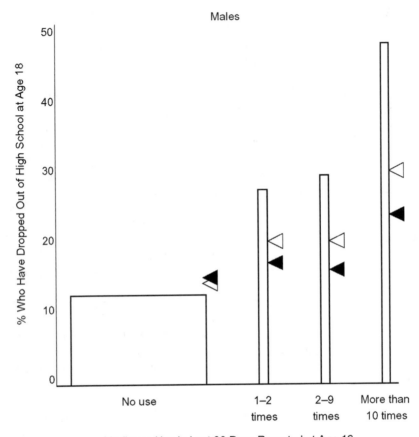

Males

The main bars are unadjusted estimates. The bar width is proportionate to the weighted number of cases in the category.

◁ Percentage adjusted for held back by 8th grade, suspended/expelled by 8th grade, race/ethnicity, population density, parents' education level, number of parents in the home, parent involvement, 10th-grade GPA, 10th-grade college plans, and 10th-grade delinquency

◀ Percentage adjusted for held back by 8th grade, suspended/expelled by 8th grade, race/ethnicity, population density, parents' education level, number of parents in the home, parent involvement, 10th-grade GPA, 10th-grade college plans, 10th-grade delinquency, and 10th-grade 30-day cigarette smoking

Figure 7.7a. Percentage of students who have dropped out of high school at age 18 (1995–1997) by frequency of marijuana use in the last 30 days reported at age 16: males.

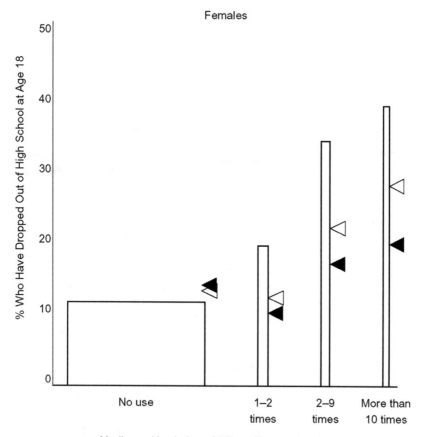

Females

The main bars are unadjusted estimates. The bar width is proportionate to the weighted number of cases in the category.

◁ Percentage adjusted for held back by 8th grade, suspended/expelled by 8th grade, race/ethnicity, population density, parents' education level, number of parents in the home, parent involvement, 10th-grade GPA, 10th-grade college plans, and 10th-grade delinquency

◀ Percentage adjusted for held back by 8th grade, suspended/expelled by 8th grade, race/ethnicity, population density, parents' education level, number of parents in the home, parent involvement, 10th-grade GPA, 10th-grade college plans, 10th-grade delinquency, and 10th-grade 30-day cigarette smoking

Figure 7.7b. Percentage of students who have dropped out of high school at age 18 (1995–1997) by frequency of marijuana use in the last 30 days reported at age 16: females.

arguments presented earlier in this chapter, differences linked to frequent marijuana use decrease further (and fall short of statistical significance). In sum, these findings suggest that frequent use of marijuana by age 16 is certainly *associated with* dropping out, but that association is primarily due to the impacts of other characteristics of the frequent marijuana users.

SUMMARY AND CONCLUSIONS

This chapter has focused on marijuana, the most widely used illicit drug in recent decades in the United States. But we found we could not focus on marijuana use among adolescents without also taking account of their use of cigarettes. The two forms of substance use are highly correlated during most of the teen years (modal ages 14–18), after which the correlation drops off a bit at age 20 and a bit more at age 22 (see Table 7.1). We attribute the decline in correlation to the fact that cigarette use typically involves a greater degree of dependency than does marijuana use. Thus, changes in roles and responsibilities may cause shifts in marijuana use, whereas cigarette use is less susceptible to change. (See Bachman et al., 1997, for an extended treatment of how new experiences in young adulthood lead to considerable shifts in use of marijuana and most other substances, but not cigarette use.)

The period from 1992 through 1997 saw substantial upward shifts in marijuana use among adolescents and young adults. Of course, the increases in marijuana use among those in our panel sample were considerably linked with age; our cross-sectional survey findings show that marijuana use was distinctly higher among 16-year-olds than among 14-year-olds at each year throughout the 1990s. But it should be kept in mind that the rises in use reported by our panel members were also influenced by the upward secular trend.

Importantly, our findings indicate that marijuana use tends to emerge somewhat later in adolescence than cigarette use. Whether that means that cigarette use *causes* the later-arriving marijuana use is a question that cannot be settled decisively with natural observations such as ours (and no one is going to conduct a proper experiment to sort it out), so we have to rely on circumstantial evidence. We noted that when adolescents learn to smoke cigarettes, they also learn the most common mode of administration for marijuana. Although the factors that predict (or correlate with) marijuana use and cigarette use are much the same, most of the links are somewhat stronger for cigarette use. Finally, explorations with structural equation models showed that 2-year lagged relationships are stronger from cigarette use to marijuana use than the reverse. Based on considerations such as these, we opted in our causal modeling to treat cigarette use as *one* of the causes of marijuana use. The other factors explored as potential contributors to marijuana use are the same as those treated as possible causes of cigarette use.

Parental education shows little consistent correlation with marijuana use; however, having both parents present in the home, as well as parental involvement in their children's lives at age 14, show some modest protective effects against marijuana use. Early educational setbacks such as grade retention, suspension, and expulsion all correlate positively with marijuana use, but any effects appear to overlap with other factors—most notably, other problem behaviors.

Problem behaviors such as cutting classes, skipping days of school, and other actions that warrant being sent to the office, all correlate positively with marijuana use. Strong correlations also appear between marijuana use and our general measure of delinquent behavior during the year prior to the end of eighth grade. Marijuana use is also above average among those adolescents who report spending frequent evenings out for fun and recreation. (Some of those evenings no doubt provide occasions for marijuana use.)

Our analyses lead us to conclude that GPAs and college plans probably have small negative (i.e., protective) effects with respect to marijuana use, both directly and indirectly, whereas scholastic setbacks after age 14 are risk factors for marijuana use at ages 16 and 18. It is also the case that those who have dropped out of high school by age 18 are more likely than average to be current marijuana users.

Does marijuana use have negative impacts on academic attainment or earlier indicators of educational success or failure? Our findings indicate that, across the broad range of adolescents, any such impacts are generally very small; indeed, in our structural equation model, not a single one of the coefficients for marijuana use causing educational outcomes reaches statistical significance in our fairly sizeable panel sample. This is not meant to deny the obvious: Any adolescent who uses marijuana heavily and frequently is likely to suffer impaired cognitive and educational outcomes (Pope, Gruber, & Yurgelun-Todd, 2001; Pope & Yurgelun-Todd, 1996). But for the overwhelming majority of adolescents in the United States, any marijuana use occurs relatively infrequently; and although such use is *correlated* with poor educational outcomes, it does not appear to be a major *cause* of such outcomes.

We are left with conclusions much like those concerning cigarette use. Early educational successes and failures are important factors in, and contributors to, a syndrome of disruptive and rebellious behaviors; these behaviors include early delinquency, cigarette use, and often also marijuana use. We thus view marijuana use as among the consequences of early educational failure. Fortunately, in contrast to cigarette users, most young people who indulge in the use of marijuana do so relatively infrequently and do not develop severe dependence. Accordingly, many are able to mature out of the behavior when they take on the responsibilities of adulthood.

Chapter 8

How Cocaine Use Is Linked With Educational Success and Failure

The previous chapter dealt with marijuana, the most widely used illicit drug in recent decades. We now turn to the use of a much more serious illicit drug: cocaine. Just as marijuana use typically begins at a later age than cigarette use, so also does cocaine use typically begin at a later age than marijuana use. In other words, in the syndrome of disruptive and rebellious behaviors, cocaine use tends to emerge later—if at all. Given the dangers associated with the use of this substance (Newcomb & Bentler, 1988; Arif, 1987), it is fortunate that only a limited subset of adolescents become involved with it, and it is also fortunate that most such adolescents use it only infrequently.

PLAN FOR THIS CHAPTER

In this chapter, we follow the same general strategy as in the previous two chapters. We begin with an examination of cocaine use rates based on cross-sectional Monitoring the Future (MTF) samples as well as our longitudinal panel of adolescents. Then, relying on regression and multiple classification analyses (MCA), we show how predictors of academic success and failure, smoking, and marijuana use are also predictors of cocaine use. The final stage of analysis examines findings on cocaine use from our structural model.

COCAINE USE IN RECENT DECADES

When marijuana use among high school seniors reached its peak in the late 1970s, fully half reported some use during the preceding 12 months (see Fig. 7.1 in the previous chapter). In contrast, during the peak years of cocaine use (1979–1986), only about one in eight (12%–13%) high school seniors reported any use during the preceding 12 months. Figure 8.1 shows that cocaine use among high school seniors dropped precipitously during the late 1980s, a period when perceptions of risk and attitudes of disapproval regarding cocaine use rose sharply following the death of two prominent athletes and the attendant publicity (Bachman et al., 1990). As the figure shows, annual use rates among high school seniors dropped below 4% in the early 1990s and rose modestly thereafter. Among 8th- and 10th-grade students, there was a similar modest rise during the mid-1990s.

During the period in which our panel respondents progressed from modal age 14 (1991–1993) to 18 (1995–1997), cocaine use was increasing among adolescents. (As noted in the previous chapter, marijuana use was also on the rise at this time.) The important difference, worth repeating, is that far fewer adolescents were involved in cocaine use. Figure 8.2 shows the age progression for panel respondents reporting use of cocaine in the past year. It shows that cocaine use was rare at eighth grade (modal age 14) and remained rare 2 years later (modal age 16). By modal age 18, annual prevalence rates rose to about 6% for males and 4% for females. By age 20, the gap between males and females widened a bit further and changed little by age 22. It is interesting to compare Figure 8.2 with Figure 7.2; not only is annual prevalence of cocaine use a great deal lower than annual prevalence of marijuana use (fewer than one quarter as many respondents reporting use), but cocaine use also appears to emerge at least 2 years later on average.

HOW COCAINE USE IS LINKED WITH USE
OF MARIJUANA AND CIGARETTES

Cocaine shares two important features with marijuana. First, both substances are typically taken by adolescents to alter consciousness—that is, to get high. Second, both substances are illicit, and for that reason alone users undertake some degree of risk (including contacts with the sorts of individuals who are involved in supplying illicit drugs). It is thus to be expected that cocaine use, like marijuana use, would be correlated with other measures of delinquency (and we see later that it is). It also seems likely that those adolescents who have experienced the risks and pleasures of marijuana use would be more willing than others to try cocaine as well, and our panel data confirm this expectation. Table A.8.1 in the appendix shows that adolescents who used marijuana on a monthly basis at modal age 18 were more likely to have also used cocaine during the past year, and the higher the frequency of marijuana use, the greater the likelihood of cocaine use (Pearson product–moment correlations range from .36 to .39; eta coefficients are virtually identical, indicating that the relationships are linear). The table also shows that current marijuana use at modal age 16 is a good predictor of annual cocaine use reported 2 years later (correlations

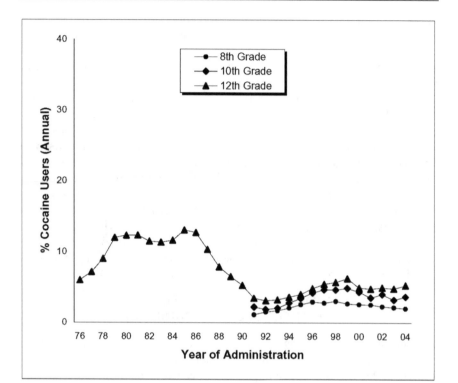

Data collected from annual national in-school surveys by Monitoring the Future.

Figure 8.1. Trends in annual prevalence of cocaine use for 8th, 10th, and 12th graders.

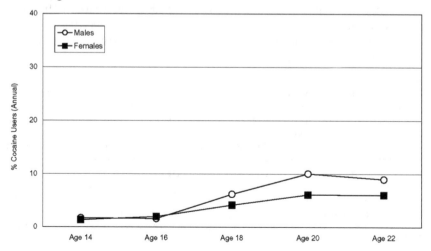

Figure 8.2. Percentage of panel respondents using cocaine in the last year: males and females.

and eta coefficients range from .27–.29). This pattern of prediction from age-16 marijuana use to age-18 cocaine use is illustrated in Figure 8.3.

It is important to keep in mind that, although marijuana use may substantially increase the likelihood of cocaine use, most marijuana users do not progress to the more serious illicit drug. Even among those who at age 16 had reported using marijuana on a daily or near-daily basis (i.e., more than 20 times during the last 30 days), 2 years later only about one third reported any use of cocaine during the past 12 months. Among those who had used marijuana less frequently, Figure 8.3 shows that cocaine use was less likely; and among those who reported no current marijuana use at age 16, few (4% of males, 2% of females) reported any cocaine use at age 18.

Cigarette use can be viewed as one of the common prior causes of marijuana and cocaine use, but the strength of association is lower for cocaine use (see the correlation matrix in Table A.3.3 in the appendix for details). Given the strong link between marijuana and cocaine, most of any effect of cigarette use on cocaine use would seem to be indirect (and that is how it is treated in our structural equation model).

MAJOR CORRELATES/PREDICTORS OF ADOLESCENT COCAINE USE

We continue the practice, employed in previous chapters, of using multiple classification analyses (MCA) and regression analyses (regression results are shown in Table A.8.2 in the appendix) to examine factors related to substance use. In this chapter, however, we predict 12-month (i.e., annual) rather than 30-day (i.e., current) substance use because current cocaine use is so infrequent among adolescents. Even annual use is sufficiently rare that the low variance constrains coefficients to be relatively low. It also produces somewhat less stable estimates (i.e., more random fluctuation) than was the case in the chapters on cigarette and marijuana use. Nevertheless, we are able to observe meaningful patterns of relationships between the predictors and cocaine use.[1]

---

[1]We continue to follow the usual nomenclature for regression analyses and refer to "predictors" of cocaine use, although we recognize that the true causal ordering does not always run entirely from predictor to outcome or dependent variable. We also remind readers that comparing MCA versus ordinary regression analyses (e.g., Tables 8.1 and A.8.2) reveals small differences in the R-squared values indicating explained variance. On the one hand, MCA captures nonlinear as well as linear relationships, which could increase explained variance. On the other hand, the MCA analyses shown here use a dichotomous dependent variable (any use of cocaine in the last year, vs. none), and that tends to lower explained variance, compared with a continuous version of the dependent variable (as used in the ordinary regression analyses). These impacts are, in the present instances, both small; moreover, they operate in opposite directions, tending to cancel each other. Thus, the results of the two multivariate analysis approaches correspond fairly closely.

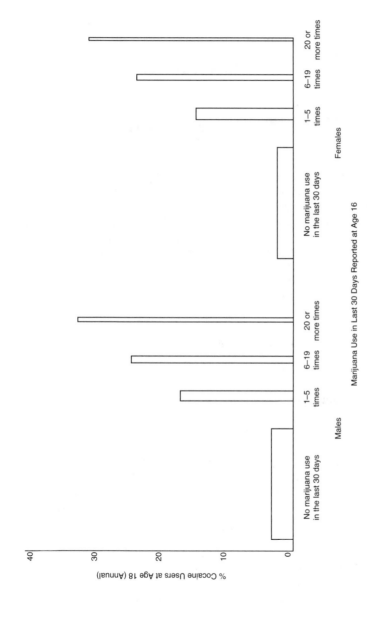

The bar width is proportionate to the weighted number of cases in the category.

Figure 8.3.   Age-18 annual cocaine use predicted from age-16 monthly marijuana use.

Race/Ethnicity

Column 1 in Table 8.1 shows that, at modal age 18, African Americans, especially African-American females, are less likely than average to have reported cocaine use during the preceding 12 months. Taking account of other predictors in the MCA or regression analyses (Tables 8.1 and A.8.2, respectively) does not diminish these differences. We note once again that a forthcoming separate publication will provide a further exploration of racial/ethnic differences.

Urban Density

Table 8.1b shows that cocaine use among females at modal age 18 is positively related to urban density—that is, use is more than twice as likely among those from large metropolitan areas, compared with those from nonmetropolitan areas. These differences among females are not reduced by controls for background and school experiences, and are reduced only slightly by controls for delinquency. Among males, however, no clear differences related to urban density emerge.

Parental Education

Tables 8.1 and A.8.2 indicate no clear pattern of correlation between parental education level and adolescent cocaine use, either bivariately or multivariately.

Presence of Both Parents in the Home

Table 8.1 shows that by the time our panel respondents reach modal age 18, cocaine use is less likely among those who lived with two parents throughout secondary school, compared with those who did not. Among females the risk is less than half as large for those in intact families, and among males the risk is less than two thirds as large. Controls for the remaining parental factors (Column 2) do not change this relationship appreciably, but controls for other factors reduce it somewhat.

Parental Involvement in Students' Lives

Just as important as having two parents present is the protective effect of early parental involvement in students' lives. Table 8.1 shows that adolescents whose parents had been least involved in their lives at modal age 14 (monitoring and participating in doing homework, requiring chores, and limiting TV viewing) are about three times as likely to have used cocaine in late adolescence (use during the past year, reported when they were 18). Controls for the remaining parental factors reduce this relationship only slightly, and controls for other factors reduce it slightly more.

Grade Retention, and Suspension or Expulsion, by End of Eighth Grade

Young men who had been held back more than once prior to the end of eighth grade are, at modal age 18, about half again as likely to have reported cocaine use during the past year compared with those not held back at all. The differences for young women are smaller. As can be seen in Table 8.1 (Column 4), once other indicators of educational success and failure are included in the equation, the held-back measure provides no additional predictive value. So our previous conclusions regarding cigarette use and marijuana use seem applicable also to cocaine use: Any effects of early grade failures are indirect via other factors.

We found in previous chapters that those who had been suspended or expelled two or more times prior to the end of eighth grade were twice as likely to be daily smokers at modal age 18 and also twice as likely to be current (monthly) marijuana users, compared with those not suspended or expelled. Table 8.1 and Figure 8.4 show essentially the same finding for cocaine use, albeit with much smaller proportions of users; cocaine use during the past year among 18-year-olds is more than twice as likely for those who had been suspended or expelled two or more times prior to the end of eighth grade, compared with those not suspended or expelled at all. These differences are changed little by controls for background and other educational experiences (Column 4 in Table 8.1), but decrease substantially when additional controls for delinquency are included (Column 5). So we can expand the conclusion stated in the previous chapter: Early misbehaviors in school appear to be part of a larger syndrome of deviant behaviors that can have lasting effects in the form of cigarette use, and then often marijuana use, and then sometimes even cocaine use.

Delinquent Behavior

Although cocaine use occurs much less often than marijuana use, and thus tends to show lower correlations with predictors, by modal age 18 delinquency correlates nearly as strongly with (annual) cocaine use as

TABLE 8.1a

Multiple Classification Analyses Predicting Percentage Who Report Any Cocaine Use in the Last Year at Age 18: Males

Grand Mean = 6.2
Effective N = 1361

	Percentage Reporting Any Cocaine Use in the Last Year					
	Col. 1	Col. 2	Col. 3	Col. 4	Col. 5	Col. 6
Variable	Bivariate	Multivariate				
Race/ethnicity						
African-American	3.1	2.6	2.1	2.1	2.9	2.9
Hispanic	9.4	8.4	8.5	8.0	8.0	8.0
Other race	8.0	7.9	7.8	7.0	7.0	7.0
White	5.9	6.2	6.3	6.6	6.4	6.4
Urban density						
Large MSA	6.4	6.2	6.0	6.3	6.0	6.1
Other MSA	6.3	6.4	6.4	6.4	6.3	6.3
Non-MSA	5.8	5.8	6.0	5.8	6.2	6.2
Parent education level						
1 (Low)	8.7	7.6	7.1	6.1	6.5	6.6
2	5.2	5.0	5.0	4.2	4.5	4.5
3	6.4	6.5	6.6	6.4	6.4	6.4
4	4.8	5.3	5.4	6.1	5.8	5.8
5 (High)	7.2	7.4	7.7	8.9	8.5	8.5
Lived with 2 parents Waves 1–3						
Yes	5.3	5.4	5.5	5.9	5.9	6.0
No	7.8	7.8	7.5	6.8	6.8	6.6
Parent involvement index						
1 (Low)	11.8	11.1	10.5	9.6	9.2	9.1
2	5.7	5.4	5.3	5.1	4.9	5.0
3	6.2	6.3	6.4	6.6	6.7	6.7
4 (High)	4.5	4.8	5.0	5.3	5.5	5.5
Held back grade 8 or earlier						
Never	6.0		6.5	6.7	6.7	6.7
Once	6.3		5.1	4.5	4.7	4.5
More than once	9.3		6.0	5.4	5.2	4.6
Suspended/expelled grade 8 or earlier						
Never	5.0		5.1	5.4	5.9	6.0
Once	6.9		6.9	5.9	5.3	5.2
More than once	11.1		10.8	10.3	8.2	7.8
Mean secondary school GPA						
D or below	21.5			17.4	16.3	15.6
C- or C	11.6			9.7	8.9	8.7
C+ or B-	7.0			6.8	6.9	6.9
B or B+	4.1			4.7	4.8	4.9
A-	3.9			4.7	5.1	5.1
A	0.1			1.5	2.7	2.7

TABLE 8.1a
Multiple Classification Analyses Predicting Percentage Who Report Any
Cocaine Use in the Last Year at Age 18: Males (*continued*)

Grand Mean = 6.2
Effective N = 1361

	Percentage Reporting Any Cocaine Use in the Last Year					
	Col. 1	Col. 2	Col. 3	Col. 4	Col. 5	Col. 6
Variable	Bivariate			Multivariate		
Mean secondary school college plans						
Definitely won't	10.6			6.6	6.3	6.0
Probably won't	10.4			7.2	7.2	6.9
Probably will	6.3			5.8	5.6	5.6
Definitely will	4.1			6.1	6.3	6.5
Serious scholastic setback W1 to W2						
None	5.0			5.2	5.6	5.6
One	9.5			8.9	7.8	7.7
Two	21.8			19.8	16.6	15.6
Serious scholastic setback W2 to W3						
None	5.0			5.3	5.5	5.5
One	9.8			8.9	8.3	8.3
Two	13.9			12.3	10.9	10.6
Delinquency (W2–3 combined)						
No incidents	2.2				3.4	3.4
1 or 2 incidents	3.0				3.5	3.5
3 or 4 incidents	5.0				5.0	5.0
5 or 6 incidents	9.3				8.4	8.4
7 or 8 incidents	14.4				12.7	12.7
9 to 14 incidents	23.5				20.9	20.8
High school dropout by W3						
Yes	12.7					8.6
No	5.0					5.7
Multiple R		.122	.147	.227	.292	.294
R Squared		.015	.022	.052	.085	.087

Factor Summary*

	eta	beta	beta	beta	beta	beta
Race/ethnicity	**.069**	.067	.073	.067	.056	.056
Urban density	.009	.011	.009	.009	.005	.004
Parents' education level	**.055**	.041	.039	.055	.048	.048
Lived with 2 parents Waves 1–3	.050	.048	.039	.018	.018	.013
Parent involvement index	**.083**	.072	.065	.054	.050	.049
Held back grade 8 or earlier	.027		.023	.038	.034	.040
Suspended/expelled grade 8 or earlier	**.091**		**.087**	**.074**	.037	.032
Mean secondary school GPA	**.146**			.102	.088	.082
Mean secondary school college plans	**.096**			.020	.023	.021
Serious scholastic setback W1 to W2	**.115**			**.098**	**.070**	.063
Serious scholastic setback W2 to W3	**.097**			**.074**	.057	.055
Delinquency (W2–3 combined)	**.236**				**.194**	**.194**
High school dropout by Wave 3	**.117**					.044

*All eta and beta statistics p<.05 are shown in **bold**.

See Table 3.3 for frequency distributions of predictor variables.

Note: W1 = Wave 1 data collection (grade 8, modal age 14), W2 = Wave 2 data collection
(modal age 16), W3 = Wave 3 data collection (modal age 18)

TABLE 8.1b

Multiple Classification Analyses Predicting Percentage Who Report Any Cocaine Use in the Last Year at Age 18: Females

Grand Mean = 4.2
Effective *N* = 1739

	Percentage Reporting Any Cocaine Use in the Last Year					
	Col. 1	Col. 2	Col. 3	Col. 4	Col. 5	Col. 6
Variable	Bivariate	Multivariate				
Race/ethnicity						
African-American	0.5	0.0 [1]	0.0 [1]	0.0 [1]	0.0 [1]	0.0 [1]
Hispanic	4.9	4.1	4.1	3.9	4.3	4.3
Other race	4.8	4.8	4.7	4.4	4.0	4.0
White	4.7	5.1	5.3	5.5	5.3	5.3
Urban density						
Large MSA	5.9	6.2	6.1	6.0	5.4	5.4
Other MSA	4.1	4.0	3.9	3.9	3.9	3.9
Non-MSA	2.5	2.3	2.6	2.8	3.3	3.3
Parents' education level						
1 (Low)	4.8	4.5	4.3	3.4	3.6	3.5
2	5.2	5.5	5.4	5.0	4.9	4.9
3	4.4	4.3	4.4	4.5	4.3	4.3
4	2.8	2.9	3.1	3.6	3.9	4.0
5 (High)	3.4	3.4	3.6	4.5	4.1	4.1
Lived with 2 parents Waves 1–3						
Yes	2.8	2.7	2.9	3.3	3.3	3.4
No	6.1	6.3	6.0	5.5	5.4	5.2
Parent involvement index						
1 (Low)	9.2	8.4	8.1	7.7	7.4	7.5
2	5.0	4.7	4.6	4.5	4.4	4.3
3	3.7	3.7	3.8	4.0	4.1	4.1
4 (High)	2.2	2.7	2.8	2.7	2.9	2.9
Held back grade 8 or earlier						
Never	4.0		4.2	4.4	4.3	4.3
Once	5.1		3.9	3.1	3.7	3.6
More than once	5.1		4.4	3.1	3.1	2.8
Suspended/expelled grade 8 or earlier						
Never	3.4		3.5	3.6	4.0	4.0
Once	8.2		7.9	6.7	5.2	5.1
More than once	8.4		8.4	7.7	5.5	5.2
Mean secondary school GPA						
D or below	17.9			12.1	10.6	9.8
C- or C	8.3			6.1	4.9	4.7
C+ or B-	5.9			5.5	5.1	5.1
B or B+	3.5			3.8	4.1	4.1
A-	1.5			2.1	2.8	2.9
A	0.8			2.3	2.8	2.9

TABLE 8.1b
Multiple Classification Analyses Predicting Percentage Who Report Any Cocaine Use in the Last Year at Age 18: Females (*continued*)

Grand Mean = 4.2
Effective N = 1739

Variable	Col. 1 Bivariate	Col. 2	Col. 3	Col. 4	Col. 5	Col. 6
			Multivariate			
Mean secondary school college plans						
Definitely won't	13.2			9.4	9.6	9.1
Probably won't	7.3			4.6	4.2	3.8
Probably will	4.5			3.7	3.5	3.5
Definitely will	3.0			4.2	4.4	4.5
Serious scholastic setback W1 to W2						
None	3.5			3.8	4.1	4.1
One	7.8			6.2	4.5	4.3
Two	8.5			6.4	5.8	5.3
Serious scholastic setback W2 to W3						
None	3.3			3.5	3.6	3.7
One	8.9			7.8	7.1	7.0
Two	5.3			4.5	4.9	4.6
Delinquency (W2–3 combined)						
No incidents	0.5				1.2	1.1
1 or 2 incidents	3.3				3.4	3.4
3 or 4 incidents	6.1				5.6	5.6
5 or 6 incidents	10.4				9.1	9.1
7 or 8 incidents	20.8				19.4	19.4
9 to 14 incidents	36.8				33.7	33.6
High school dropout by Wave 3						
Yes	9.8					6.2
No	3.2					3.8
Multiple R		.166	.183	.224	.319	.320
R Squared		.027	.034	.050	.102	.103

Factor Summary*

	eta	beta	beta	beta	beta	beta
Race/ethnicity	.072	.100	.116	.120	.106	.103
Urban density	.060	.070	.065	.059	.038	.039
Parents' education level	.045	.046	.039	.030	.022	.023
Lived with 2 parents Waves 1–3	.080	.089	.077	.055	.051	.044
Parent involvement index	.094	.075	.068	.064	.058	.058
Held back grade 8 or earlier	.020		.006	.023	.012	.015
Suspended/expelled grade 8 or earlier	.087		.083	.063	.025	.021
Mean secondary school GPA	.124			.077	.051	.047
Mean secondary school college plans	.089			.038	.041	.040
Serious scholastic setback W1 to W2	.079			.043	.012	.007
Serious scholastic setback W2 to W3	.098			.075	.061	.058
Delinquency (W2–3 combined)	.273				.240	.240
High school dropout by Wave 3	.116					.041

*All eta and beta statistics p<.05 are shown in **bold**.

See Table 3.3 for frequency distributions of predictor variables.

Note: W1 = Wave 1 data collection (grade 8, modal age 14), W2 = Wave 2 data collection (modal age 16), W3 = Wave 3 data collection (modal age 18)

[1]Negative values were set to 0.

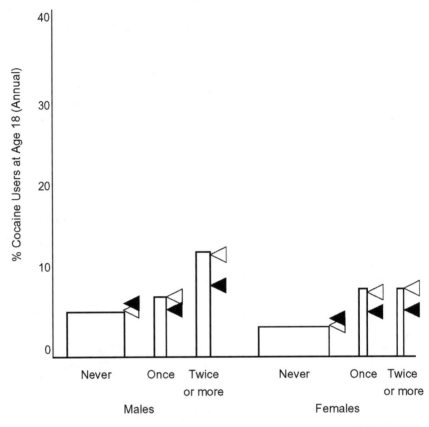

The main bars are unadjusted estimates. The bar width is proportionate to the
weighted number of cases in the category.

◁ Percentage adjusted for race/ethnicity, population density, parents' education,
number of parents, parental involvement, and held back (Column 3 in Table 8.1a & b)

◀ Percentage adjusted for race/ethnicity, population density, parents' education,
number of parents, parental involvement, held back, GPA, college plans, serious
scholastic setback between grades 8 and 10 and 10 and 12, delinquency, and
dropout by age 18 (Column 6 in Table 8.1a & b)

Figure 8.4. Percentage of age-18 annual cocaine use by number of times
suspended or expelled Grade 8 or earlier: males and females.

with (monthly) marijuana use (product–moment correlations of .20 versus .28 for males, and .20 versus .23 among females) (see Tables A.8.2 vs. A.7.1). As shown in Figure 8.5 (see also Table 8.1), among 18-year-olds who had a history of high delinquency (9–14 incidents), nearly one in four males (24%) and more than one in three females (37%) had used cocaine at least once during the previous 12 months, whereas among those with no delinquency, only 2% of males and fewer than 1% of females had used cocaine. Including other predictors produces almost no change, as shown in Table 8.1, so it appears that a good deal of the association between general delinquency and cocaine use in adolescence does not overlap with background or early educational successes and failures.

Grade Point Average

Grade point average (GPA) is a negative predictor of cocaine use, just as it was for other substances in previous chapters. Figure 8.6 shows that among the few students who had D or lower averages throughout secondary school, about one in five (22% of males, 18% of females) had used cocaine during the 12 months prior to the third survey wave (end of high school for most). Among the straight-A students, less than 1% had used cocaine during the past 12 months. Multivariate analyses controlling background, and including delinquency and other indicators of academic success and failure (see Tables A.8.2 and 8.1), show that GPA overlaps considerably with other factors.

College Plans

Cocaine use is also negatively related to college plans. Cocaine use at age 14, although quite rare in our panel sample, shows stronger negative correlations with college plans than with grade point average (see Table A.8.2). Here again, the multivariate analyses show considerable overlap with other factors.

Serious Scholastic Setbacks During High School (After Eighth Grade)

Among those who had been held back, or suspended or expelled, during the years after eighth grade, the likelihood of cocaine use at modal age

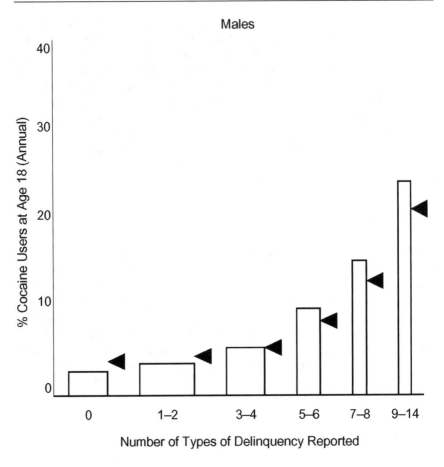

The main bars are unadjusted estimates. The bar width is proportionate to the weighted number of cases in the category.

◀ Percentage adjusted for race/ethnicity, population density, parents' education, number of parents, parental involvement, GPA, college plans, held back, suspension/expulsion, serious scholastic setback between grades 8 and 10 and 10 and 12, and dropout by age 18 (Column 6 in Table 8.1a)

Figure 8.5a. Age-18 annual cocaine use by delinquency index (ages 16 and 18 combined): males.

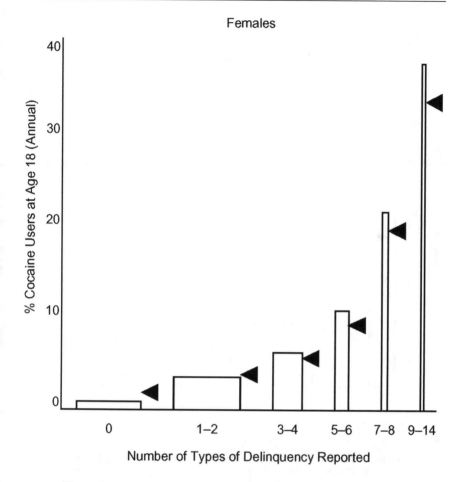

Figure 8.5b. Age-18 annual cocaine use by delinquency index (ages 16 and 18 combined): females.

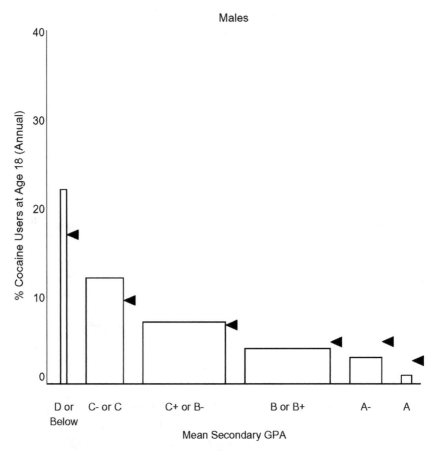

The main bars are unadjusted estimates. The bar width is proportionate to the weighted number of cases in the category.

◄ Percentage adjusted for race/ethnicity, population density, parents' education, number of parents, parental involvement, GPA, college plans, held back, suspension/expulsion, serious scholastic setback between grade 8 and 10 and 10 and 12, and dropout by age 18 (Column 6 in Table 8.1a)

Figure 8.6a. Age-18 annual cocaine use by mean secondary school GPA (Grades 8, 10, and 12 combined): males.

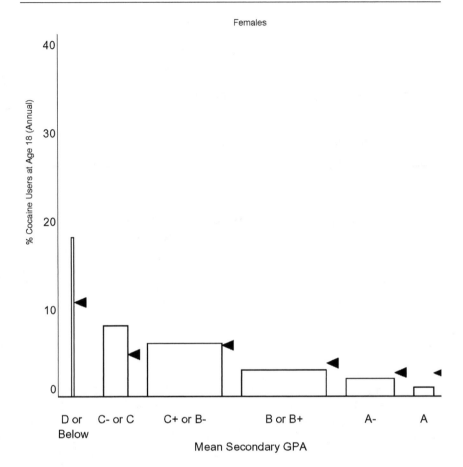

The main bars are unadjusted estimates. The bar width is proportionate to the weighted number of cases in the category.

◀ Percentage adjusted for race/ethnicity, population density, parents' education, number of parents, parental involvement, GPA, college plans, held back, suspension/expulsion, serious scholastic setback between grade 8 and 10 and 10 and 12, and dropout by age 18 (Column 6 in Table 8.1b)

Figure 8.6b. Age-18 annual cocaine use by mean secondary school GPA (Grades 8, 10, and 12 combined): females.

18 is several times higher compared with those who experienced no such scholastic setbacks (see Table 8.1). The multivariate analyses (Tables A.8.2 and 8.1) indicate considerable overlap with other predictors.

Dropping Out of High School by Age 18

High school dropouts are two to three times more likely than non-dropouts to report annual use of cocaine at modal age 18 (see Table 8.1). Regression analyses (Table A.8.2) indicate considerable overlap with other predictors.

ADDITIONAL CORRELATES/PREDICTORS
OF ADOLESCENT COCAINE USE

In this section, we consider other predictors that were not included in our structural equation model, but which have shown some bivariate relationships with substance use in previous chapters.

Various Problem Behaviors

We learned in previous chapters that students who misbehave in school (cutting classes, skipping days of school, or getting sent to the office) are at increased risk for being smokers and marijuana users. Table A.8.2 shows that those who misbehave in school are also more likely to be cocaine users. The table also shows that these misbehaviors overlap considerably with other problem behaviors, and by modal age 18 the general measure of delinquency is a distinctly stronger predictor of cocaine use.

Evenings Out for Fun and Recreation

Frequency of evenings out for fun and recreation at modal age 18 is modestly correlated with annual cocaine use reported at age 18 (product–moment correlations of .10 for males and .09 for females; see Table A.8.2). These relationships overlap largely with other predictors.

Actual and Preferred Work Hours

Much the same as we found for marijuana use, cocaine use shows mostly positive correlations with preferred and actual hours of part-time work during the school year. However, these relationships are all quite small, especially among young women, and most are reduced to near zero in the presence of other predictors (see Table A.8.2). It thus appears that part-time work desires and behaviors do not contribute much to illicit drug use or vice versa.

Religious Attendance and Importance

Adolescents who frequently attend religious services, and those (often the same individuals) who rate religion as important in their lives, are less likely than average to smoke or use marijuana or alcohol, and are also slightly less likely to use cocaine. The links with cocaine use are distinctly weaker than those with marijuana use (based on comparison of Tables A.7.1 and A.8.2). The multivariate findings suggest that any protective effects are likely to be indirect via other factors.

Self-Esteem

The self-esteem measures, like those involving religion, show mostly negative bivariate correlations with cocaine use. Here again, however, the bivariate correlations are quite small, and the multivariate coefficients are close to zero (only 1 out of 18 reaches the threshold of significance; see Table A.8.2).

STRUCTURAL EQUATION MODEL: ACADEMIC ATTAINMENT AND COCAINE USE

The structural equation model presented in this chapter was first introduced in chapter 5. As we mentioned then, and for conceptual reasons discussed earlier in this chapter, we opted to treat cocaine use as influenced by marijuana use. We treat cocaine use as influenced also by delinquency and by factors related to educational success and failure. We did not find it necessary, however, to model direct causal effects of cigarette use on cocaine use; the indirect effects via marijuana use proved to capture the relationship well. We also did not find it necessary to model any direct causal links between alcohol use and cocaine use.

We continue to focus on annual rather than monthly cocaine use, primarily because monthly use of cocaine by adolescents is so rare. Thus, because the cocaine-use measure covers the 12-month period preceding the survey, we treat the causation from marijuana use to cocaine use as lagged, as shown in Figure 8.7. Specifically, we treat marijuana use for the 30-day period preceding the first survey wave as among the causes of cocaine use during the 12-month period preceding Wave 2; similarly, marijuana use reported at the second survey wave is a cause of cocaine use at Wave 3. We also use lagged prediction from college plans to cocaine use, again in order to preserve measurement chronicity. Other predictors of cocaine use such as delinquency, GPA, and serious scholastic setbacks all cover events spanning about 1 year or longer, and we felt that lagged prediction was not necessary in these cases.[2]

Structural Model Findings

As in previous chapters, we highlight findings for the focal drug, in this case cocaine, based on the total model including all substances. The highlighted findings appear in Figure 8.7 and Table 8.2. Additional findings for the total model are provided in the appendix in Tables A.3.4–10. One general observation is that because cocaine use is much more rare among adolescents, even when the reporting period is a full 12 months, the coefficients involving cocaine use are generally smaller than those involving either cigarette use or marijuana use.

Most of the exogenous background factors show only small and nonsignificant total effects on cocaine use at each of the three modal ages, although they are generally consistent with the findings reported earlier in this chapter. Parental involvement in adolescents' lives (as of age 14) is one factor that shows significant negative (i.e., protective) effects on cocaine use at all three ages for females, and at modal ages 14 and 18 for males. One other exogenous factor showing significant total effects is suspension or expulsion prior to the end of eighth grade; in this case the relationships are positive (i.e., early suspensions or expulsions constitute risk factors).

We reported in earlier chapters that the stability estimates are quite high for cigarette use from modal ages 14 to 18, but only from ages 16 to 18 for marijuana use. In the case of cocaine use, stability estimates are not very high between any of the three survey waves, consistent with

---

[2]This leaves open the possibility, of course, that cocaine use earlier in the 12-month reporting interval might have influenced grades or delinquent behavior later in the 12-month period; however, given the relatively late emergence of cocaine-using behavior, and the high stability of other factors such as GPA, we judged that lagged prediction was not necessary. Moreover, lagged prediction in this case would have produced poorer model fit statistics. In contrast, the lagging of the marijuana-use causation of cocaine was necessary from a modeling standpoint in order to avoid instability due to excess multicollinearity.

TABLE 8.2
Direct and Total Effects of Predictors on Annual Cocaine Use at Wave 1, Wave 2, and Wave 3*

Predictors	Annual Cocaine Wave 1 Males Direct	Males Total	Females Direct	Females Total	Annual Cocaine Wave 2 Males Direct	Males Total	Females Direct	Females Total	Annual Cocaine Wave 3 Males Direct	Males Total	Females Direct	Females Total
African-American	.017	.009	-.058	-.069	-.024	-.033	-.049	**-.082**	-.029	-.054	**-.077**	**-.130**
Hispanic	.005	.008	.049	.057	.021	.024	.054	.058	.019	.031	-.024	-.030
Other race	-.006	-.010	.030	.045	.009	.014	-.048	-.029	-.010	.011	-.024	-.039
Large MSA	-.040	-.033	-.040	-.038	-.023	-.029	-.036	-.037	.006	.002	-.010	.017
Non-MSA	-.052	-.056	-.021	-.039	.003	-.017	-.023	-.053	.013	-.005	.007	-.032
Parents' education level	-.001	.002	-.003	-.017	-.042	-.052	.033	.003	.057	.031	-.025	-.037
Lived with 2 parents Waves 1–3	-.019	-.019	.032	.014	.021	.013	-.003	-.027	-.010	-.024	-.046	**-.073**
Parent involvement index	-.109	**-.132**	-.077	**-.122**	.022	-.053	-.021	**-.100**	-.054	**-.104**	-.031	**-.098**
Held back grade 8 or earlier	.044	.047	.033	.030		.029		.019		.028		.020
Suspended/expelled grade 8 or earlier	.085	**.129**	.066	**.147**		.067		.097		.063		.069
GPA Wave 1	.024	.002	.008	-.041		-.076		**-.100**		-.098		**-.122**
GPA Wave 2					-.021	-.038	-.014	-.050		-.082		**-.107**
GPA Wave 3									-.034	-.045	-.050	-.070
College plans Wave 1		-.005		-.026	-.023	-.034	-.053	-.083		-.030		-.027
College plans Wave 2						-.005		-.009	-.012	-.032	.022	.000
College plans Wave 3										.001		-.006
Serious scholastic setback W1 to W2					.040	.059	-.039	-.005		.050		.036
Serious scholastic setback W2 to W3									.058	.081	-.009	.010
Delinquency Wave 1	**.135**	**.135**	**.278**	**.278**		**.119**		**.165**		**.119**		**.127**
Delinquency Wave 2					**.150**	**.150**	**.231**	**.231**		**.219**		**.229**
Delinquency Wave 3									**.213**	**.213**	**.203**	**.203**
30-day cigarette smoking Wave 1						**.086**		**.119**		.051		.080
30-day cigarette smoking Wave 2										.039		.090
30-day cigarette smoking Wave 3												
30-day marijuana Wave 1					**.198**	**.196**	**.252**	**.251**		.078		.080
30-day marijuana Wave 2									.098	**.101**	**.244**	**.244**
30-day marijuana Wave 3												
Annual cocaine Wave 1					.075	.073	.049	.049		.024		.004
Annual cocaine Wave 2									**.344**	**.341**	**.166**	**.165**
Annual cocaine Wave 3												

Direct and Total Effects of Annual Cocaine Use at Wave 1, Wave 2, and Wave 3 on Education Factors*

Predictors		GPA Wave 2 Total	College Plans Wave 2 Total	Serious Scholastic Setback W1 to W2 Direct	Total	GPA Wave 3 Total	College Plans Wave 3 Total	Serious Scholastic Setback W2 to W3 Direct	Total	High School Dropout Wave 3 Direct	Total	Academic Attainment Wave 5 Direct	Total
Annual cocaine Wave 1	Males	.004	.003	-.035	-.035	.003	.003		-.004		.002		.004
	Females	.005	.011	-.098	-.098	.004	.007		-.004		-.017		.008
Annual cocaine Wave 2	Males					.005	.004	-.045	-.045	**.092**	**.092**		-.004
	Females					.002	.002	-.037	-.037	-.005	-.005		.001
Annual cocaine Wave 3	Males											.028	.028
	Females											-.014	-.014

*Coefficients that are p<.05 (two-tailed) are shown in **bold**.

Note: W1 = Wave 1 data collection (grade 8, modal age 14), W2 = Wave 2 data collection (modal age 16), W3 = Wave 3 data collection (modal age 18)

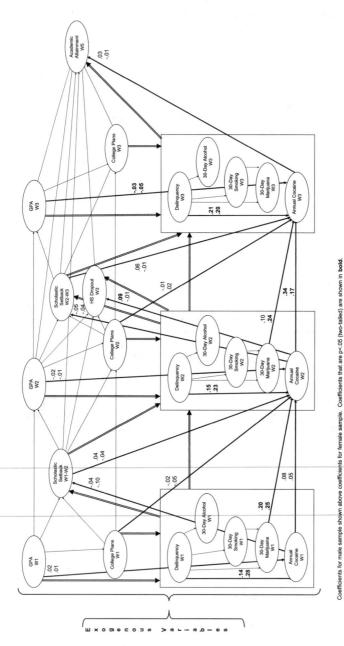

Coefficients for male sample shown above coefficients for female sample. Coefficients that are p<.05 (two-tailed) are shown in **bold**.

Note: W1 = Wave 1 data collection (grade 8, modal age 14), W2 = Wave 2 data collection (modal age 16), W3 = Wave 3 data collection (modal age 18), W5 = Wave 5 data collection (modal age 22)

Model Fit Statistics

	Males	Females
Comparative Fit Index (CFI)	.996	.995
Root Mean-Square Error of Approximation (RMSEA)	.023	.027
Chi-Square	549	712
Degrees of Freedom	316	316

Figure 8.7. Structural equation model of academic attainment and substance use, focusing on cocaine use.

the fact that annual cocaine use among adolescents is almost entirely absent until the late teen years (see Fig. 8.2). Indeed, Figure 8.7 shows that among behaviors influencing or predicting cocaine use reported at age 16, monthly marijuana use reported at age 14 is a stronger predictor than cocaine use reported at age 14. For cocaine use reported at age 18, the story is more complicated and appears to differ between males and females.[3]

The direct effects of delinquency on cocaine use vary by gender and modal age, as can be seen in Figure 8.7, although all are significant and positive. The total effects of early delinquency on later cocaine use are clearer and somewhat more consistent; for example, delinquency reported at age 14 shows significant effects on cocaine use reported at age 18 (coefficients of .12 for males and .13 for females; see Table 8.2).

As noted previously, the lagged effects of marijuana use on cocaine use are important, but also vary by gender and age. The effects of cigarette use on cocaine use are only indirect, via marijuana use; all are statistically significant, albeit rather modest. So cocaine use does appear to be part of a problem behavior syndrome—influenced by the use of other substances, as well as by general delinquent behavior. But it is clearly a late-emerging part of such a syndrome, and fortunately it does not emerge at all among most adolescents.

Do educational successes and failures also contribute to cocaine use? We already noted that those who experienced early suspension or expulsion from school are more likely than others to become cocaine users. The model also shows some positive impacts of later scholastic setbacks on cocaine use, although the effects are small. GPA shows near-zero direct effects on cocaine use, but the total effects of earlier GPA on later cocaine use are negative and significant. Effects of college plans are generally close to zero and nonsignificant. We thus conclude that educational experiences—particularly educational setbacks and poor performance—do seem to contribute to cocaine use, albeit rather modestly.

What about a reverse causal contribution? Does cocaine use impede academic success? For the levels of cocaine use reported by our panel sample, our structural model yields a largely negative answer to that question. Impacts of cocaine use on age-22 academic attainment are essentially zero, and impacts on other indicators of educational success or failure are also nonsignificant and mostly near zero, with just one exception: cocaine use reported by males at modal age 16 shows a significant

---

[3]Given the rarity of cocaine use in earlier adolescence, we are not inclined to give much credence to the gender differences in coefficient size.

positive impact on dropping out by age 18 (direct effect of .09), but for females this relationship is essentially zero (a coefficient of -.005).

To explore further the question of whether cocaine use reported at age 16 contributes to dropping out within the following 2 years, we conducted multiple classification analyses similar to those in the previous two chapters. The results (in Table A.8.3 in the appendix) provide some additional perspective beyond that from the structural equation model findings. At modal age 16, just below 2% of the young men and just over 2% of the young women reported any cocaine use during the preceding year. Among these small subsets, the likelihood of dropping out in the next 2 years is nearly quadruple among the men and nearly triple among the women. Controls for other factors (similar to those in the structural equation model) reduce the differences, but the remaining cocaine effect is more than a doubling of the risk of dropping out for young men and somewhat less for young women. These findings are entirely consistent with those from the structural model. Nevertheless, given the small numbers of users and the lack of consistency between male and female findings, we remain cautious about concluding that cocaine use makes an independent contribution to dropping out.

SUMMARY AND CONCLUSIONS

Fortunately, the great majority of adolescents and young adults these days do not use cocaine. Nearly all of those who do use this drug have already tried cigarettes and marijuana, and their use of cocaine tends to emerge later (i.e., at older ages). Because cocaine use is relatively rare, and the variance for this behavior is thus low, the coefficients (correlation, regression, and path coefficients) involving cocaine use also tend to be low. Nevertheless, we have been able in this chapter to observe a number of now-familiar patterns of relationships with background and educational factors.

Cocaine use is less likely to emerge among adolescents who have the benefit of the following protective factors: both of their parents live at home with them throughout secondary school; their parents are actively involved in their lives, including their schoolwork; they have high GPAs; and they plan to enter and complete college, although it is not clear that college plans have any protective effect above and beyond the other factors.

Cocaine use is more likely among adolescents with the following risk factors: poor scholastic performance as evidenced by low grades or grade retention (being held back); poor scholastic adjustment as evidenced by truancy, school misbehavior warranting trips to the office, suspension, and/or expulsion; and, in addition to such school-related events, a history of other delinquent behaviors.

Does poor scholastic performance and adjustment, as summarized previously, make a causal contribution to cocaine use? Does the use of marijuana also contribute to cocaine use? Our structural equation modeling assumes these causal patterns; the coefficients are generally consistent with the assumptions, and the fit indicators for the model meet general standards for acceptability. But that certainly does not constitute definitive proof; rather, it is the usual kind of evidence available from correlational analyses—we did not *disprove* our assumptions. Moreover, the fact that cocaine use tends to emerge late in adolescence, if at all, is consistent with the general conclusion that has appeared in previous chapters.

Specifically, we believe that early (and continuing) educational failure is an important contributor to cocaine use. Extending our conclusions from the previous chapter, we consider educational failure and disengagement to be a key component in a syndrome of disruptive and rebellious behaviors that include delinquency, cigarette use, often marijuana use, and sometimes even cocaine use.

Does cocaine use make any contribution of its own to this syndrome? At least at one level, the answer is obviously positive. After all, only relatively few adolescents reach this pinnacle of problem behavior, so cocaine use becomes in one sense a defining characteristic. But the more meaningful questions are: Does cocaine use add to academic problems, and does it impede long-term academic attainment? The answers to those questions, at least as provided by our structural equation model, are a very guarded "Yes and No." The answer "No" refers to the lack of any significant impact of cocaine use on academic attainment at age 22; the total effects are essentially zero. Again, of course, we do not mean to deny the obvious: any adolescent using cocaine heavily and frequently is likely to suffer academically. But such individuals are very rare (and, alas, they tend not to enter or remain in longitudinal survey studies). The answer "Yes" refers to our finding that cocaine use reported at modal age 16 appears to contribute to dropping out of high school. Indeed, for the handful of young men in our panel who used cocaine at all during the year prior to the second survey wave, it appears to have doubled the risk of dropping out. But we remain cautious due to the smaller and nonsignificant cocaine effect among young women, above and beyond the effects attributable to background and earlier scholastic experiences. We are thus not able to reach firm answers to the earlier questions based on the evidence available from our panel analyses. For what it is worth, however, we suspect that there would be clear evidence of negative academic consequences if cocaine use among adolescents were as frequent as marijuana use. Fortunately, it is not.

Chapter 9

How Alcohol Use Is Linked With Educational Success and Failure

Each of the previous chapters has dealt with a substance that is generally disapproved not just for adolescent use, but also for adult use. Although the purchase and use of tobacco is legal for adults, use is severely restricted and widely disapproved because of the attendant health risks to smokers, as well as to others nearby due to second-hand smoke. Marijuana and cocaine are illicit drugs, with possession and sale carrying penalties—sometimes quite severe. At the end of the 20th century, there was little official ambiguity about these substances in the United States—all were seen and continue to be seen as wrong to use, especially if the users are adolescents.

Now the story changes as we turn to alcohol, a substance that has been used and enjoyed by humankind for millennia. Nevertheless, there has been, and continues to be, a great deal of ambiguity in the United States about the use of alcohol. Its sale is legal in most, but not all, counties. Its use is disapproved by some religious groups, but accepted by others. Beer, wine, and hard liquor advertising is permitted and widespread in the electronic media, in sharp contrast to the current situation for cigarettes. Indeed, it is now generally accepted in the medical literature that for most adults the positive effects of moderate alcohol use clearly outweigh the negative effects, provided use does not exceed two drinks per day for men and one drink per day for women (Baum-Baicker, 1985; Klatsky, 1999; Reynolds et al., 2003; U.S. Department of Health and Human Services & U.S. Department of Agriculture, 1995). Use of greater quantities remains widely disapproved because of short-term risks such as accidents as well as long-term risks such as alcoholism and liver damage.

Where do adolescents fit into these relatively complex and nuanced views about the use of alcohol? The official view in the United States, of course, is that no one under the age of 21 should use alcohol. It is illegal for them to buy it, and their use of it on school property is grounds for serious penalties such as suspension. Yet many adolescents frequently see their parents or other adults enjoying the use of alcohol, often with no evident negative consequences. Thus, they can expect, quite reasonably, that they will also come to use and enjoy alcohol as adults. Moreover, they are likely to view alcohol use as a badge of adulthood, and some adolescents may engage in alcohol use as part of what has been called a *premature adulthood syndrome* (Arbeau, Galambos, & Jansson, in press; Newcomb & Bentler, 1988), *pseudomaturity* (Jessor & Jessor, 1977), or *pseudoadulthood* (Greenberger & Steinberg, 1986). To the extent this is true, we might expect that use relatively early in adolescence (e.g., age 14), when it is least typical, might be most likely to be linked with other sorts of problem behaviors.

PLAN FOR THIS CHAPTER

This chapter employs the same analytic approach as previous chapters, beginning with cross-sectional data from the larger Monitoring the Future (MTF) school surveys, then examining regression and multiple classification analyses (MCAs), and concluding with the structural equation model. Whereas chapters 6 to 8 focused on a single dimension of behavior, we focus here on two aspects of alcohol use: frequency of use during the past 30 days (as we did with cigarettes and marijuana), and more risky use—the consumption of five or more drinks in a row in the past 2 weeks, referred to as *occasions of heavy drinking.*

Obviously these two forms of drinking behavior are closely connected because the instances of heavy drinking are included among the overall instances of alcohol use. Nevertheless, it seems important to determine whether the two dimensions of alcohol use show similar patterns of relationship with other factors. For one thing, although some might be tempted to dismiss "having a drink or two" as "no big deal" for an adolescent, it is hard to dismiss five or more drinks in a row as something other than problem behavior—especially when that behavior occurs among adolescents who are likely to be more susceptible to alcohol intoxication than adults. As we show later in this chapter, even as early as eighth grade, fully half of those who reported any drinking in the past 30 days also reported having five or more drinks in a row at least once during the past 2 weeks. So, much of what we report here can properly be termed alcohol misuse.

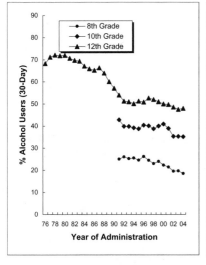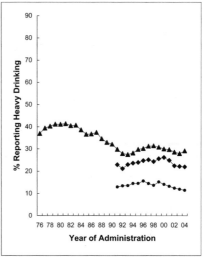

Any Alcohol Use in the Last 30 Days   Any Heavy Drinking in the Last Two Weeks

Data collected from annual national in-school surveys by Monitoring the Future.

Figure 9.1.   Trends in 30-day prevalence of alcohol use and prevalence of five or more drinks in a row during the last 2 weeks for 8th, 10th, and 12th graders.

ALCOHOL USE IN RECENT DECADES

Figure 9.1 shows recent trends in alcohol use based on the MTF cross-sectional surveys of students. Major declines in proportions of 12th graders using alcohol occurred during the 1980s, when many states raised the minimum legal age for purchasing alcohol to 21. In recent years, trends have been much less pronounced and seem unlikely to confound any of the panel analyses reported here. Even after the declines during the 1980s, it still remains true that nearly half of all 12th graders report some consumption of alcohol during the past 30 days, and even among 8th graders the figure is nearly one in five. The rates are distinctly higher for use during the past 12 months; among 12th graders, more than two thirds report some alcohol use, and most of these (52% of the total sample) report having been drunk at least once; among 8th graders, more than one third report some use, and nearly half of these (15% of the total sample) report having been drunk at least once (Johnston et al., 2005b).

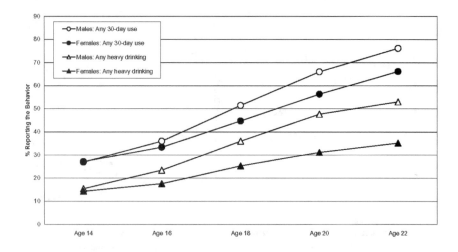

Figure 9.2. Percentage of young people using alcohol in the last 30 days or drinking heavily in the last 2 weeks: males and females.

Figure 9.2 shows that alcohol usage rates for our panel respondents roughly match rates from the cross-sectional surveys shown in the previous figure. Figure 9.2 also shows gender differences that begin by modal age 16 and increase thereafter. The figure further shows that proportions of respondents using alcohol continue to increase after high school (modal age 18, for most), so that by age 22 three quarters of men and two thirds of women report some use of alcohol during the preceding 30 days. More troubling is the finding that most of these young drinkers use large quantities of alcohol at least some of the time. More than half of all men and more than one third of all women at age 22 report having five or more drinks in a row at least once during the preceding 2 weeks, and the frequencies at age 20 are nearly as large.

MAJOR CORRELATES/PREDICTORS OF ADOLESCENT ALCOHOL USE

In this section, we provide multiple classification analyses for both dimensions of alcohol use (see Tables 9.1 and 9.2). We also rely heavily on regression analyses, shown in Table A.9.1 for current alcohol use (i.e., any use in the last 30 days) and in Table A.9.2 for recent instances of heavy drinking (i.e., five or more drinks in a row during the past 2 weeks).

Race/Ethnicity

African-American adolescents report substantially lower than average alcohol use. This holds true in both bivariate and multivariate analyses. A subsequent publication will present further detail on racial/ethnic differences along all of the substance-use dimensions.

Urban Density

Alcohol-use levels are fairly similar across the three categories of urban density.

Parental Education

Among eighth graders, alcohol use in general, as well as instances of heavy drinking, occurs less frequently among those with more highly educated parents. This negative relationship disappears, however, when other factors are controlled in multivariate analyses. Moreover, as adolescents grow older, even the bivariate link with parental education disappears. This may be related to similar shifts in relationships involving college plans and other factors discussed in the following sections.

Presence of Both Parents in the Home

Alcohol use, including instances of heavy drinking, occurs less often among young people who have both parents present in their home. Here again the relationships are reduced somewhat when other factors are included in multivariate analyses, and the links tend to grow weaker as respondents grow from modal ages 14 to 18.

Parental Involvement in Students' Lives

Students whose parents are most involved in their lives are least likely to use alcohol at age 14; that pattern continues into the later teens, but the correlations grow weaker with increasing age. Once again, the coefficients are generally diminished when other factors are included as predictors.

TABLE 9.1a
Multiple Classification Analyses Predicting Percentage Who Report Any
Alcohol Use in the Last 30 Days at Age 18: Males

Grand Mean = 51.4
Effective N = 1361

Variable	Col. 1 Bivariate	Col. 2	Col. 3	Col. 4	Col. 5	Col. 6
		Multivariate				
Race/ethnicity						
African-American	38.5	36.7	35.2	34.9	36.1	36.1
Hispanic	53.0	54.0	53.8	52.9	52.1	52.1
Other race	50.2	50.4	49.9	48.2	48.2	48.2
White	54.2	54.4	54.9	55.5	55.4	55.4
Urban density						
Large MSA	46.4	46.9	46.7	47.1	46.4	46.4
Other MSA	52.9	52.9	53.0	52.9	52.6	52.6
Non-MSA	54.0	53.5	53.6	53.2	54.5	54.5
Parents' education level						
1 (Low)	50.7	48.6	46.9	44.7	45.1	45.2
2	54.3	54.3	54.0	52.0	52.8	52.8
3	51.3	51.5	51.6	51.1	51.2	51.2
4	50.6	51.3	51.7	53.2	53.2	53.2
5 (High)	50.1	50.8	51.8	55.3	53.6	53.6
Lived with 2 parents Waves 1–3						
Yes	49.4	48.8	49.3	50.0	50.1	49.4
No	55.2	56.4	55.4	54.0	54.0	55.2
Parent involvement index						
1 (Low)	54.2	53.3	51.6	50.3	49.2	49.2
2	54.3	53.9	53.7	53.3	52.8	52.8
3	52.6	52.7	52.9	52.8	53.1	53.1
4 (High)	46.2	46.7	47.3	48.3	48.7	48.7
Held back grade 8 or earlier						
Never	50.2		50.8	51.4	50.9	51.0
Once	53.9		52.4	50.5	51.9	51.9
More than once	61.5		58.6	57.4	58.0	57.8
Suspended/expelled grade 8 or earlier						
Never	49.0		48.9	49.7	51.1	51.1
Once	54.8		54.9	52.7	51.0	51.0
More than once	59.5		59.8	58.3	53.3	53.2
Mean secondary school GPA						
D or below	62.4			62.4	49.8	49.7
C- or C	60.5			60.5	55.3	55.2
C+ or B-	54.0			54.0	53.3	53.3
B or B+	50.0			50.0	51.3	51.3
A-	45.8			45.8	49.2	49.2
A	27.4			27.4	34.3	34.3

TABLE 9.1a
Multiple Classification Analyses Predicting Percentage Who Report Any
Alcohol Use in the Last 30 Days at Age 18: Males (*continued*)

Grand Mean = 51.4
Effective *N* = 1361

Variable	Percentage Reporting Any Use of Alcohol in the Last 30 Days					
	Col. 1	Col. 2	Col. 3	Col. 4	Col. 5	Col. 6
	Bivariate			Multivariate		
Mean secondary school college plans						
Definitely won't	59.6			59.6	52.8	52.7
Probably won't	62.1			62.1	57.0	56.9
Probably will	53.5			53.5	51.1	51.1
Definitely will	44.7			44.7	49.5	49.5
Serious scholastic setback W1 to W2						
None	49.5			49.5	50.6	50.6
One	58.1			58.1	54.4	54.4
Two	66.5			66.5	58.0	57.7
Serious scholastic setback W2 to W3						
None	48.9			48.9	50.2	50.2
One	60.8			60.8	56.8	56.8
Two	51.7			51.7	45.8	45.8
Delinquency (W2–3 combined)						
No incidents	32.7				34.2	34.2
1 or 2 incidents	47.3				48.0	48.0
3 or 4 incidents	56.8				57.4	57.4
5 or 6 incidents	62.6				61.2	61.2
7 or 8 incidents	71.2				68.4	68.4
9 to 14 incidents	72.2				68.0	68.0
High school dropout by W3						
Yes	60.8					52.1
No	49.7					51.3
Multiple *R*		.155	.180	.247	.325	.325
R Squared		.024	.032	.061	.106	.106

Factor Summary*

	eta	beta	beta	beta	beta	beta
Race/ethnicity	**.103**	**.116**	**.130**	**.138**	**.129**	**.129**
Urban density	.063	.056	.058	.053	.063	.063
Parents' education level	.029	.034	.042	.063	.056	.056
Lived with 2 parents Waves 1–3	**.056**	**.072**	**.058**	.038	.038	.037
Parent involvement index	**.065**	.058	.051	.042	.040	.040
Held back grade 8 or earlier	.051		.032	.026	.028	.028
Suspended/expelled grade 8 or earlier	**.079**		**.082**	.062	.016	.015
Mean secondary school GPA	**.139**			**.106**	.085	.085
Mean secondary school college plans	**.129**			.060	.052	.051
Serious scholastic setback W1 to W2	**.079**			.062	.035	.034
Serious scholastic setback W2 to W3	**.096**			**.071**	.057	.057
Delinquency (W2–3 combined)	**.253**				**.225**	**.225**
High school dropout by Wave 3	**.080**					.006

*All eta and beta statistics p<.05 are shown in **bold**.

See Table 3.3 for frequency distributions of predictor variables.

Note: W1 = Wave 1 data collection (grade 8, modal age 14), W2 = Wave 2 data collection
(modal age 16), W3 = Wave 3 data collection (modal age 18)

TABLE 9.1b
Multiple Classification Analyses Predicting Percentage Who Report Any Alcohol Use in the Last 30 Days at Age 18: Females

Grand Mean = 44.75
Effective N = 1739

Variable	Col. 1 Bivariate	Col. 2	Col. 3	Col. 4	Col. 5	Col. 6
		Multivariate				
Race/ethnicity						
African-American	29.4	26.8	25.5	24.5	25.4	25.6
Hispanic	42.5	42.2	42.3	41.6	42.3	42.3
Other race	41.7	41.8	41.6	41.1	41.2	41.2
White	49.3	49.9	50.2	50.7	50.3	50.3
Urban density						
Large MSA	48.1	48.7	48.4	47.9	46.6	46.6
Other MSA	44.3	43.9	43.8	43.5	43.8	43.7
Non-MSA	42.0	42.2	42.6	43.6	44.6	44.6
Parents' education level						
1 (Low)	42.5	42.6	42.3	41.7	42.3	42.1
2	44.8	45.7	45.4	45.1	45.1	45.2
3	43.3	43.2	43.2	43.0	42.7	42.7
4	47.1	46.7	47.0	47.5	47.9	48.0
5 (High)	47.1	46.5	46.6	47.9	46.5	46.5
Lived with 2 parents Waves 1–3						
Yes	42.3	41.0	41.3	41.6	41.9	42.0
No	48.3	50.3	49.8	49.3	49.0	48.8
Parent involvement index						
1 (Low)	46.0	45.5	44.8	45.7	45.3	45.3
2	50.9	50.7	50.6	50.6	49.9	49.8
3	43.3	43.1	43.2	43.0	43.2	43.2
4 (High)	40.4	41.1	41.2	41.2	41.9	41.9
Held back grade 8 or earlier						
Never	45.2		45.3	45.3	45.1	45.2
Once	43.3		42.8	42.1	43.3	43.2
More than once	33.0		35.5	37.3	37.6	37.2
Suspended/expelled grade 8 or earlier						
Never	44.1		43.5	43.6	44.0	44.1
Once	44.6		46.9	46.2	44.3	44.2
More than once	54.1		58.9	58.5	54.9	54.5
Mean secondary school GPA						
D or below	58.1			54.1	51.5	50.5
C- or C	43.8			43.1	41.0	40.7
C+ or B-	45.9			46.3	45.3	45.2
B or B+	47.2			47.6	47.8	47.9
A-	41.8			41.2	42.8	42.9
A	36.8			36.3	37.9	38.0

TABLE 9.1b
Multiple Classification Analyses Predicting Percentage Who Report Any Alcohol Use in the Last 30 Days at Age 18: Females (continued)

Grand Mean = 44.75

Effective N = 1739

	Percentage Reporting Any Use of Alcohol in the Last 30 Days					
	Col. 1	Col. 2	Col. 3	Col. 4	Col. 5	Col. 6
Variable	Bivariate			Multivariate		
Mean secondary school college plans						
Definitely won't	35.1			32.0	33.4	32.7
Probably won't	44.7			42.4	41.8	41.2
Probably will	46.4			46.1	45.7	45.7
Definitely will	43.9			44.7	45.1	45.2
Serious scholastic setback W1 to W2						
None	44.5			44.5	45.0	45.1
One	46.6			46.6	43.9	43.5
Two	42.1			41.5	38.7	38.1
Serious scholastic setback W2 to W3						
None	43.7			43.8	44.0	44.1
One	50.3			49.8	48.4	48.3
Two	50.7			50.9	50.5	50.1
Delinquency (W2–3 combined)						
No incidents	46.8				34.4	34.4
1 or 2 incidents	54.8				46.4	46.5
3 or 4 incidents	59.3				53.6	53.6
5 or 6 incidents	62.0				58.5	58.4
7 or 8 incidents	65.2				62.5	62.4
9 to 14 incidents					62.6	62.6
High school dropout at W3						
Yes	50.1					47.2
No	43.8					44.3
Multiple R		.190	.204	.225	.281	.282
R Squared		.036	.042	.051	.079	.079

Factor Summary*

	eta	beta	beta	beta	beta	beta
Race/ethnicity	**.137**	**.158**	**.170**	**.181**	**.172**	.170
Urban density	.046	.050	.046	.039	.024	.024
Parents' education level	.038	.034	.037	.047	.044	.046
Lived with 2 parents Waves 1–3	**.059**	**.092**	**.085**	**.076**	**.070**	**.067**
Parent involvement index	**.077**	**.073**	.071	.072	.062	.061
Held back grade 8 or earlier	.032		.029	.030	.022	.023
Suspended/expelled grade 8 or earlier	**.049**		**.077**	**.074**	.054	.051
Mean secondary school GPA	**.064**			.070	.061	.061
Mean secondary school college plans	.035			.041	.038	.042
Serious scholastic setback W1 to W2	.016			.017	.017	.019
Serious scholastic setback W2 to W3	**.049**			.045	.034	.032
Delinquency (W2–3 combined)	**.195**				**.178**	**.178**
High school dropout by Wave 3	.045					.021

*All eta and beta statistics p<.05 are shown in **bold**.

See Table 3.3 for frequency distributions of predictor variables.

Note: W1 = Wave 1 data collection (grade 8, modal age 14), W2 = Wave 2 data collection (modal age 16), W3 = Wave 3 data collection (modal age 18)

TABLE 9.2a

Multiple Classification Analyses Predicting Percentage Who Report Any Heavy Drinking in the Last Two Weeks at Age 18: Males

Grand Mean = 36.0
Effective *N* = 1361

	Percentage Reporting Heavy Drinking in the Last Two Weeks					
	Col. 1	Col. 2	Col. 3	Col. 4	Col. 5	Col. 6
Variable	Bivariate			Multivariate		
Race/ethnicity						
African-American	27.4	26.4	25.2	25.0	26.4	26.3
Hispanic	38.2	38.9	38.7	37.8	36.9	36.8
Other race	35.2	35.5	35.0	33.8	33.8	33.8
White	37.7	37.7	38.1	38.6	38.4	38.5
Urban density						
Large MSA	31.7	31.7	31.7	32.0	31.4	31.5
Other MSA	36.6	36.6	36.7	36.6	36.3	36.3
Non-MSA	39.4	39.2	39.1	38.9	40.0	40.0
Parents' education level						
1 (Low)	36.8	34.5	33.1	31.6	32.0	32.1
2	35.6	35.5	35.2	33.9	34.7	34.7
3	37.8	38.1	38.2	37.8	37.9	37.8
4	34.0	34.6	35.1	36.1	36.0	36.0
5 (High)	35.9	36.9	37.8	40.2	38.7	38.6
Lived with 2 parents Waves 1–3						
Yes	34.4	34.0	34.4	35.0	35.0	35.1
No	39.1	39.7	38.9	37.9	37.9	37.7
Parent involvement index						
1 (Low)	38.2	37.4	35.9	35.1	34.0	34.0
2	39.0	38.7	38.5	38.2	37.7	37.8
3	36.3	36.3	36.5	36.4	36.7	36.7
4 (High)	32.2	32.7	33.1	33.8	34.2	34.2
Held back grade 8 or earlier						
Never	34.7		35.0	35.3	35.0	35.1
Once	38.4		37.6	36.3	37.5	37.2
More than once	49.0		46.7	46.5	47.0	46.1
Suspended/expelled grade 8 or earlier						
Never	34.5		34.7	35.2	36.5	36.7
Once	36.8		36.6	35.1	33.5	33.4
More than once	42.1		41.5	40.5	35.7	35.2
Mean secondary school GPA						
D or below	41.9			34.4	31.8	30.8
C- or C	43.5			40.2	38.9	38.6
C+ or B-	37.3			36.7	36.6	36.7
B or B+	35.2			36.4	36.2	36.4
A-	32.5			34.7	35.6	35.6
A	17.5			19.8	23.9	23.9

TABLE 9.2a
Multiple Classification Analyses Predicting Percentage Who Report Any
Heavy Drinking in the Last Two Weeks at Age 18: Males (*continued*)

Grand Mean = 36.0

Effective N = 1361

	Percentage Reporting Heavy Drinking in the Last Two Weeks					
	Col. 1	Col. 2	Col. 3	Col. 4	Col. 5	Col. 6
Variable	Bivariate	Multivariate				
Mean secondary school college plans						
Definitely won't	38.9			34.0	33.6	33.1
Probably won't	44.4			39.9	40.0	39.6
Probably will	37.8			37.0	36.1	36.1
Definitely will	30.9			33.8	34.6	34.8
Serious scholastic setback W1 to W2						
None	34.7			34.9	35.6	35.7
One	40.3			39.6	37.2	37.0
Two	49.2			46.4	41.7	40.3
Serious scholastic setback W2 to W3						
None	33.9			34.4	34.9	34.9
One	43.5			41.9	40.4	40.4
Two	38.5			35.8	33.5	33.1
Delinquency (W2–3 combined)						
No incidents	20.8				21.5	21.5
1 or 2 incidents	31.4				31.7	31.8
3 or 4 incidents	38.6				39.1	39.1
5 or 6 incidents	48.8				48.0	48.0
7 or 8 incidents	53.7				52.1	52.1
9 to 14 incidents	55.4				53.1	53.0
High school dropout at W3						
Yes	45.6					39.4
No	34.2					35.4
Multiple R		.122	.144	.198	.284	.285
R Squared		.015	.021	.039	.081	.082

Factor Summary*

	eta	beta	beta	beta	beta	beta
Race/ethnicity	**.071**	**.079**	**.090**	**.095**	**.085**	**.085**
Urban density	**.060**	.059	.058	.055	.066	.066
Parents' education level	.029	.031	.038	.055	.045	.044
Lived with 2 parents Waves 1–3	.047	**.056**	.045	.029	.028	.025
Parent involvement index	**.054**	.046	.041	.033	.031	.031
Held back grade 8 or earlier	**.064**		.051	.046	.052	.047
Suspended/expelled grade 8 or earlier	**.057**		.051	.041	.021	.024
Mean secondary school GPA	**.109**			.082	.062	.061
Mean secondary school college plans	**.102**			.047	.040	.036
Serious scholastic setback W1 to W2	**.060**			.049	.021	.017
Serious scholastic setback W2 to W3	**.081**			.062	.047	.047
Delinquency (W2–3 combined)	**.234**				**.218**	**.217**
High school dropout by Wave 3	**.086**					.031

*All eta and beta statistics p<.05 are shown in **bold**.

See Table 3.3 for frequency distributions of predictor variables.

Note: W1 = Wave 1 data collection (grade 8, modal age 14), W2 = Wave 2 data collection
(modal age 16), W3 = Wave 3 data collection (modal age 18)

TABLE 9.2b
Multiple Classification Analyses Predicting Percentage Who Report Any Heavy Drinking in the Last Two Weeks at Age 18: Females

Grand Mean = 25.3
Effective *N* = 1739

Variable	Col. 1 Bivariate	Col. 2	Col. 3	Col. 4	Col. 5	Col. 6
		Multivariate				
Race/ethnicity						
African-American	17.0	15.0	13.6	13.0	14.0	14.0
Hispanic	25.5	24.5	24.5	23.9	24.5	24.5
Other race	23.4	23.2	23.0	22.3	22.1	22.1
White	27.6	28.2	28.6	29.0	28.7	28.7
Urban density						
Large MSA	25.0	25.3	25.3	24.9	23.7	23.7
Other MSA	25.8	25.7	25.6	25.3	25.4	25.4
Non-MSA	24.6	24.6	24.9	25.8	26.8	26.8
Parents' education level						
1 (Low)	27.2	26.6	26.1	25.0	25.5	25.5
2	24.2	24.5	24.3	23.7	23.6	23.6
3	25.7	25.6	25.7	25.5	25.2	25.2
4	22.9	23.0	23.3	24.1	24.5	24.5
5 (High)	27.8	28.3	28.6	30.4	29.3	29.3
Lived with 2 parents Waves 1–3						
Yes	22.8	22.2	22.5	23.0	23.1	23.1
No	29.0	29.9	29.5	28.7	28.5	28.5
Parent involvement index						
1 (Low)	28.8	27.4	26.8	27.1	26.7	26.7
2	30.1	29.9	29.7	29.6	29.1	29.1
3	23.7	23.8	23.9	23.9	24.0	24.0
4 (High)	21.7	22.4	22.6	22.5	23.1	23.1
Held back grade 8 or earlier						
Never	25.0		25.2	25.5	25.3	25.3
Once	26.6		25.3	23.8	24.9	24.9
More than once	29.2		28.4	27.8	27.9	27.9
Suspended/expelled grade 8 or earlier						
Never	24.5		24.4	24.6	25.1	25.1
Once	27.2		27.4	26.0	24.0	24.0
More than once	33.9		35.0	33.6	30.0	30.0
Mean secondary school GPA						
D or below	40.7			36.8	34.1	34.2
C- or C	29.6			28.0	26.1	26.1
C+ or B-	28.1			28.1	27.2	27.2
B or B+	26.7			27.1	27.4	27.4
A-	19.1			19.2	20.6	20.6
A	16.7			17.1	18.4	18.4

TABLE 9.2b

Multiple Classification Analyses Predicting Percentage Who Report Any Heavy Drinking in the Last Two Weeks at Age 18: Females (*continued*)

Grand Mean = 25.3

	Percentage Reporting Heavy Drinking in the Last Two Weeks					
Effective *N* = 1739	Col. 1	Col. 2	Col. 3	Col. 4	Col. 5	Col. 6
Variable	Bivariate	Multivariate				
Mean secondary school college plans						
Definitely won't	25.4			19.2	20.1	20.1
Probably won't	28.5			24.3	23.6	23.6
Probably will	27.3			26.2	25.8	25.8
Definitely will	23.3			25.1	25.5	25.5
Serious scholastic setback W1 to W2						
None	25.0			25.4	25.8	25.8
One	27.3			25.1	22.3	22.4
Two	27.3			24.8	22.8	22.9
Serious scholastic setback W2 to W3						
None	24.1			24.3	24.6	24.5
One	32.0			30.5	29.2	29.2
Two	31.5			30.5	30.5	30.6
Delinquency (W2–3 combined)						
No incidents	16.5				17.4	17.4
1 or 2 incidents	25.6				25.6	25.6
3 or 4 incidents	32.4				31.2	31.2
5 or 6 incidents	39.0				37.6	37.6
7 or 8 incidents	45.2				44.4	44.4
9 to 14 incidents	58.4				56.8	56.8
High school dropout at W3						
Yes	31.1					25.1
No	24.3					25.3
Multiple *R*		.147	.158	.192	.256	.256
R Squared		.021	.025	.037	.065	.065

Factor Summary*

	eta	beta	beta	beta	beta	beta
Race/ethnicity	**.084**	**.104**	**.118**	**.127**	**.118**	**.118**
Urban density	.012	.010	.006	.008	.026	.026
Parents' education level	.040	.038	.037	.047	.038	.038
Lived with 2 parents Waves 1–3	**.071**	**.087**	**.079**	**.065**	**.061**	**.061**
Parent involvement index	**.076**	.067	.063	.063	.054	.054
Held back grade 8 or earlier	.017		.009	.016	.008	.008
Suspended/expelled grade 8 or earlier	**.055**		**.061**	.051	.029	.029
Mean secondary school GPA	**.100**			**.096**	.076	.076
Mean secondary school college plans	**.049**			.023	.022	.021
Serious scholastic setback W1 to W2	.019			.003	.028	.028
Serious scholastic setback W2 to W3	**.066**			.051	.040	.040
Delinquency (W2–3 combined)	**.198**				**.181**	**.181**
High school dropout by Wave 3	.055					.002

*All eta and beta statistics p<.05 are shown in **bold**.

See Table 3.3 for frequency distributions of predictor variables.

Note: W1 = Wave 1 data collection (grade 8, modal age 14), W2 = Wave 2 data collection (modal age 16), W3 = Wave 3 data collection (modal age 18)

Grade Retention, and Suspension or Expulsion, by End of Eighth Grade

Tables A.9.1 and A.9.2 show that eighth graders who were previously held back one or more grades in school are more likely to use alcohol and to report instances of heavy drinking, but again the correlations are weaker for drinking at later ages. Turning to suspension or expulsion prior to the end of eighth grade, we see even stronger links with 30-day alcohol use and instances of heavy drinking. The bivariate correlations with the alcohol-use measures at eighth grade range from .23 to .29; however, correlations with alcohol-use measures 4 years later (modal age 18) are much smaller, ranging from .04 to .07. All of these relationships are diminished when other factors are included as predictors. Tables 9.1 and 9.2 show that, among those who had been suspended or expelled more than once prior to the end of eighth grade, rates of 30-day alcohol use and instances of heavy drinking at modal age 18 are 6 to 9 percentage points above the overall averages. Here again most of these differences are reduced when other factors are controlled.

Delinquent Behavior

Delinquency and alcohol use seem to go hand in hand, as can be seen clearly in Tables A.9.1 and A.9.2. The unadjusted correlations between the alcohol-use measures and delinquency (reported for the previous 12 months) range from .31 to .39 at eighth grade. Four years later, the relationships are still substantial, ranging from .20 to .27. Multivariate controls for other factors reduce, but by no means eliminate, these connections between drinking and delinquency. Some of the delinquency–alcohol links are shown in greater detail in Tables 9.1 and 9.2. By age 18, those with the highest rates of delinquency during their mid-teens are two to three times as likely to be drinkers, and occasional heavy drinkers, compared with the least delinquent. Controls for background characteristics and measures of scholastic success or failure have almost no effect on these strong relationships.

Grade Point Average

As shown in Tables A.9.1 and A.9.2, students with poor grades are somewhat more likely than average to drink and occasionally drink heavily. Drinking is not as strongly correlated with GPA as it is with delinquency, and the relationships are sharply reduced or disappear when other factors are controlled. Nevertheless, Tables 9.1 and 9.2 show that at the extremes of GPA there are some important differences in alcohol use. For example, at modal age 18, instances of heavy drinking are reported by only about 17% of those who were straight-A students throughout high school, compared with roughly twice as many of the C or lower students (43% for males, 30% for females). Even after controlling for other factors, the students with the lowest grades are about half again as likely as the top students to be occasional heavy drinkers.

College Plans

Tables A.9.1 and A.9.2 show that alcohol use is related to college plans in much the same way as it is related to grades. At the end of eighth grade, those expecting to complete college are less likely than average to drink or drink heavily. By modal age 18 (the end of high school for most), the relationships are weaker among young men and essentially zero among young women. All of these bivariate relationships are sharply reduced or eliminated when other factors are included in multivariate analyses.

Serious Scholastic Setbacks During High School (After Eighth Grade)

As can be seen most clearly in Tables 9.1 and 9.2, those who were held back, suspended, or expelled during high school are generally more likely than average to be alcohol users at modal age 18.[1] The multivariate analyses suggest considerable overlap with other predictors.

Dropping Out of High School by Age 18

Those who have dropped out of high school by modal age 18 are somewhat more likely than average to be alcohol users and occasional heavy drinkers, especially among young men (shown most clearly in Tables 9.1–9.2). The multivariate analyses, however, show that these relationships overlap almost entirely with other predictors.

---

[1]The one exception is that, for young women, such setbacks between Grades 8 and 10 were not associated with higher alcohol use.

A more interesting finding, shown by the bivariate correlations in Tables A.9.1 and A.9.2, is that dropping out is correlated most strongly with alcohol use at modal age 14 and least strongly with alcohol use at modal age 18. In other words, precocious alcohol use is one of the *predictors* of dropping out. However, the multivariate analyses in Tables A.9.1 and A.9.2 show that the links between dropping out and alcohol use are reduced substantially in the presence of other predictors. The structural equation model findings, reported later in this chapter, also indicate no separate contribution of early alcohol use to dropping out. In sum, it appears that early alcohol use has relatively little *causal* impact on dropping out; rather, it is a *predictor* because of its correlation with other more fundamental causes.

ADDITIONAL CORRELATES/PREDICTORS OF ADOLESCENT ALCOHOL USE

Various Problem Behaviors

Earlier chapters revealed that students who misbehave in school (cutting classes, skipping days, or getting sent to the office) are also more likely than average to be users of cigarettes, marijuana, and cocaine. Tables A.9.1 and A.9.2 show that such individuals are also more likely to use alcohol. These correlations are strongest at modal age 14 and drop off appreciably by modal age 18, especially among young women. As with other substances, the multivariate analyses show that there is a substantial overlap between these school-related behaviors and other problem behaviors as predictors of alcohol use.

Evenings Out for Fun and Recreation

Not surprisingly, evenings out for fun and recreation are positively correlated with both measures of alcohol use (see Tables A.9.1 and A.9.2). Here, in contrast to the school-related problem behaviors noted previously, the strength of correlation generally increases from modal ages 14 to 18. It is also notable that, by age 18, a good deal of the relationship remains after other factors are controlled in multivariate analyses. We showed in earlier reports that evenings out are an important mediating factor in accounting for alcohol use among young adults (Bachman et al., 2002), and the present findings indicate the same is likely the case for late adolescents. As we proposed with other substances, some of this relation is likely due to adolescents' decisions to spend evenings away from home so that they can drink.

Actual and Preferred Work Hours

Eighth-grade students who work long hours during the school year are more likely than average to use alcohol and use it heavily, and the same is true for those who *prefer* to work long hours (see Tables A.9.1 and A.9.2). On the whole, these bivariate relationships tend to grow smaller with increasing age, but many of them remain statistically significant. Multivariate analyses reduce most of these coefficients to near zero, suggesting that there is little or no causal connection between part-time work during the school year and alcohol use.

Religious Attendance and Importance

Religious attendance and importance are negatively correlated with both dimensions of alcohol use at modal ages 14 to 18, as shown in Tables A.9.1 and A.9.2. Virtually all of the correlations are statistically significant, but all are modest in size. However, the multivariate coefficients are generally quite small and often near zero.[2] It thus appears again that any protective effects of religiosity are probably indirect via other factors.

Self-Esteem

Correlations between the self-esteem and alcohol-use measures are negative and generally modest, with multivariate coefficients mostly approaching zero (see Tables A.9.1 and A.9.2). It may be of interest that the strongest correlations between self-esteem and alcohol use are evident at modal age 14, and at that age the relations are somewhat more pronounced for girls ($r = -.17$ for 30-day use, $r = -.15$ for the 2-week measure of heavy drinking) compared with boys (corresponding r values $= -.12$ and $-.10$). The multivariate coefficients are all nonsignificant, indicating large overlaps with other factors—most likely those having to do with educational success or failure.

---

[2]Only 4 out of 72 multivariate coefficients reach the .05 significance threshold (with one of them positive rather than negative)—not much different from what would be expected by chance.

THE PATTERN OF WEAKER CORRELATIONS
WITH INCREASING AGE

Tables A.9.1 and A.9.2 reveal a number of instances in which links with alcohol use tend to decline as adolescents move from modal ages 14 to 18. These links involve direct or indirect indicators of academic success or failure, such as college plans or various misbehaviors in school, as well as background factors that contribute to longer term academic attainment, such as parental education and having both parents present in the home. This pattern of declining correlations is evident for both genders, but tends to be more pronounced among young women. The pattern has interesting implications for our structural equation model findings presented later, and we discuss it further at the end of the chapter. For now, however, let us suggest that in addition to the idea that alcohol use becomes more normative for all young people as they progress through high school (thus, previous protective factors tend to lose their power), there is a further explanation that is more specific to the college-bound.

High school students tend to associate most frequently with their agemates, but they also associate with young people a few years younger and older. Importantly, the slightly older friends and siblings are often role models. It is also the case that students heading toward college tend to associate with college-bound friends, or with older friends and siblings who already attend college. As we have shown elsewhere (Bachman et al., 1997), the living arrangements associated with college attendance (being unmarried and often living away from parents) contribute to substantial increases in alcohol use and instances of heavy drinking. The shifting correlations we have observed in Tables A.9.1 and A.9.2 may reflect a sort of anticipatory process, in which those headed for college begin to take on the alcohol-consuming behaviors of their older friends and siblings, many of whom are already part of the college scene. Moreover, the gender differences we observed may result from the tendency for some young women in their last year or two of high school to date college men.

This pattern of findings for alcohol use differs from those for other forms of substance use. In particular, it stands in sharp contrast to the findings for cigarette use. We return to this phenomenon in our final section, after first considering how it plays out in our structural model.

STRUCTURAL EQUATION MODEL: ACADEMIC
ATTAINMENT AND ALCOHOL USE

Two structural equation models are necessary for this chapter, because the two measures of alcohol use are so highly correlated that we preferred not to treat them simultaneously in one model (such high correlations can sometimes cause identification problems, contributing to what can be viewed as misspecified models). The model used for chapters 6 to 8 includes the measure of alcohol use during the past 30 days, and that model is the focus of most of our attention in this chapter. A second model, presented in Figure A.9.1 in the appendix, is identical to the first (Fig. 9.3) in all respects except that it uses the measure of five or more drinks during the past 2 weeks in place of the 30-day alcohol-use measure. The results for the two dimensions of alcohol use are highly similar.

As is the case for all of the other forms of substance use, we treat delinquency as a potential cause of alcohol use measured at the same survey wave. It should be recalled that the delinquency measure covers the 12-month interval prior to each survey, whereas the alcohol measure covers the prior 30 days—or 2 weeks, for instances of heavy drinking. We opted not to impose any causal ordering between alcohol use and the other forms of substance use, and instead simply permitted the disturbance terms to correlate within wave. We consider this a more parsimonious approach, given that preliminary analyses failed to reveal any clear causal ordering between alcohol use and use of the other substances, and the measures of fit indicate that the lack of such causal connections does not result in serious distortions. Figure 9.2 presents the model that includes drinking during the previous 30 days, and key results are presented in Table 9.3; as noted previously, it is the same model used in chapters 6 to 8, but this time we have highlighted that portion of the findings concerning alcohol use. Additional findings for the total model are provided in the appendix in Tables A.3.3 to A.3.10, as are findings for the alternate version of the model that includes instances of heavy drinking.

Structural Model Findings

The effects of exogenous factors in the structural model are generally consistent with the findings reported earlier in the chapter based on regression analyses and MCAs. Among the more noteworthy findings from the structural model are modest direct effects and strong total effects of suspension or expulsion prior to eighth grade, indicating that it is a risk factor for alcohol use at modal age 14. Total effects on 30-day alcohol use appear to be a bit stronger for girls (.26) than boys (.19), and the effects as well as the gender differences are larger for instances of heavy drinking (.36 for girls, .25 for boys). The impacts of early suspension or expulsion grow much weaker over time, but remain statistically significant at modal ages 16 and 18. Another finding is that

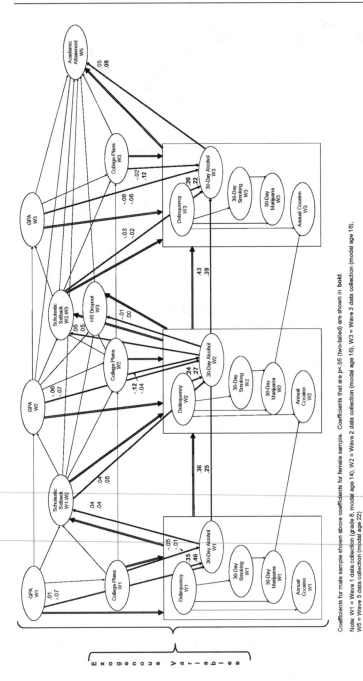

Coefficients for male sample shown above coefficients for female sample. Coefficients that are p<.05 (two-tailed) are shown in **bold**.

Note: W1 = Wave 1 data collection (grade 8, modal age 14), W2 = Wave 2 data collection (modal age 16), W3 = Wave 3 data collection (modal age 18), W5 = Wave 5 data collection (modal age 22)

Model Fit Statistics

	Males	Females
Comparative Fit Index (CFI)	.996	.995
Root Mean-Square Error of Approximation (RMSEA)	.023	.027
Chi-Square	549	712
Degrees of Freedom	316	316

Figure 9.3. Structural equation model of academic attainment and substance use, focusing on 30-day alcohol use.

TABLE 9.3
Direct and Total Effects of Predictors on 30-Day Alcohol Use at Wave 1, Wave 2, and Wave 3*

Predictors	30-Day Alcohol Wave 1 Males Direct	Males Total	Females Direct	Females Total	30-Day Alcohol Wave 2 Males Direct	Males Total	Females Direct	Females Total	30-Day Alcohol Wave 3 Males Direct	Males Total	Females Direct	Females Total
African-American	-.027	-.048	-.083	-.101	-.048	-.085	-.091	-.126	-.100	-.142	-.153	-.198
Hispanic	-.009	.000	.036	.050	-.003	-.004	-.005	.002	-.029	-.028	-.041	-.040
Other race	-.008	-.012	-.005	.026	-.071	-.068	-.061	-.036	-.025	-.040	-.076	-.089
Large MSA	-.039	-.024	-.010	-.010	-.017	-.022	-.015	.000	-.063	-.067	.009	.039
Non-MSA	.001	-.004	.000	-.036	.075	.070	.044	.013	-.016	.004	.018	-.001
Parents' education level	.016	.005	.036	-.008	.042	.014	.035	-.009	.022	.014	.056	.071
Lived with 2 parents Waves 1–3	.014	.009	-.029	-.071	-.043	-.061	-.043	-.098	-.030	-.064	-.051	-.084
Parent involvement index	-.191	-.263	-.125	-.207	-.044	-.198	.024	-.072	.043	-.059	-.070	-.105
Held back grade 8 or earlier	.075	.104	-.002	.011		.068		.021		.043		.012
Suspended/expelled grade 8 or earlier	.060	.189	.111	.262		.121		.114		.084		.059
GPA Wave 1	.008	-.064	-.074	-.160		-.157		-.175		-.133		-.104
GPA Wave 2					-.055	-.119	-.067	-.119		-.124		-.093
GPA Wave 3									-.056		-.058	-.060
College plans Wave 1	-.045	-.058	-.011	-.053		-.082		-.050		-.045		.002
College plans Wave 2					-.119	-.128	-.039	-.049		-.070		.038
College plans Wave 3									-.018	-.017	.124	.117
Serious scholastic setbacks W1 to W2					.042	.085	.053	.100		.059		.050
Serious scholastic setbacks W2 to W3									-.028	.003	-.019	-.007
Delinquency Wave 1	.345	.345	.462	.462		.231		.229		.162		.130
Delinquency Wave 2					.240	.240	.272	.272		.253		.212
Delinquency Wave 3									.260	.260	.215	.215
30-day cigarette smoking Wave 1						.002		.005		.002		.002
30-day cigarette smoking Wave 2										.000		-.001
30-day cigarette smoking Wave 3												
30-day marijuana Wave 1						-.003		.009		-.002		.005
30-day marijuana Wave 2										.000		.000
30-day marijuana Wave 3												
Annual cocaine Wave 1						-.003		-.010		-.002		-.005
Annual cocaine Wave 2										.000		.000
Annual cocaine Wave 3												
30-day alcohol Wave 1					.364	.367	.251	.255		.157		.099
30-day alcohol Wave 2									.426	.427	.387	.387
30-day alcohol Wave 3												

Direct and Total Effects of 30-Day Alcohol Use at Wave 1, Wave 2, and Wave 3 on Education Factors*

Predictors		GPA Wave 2 Total	College Plans Wave 2 Total	Serious Scholastic Setback W1 to W2 Direct	Total	GPA Wave 3 Total	College Plans Wave 3 Total	Serious Scholastic Setback W2 to W3 Direct	Total	High School Dropout Wave 3 Direct	Total	Academic Attainment Wave 5 Direct	Total
30-day alcohol Wave 1	Males	-.004	-.003	.036	.036	-.005	-.004		.023		.002		.003
	Females	-.002	-.005	.043	.043	-.002	-.004		.014		.008		.003
30-day alcohol Wave 2	Males					-.006	-.005	.061	.061	-.010	-.010		.019
	Females					-.003	-.003	.052	.052	.004	.004		.027
30-day alcohol Wave 3	Males											.054	.054
	Females											.080	.080

*Coefficients that are p<.05 (two-tailed) are shown in bold.

Note: W1 = Wave 1 data collection (grade 8, modal age 14), W2 = Wave 2 data collection (modal age 16), W3 = Wave 3 data collection (modal age 18)

early parental involvement and supervision has protective effects against 30-day alcohol use and instances of heavy drinking that are fairly strong at age 14 (total effects range from −.14 to −.21), and decline thereafter.

Both dimensions of alcohol use show moderate stability between modal ages 14 and 16, and higher stability between modal ages 16 and 18.[3] Comparing across substances, it appears that during the earlier age 14 to 16 interval alcohol use is less stable than cigarette use, but more stable than illicit drug use; across the later age 16 to 18 interval the differences in stability are less pronounced.

Early delinquency is a strong predictor of early alcohol use (direct effects range from .33–.46, across genders and dimensions of use). Early delinquency also shows important indirect effects on later alcohol use (see Tables 9.3 and A.9.3). Later delinquency also has significant direct effects on later alcohol use. Overall, this pattern of findings seems quite consistent with our interpretation that delinquency is a relatively early-emerging aspect of a problem behavior syndrome.

What about any protective effects of grades and college plans against alcohol use during adolescence? We noted earlier in the chapter that alcohol use at age 14 is lower than average among those with good grades and high college aspirations, but that such relationships are greatly reduced when other factors are included in multivariate analyses. The structural model findings support these earlier observations by showing that much of any effects of grades and college plans are indirect via other factors (notably delinquency).

Scholastic setbacks between ages 14 and 16 appear to be risk factors, again largely indirectly.[4] Scholastic setbacks between ages 16 and 18 show no significant effects, direct or indirect, on either measure of alcohol use.

Now let us consider what the model findings suggest about whether adolescent alcohol use has negative effects on later academic outcomes.

---

[3]It should be recalled that stability coefficients include adjustments to correct for measurement error, and these adjustments are larger for the alcohol-use measure than for the cigarette-use measure. For instances of heavy drinking, in particular, the 2-week reporting interval contributes to error—quite apart from any errors in recall. As also pointed out in earlier chapters, the adjustments in the structural equation models are designed to correct all such measurement errors, thereby providing a truer representation of cross-time stability in *general tendencies* to use each substance.

[4]As can be seen in the figures, the direct effect estimates all fall short of statistical significance, and some are near zero. Most total effects reach significance, although they are relatively small. The small size of the coefficients reflects, at least in part, the fact that only small proportions of respondents experience these significant scholastic setbacks after eighth grade.

First, we note that the figures show no significant direct effects of alcohol use on scholastic setbacks or dropping out, nor does the accompanying tabular data show any significant total effects on setbacks, dropping out, grades, or college plans. The only statistically significant effects of adolescent alcohol use on an academic outcome, as shown in the model, involve academic attainment at age 22; they reach significance only for young women and, most notably, they are in the "wrong" direction. Specifically, Figure 9.2 shows positive coefficients of .05 for males and .08 for females between 30-day alcohol use at age 18 and academic attainment. In other words, once we take account of background, earlier academic experiences, and delinquency, young women who drink more at the end of high school are headed toward slightly higher academic attainment by age 22. This does not come as a complete surprise given some of the findings reported earlier in this chapter (Schulenberg et al., 1994), but it does call for further discussion, and we turn to that at the end of the next section.

SUMMARY AND CONCLUSIONS

This chapter has dealt with one of the most widely used substances in the United States for centuries and in the world for millennia. Of all the substances considered in this volume, alcohol is by far the most widely used by adolescents and young adults in the contemporary United States. Nearly one third of eighth graders report use during the preceding year; by the time they reach age 18, nearly three quarters report having used it during the preceding year, and half the young men and nearly as many young women report use during the preceding 30 days.

Far more serious is the fact that, by age 18, more than one third of young men and fully one quarter of young women report having had five or more drinks in a row on at least one occasion during the preceding 2 weeks, as shown in Figure 9.2. The figure also shows that, by the time they reach age 22, when it is legal for them to purchase alcohol, the proportions reporting occasions of heavy drinking increase to more than half of the men and more than one third of the women. So although alcohol use in moderation (one or two drinks per day) may be a boon to most adults, it is clear that many adolescents and young adults on some occasions consume far more than that, with all the accompanying risks of accidents and long-term health consequences.

Alcohol use was even higher among high school seniors during the early 1980s, as shown in Figure 9.1. A variety of factors led to subsequent declines, including greater attention given to the risks of drunk driving and, probably more important, the widespread change to age 21 as the minimum age for legal purchase (O'Malley & Wagenaar, 1991).

We found differences, of course, between our measure of current alcohol use (total instances of any use during the preceding 30 days) and our measure of occasional heavy drinking (instances of five or more drinks in a row during the preceding 2 weeks). There are some adolescents who use alcohol without indulging in five or more drinks in a row (at least during the preceding 2 weeks), and this is particularly true among 14-year-olds. Nevertheless, the two measures show closely parallel relationships with other factors, such that we can summarize our findings for alcohol use mostly in general terms referring to both of the use dimensions.

Early alcohol use is clearly correlated with other problem behaviors, most notably delinquency and misbehaviors in school. It is also negatively correlated with grades and college plans, although here the relationships grow considerably weaker as adolescents move from modal ages 14 to 18. The multivariate analyses suggest that the effects of grades and college plans are mostly indirect via delinquent behaviors. So our findings suggest that doing well in school does offer some protection against alcohol use during early adolescence; however, a few years later any such effects are diminished, especially among young women.

We suggested earlier that this pattern of weakening correlations with age arises because of a competing influence, an influence that is especially strong among young people headed for college. Of course, this is in the context of the overall increased normativeness of alcohol use during high school, such that earlier protective factors start losing their power during the later years of high school. Young people sometimes associate with others who are a few years older (friends, siblings, and friends of siblings). Such older individuals can serve as role models, and they can also be sources of alcohol—especially if they are old enough to purchase alcohol legally. Although our survey did not measure it, we think it is safe to assume that young people headed for college are more likely than their non-college-bound peers to associate with others who are already in college. College students, especially those living away from their parents' homes, are more likely than average to use alcohol and sometimes use it heavily. So college-bound students, while still in high school, might be expected to anticipate the increases in alcohol use that are often part of the college lifestyle. (This process has been called *anticipatory socialization* and has been invoked in studies of high school marijuana use [Mauss, 1969] and medical students [Becker, Hughes, Geer, & Strauss, 1961; Schulenberg & Maggs, 2002].) In addition, because some young women in high school date college men several years older than they, we could expect this precocious shift toward college drinking patterns to be more pronounced among the women. Our panel findings clearly match these expectations, as can be seen by returning to Figure 1.4 presented in chapter 1.

Figure 1.4 shows age 14 to 22 trend lines in proportions reporting any instances of heavy drinking in the past 2 weeks. The figure distinguishes four levels of educational attainment reached by age 22: those with no high school diploma or only a GED, those with a high school diploma but no college, those with 1 or 2 years of college, and those with 3 or more years of college.[5] Turning first to the young women, we see the striking cross-over in relationships between alcohol use and academic attainment; those headed for 3 or more years of college were least likely to use alcohol at age 14, but by ages 20 and 22 they were the most likely. In contrast, the young women destined to become dropouts were most likely to be alcohol users at ages 14 and 16. Among young men, the cross-over appears a bit later; at ages 14 through 18, those destined to complete 3 or more years of college were least likely to use alcohol, and those who become dropouts were most likely to be users, but by ages 20 and 22, the college students had caught up to (or slightly surpassed) their age-mates.

The question arises as to whether the positive relationship between educational attainment and alcohol use, evident at age 22, is maintained or even enlarged after the college years; the answer as shown in Figure 1.4 is clearly negative. Although our adolescent panel data do not extend far enough to provide that answer, the MTF panels that began with high school seniors now extend well into adulthood. In other analyses of these MTF panels (Bachman et al., 1997), we found that substance use in general, including 30-day alcohol use and especially instances of heavy drinking, seems to respond primarily to the respondents' *current* environments, rather than their environments a few years earlier. In other words, it appears that the alcohol excesses associated with the college lifestyle do not have long-term impacts on the large majority—they seem to outgrow it when they take on adult responsibilities such as marriage and parenthood. But that sanguine conclusion does not, of course, take account of the small proportion whose lives are ended or permanently altered by accidents or health complications caused by alcohol abuse.

We conclude, then, that educational success makes some contribution as a protective factor against alcohol use during early adolescence, just as educational failures and setbacks act as risk factors. To put it another way, it

---

[5]Recall that these four categories are a collapsed version of the eight-category measure of educational attainment used throughout this volume. We adopted this simplified (and much easier to read) version only after first examining similar figures using the full eight categories.

appears that early alcohol use is part of the syndrome of problem behavior. Over the longer term, however, the early negative correlation with educational success seems largely overwhelmed by the social environment of college life, with its emphasis on consumption or overconsumption of alcohol. As for reverse patterns of causation, we find little evidence that alcohol use has negative impacts on eventual academic attainment— again, of course, with the exception of those few whose lives are so seriously damaged by alcohol that they tend not to remain in panel survey studies such as ours. Perhaps a better way of saying it is that those who were good students in early adolescence tend to do well in college despite their participation in the typical student drinking behaviors.

Chapter 10

Summary, Conclusions, and Implications

We began this book by contrasting two "headlines":

1. *Doing well in school protects your teenager from drug use.*
2. *Drug use threatens your teenager's success in school.*

Both headlines take as their starting point the fact that adolescent substance use is negatively correlated with success in school—a fact that has been demonstrated by numerous research studies. But the two headlines involve distinctly different causal interpretations of that negative correlation, and they have different policy implications. In chapter 1, we previewed our findings by stating our broad conclusions: *Adolescent substance use is negatively correlated with educational success (a) because both sets of behaviors share common prior causes, (b) because educational successes protect against substance use whereas educational failures are risk factors, and (c) to a lesser extent because some substance use can impair educational success.* We also noted that our findings differ from one substance to another and from one age or developmental period to another.

Now, at the end of the book, we are in a position to look back over the evidence we provided and revisit our conclusions. In this chapter we summarize what we accomplished, state our conclusions, and consider the implications. We reported findings based primarily on analyses of a longitudinal panel of several thousand adolescents surveyed at 2-year intervals, starting when they were at the end of eighth grade in 1991 to 1993, and tracked to modal age 22. In chapter 1 we also reported findings from other longitudinal panels extending from modal ages 18 to 40, and in later chapters we summarized findings from many cross-sectional surveys involving hundreds of thousands of respondents. All of these data are from the Monitoring the Future (MTF) project collected over a period spanning more than a quarter century. After we reviewed relevant literature in chapter 2 and outlined our data sources and methods in chapter 3, we looked in considerable detail at educational attainment (chap. 4), delinquency (chap. 5), cigarette use (chap. 6), marijuana use (chap. 7), cocaine use (chap. 8), and alcohol use (chap. 9). We saw that the findings do, indeed, vary from one set of behaviors to another and from one age range to another. We also noted historical shifts (secular trends) in substance use during the decade in which our panel data were collected. Nevertheless, despite these nuances and complications, there are more than enough common threads in these different chapters to leave us confident in our broad conclusions stated at the outset and repeated at the beginning of this chapter.

Stated as broad conclusions, our findings suggest that background characteristics including parental education, parental presence and involvement, and early educational successes and failures all influence later academic attainment as well as adolescent delinquency and substance use. In addition, we found that educational outcomes during adolescence also play a role in adolescent delinquency and substance use. Finally, we found that substance use, at least among the great majority of adolescents, seems to have at most only modest additional impacts on long-term academic attainment. We discuss these conclusions in more detail later, but first set the stage with conceptual considerations and methodological detail. We believe that substantive conclusions should rest on a firm understanding of the methodological strengths and weaknesses of the data collection and analytic efforts; the reader who already has that understanding (or simply disagrees with our view about its importance) may wish to skip the following section entitled "Three Goals of This Book" and proceed directly to the section entitled "Summary of Findings: What We Think We Learned."

THREE GOALS OF THIS BOOK

Our reporting in this book has been guided by three goals. First, we tried to sort out the complex interconnections among (a) educational successes and failures, (b) delinquent behaviors in general, and (c) several kinds of substance use in particular, to gain a clearer understanding of the underlying causal processes. Second, because we made use of nationally representative data, we took special pains to present our findings in ways designed to preserve descriptive accuracy. Third, we employed multiple analytic approaches in order to strengthen our findings, and we tried to present these analysis methods and their rationales so as to be meaningful to a wide range of readers. We next say a bit more about our efforts to achieve each of these goals, after which we summarize our findings and conclusions and consider their implications.

Sorting Out Causal Connections

It is universally agreed that correlation does not equal causation. There are usually several plausible causal hypotheses that could explain any observed correlation. So the challenge for those trying to infer causation from observational or correlational data is to tease out additional relationships that may shed further light on which causal interpretations are most plausible. That is the sort of logical inductive exercise in which we have been engaged throughout much of this book.

We reported many significant correlations between educational successes or failures and adolescent substance use. We also examined these relationships across time so as to find additional evidence about whether A causes B (educational successes and failures influence adolescent substance use) or B causes A (substance use contributes to educational failures and impairs success). To gain still more leverage in our efforts to extract causal conclusions from correlational data, we examined a number of likely prior causes, searching for evidence that C (background and prior experiences) may cause both A (educational successes or failures) and B (adolescent substance use). As expected, we found some evidence supporting each causal interpretation, but the B–causes–A interpretation received much less support than the others (as noted in chap. 1 and summarized later in this chapter).

This separation of factors into A, B, and C categories is useful in distinguishing alternative causal interpretations, but we recognize that it is in some respects arbitrary. A notable example is that we found it useful in our analyses to treat early experiences of suspension or expulsion as part of educational background (i.e., among the C factors in the C-causes-A-and-B interpretation), but educational background factors could also be treated as among the A factors in the A–causes–B interpretation. Thinking in terms of a *problem behavior syndrome* may run the risk of blurring some of the sharp distinctions drawn earlier in this chapter, but it is also perhaps a more realistic approach to understanding the complex interrelationships among the factors we have studied in this book.

Among the concepts included in this syndrome notion is that some problem behaviors emerge earlier than others. Our findings indicate that delinquent behaviors such as petty theft, vandalism, fighting, and the like emerge relatively early in adolescence (if they emerge at all); smoking and drinking emerge a bit later; marijuana use emerges still later; and cocaine use emerges still later. Where do educational problems fit into this sequence? Our findings indicate that educational problems (and successes) are among the earliest emerging behaviors. Our findings indicate further that, by the time late adolescence is reached, educational experiences still influence substance use much more than the reverse. That is where the A-causes-B-more-than-B-causes-A type of distinction, albeit a simplification, seems useful.

In the end, we are not so presumptuous as to claim that we have "proved" any particular causal conclusions; however, we do believe we have been able to go further than is usually the case with correlational data, thanks in large measure to our use of national panel data covering an exceedingly important developmental period—modal ages 14 to 22.

Presenting Descriptively Accurate Findings

The panel data that are the primary focus of this book have an important advantage compared with panel data often available to social scientists: The present data are nationally representative. Actually, we suspect that our *relational* findings would be much the same if we had analyzed the same measures obtained from a less broadly representative panel; the consistencies between our findings and many of the studies cited in chapter 2 suggest that would be the case. But given that we began the collection of our panel data with a nationally representative sample, we considered it important to retain that representation to the extent possible.

In an ideal world for survey researchers, everyone selected for a panel study would agree to participate, they would not miss any of the data collections, and they would never skip over questions without answering them. In such a world, maintaining representativeness would not be a problem. Of course, things do not happen that way in the real world. Not only do considerable numbers of individuals drop out of panel studies, they do it in a decidedly nonrandom fashion. In our study, like most others, the panel losses were more severe among males, non-Whites, and those who were less successful in school. Fortunately, our initial efforts to oversample those students most likely to drop out of high school (as discussed in chap. 3) meant that the loss of *numbers* in these categories was not as serious as it otherwise would have been.

Nevertheless, such disproportionate panel losses produce *biases* in the retained sample unless corrective efforts are undertaken.

A preliminary step in developing a descriptively accurate panel sample was to determine what data, from which respondents, to include or exclude. As noted in chapter 3 and discussed at some length in the appendix, this is not as simple a matter as it might seem. If we had excluded anyone who missed one of the follow-up surveys, or (more drastically) if we had excluded anyone who had missing data on any of the measures important to the analyses, we would have been throwing out a considerable amount of good data from incomplete respondents and would have run the risk of biasing the sample more severely than necessary. But we also would have had problems if we had included everyone, no matter how extensive the missing data, because we would have included some for whom we had no good data on academic attainment. Our solution was to strike a middle ground. Specifically, we retained for our follow-up panel analyses any respondent who participated in either the fourth (modal age 20) or fifth (modal age 22) survey wave (or both, as was usually the case), and who provided us with academic-attainment data. That left us with two problems: how to deal with the biases resulting from excluding some respondents (those who failed to participate in both the age-20 and age-22 surveys), and how to deal with missing data for many of those who were included in the retained panel sample.

The first problem—bias from excluding nonrespondents—was addressed using poststratification; we reweighted the selected panel sample so as to approximate closely the initial (base-year) sample in terms of race/ethnicity, key educational factors, and substance use (see chap. 3 and appendix). In effect, we gave additional weight to panel participants who were most like those who dropped out of the panel; this meant, for example, that we increased the sample weights for male minority respondents, and we also reduced the sample weights for females who planned to complete college. We do not suppose that male minority respondents who *did* continue in the panel had just the same levels of substance use, on average, as their counterparts who did not continue. But we do believe that the reweighting appreciably *reduced* the biases (and we provide some evidence in the appendix to support that view).

The second problem—missing data in the retained panel sample—was addressed using multiple imputation. In effect, the multiple imputation program uses all available information to make the best possible estimate about what each missing answer would have been if the respondents had provided the data. The program is not assumed to produce a single true value, and results (given random start points) vary from one application to the next (although the input data are the same). Accordingly, we repeated each application 10 times and then averaged the results (see chap. 3 and the appendix for details of the procedure).

These corrective efforts yielded results that remain subject to some limitations. To take a specific example, we surely underestimate those who were incarcerated at age 20 or 22 and were thus unwilling or unable to participate in those follow-up surveys; unfortunately, no amount of upweighting of data from classmates who were similar to them at age 14 will fully solve that problem. More generally, we probably underestimate substance use and overestimate educational attainment to at least a small degree. So some inaccuracies surely remain. Nevertheless, the findings presented in this book are as descriptively accurate as we could manage, and certainly more accurate than would be the case had we not undertaken the corrective efforts noted previously.

Using Multiple Analysis Methods

The analytic and reporting methods used in this book range from relatively simple descriptive graphs showing percentages of individuals reporting use of a substance (prevalence rates) to complex multivariate structural equation models. We also used other less complex multivariate methods, such as multiple regression and multiple classification analysis.

Why use so many methods? One reason is that they illuminate different aspects of the topic being studied. Prevalence rates are fine for showing whether use of a particular substance has been rising or falling—especially during the time period in which we surveyed our adolescent panel. Multiple regression is good for showing how possible predictors overlap in their relationship to one particular outcome (dependent) variable, and multiple classification analysis (a particular form of multiple regression) provides some additional useful information that facilitates interpretation. The structural equation models also show overlaps, but do so within the constraints of a particular set of assumptions about causal directions. A second reason for using multiple methods is that different readers may be familiar with different methods, and we have tried to make our evidence available in several forms to accommodate such differences. The third and most important reason is that we do not believe there is only one right method, and we are more confident of findings that emerge consistently across the several different methods. We have tried to emphasize those consistently emerging findings in our reporting in chapters 4 through 9, and we do so again in this summary chapter. But we have also provided many of the summary data tables in the appendix—including nearly all of the tabular material that we used as we wrote the chapters—so that readers who wish to examine these tabulations in detail are able to do so.

We conducted and reported our analyses separately for males and females, again for a number of reasons. First, our emphasis on representativeness and descriptive accuracy argued against combining data for males and females, especially given their very different rates of delinquency, their somewhat different rates of use of some substances, and their differences in educational outcomes both during secondary school and afterward. Second, we wanted to avoid missing any male–female differences in patterns of relationship, and we did discover several worth reporting. Fortunately, for the sake of parsimony, the large majority of findings were very similar for males and females. That heightens our confidence in the findings, because we think most of the underlying causal mechanisms should operate in much the same way for young men and women.

A word may be in order concerning the nature of our regression analyses and structural models. We included a large number of measures in the regressions and then narrowed the list for the structural models. Neither set of analyses would be characterized as parsimonious, but we were concerned not to omit any important prior causal factors (as in "C causes both A and B"). We used the regressions to reduce the number of measures included in the structural models. Then, in the structural models, we controlled the exogenous factors by allowing them to predict all of the endogenous factors. We certainly could have striven for more parsimony in dealing with the exogenous factors, but that was not our primary purpose; rather, we were seeking to focus attention on the interrelationships among the endogenous factors while assuring that the exogenous factors were fully controlled. Others may prefer a more closely restricted approach; a covariance matrix is available for those who may wish to try their hand at it.

One aspect of our multiple methods approach was to repeat key analyses with our sample restricted to White respondents only. A more complete examination of racial/ethnic differences in our findings must await a later publication, but it was important to us in our reporting here that we not mistake complex differences related to race/ethnicity for other effects and thus reach spurious conclusions about how educational attainment and substance use are related to each other. We know that there are substantial differences in the use of various substances among racial/ethnic subgroups. We dealt with this potential complexity, at least in part, by including a set of race/ethnicity variables in all of our multivariate analyses, thereby controlling for any additive main effects. But complex interactions remained a potential problem. By repeating key analyses with White respondents only, we were able to see whether any of our total sample findings were significantly changed. If race/ethnicity effects had been producing spurious findings, a Whites-only analysis should have shown a reduction, elimination, or exaggeration of such findings. In fact, there were no important changes in parameter estimates, thus leaving us confident that our findings are not spurious results of complex race/ethnicity differences.

SUMMARY OF FINDINGS: WHAT WE THINK WE HAVE LEARNED

We now state our findings and conclusions in a series of brief declarative sentences, followed in each case by elaborations, caveats, and whatever else seems helpful or relevant. Throughout the book, we have reported that evidence in sufficient detail so that readers can examine it extensively, if they wish, and then form their own conclusions.

In Adolescence, Substance Use Is Negatively Linked With Educational Success

All four substances studied here—tobacco (cigarettes), marijuana, cocaine, and alcohol—are more likely to be used by adolescents who are not doing especially well in school and who are less likely than average to enter or complete college during their postadolescent years. This conclusion is not at all surprising; we knew this much before we began! Indeed, it was the basic premise for the book, and our purpose was to gain a better understanding of the nature and direction of the negative link. But we have seen that this simple assertion of a negative linkage applies clearly to substance use only up to age 16 or so. After that, the story becomes a good deal more complicated and differs from one substance to another. So later in this summary of findings, we look at the several forms of substance use separately and spell out those differences. But in the earlier years—the typical age of onset for most forms of substance use—the correlates and predictors of use show a good deal of similarity across substances.

Similar Correlates for Delinquency Suggest a
Problem Behavior Syndrome

It became evident early in our analyses that delinquent behavior is a central correlate of substance use in adolescence. We also found that, in general, the causes of delinquent behavior overlap considerably with the causes of specific substance-using behaviors in adolescence. Accordingly, we decided to include a measure of delinquent behavior as an early emerging part of a syndrome of problem behavior or general deviance. In our structural equation modeling, we view our seven-item measure of delinquency as a proxy for a much wider range of delinquent behaviors, including some school-related misbehaviors that are included only in our regression analyses. The tendency toward delinquent behaviors, as captured in our model, is an important mediating variable between various background factors and substance use.

This finding of similarities in the correlates of delinquency and substance use, at least during early and middle adolescence, seems highly consistent with theoretical views of a general syndrome of problem behaviors (e.g., Jessor & Jessor, 1977). We can thus review what we judge to be the causes of problem behaviors in general, summarizing key relationships that appear fairly consistently across chapters 5 through 9.

Background Factors That Contribute to Educational
Success Also Protect Against Problem Behaviors

Many of the variables that correlate positively with problem behaviors also correlate—in the opposite direction, of course—with educational success. Here we refer not only to educational success during adolescence, but also to academic attainment reached by young adulthood. It thus appears that, to some extent at least, the negative relationships between educational success and problem behaviors can be attributed to common causes (i.e., C causes both A and B)—and this is the first of our broad conclusions, as summarized at the start of this chapter. We begin by reviewing some of those common causes, focusing primarily on those that we found useful to include as exogenous factors in our structural models.

Following roughly the same ordering of factors used in chapters 5 through 9, we start with two aspects of demographic background—race/ethnicity and urban density. These two factors actually do not fit the pattern of showing opposite directions of association with educational success and problem behaviors. Although we were tempted to omit them from our multivariate analyses in the interest of parsimony, we opted to retain them to reduce possibilities of spurious findings due to these factors. Additionally, because we assumed questions about controls for race/ethnicity and urban density would arise for many readers, we thought it better to include these factors in the analyses.

Demographic Background: Race/Ethnicity. Our study, like virtually all others dealing with academic attainment, showed racial/ethnic differences: Attainment is lower for African-American and Hispanic young adults compared with White young adults. As shown in chapter 4, these differences overlap substantially with socioeconomic and other background factors. Our findings are thus consistent with the view that racial/ethnic educational inequality is largely a socioeconomic matter. We hasten to add that this finding in no way explains away the racial/ethnic differences; they remain important and worthy of further research and policy consideration. Such consideration, however, lies beyond the scope of the present volume.

Given our finding that substance use and educational success are negatively related in adolescence, and also given the general pattern of findings that background factors show opposite directions of correlation with educational success and problem behaviors, it might be expected that African-American and Hispanic adolescents would be above average in substance use. But here is the exception to that general pattern of findings: African-American and Hispanic students are distinctly below Whites in use of cigarettes; additionally, African-American students are far below average in alcohol use and occasional heavy drinking, and overall they are somewhat less likely than others to be users of illicit drugs.

We included race/ethnicity variables in all of our multivariate analyses to control any additive effects on the relationships between educational factors and various dimensions of substance use. The findings are reported in chapters 5 through 9. We also repeated key analyses with only the White respondents included, and that strengthened our conclusion that racial/ethnic differences did not produce spurious findings. Future separate publications will focus on possible racial/ethnic differences in the links between educational success and substance use.

Demographic Background: Urban Density. Urban density is another exception to the general pattern of background factors predicting in opposite directions to educational success and substance use. Here the reason is that urban density differences in substance use are not large and do not predict in consistent directions. As for academic attainment, there seem to be modest advantages to living in large metropolitan areas and modest disadvantages to living in nonurban areas. These differences are reduced somewhat by controls for family socioeconomic status (SES) and other factors; but even after these and other controls, academic attainment remains slightly higher among adolescents who live in large cities or suburbs, compared with those from nonmetropolitan areas.

Delinquency rates are also somewhat positively correlated with urban density, which is the opposite of what would be expected if urban density were an important contributor to the negative association between delinquency and educational success. The various substance-use dimensions generally relate only modestly, if at all, to urban density; moreover, any such relationships are not consistent from one substance to another, and often not consistent across genders. So in chapters 5 through 9, we report the urban density differences we have observed, and we consider it worthwhile to have included urban density as a control factor in our multivariate analyses; however, we conclude that urban density is not an important contributor to the links between substance use and academic attainment.

Family Background: Parental Education. Parental education is a key ingredient and indicator of family socioeconomic level, but it also represents a good deal more in terms of family educational level and environment. Highly educated parents are most likely to encourage and facilitate their children's educational success, from preschool through high school and beyond. Additionally, well-educated parents are likely to have higher than average incomes, and are thus better able to provide financial resources for their children's college education. For these reasons, parental education is a strong positive contributor to children's educational attainment—it shows direct effects (with other things controlled), as well as indirect effects via their children's grades and college plans.

Parental education is also negatively linked with adolescent substance use, although these links are not as strong as the positive links with educational success. Parental education shows modest preventive effects—primarily indirectly via early educational success—on smoking, drinking, and marijuana use during earlier adolescence (i.e., by the end of eighth grade). The story for later substance use is more complicated, as we note later in this summary, and as we reported in detail especially in chapter 9.

Family Background: Presence of Both Parents in the Home. Having both parents present in the home throughout the high school years (i.e., modal ages 14, 16, and 18) makes a positive contribution to academic attainment. Much of this effect appears to be indirect via grades and college plans, but a modest portion is direct—perhaps because families with both parents present are most likely to be able to contribute to college expenses.

Adolescents with two parents present in the home are less likely to be involved in delinquent behavior, although the effects appear largely indirect via early educational experiences. Adolescents with both parents present are also less likely to engage in substance use, with only some of the impacts indirect via educational successes or failures.

Family Background: Parental Involvement in Students' Lives. Although some of them might not always be happy about it, 14-year-olds are generally better off when their parents are involved in their lives, as indicated by parents checking on and perhaps helping with homework, requiring chores, and limiting TV viewing. These benefits are reflected in better grades and lower likelihoods of delinquency, smoking, drinking, and illicit drug use. The beneficial effects of parental involvement are strongest at age 14 and generally much weaker by age 18. Academic attainment at age 22 is positively correlated with early parental involvement, but our structural analyses suggest that this association is primarily due to other common causes. The structural analyses do, however, indicate that parental involvement has important protective effects against adolescent substance use.

Educational Background: Having Been Held Back Prior to Eighth Grade. A significant minority of boys (about one in four) and fewer girls (about one in six) are held back a grade in school prior to the end of eighth grade. Despite its infrequent occurrence, grade retention clearly predicts low academic attainment by age 22 (see Fig. 4.4). The analyses in chapter 4 show that any impacts of grade retention are at least partly indirect via high school grades and college plans. Moreover, we note that grade retention is clearly a *symptom* of considerable academic difficulties, and whether this symptom is also a cause of further difficulties in its own right is beyond our ability to disentangle.

Problem behaviors, including delinquency and the various forms of substance use, are all greater than average among those having been held back; however, these relationships evident at the bivariate level tend to diminish greatly or disappear when multivariate controls for other factors are included. On the whole, we conclude that having been held back has little direct effect on the problem behaviors, and the relationships largely reflect the effects of other factors. One of those other factors worth noting is simply age; those held back are among the oldest students at the end of eighth grade, and age is positively related to the initiation of substance use.

Educational Background: Suspension or Expulsion Prior to Eighth Grade. Suspension or expulsion is usually the consequence of fairly serious misbehavior having to do with school. It is also a good predictor of later academic attainment; those who were suspended or expelled prior to the end of eighth grade are only about half as likely to complete a year or more of college by age 22, compared with those not suspended or expelled.

Not surprisingly, early suspension or expulsion is also strongly correlated with delinquency, cigarette use, illicit drug use, and early alcohol use. These correlations with general delinquency and substance use are only modestly reduced when other factors are controlled in regression analyses and the structural equation models. We thus view suspension and expulsion prior to eighth grade as clear indicators of, and contributors to, a syndrome of problem behaviors.

Summary of Findings Thus Far. We began this section with the assertion that predictors of educational success also negatively predict substance use (or C causes both A and B). We have reviewed all dimensions included as exogenous factors in our structural model. We found mixed results for the demographic background factors of race/ethnicity and urban density, with little support for the C-causes-both-A-and-B interpretation. For family background factors, the pattern is clearer: High levels of parental education, having both parents living in the home, and high levels of parental involvement all contribute to educational success, and all appear to provide some protection against substance use during adolescence—especially through age 16. Early scholastic setbacks such as grade retention, suspension, or expulsion are associated with below-average levels of academic attainment; these setbacks are also linked with above-average levels of substance use (although the link with grade retention may be attributable to overlap with other factors).

We think there is a good deal of support in these findings for the assertion that part of the negative connection between academic success and adolescent substance use is attributable to their sharing common prior causes. But this is also a good point to acknowledge again that the sorting of factors into exogenous and endogenous—particularly the selection of some dimensions as background factors or prior causes—is necessarily arbitrary. Most notably, we have treated early experiences of grade retention, suspension, and expulsion as educational background, whereas we treat similar events occurring later (after eighth grade) as contemporary (endogenous) factors. We made this distinction to take appropriate account of the chronology of behaviors and experiences we were examining, but we do not want to imply that modal age 14 is a clear and distinct point of separation. That happened to be the modal age at which we obtained the first in our series of panel surveys, but if it could have been earlier (e.g., age 10 or 12), then that would have been the logical dividing line between exogenous and endogenous factors.

Other Factors Linked With Educational Success or Failure Are Also Linked With Problem Behaviors

We explored several additional dimensions that have shown linkages with academic attainment and also (inversely) with problem behaviors. As we stated in chapter 4, these "additional correlates ... contribute rather little to the prediction of academic attainment, above and beyond the prediction provided by grades, college plans, and background factors...." We certainly do not consider these other dimensions unimportant; however, we found that the need for some parsimony in modeling outweighed our tendency to be inclusive. Nevertheless, we reported regression analyses in chapter 4 linking these other factors with academic attainment, and in chapters 5 through 9 we included these factors in the regression analysis tables so as to document their linkages with adolescent delinquency and substance use. We provide a brief summary here.

School Misbehaviors.   Not surprisingly, the students who tend to cut classes, skip whole days of school, or misbehave in ways that earn them a trip to the office are the students who get poorer grades and complete fewer years of education. They are also more likely than average to report engaging in other deviant or delinquent behaviors, including using cigarettes, alcohol, and illicit drugs. Once grades, college plans, and delinquency are included as predictors, these school misbehavior measures make little or no additional contribution to explaining academic attainment or problem behaviors. Accordingly, we were able to omit them from the structural model. We view them as additional aspects of the problem behavior syndrome, but they are adequately represented in the model by the general measure of delinquency as well as the other indicators of school performance and adjustment.

Evenings out for Fun and Recreation.   Adolescents who spend frequent evenings out for fun and recreation are somewhat more likely than average to engage in delinquent behaviors and substance use. Indeed, their frequent evenings out probably provide the occasions and opportunities for some of these problem behaviors. It is not the case, however, that frequency of evenings out shows any strong association with long-term academic attainment. So we have recorded the links with the various substance-using behaviors in our regression analyses, but this dimension seemed unnecessary in our structural model.

Actual and Preferred Hours of Work During the School Year. The connections between long hours of part-time work during the school year and substance use and academic performance are complicated and subject to various conflicting interpretations. In our current study, we have two important advantages: First, we begin at modal age 14, before most students are able to work long hours during the school year; second, our surveys asked students how many hours they would *like* to work during the school year, as well as the number of hours per week actually worked. Our interpretation of the relationships—which is guided by our panel data, if not necessarily "proved"—is as follows: Adolescents who are not doing well in school, and are thus likely to have below-average academic attainment by young adulthood, are more likely than average to *wish to work* long hours while they are in school—although most of them at the end of eighth grade are too young to be able to do so. Then, a few years later, these same individuals are likely to have part-time jobs in which they actually do work long hours during the school year. Finally, these same individuals who are not doing well in school are more likely than average to become involved in the various forms of substance use. In other words, we think that poor school performance during early and middle adolescence underlies much of the association between long hours of part-time work and student drug use.

The regression analysis findings involving the part-time work measures generally show zero-order correlations that are consistent with the previously stated interpretation. All of the multivariate coefficients are quite small, many essentially zero, and this degree of overlap is also consistent with the previously stated interpretation. We thus conclude that part-time work preferences and actual behaviors, whereas correlated to some degree with educational outcomes and problem behaviors, are probably not very important causes of either.

Religious Attendance and Importance. As we noted in chapter 4, students and young adults who rate religion as important in their lives and attend services frequently are less likely to be substance users. The analyses in this book confirm that religiosity is negatively linked with drug use, and also with adolescent delinquency. It thus appears that religion is a protective factor against these forms of deviant behavior.

We also found, and reported in chapter 4, that religious attendance is positively correlated with age-22 academic attainment. The regression analyses indicate little independent contribution of the religion dimensions that is not explained or mediated via other variables. In other words, it appears that any impacts of religiosity on adolescent educational outcomes and substance use are indirect via other factors such as earlier educational successes or failures.

Self-Esteem. The measure of self-esteem used in our analyses shows positive correlations with age-22 academic attainment and negative correlations with delinquency and the substance-use measures. These relationships appear to overlap mostly or entirely with other factors in our regression analyses. Accordingly, we were content to document the self-esteem findings in our tables of regression analyses, but did not attempt to include self-esteem in the structural models.

Educational Experiences During Adolescence Have Impacts on Problem Behaviors as Well as Long-Term Academic Attainment

The factors listed in this section are all treated as endogenous in our structural equation models of academic attainment and problem behaviors. All were expected to contribute to academic attainment by age 22, and the findings reported in chapter 4 indicate that all do. Of greater interest, perhaps, are the findings that these factors also contribute to problem behaviors—delinquency and the various forms of substance use—as reported in chapters 5 through 9. This set of findings supports the second of our broad conclusions (A causes B), as summarized at the start of this chapter.

Adolescent Educational Experiences: Serious Setbacks After Eighth Grade. Setbacks that occurred prior to the end of eighth grade were included among the (exogenous) educational background factors, as summarized earlier in this chapter. We treated instances of grade retention, suspension, or expulsion that took place after eighth grade as separate factors in our analyses, because they could be examined among other contemporaneous (endogenous) factors occurring during adolescence. We found that these more recent setbacks, like the earlier ones, are linked negatively with academic attainment. They are also linked positively with delinquency and substance use. These effects, of course, overlap to some extent with effects of other factors, but often retain some independent contribution as well.

Adolescent Educational Experiences: Grade Point Average. Of all the measures obtained in the initial surveys at the end of eighth grade, grade point average (GPA) for the past year is by far the best predictor of eventual (i.e., age-22) academic attainment. GPA at the end of 10th grade is an even stronger predictor. Although they overlap considerably with other predictors of academic attainment, grades retain a key position in the multivariate analyses in general, and in the structural equation model in particular. The structural model treats grades as an important direct contributor to college plans, and the findings seem fully consistent with that assumption. The model findings also indicate a high degree of stability in grade point averages—students who do well in eighth grade are also very likely to do well in later grades. Given this overall stability during adolescence, it seems highly likely that those students who were successful in secondary school were also successful in earlier grades.

Not only are adolescents with good grades more likely to enter and complete college, they are also less likely to be involved in problem behaviors. Successful students are less likely to be delinquent, less likely to smoke cigarettes, less likely to use illicit drugs, and—in early adolescence at least—less likely to use alcohol. Again, all of these relationships overlap with other prior causes; nevertheless, the structural model findings show a continuing protective function of good grades. Indeed, even for 30-day alcohol use and instances of heavy drinking occurring at age 18, a time when the college-bound students seem to be catching up with their age-mates, the model findings indicate that the students with a history of high grades are less likely than their peers to use alcohol.

Adolescent Educational Experiences: College Plans. College plans are also strong predictors of eventual academic attainment, although here the pattern is somewhat different from what we observe for GPAs. College plans (or, more accurately, expectations) are less stable than grades; they grow increasingly accurate as students move from 8th to 10th to 12th grade. In fact, by the end of 12th grade (the time of the third survey wave for most of our panel respondents), most adolescents have made fairly firm short-term decisions about what they will be doing after high school, and many have applied to and been accepted by one or more colleges or universities. But even if we focus on plans 2 years earlier (end of 10th grade), it is clear that adolescents' expectations about college are by that time highly predictive of their age-22 academic attainment.

Adolescents who expect to complete college are also less likely to be involved in problem behaviors including delinquency, cigarette use, and illicit drug use. The story for alcohol use at the end of high school is more complicated, as we discussed in chapter 9 and note again in the next section of this chapter. But at least from 8th grade through the end of 10th grade, college-bound students are less likely to use alcohol.

There Are Important Differences Across Types of Substance Use

We noted earlier in this summary of findings that, at least up to modal age 16, our findings indicate substantial similarities across types of substance use in terms of their links with educational successes and failures, with delinquent behaviors, and with what has been termed more generally as problem behavior. However, we have also reported a number of important distinctions among the types of substance use, not only in typical ages of onset, but also in longer term links with academic attainment. We summarize some of those distinctions now.

Cigarette Use. Cigarette use is among the earliest emerging forms of substance use among adolescents. Among all the forms of substance use we examined, smoking also shows the strongest initial linkages with educational success or failure. Most strikingly, the links between smoking and educational outcomes remain impressively strong well into middle adulthood, as illustrated in Figure 1.1 in chapter 1. Why do these connections remain so strong? The obvious answer is that smoking, like educational attainment, is a very stable form of behavior. Adolescents who have not made a good adjustment to school are disposed to become involved in a variety of problem behaviors, including delinquency, smoking, drinking, and illicit drug use. But of all these adolescent problem behaviors, cigarette use is by far the most difficult for most individuals to quit. The typical smoker engages in the behavior multiple times during each day—a level of involvement far exceeding what is typical for the other forms of substance use—and that helps set the stage for what often becomes a lifetime of dependence.

Cigarette use may make a small negative contribution to academic attainment, in part by contributing to the likelihood of dropping out of high school. Smokers spend time with other smokers, and adolescent smokers on the whole have lower than average success with and enthusiasm for education. So among the reasons for the lower academic attainment of smokers may be that they associate with, and to some extent model the behavior and attitudes of, other smokers. In any case, it seems clear that the impacts of educational successes and failures on smoking are a good deal stronger than any impacts in the opposite direction (i.e., A causes B much more than B causes A).

Marijuana Use. Marijuana has been the most widely used illicit drug in the United States in recent decades. We found marijuana use to be highly correlated with cigarette use during adolescence, but less so during early adulthood. We attribute this decline in correlation to the relatively lower dependence associated with typical adolescent marijuana use, in contrast to the high dependence for cigarette use. So when new experiences occur in young adulthood (leaving the parental home, marriage, parenthood, etc.), marijuana use is much more likely than cigarette use to change in response to those new experiences. As noted in chapter 7, our analyses suggest that for the large majority of adolescents, the use of marijuana tends to be *correlated* with poor educational outcomes, but is not a primary *cause* of such outcomes (again, little evidence that B causes A).

Cocaine Use. Cocaine use does not occur among the great majority of adolescents in the United States. When it does occur, it tends to emerge at somewhat later ages than the other forms of substance use reported here. Nevertheless, the links with background and educational factors are similar to those found for cigarette, marijuana, and (perhaps to a lesser extent) alcohol use. So we view cocaine use as a late (and, fortunately, infrequently) emerging aspect of the problem behavior syndrome. By the time it does emerge, the key differences in educational experiences, attitudes, and aspirations are already largely in place, and seem little influenced by the kinds of cocaine use we have been able to measure (once more, little evidence that B causes A).

Alcohol Use. Alcohol use, like cigarette use, emerges fairly early in adolescence. It involves larger proportions of adolescents, but to a far less intensive degree than cigarette use. At modal ages 14 and 16, alcohol use, including occasions of heavy drinking, is more likely among students who are not doing very well in school (i.e., A causes B, much as we observed for cigarette use). By age 18, however, the story changes substantially, and by their early 20s the college students surpass their less educated age-mates in their use of alcohol—especially in occasions of heavy use (five or more drinks in a row). This cross-over pattern is clearly evident in Figure 1.4. Earlier analyses of MTF data tracking high school seniors into adulthood (Bachman et al., 1997) have shown that these shifts in behavior are largely attributable to changes in lifestyle environments—compared with their age-mates, college students are more likely to have left their parents' homes, but less likely to have assumed the responsibilities associated with marriage (and perhaps also parenthood). So although alcohol use among college students—especially occasions of heavy use—certainly deserves to be characterized as problem behavior, this use in the late teens and early 20s does not fit very well within the problem behavior syndrome as discussed here, but may be more of a reflection of a "single's scene partying syndrome" that happens to correlate with educational status during the early 20s. There is little evidence, however, that alcohol use makes much of a contribution to educational success (i.e., little evidence that B causes A).

CONCLUSIONS AND IMPLICATIONS

The "Big Picture" Revisited

Patterns of educational success or failure seem well established by the time adolescents reach the end of eighth grade. GPAs show high levels of stability across the next 4 years, and college expectations show a good deal of stability as well. The various forms of substance use, in contrast, are mostly still emerging at the end of eighth grade. As they emerge, they consistently show that students who are doing well in school are less likely to engage in such behaviors, whereas those doing poorly are more likely to do so. We have tried to be appropriately cautious in drawing causal conclusions from correlational data; nevertheless, some aspects of our findings seem rather obvious. As we noted at the outset in chapter 1, marijuana use at age 16 or cocaine use at age 18 cannot, by any stretch of the imagination, *cause* a low GPA at age 14; however, the reverse pattern of causation (A causes B) seems quite plausible. Adolescents with a history of poor educational adjustment clearly seem at increased risk for substance use. Part of that risk seems to be the result of background factors, including disrupted homes (living with fewer than two parents) and low parental involvement (C causes both A and B). But a considerable amount of the risk seems directly linked to how the students have been doing in school.

Where does that leave the question of whether the substance-using behaviors cause further decrements in academic attainment (B causes A)? Here the findings provide a good deal less support. Smoking may make matters a little bit worse, but there is little evidence of negative impacts of marijuana use or cocaine use on the academic attainment of the great majority of young people in the United States these days. The story for alcohol use is more complicated, as summarized earlier in this chapter, but it seems clear that it does not contribute much in the way of negative long-term effects overall. It must be kept in mind that all of those negative findings are based on panel data from those who continued in our study from age 14 through at least age 20 or 22. Our panel retention was good, and we made considerable efforts to counter panel attrition biases; nevertheless, our panel data cannot include the individuals who never made it to young adulthood because they lost their lives due to alcohol abuse, or those whose use of illicit drugs was so extensive that they were unwilling or simply unable to provide survey responses. Fortunately, such events are rare; but they do occur, and we would not want to be misunderstood as suggesting that illicit drug use and abuse of alcohol seem to have no long-term consequences. One form of substance use that is, alas, not rare (and unfortunately becomes habitual in most cases) is the use of cigarettes. This is an additional consequence of poor educational adaptation that can last a lifetime—all too often a shortened lifetime.

Policy Implications

There are many good reasons for encouraging adolescents and preadolescents to do well in school, and to help them to do well. The long-term economic and cultural benefits of a good education are widely recognized and appreciated. The findings of this research suggest an additional class of benefits: Early educational success provides considerable protection against a wide range of problem behaviors, including delinquency, smoking, drinking, and illicit drug use. So although the educational benefits alone are more than enough reason for us to strive to "leave no child behind," substance-use prevention also belongs in the list of reasons for investing in educational success for all children.

There are also many good reasons for encouraging adolescents to avoid substance use, because it can have a variety of serious consequences. Smoking cigarettes frequently leads to long-term dependence, resulting in substantial health risks and less longevity. Instances of heavy drinking can lead to accidental death or injury, and in some cases can be a precursor to dependence. Illicit drug use can also lead to dependence, as well as to legal problems and a variety of other risks. Should educational benefits also be high on the list of reasons for avoiding substance use? Our findings cast some doubt on that proposition. Rather, our findings indicate that educational failures tend to come early in the sequence of problem behaviors, followed by adolescent delinquency, smoking, drinking, and illicit drug use. In general, substance use appears to be largely a *symptom*, rather than a *cause*, of poor academic adjustment, although one can easily imagine specific examples to the contrary.

To put it more pointedly, it is probably wishful thinking to suppose that reducing adolescent substance use will lead to substantial increases in educational success. Instead, an alternative view seems more plausible: Whatever can be done to improve the educational successes of children and adolescents will likely have a valuable fringe benefit—reductions in substance use.

Again we need to stress that we do not view these findings as any reason for slackening efforts to reduce adolescent substance use. There are already more than enough good reasons for discouraging such use, even if we look no further than the potential health consequences. What our findings do suggest is this: One particularly important way to reduce or prevent adolescent involvement in substance use is to help them succeed in school—and to do so well before they reach adolescence.

Does our research tell us anything about how to improve educational success? Although that was not the primary purpose of the study, our analyses of the predictors of academic attainment and earlier educational outcomes provide some useful clues. As we noted in chapter 4, a key to good academic health is to choose the right parents: It helps if they are well educated, reasonably compatible with each other (i.e., not divorced, separated, or on the verge of separation), and actively involved in monitoring the homework and other behaviors of their children. Public policy cannot do much to raise the educational levels of parents or increase their compatibility. But perhaps parents could be encouraged to become more involved with their children's education. Public policy also could do more to deal with one of the disadvantages of low parental education: limited ability to finance college for their children.

Our findings in chapter 4 point to the long-term advantages of good grades and college aspirations, as well as the disadvantages of setbacks such as grade retention, suspension, or expulsion. The implication is that we should find ways to help students succeed in their schoolwork and avoid the behaviors that lead to suspension or expulsion. If the solution were as simple as assigning every student high grades and banning grade retention, suspension, and expulsion, that already would have been tried.

Alas, except for the mythical Lake Wobegon where "… all the children are above average," such a policy of assigning top scores to everyone would be recognized as a farce. Instead, it is almost universally agreed that children really do need to be able to read and develop other skills and knowledge associated with educational success. Being told that one is a success, and not getting messages that one is a failure, is certainly part of the solution; but another part of the solution are the feelings associated with actually being successful.

It does seem clear that overcoming *early* educational problems is particularly important. As we noted in chapter 2, educational research is showing that there are successful alternatives to grade retention and ways to help children deal with and overcome early educational failures. For example, teachers and curriculum developers can provide students with experiences in which they feel competent and lessons that highlight the value of their schoolwork. Even students who struggle in school can remain motivated to persist in the face of failures, provided they believe that additional effort can result in personal growth and success. Our statement at the conclusion of chapter 2 bears repeating here: Early educational interventions and additional support for low-achieving students are among the best ways to decrease adolescent substance use and delinquency. That, it seems to us, is a worthy policy goal.

Appendix

This appendix consists of written material, organized into three sections, plus many supplementary tables and a few figures all placed at the end. The third and final text section presents structural equation model technical decisions and their rationales. The second section describes our sampling and survey procedures in greater detail than in chapter 3. The section we present first provides a broad overview of the many factors involved in developing sample weights and deciding what numbers of cases should be assumed when conducting statistical tests of significance. This first section touches on a wide range of survey design and analysis issues that have a lot to do with how much confidence can be placed in various findings. So we recommend it to readers who want a fuller understanding of how the authors sorted through issues of prestratification, poststratification, multiple imputation calculations, and design effects. Other readers, of course, may want to skip selectively to certain portions of the appendix; the table of contents and index should help them find what they seek.

N—OR, WHAT'S IN A NUMBER? THE QUEST FOR PRACTICAL AND REALISTIC VALUES OF N TO USE IN ESTIMATING SAMPLE PRECISION

Introductory note: *Readers of a certain age may recall the brilliantly funny Tom Lehrer, a Harvard mathematics professor whose record albums included "That Was the Year That Was." One of his songs was entitled "New Math," in which Lehrer took the audience—at breakneck speed—through a set of arithmetic calculations. All would have been fine, except that Lehrer, providing an example of new math, was doing everything using the base eight rather than the familiar base ten. (As he pointed out, "Base eight is just like base ten—if you're missing two fingers.") This appendix section reminded us of "New Math"—and that may be a clue as to what lies ahead. We will try to be less confusing than Lehrer's song—although, arguably, our task is more challenging.*

Assessment of the significance of many statistics often uses an assumption of simple random samples. Survey researchers, however, seldom have the luxury of simple random samples. On the contrary, survey researchers have to deal with issues arising from complex sample designs, including the effects of sampling by strata and clusters, and of course, response rates. For those survey researchers who use longitudinal panel data, there is the additional challenge of dealing with panel attrition.

We deal with matters of sample design and adjustments for panel attrition in chapter 3 and also elsewhere in this appendix. In this section, we focus on matters having to do with numbers of cases (*N*s) because they figure crucially in our estimates of statistical significance. Everyone who has taken Statistics 101 knows (or once knew) that probability samples with larger numbers of cases generally (assuming other things equal) result in inferences with greater levels of precision. In other words, bigger *N*s equal smaller standard errors. Some may also recall that the precision of a simple random sample increases in direct proportion not to *N*, but to the square root of *N*; accordingly, if one wants to double accuracy, for example, one has to quadruple sample size (because the square root of four equals two). So *N* matters—big time.

But what, exactly, is *N*? We said a moment ago that it is the number of cases. That is fine for simple random samples, but for us it is only the starting point. In our analyses, we have had to distinguish several different kinds of *N*, including: (a) the *Raw* N—the actual number of people whose data we included in the analyses; (b) an *Initial Selection Weighted* N—the number that results when we apply weights to correct for initial stratification; (c) a *Down-Weighted Initial Selection Weighted* N; (d) *Poststratification Weighted* N—which attempts to correct for differential panel attrition; and (e) an *Effective* N—an artificial number that takes account of the complexities of the actual sample design, such that simple random sample statistics can be applied using *that* number (i.e., the Effective *N*) rather than the Raw *N*. Here we use the term *Effective N* in the same spirit (we hope) as Kish (1965) and others used it in their exposition of the concept of design effect; however, our usage includes adjustment not only for the effects of initial sample design, but also for the effects of poststratification and imputation.

It is worth mentioning that many of the elegant statistics that utilize an assumption of a simple random sample actually are quite robust in a number of respects, and they seem to work well despite various violations of the underlying assumptions. That is a good thing for those of us who often have to analyze data that violate the assumptions. But one of the things we do, perhaps as one way of compensating for all those violations, is to try to take account of our various sampling and weighting machinations by developing an Effective *N* that will prevent us (or others) from claiming more precision than is justified by our data. That generally amounts to some discounting of sample size—some reduction from the Raw N or actual number of observations.

There were several steps involved in choosing an Effective N approach that would work for our total sample and also for subgroups. We review some of the major considerations that shaped what, in the end, turned out to be a fairly simple solution.

Raw N Versus Initial Selection Weighted N

We note first that our Initial Selection Weighted Ns were different from—in fact, larger than—the raw numbers of observations. This was true for both males and females, albeit in different degrees. As discussed briefly in chapter 3, and spelled out further in the appendix section "Initial Stratification for Selecting Target Panel Samples," our original specification for target samples involved four strata, differing in likelihood of dropping out of high school—which amounts to differing degrees of educational success or failure up to the end of eighth grade. We oversampled those at greatest risk of dropping out of high school, and undersampled those at lowest risk. The primary purpose of this differential sampling was to increase the raw numbers of high school dropouts in the follow-up samples. These differential sampling proportions also had some advantages in terms of panel attrition, because the same factors that predict dropping out of high school also do a pretty good job of predicting who is more likely to drop out of panel studies. In effect, oversampling of those at high academic risk had the side effect of compensating for their greater than average attrition in the follow-up surveys.

The initial selection weights were assigned simply to correct for the oversampling of the high-risk respondents and the undersampling of the low-risk respondents in the follow-up surveys. For example, if a low-risk college-bound eighth grader were sampled with only .6 probability compared with the overall average, then the initial weight for that respondent would be 1.67 (because 1 divided by .6 = 1.67). Conversely, if a high-risk eighth grader were sampled with 2.0 probability compared with the average, then the initial weight for that individual would be .5 (because 1 divided by 2 = .5). This approach would yield weighted Ns equal to the raw Ns if the strata did not differ in follow-up participation rates. In fact, of course, the response rates differed quite a bit, as can be seen in Table A.3.1. Specifically, those low-risk individuals with the low initial selection probability and the corresponding high compensatory weights were the most likely to participate, and after weighting they counted as a good many more cases than their actual numbers. The reverse was true for the high-risk respondents; each one of them got weighted down. Because there were a lot more of the low-risk than high-risk individuals in the initial eighth-grade cross-sections (which our weighted follow-up samples were intended to duplicate insofar as possible), these up-weighted low-risk individuals boosted the Initial Selection Weighted Ns to higher overall values than the Raw Ns (i.e., the actual numbers of obtained observations). In short, the initial weights turned out not to be N-neutral (a term that we just made up because it is analogous to the widely used term *revenue-neutral*).

So what is the problem with the Initial Selection Weighted N being a bit large (or overweight)? There are two problems—or two parts of the same problem. First, the Initial Selection Weighted Ns for *total* samples could mislead readers, giving a false impression of (slightly) greater precision because they are larger than the actual numbers of cases (Raw Ns) on which they are based. Second, and more serious perhaps, certain *subgroup* weighted Ns—most notably those for the lowest risk stratum—could be still more misleading because the Raw Ns would be a good deal lower than the weighted Ns. Well then, what good are these initial weighted Ns? One thing they are good for is calculating response rates because they approximate closely the kinds of response rates we would have gotten had our follow-up sampling used equal probabilities and skipped all the complications of initial stratification. For that reason the response rates reported in chapter 3 are based on the original weighted Ns.

But now let us get back to the problem of weighted Ns being higher than Raw Ns, particularly among low-risk individuals like the college-bound. We did not want to provide misleadingly high numbers of weighted cases in such categories. We would prefer, instead, to be statistically conservative and provide misleadingly *low* numbers in the other categories. So we looked at all four of the initial sampling strata separately for males and females, and discovered that if we down-weighted the original weighted Ns in the low-risk categories by one quarter (i.e., multiplied all of the initial weights by a factor of .75), the resulting new weighted Ns never exceeded the underlying Raw Ns (i.e., the actual numbers of observations). The same was true, of course, for the higher risk categories, although their new weighted Ns were substantially lower than the underlying Raw Ns.

Summarizing our progress thus far, we found that when we take the (slightly oversized) Initial Selection Weighted Ns and reduce them to three-quarter size, that leaves us with some categories (the lowest risk ones) in which these new (down) weighted Ns are just slightly smaller than the underlying Raw Ns, and other (high-risk) categories in which the new weighted Ns are substantially smaller. To put it in more meaningful terms, we found that this possible new weighting scheme would, for all major categories of interest to us, give us *N*s that always reflect an equal or greater number of actual observations—that is, the Raw *N* would always equal or exceed the new (down) weighted *N*. Moreover, for some smaller but very important categories such as high school dropouts, our actual degree of precision would be slightly higher than that implied by the (down) weighted *N*.

It also occurred to us that if we were lucky, this proposed down-weighting of the initial weighted *N* might be sufficient to take care of some other potentially pesky problems—increased (random) error attributable to poststratification, imputation, and sample design effects. We cover each of those matters next.

Effects of Poststratification

As discussed in chapter 3, one of our techniques for handling the effects of panel attrition was to poststratify. We developed a new (yet another) set of weights that reproduced the original (i.e., eighth-grade) distributions along a number of dimensions (race/ethnicity, grade point average and other educational success/failure indicators, substance use, and of course gender). This new poststratification weight was designed to be truly *N*-neutral, in that the Poststratification Weighted *N* was identical (within rounding error) to the Initial Selection Weighted *N*. (That meant, of course, that it was equally overweight compared with the Raw *N*. So that problem has not gone away.)

The question of interest here is: What effects did poststratification have on the precision of our follow-up sample? The short answer, we think, is: Not very much. By way of explanation, let us outline briefly a topic we cover more completely in the appendix section that shows the details of poststratification as carried out for this book. We arrived at our poststratification weights by, in effect, sorting the members of our *target* panel sample into bins according to the various factors noted in the preceding paragraph, and counted the contents of each bin. We next looked at the *obtained* panel sample (in this case defined as those who participated in one or both of the age-20 and age-22 follow-up surveys) and again counted the contents of each bin. In some bins (such as those getting good grades, planning on college, not smoking, etc.), most of the 14-year-olds stayed in the panel and participated in follow-ups at ages 20 and/or 22. In some other bins (poor grades, no college plans, daily smoker, etc.), smaller proportions stayed in the panel. Now the logic of poststratification is this: We think we will do a better job of representing the whole age cohort if we do not allow the poor students and early smokers to be underrepresented in our tabulations. As a *partial* solution to that, we take those in such low-participation categories who *did* stay in the panel and give them a somewhat increased weight (with our poststratification weighting scheme), whereas those in the high-participation categories get a somewhat reduced weight. That has the effect of making the retained panel sample look a great deal like the original target sample *in terms of factors measured at the initial (eighth-grade) survey*. What it cannot do, alas, is tell us exactly what the nonparticipants looked like at age 22, for example. We know that those who were smoking at age 14 are more likely than average to also be smoking at age 22. But what cannot be known from our data is whether, among all those who smoked at age 14, those who drop out of the panel are more likely to remain smokers at age 22, compared with those age-14 smokers who stayed in the panel. Our guess is that, if anything, the panel nonparticipants tend to be doing less well than the participants, even after we match for age-14 characteristics. If so, then our poststratification is only partly successful. Nevertheless, the partial success seems pretty good, at least in terms of substance use, as indicated by earlier analyses comparing poststratified panel data and data from Monitoring the Future (MTF) annual cross-sections (Bachman, Johnston et al., 2006).

How would all of this affect sampling precision? That depends, to a considerable extent, on whether the new weights are more widely dispersed than the initial selection weights. Recall that individuals at high risk of dropping out of high school were substantially oversampled in our initial panel sample selection (with a consequent low initial selection weight). These are the individuals least likely to participate fully in the panel follow-ups, and thus most likely to be up-weighted by poststratification. The effect, therefore, is to reduce rather than increase the variability of the weights, and that (other things equal) results in a sample that is more efficient. So we conclude that the poststratification involved in these analyses did not lessen sample precision. To put it in more practical terms, poststratification as applied here does not require us to reduce the Ns we claim as Effective Ns when applying significance tests, and so on, based on simple random samples.

Impacts of Imputation

Imputation of missing data can seem to be a bit of black magic. A computer program takes account of everything (or at least a whole lot) that we know about a survey respondent and feeds that information into an explicit statistical model in order to make a guess (a good guess, we hope) about what that respondent would have answered for questions omitted—or sometimes for a whole survey unreturned. The program needs to be told a lot about the nature of the variables being imputed, and if one inadvertently gives the program the wrong instruction, one can get back very strange-looking imputed data. (Never mind how we know that!)

In any case, if one does a decent job of all the initial specifications, and allows the computer to run for an impressively long while (at least with our data), out comes a data set with *no missing data*! That is really great because it can avoid all sorts of missing data problems in complex multivariate analyses. If one then does the same thing again, with exactly the same input information, out comes another data set—again with no missing data. But here is the catch: the second data set will not look exactly like the first. Oh, to be sure, all the *nonimputed* data will be exactly the same; but the *imputed* data will differ, to some extent, from one data set to the other. That takes a little getting used to, at least for those of us who are accustomed to getting exactly the same answers any time we feed the same data into a correlation matrix or a regression equation. The imputation program is not quite like that because it incorporates a chance or stochastic process into its estimation of the missing data.

We sometimes find it useful to think of the imputed data sets as cloned from the original. Actually, we think of each particular imputed *case* as a clone of his or her original parent data case, except that the clones have no missing data. In the previous example, each parent case (which is no longer used in analyses) has two clones, which differ only in the data that were imputed—and only some of the time on even those dimensions.

So which of the two data sets should we use? Our answer was: Use both of them, plus more because we increase accuracy by doing multiple imputations. In our analyses we ran 10 sets of imputations, all done separately for males and females, in order to feel we had enough to average out the fluctuations from one pass through the program to another.

Assuming the computer has done its thing successfully, and one now has 10 data sets in hand, what comes next? The statistically correct approach is to run the full set of desired analyses separately on each of the 10 data sets and then combine the results using an approach such as that offered by Rubin (1987; see also Li, Raghunathan, & Rubin, 1991). The outcome of this process is that the statistic in question—let us suppose it is a coefficient—will be, in effect, an average of the 10 separate ones. The standard error of that coefficient, however, will be derived by taking account of two kinds of information—the corresponding standard errors from each of the 10 data sets, along with the degree of dispersal among the 10 coefficients. If the 10 different coefficients agree closely, then the resulting combined standard error will look much like the standard error from any of the individual data sets; however, if the 10 different coefficients are more varied, then the combined standard error will be larger than most or all of the ingredient standard errors. In other words, if the imputation process comes up with just about the same answer each time, not much error has been added; but if the results differ appreciably, then sampling precision is (quite appropriately) estimated to be lower.

Well, we did all of that. We followed the statistically correct procedures just described to assign significance levels to all of the ordinary least-squares regression coefficients reported in this book (specifically Tables 4.1, 5.1, A.6.2, A.7.1, A.8.2, A.9.1, and A.9.2). As input to the Rubin (1987) procedure, we used the output from the SAS PROC REG program. That SAS program uses weighted data in calculating the coefficients, but uses the raw number of observations in calculating standard errors. We considered the Raw Ns a reasonable starting point for a procedure that was then going to make an empirical assessment of additional error. An examination of the standard errors that emerged from this process revealed that the combined ones were only modestly larger than the average of their ingredients. We thus tentatively concluded that the imputation process was not adding much error to our sample estimates. This was not surprising given that only modest portions of data needed to be imputed because we excluded from the panel those who had failed to participate in either of the final (i.e., age-20 or age-22) follow-up surveys.

It may be worth noting here that we did some preliminary explorations with more liberal rules for panel inclusion, which thus required considerably more imputation. We found (again, not surprisingly) that this resulted in a good deal more variation from one imputed data set to another, leaving us not entirely confident about imputing substantially larger proportions of data. These preliminary explorations were among the factors we considered in deciding how stringently to restrict membership for inclusion in our panel analyses.

The statistically correct procedure requires conducting every analysis multiple times—10 times in our case—then putting the results (e.g., coefficients and their standard errors) into some format that permits wholesale processing through the Rubin (1987) formula. We were able to semiautomate that process for the regression analyses, but the other sorts of analyses widely used in this book—multiple classification analyses and structural equation modeling—did not so readily lend themselves to such streamlining. Given the many thousands of separate statistics involved, it was a truly daunting prospect to consider doing all of the computations 10 times over (not all that hard) and then plucking out bits and pieces from each of 10 sets of output and feeding them through the Rubin formula (harder, and dreadfully tedious). The idea of doing all that just so as to make very fine-grained adjustments to significance tests seemed an unnecessary extravagance—all the more so when we considered that close calls on significance tests are not really what this book is about.

The alternative we considered was to combine all 10 data sets together and run our analyses once, rather than 10 times over. We gave that a try, and this now quite large data set yielded coefficients virtually identical to those coming out of the much more elaborate statistically correct procedure. As for computing standard errors and significance tests, we of course had to be sure that we down-weighted everything by a factor of 10—but that was easily accomplished, and it worked fine so long as we were dealing with statistical programs that used the weighted Ns rather than actual numbers of observed cases in computing significance tests. We found again that results from this shortcut method were not much different from those following statistically correct procedures; however, there were a few borderline cases that just slipped over the threshold of significance following this particular shortcut, but fell just short when following the Rubin (1987) approach.

"Effective N Weighting" to the Rescue

At this point, we returned to the "Effective N" notion. We were faced with 10 data sets—actually 20 given that we did everything separately by gender and thus had 10 data sets for males and 10 for females. Rather than take the weights resulting from the poststratification process and multiply them all by a factor of .10, we down-weighted a bit further, and instead multiplied all of the poststratification weights by a factor of .075. That value did not arrive by magic, of course. It is the same factor of .75 discussed many paragraphs ago, modified because now we are dealing with 10 times as many cases. Shrinking a sample by one quarter, which is what we proposed to do with our (slightly oversized, remember) initial weighted sample, had the effect of increasing standard errors, confidence intervals, and significance thresholds by just over 15%.[1] This modest increase in confidence intervals was more than sufficient to account for the modest increases in error that seemed to result from applying the imputation process to our data.

---

[1]Why? Because if N is dropped to .75 of the original, the square root of N drops to .866 of the original, and 1 divided by .866 equals 1.1547.

One of our ways for checking the accuracy of this adjustment—which we call *Effective N Weighting* for want of a better term—was to compare the regression analyses in chapters 6 through 9 with the corresponding multiple classification analyses. The regression analyses, the reader may recall, used the statistically correct (Rubin, 1987) method in computing significance levels, whereas the multiple classification analyses used our shortcut approach—all 10 imputed data sets combined into one large data set, with each clone in that large data set weighted by the poststratification weight multiplied by .075. This is the weighting used in all analyses except the regression analyses, and it is what gives rise to the Effective *N*s shown in the tables. Interested readers are invited to compare significance thresholds from regression tables and multiple classification analysis tables; they will find them very similar.

We have nearly finished our odyssey in search of *N*, and the Effective *N* approach outlined previously looks promising. But first we must confront one last challenge—what to do about design effects.

Design Effects[2]

As noted earlier, sample precision generally increases directly proportionate to the square root of *N*. In the case of simple random samples, one can for example compute the standard error essentially by dividing the standard deviation by the square root of *N*. But complex probability samples such as ours make use of stratification, clustering, and differential weighting of respondents. Stratification tends to heighten precision, whereas clustering and weighting tend to reduce precision (compared with a simple random sample of the same size). Methods exist for taking account of these departures from simple random sampling. Kish (1965) defined a correction term called the *design effect*, which consists of the actual sampling variance (from a complex sample) divided by the expected sampling variance from a simple random sample of the same size.

This correction term is clear and simple enough; it is the amount by which one must divide an actual sample *N* to get an Effective *N* that can then be used in simple random sample statistics. Thus, for example, a complex sample with a design effect of 2.0 and based on 2,000 cases would have precision equivalent to a simple random sample of 1,000. But although *using* design effects can be a relatively simple matter, *computing* them (i.e., carrying out computations to decide what a design effect should be) is not

---

[2]The first portion of this section is adapted from Bachman et al. (2005) and Bachman, Johnston et al. (2006).

so simple, and explaining such computations lies outside the scope of this book. Fortunately, there are now computer programs available to carry out such computations, provided one has available the necessary information about stratification, clustering, and weighting.

In an earlier set of analyses with the present panel sample, in this case tracked through three follow-ups (to modal age 20), we calculated a number of design effects for cigarette use, alcohol use, and marijuana use.[3] The results, reported in Bachman, Johnston et al. (2006), were a range of design effect estimates (each statistic actually gets its own). The important finding from that effort is that the design effects for the approach most similar to the one used in this book tended to vary around 1.0 (out of 16 such design effects, 7 were lower than 1.0 and 9 were higher), suggesting that the positive effects of stratification and the negative effects of clustering and differential weighting were just about an even tradeoff. This might leave some readers wondering why these design effects were so low, whereas typical design effects on MTF samples of 15,000 would be on the order of 3.5. A substantial part of the answer is that the average cluster size is far greater in the large cross-sectional samples, and design effects increase with cluster size. Furthermore, weighting across individuals varies more widely in the cross-sectional samples than in our panel samples of eighth graders. In short, the present samples are far more efficient, in sampling terms, than our much larger in-school surveys.

As noted previously, each statistic has its own design effect. In reports of the MTF cross-sectional surveys of 12th graders, we have shown how design effects vary systematically as a function of the sizes of samples and subgroups, and it can readily be seen how larger sizes (and corresponding sizes of clusters) in these samples impact the sizes of design effect estimates (Bachman et al., 2005). It can also be seen that useful generalizations can be developed, such that calculating separate design effect estimates for each and every statistic is unnecessary. This latter point is particularly important in work such as the present book, which involves many thousands of different statistics. Estimating separate design effects for each of these would hugely complicate an already demanding analysis task.

What should we do about design effects in the present book? Based on our earlier analyses of these data, as summarized in the preceding paragraphs, we concluded that the modest downsizing of the obtained samples is adequate to account for design effects for our samples.

---

[3]These design effects were estimated using IVEware software developed at the University of Michigan by T. E. Raghunathan, P. W. Solenberger, and J. Van Hoewyk (Raghunathan et al., 2001, 2002). IVEware calculates sample variances using the Taylor series expansion method.

In sum, we believe the values of N shown throughout this book are, if anything, slightly conservative—especially when it comes to individuals at high academic risk who were oversampled in the initial selection of follow-up target samples. The N values take account of (a) the initial pre-stratification, (b) poststratification to adjust for differential panel attrition, (c) effects of multiple imputation, and (d) design effects. The actual numbers of cases are equal to or larger than the corresponding N values shown in tables. We have thus felt confident in using .05 (two-tailed) confidence levels as the basis for declaring a finding to be statistically significant.

SAMPLING AND SURVEY PROCEDURES

In this section, we provide greater detail about several matters noted in the previous portion of this appendix and in chapter 3. We first describe the initial cross-sectional surveys of eighth-grade students, which provided the relatively large pool from which we drew our follow-up panel samples. We then describe the stratification procedure used in selecting individuals for inclusion in the target panel samples. Next we describe the follow-up survey procedures. Then we provide full details on how we poststratified our retained panel sample so as to closely approximate the original target sample (in terms of key characteristics measured in the original eighth-grade survey).

Samples and Surveys of Eighth-Grade Students

The sampling of eighth-grade students involved a multistage procedure: The first stage consisted of geographic areas (the Survey Research Center's primary sampling areas located throughout the coterminous United States), the second stage was the selection of one or more schools in each primary sampling area (generating a total of approximately 160 schools, both public and private), and the third stage was the random selection of up to 350 students—if the number of eighth graders in the school was larger than that.

As noted in chapter 3, the numbers of participating schools in the surveys of eighth-grade students were 162 in 1991, 159 in 1992, and 156 in 1993; the numbers of students surveyed were 17,844, 19,015, and 18,820, respectively.

The eighth-grade participants completed questionnaires during survey sessions conducted by professional interviewers on the staff of the

University of Michigan's Survey Research Center. Ordinarily these sessions were held in regular classroom settings, with teachers present but not actively participating in data collection. The questionnaires consisted entirely of closed-ended multiple-choice items formatted for optical scanning. Students provided names and mailing addresses on a tear-off portion of the back cover to the questionnaire booklet. Booklets and the tear-off mail information were identifiable by two different sets of code numbers that could be linked only by a data file maintained under strict security at the University of Michigan. Respondents were informed at each survey that such links are used only to match data across time, never to link individuals' names to their answers.[4]

Initial Stratification for Selecting Target Panel Samples

From each of the three eighth-grade cross-sectional samples in 1991 to 1993, approximately 2,000 respondents were selected as potential participants in the follow-up panels. These targets were selected so as to overrepresent those eighth graders most likely to drop out of school before graduating. To accomplish that, we assigned each respondent an *Academic Risk Score* based on factors known to predict academic attainment. These self-reported factors include (a) parental educational attainment, (b) student GPA, (c) student truancy, and (d) a composite of student grade retention, required attendance at summer school, and/or suspension or expulsion. This risk score was bracketed to produce four strata; of the initial samples, 43% fell into the lowest risk stratum, 26% in the next lowest, 18% in the next, and 13% in the highest risk stratum. We then used stratified random procedures to select 500 from each risk stratum as target follow-up participants (yielding the total target each year of 2,000). Thus, although those at highest risk of dropping out amounted to only 13% of eighth graders, they constituted 25% of the target follow-up sample; conversely, those at lowest risk made up 43% of eighth graders, but they also constituted 25% of the follow-up targets. As a consequence of this sampling strategy, a student at high risk of dropping out was several times more likely to be included than a student likely to complete college. This, of course, requires the use of corrective weights in analysis, with lower weights assigned to the (originally oversampled) high-risk individuals; otherwise, the samples would be distorted and show disproportionately large numbers of individuals with low grades and poor school experiences.

---

[4]The more recent MTF surveys of eighth-grade students do not involve any follow-up component. Consequently, the name identification procedures have been dropped.

Follow-Up Procedures

The survey procedures for the follow-up samples involved a series of mailings. The first was a letter explaining that the respondent had been chosen for a follow-up study and expressing the hope that he or she would participate. There were also annual newsletters mailed in December as a means of maintaining respondent interest and also keeping addresses up to date. Then, approximately 2 years after the initial eighth-grade survey, a questionnaire was sent in April, along with a check for $5 in the respondent's name. The cover letter explained that the check was an expression of appreciation, and that an additional check for $15 would be sent on receipt of a completed questionnaire. The questionnaire content was largely similar to the in-school survey and consisted of closed-ended multiple-choice items formatted for optical scanning. An address correction form was attached to the back of the questionnaire, and the mailing label containing the respondent's name and address was affixed to that form. The respondent was asked to detach the form (containing a code number) and mail the questionnaire (now identified only by a different code number) using the return postage-paid envelope provided. Respondents were asked to update the address form as needed and mail it back separately (also postage-paid) or discard it if no changes were required.

An additional set of follow-up contacts was employed as needed. About 1 week after the initial questionnaire mailing, postcards were sent to all target respondents, thanking those who had already returned their questionnaires and reminding the others of the importance of the study and our hopes for their early response. About 4 weeks after the questionnaire mailing, letters were sent to all who had not yet responded, urging them to complete and return the questionnaires as soon as possible. Several weeks after that, the Survey Research Center telephone-interviewing staff attempted to contact all remaining target respondents in order to prompt their response (and to arrange for an additional questionnaire to be sent if the original was misplaced).

These questionnaire mailing and tracking procedures were repeated five times at 2-year intervals, corresponding to modal ages 14 (the in-school survey, in 1991–1993), 16 (the first follow-up), 18 (second follow-up), 20 (third follow-up), 22 (fourth follow-up, in 1991–2001), and 24 (fifth follow-up, not used in most analyses in this volume).

The follow-up procedures outlined previously were successful in maintaining acceptable response rates, although researchers nearly always would prefer to do better—and we are no exception. Response rates are discussed in chapter 3 and shown in Table 3.1, and also in Table

A.3.1. We also discussed in chapter 3 the two procedures for dealing with less-than-perfect follow-up response: poststratification (i.e., reweighting of the obtained sample so as to more closely approximate initial target sample characteristics) and imputation (i.e., calculating estimated values to act as substitutes for missing data). Some details of our poststratification procedure are provided in the next section.

Poststratification Details

In the earlier appendix section entitled "N—or, What's in a Number?," we provide an overview of our poststratification strategy and rationale. Because it provides a good orientation to this section, we repeat a portion of that overview in the next paragraph.

We arrived at our poststratification weights by sorting the members of our *target* panel sample into categories according to several factors spelled out later in this appendix, and checking the *retained* panel sample (in this case defined as those who participated in one or both of the age-20 and age-22 follow-up surveys) to see what proportion of the target sample had been retained. In some categories (e.g., those who as 14-year-olds reported good grades and no substance use), most of the individuals stayed in the panel and participated in follow-ups at ages 20 and/or 22. In some other categories (e.g., those who reported poor grades and daily smoking or other substance use), smaller proportions stayed in the panel. The logic of poststratification is that we expect to do a better job of representing the whole age cohort if we do not allow the poor students and early smokers to be underrepresented in our analyses. As a *partial* solution to that, we take those in such low-participation categories who *did* stay in the panel and give them a somewhat increased weight (with our poststratification weighting scheme), whereas those in the high-participation categories get a somewhat reduced weight. That has the effect of making the retained panel sample look similar to the original target sample *in terms of factors measured at the initial (eighth-grade) survey.* What it cannot do is tell us exactly what the nonparticipants looked like at age 22. We know that those who were smoking at age 14 are more likely than average to also be smoking at age 22. But what cannot be known from our data is whether, among all those who smoked at age 14, those who drop out of the panel are more likely to remain smokers at age 22, compared with those age-14 smokers who stayed in the panel. Our guess is that, if anything, the panel nonparticipants tend to be doing less well than the participants in terms of substance use, even after we match for age-14 characteristics. If so, then our poststratification is only partly successful. Nevertheless, the partial success seems pretty good, at least in terms of substance use, as indicated by earlier analyses comparing poststratified panel data and data from MTF annual cross-sections (Bachman, O'Malley et al., 2001).

One part of the process that is not so simple is defining the categories into which we sort respondents for purposes of reweighting. We developed a set of 64 categories based on four dimensions:

1. Gender: males and females. (two groups)
2. Race/ethnicity: We distinguished African-American and Hispanic target respondents (combined) versus all others because these two groups showed distinctly lower than average follow-up participation rates (two groups).
3. Eighth-grade substance use: We distinguished two levels—(a) those who in the eighth-grade survey reported one or more of the following behaviors: any heavy drinking (five or more drinks at one time) during the past 2 weeks, daily smoking during the past 30 days, any marijuana use during the past 30 days, any cocaine use during the last 12 months; versus (b) all others (two groups).
4. Educational successes and failures by the end of eighth grade: we developed a total of eight levels, derived by using the initial four-level follow-up sampling stratification code (which took account of parental education plus educational problems reflected in low grades, truancy, suspension, expulsion, grade retention, and need to attend summer school) and combining it with the full range of GPAs in eighth grade. We reduced a much larger set of cells to eight to capture a wide range of educational success or failure while also retaining sufficient cases at each of the eight levels (eight groups).

Combining these four dimensions yielded 2 x 2 x 2 x 8 = 64 categories. The numbers of cases in each of these categories were large enough to permit the poststratification as outlined previously.

The advantages of this categorical approach to poststratification are that it is relatively straightforward to describe and implement, and it captures any interaction among the four ingredients.

The success of our poststratification effort is indicated, to some extent, by the comparisons between the panel data and the large-scale MTF cross-sectional samples as reported in chapters 6 through 9. Further evidence of the efficacy of this general approach was provided in preliminary analyses reported elsewhere, which led us to the following conclusions:

The post-stratification re-weighting approach ... takes data which are already weighted—necessarily so—and revises the weights so as to reproduce the original sample more accurately. Moreover, the new weighting scheme shows a somewhat narrower distribution of weights, with the result that the sample is more "efficient" than if the original weights were used. Most importantly, the sample estimates resulting from the new weighting scheme are quite realistic in terms of substance use, as well as educational success. ... " (Bachman, O'Malley et al., 2001, p. 15)

STRUCTURAL EQUATION MODEL TECHNICAL DECISIONS AND RATIONALE

Technical decisions for the structural equation model, along with the underlying rationale, are spelled out in the text chapters as follows:

In chapter 4, the section entitled "A Structural Equation Model of Academic Attainment" lays out a large portion of what later becomes our full structural equation model. This initial model includes relevant background factors; educational experiences measured at modal ages 14, 16, and 18; and academic attainment measured at modal age 22. The section explains the causal orderings we imposed and our reasons for doing so.

In chapter 5, the section entitled "Adding Delinquency to the Structural Equation Model of Academic Attainment" does just what the title indicates. It shows how we expand the model to incorporate delinquent behaviors measured at modal ages 14, 16, and 18. Later in chapter 5, the section entitled "Expanding the Structural Equation Model to Include Substance Use" again does what the title indicates: It outlines how we further expand the model to include cigarette use, marijuana use, cocaine use, and alcohol use, each measured at modal ages 14, 16, and 18. For both of these expansions, we explain the causal orderings imposed and our reasons for choosing them.

The full model, as described at the end of chapter 5, is estimated separately for males and females. There are some differences between genders, but our overall conclusion is that findings are generally quite similar for males and females.

The primary model includes measures of 30-day alcohol use, but an additional model replaces those with measures of instances of heavy drinking (five or more drinks in a row) during the past 2 weeks, as detailed in chapter 9. Comparing the model findings across the two alcohol measures reveals virtually identical findings for all other aspects (as can be seen by comparing Tables A.3.8 and A.3.9 in the appendix). Accordingly, all of our presentations of findings focus on the primary version that includes the 30-day alcohol-use measures, except for the portion of chapter 9 dealing with instances of heavy drinking.

Aspects of the model having to do with each form of substance use are treated in sections entitled "A Structural Equation Model Including Academic Attainment and Smoking (chap. 6), ... Marijuana Use (chap. 7), ... Cocaine Use (chap. 8), and ... Alcohol Use" (chap. 9).

Many details of the models and their findings are presented in the appendix in the following tables:

Table A.3.4 provides all factor loadings used in the structural models. Factors were defined by either multiple indicators or single indicators. Factor loadings for the multiple indicators were estimated by the EQS program (Bentler, 1995). For single-indicator factors, the loadings were set equal to the square root of the estimated reliability of the indicator. As indicated in the text, some reliabilities were assumed to equal 1; other reliabilities were assumed to equal .81 (yielding loadings of .90); the remaining reliabilities were estimated from repeated measures of the indicators, using procedures described in O'Malley et al. (1983). The error variances of the multiple indicators were estimated by the program; the error variance of each single indicator was set equal to (1 minus reliability) times the indicator's observed variance.

Table A.3.5 shows model fit statistics for males and females and both alcohol-use measures. Decisions about which statistics to show were guided by recommendations in Byrne (2006) and McDonald and Ho (2002).

Tables A.3.6 and A.3.7 show variance in endogenous factors explained by all prior causal factors in the models for each of the alcohol-use measures.

Tables A.3.8 and A.3.9 present bivariate factor correlations, direct effects, and total effects of each predictor in the model on academic attainment for the models for each of the alcohol-use measures.

Table A.3.10 provides a full tabular summary of findings for the primary structural equation model—the one including the 30-day alcohol-use measures. Given the similarities across the two models shown in Tables A.3.4 to A.3.9, we considered it unnecessary to produce a full tabular summary for the model including the 2-week heavy drinking measures.

Appendix Tables and Figures

Table A.1.1a
Percentage Reporting Any Daily Smoking in the Last 30 Days
by Academic Attainment: Males

8th-Grade Classes 1991–1993 (combined)

						Pearson Product
Weighted N	198	364	381	419	1362	Moment
% in Subgroups	14.5	26.7	28.0	30.8	100.0	Correlation*
	H.S. Dropouts	H.S. Diploma	1–2 Years College	3+ Years College	Total	
Age 14	19.2	9.1	7.1	2.4	7.9	-.20
Age 16	33.8	16.5	12.9	5.3	14.5	-.26
Age 18	44.9	31.0	23.4	12.4	25.2	-.25
Age 20	53.0	35.8	28.9	18.4	31.0	-.25
Age 22	56.1	36.5	31.2	19.4	32.6	-.25

12th-Grade Classes 1988–1994 (combined)

						Pearson Product
Weighted N		778	1073	1046	2897	Moment
% in Subgroups		26.9	37.0	36.1	100.0	Correlation*
	H.S. Dropouts	H.S. Diploma	1–2 Years College	3+ Years College	Total	
Age 18		26.0	15.8	9.8	16.4	-.19
Ages 19–20		30.5	17.9	11.6	19.0	-.19
Ages 21–22		29.4	21.7	13.6	20.8	-.17
Ages 23–24		30.3	20.4	13.7	20.7	-.18
Ages 25–26		29.0	19.8	12.9	19.8	-.17
Ages 27–28		27.6	17.1	11.2	17.8	-.18

12th-Grade Classes 1976–1982 (combined)

						Pearson Product
Weighted N		1070	1018	808	2895	Moment
% in Subgroups		37.0	35.2	27.9	100.0	Correlation*
	H.S. Dropouts	H.S. Diploma	1–2 Years College	3+ Years College	Total	
Age 18		33.1	16.9	10.1	21.0	-.23
Ages 19–20		36.1	21.3	12.1	24.2	-.23
Ages 21–22		37.0	21.4	14.8	25.3	-.22
Ages 23–24		35.2	21.2	14.3	24.4	-.20
Ages 25–26		33.8	20.1	13.6	23.4	-.20
Ages 27–28		34.7	20.3	13.6	23.7	-.21
Ages 29–30		30.8	18.6	13.0	21.6	-.20
Ages 31–32		31.2	17.7	12.4	21.2	-.21
Age 35		31.3	17.0	11.8	20.8	-.21
Age 40		29.1	15.2	11.2	19.2	-.21

*Correlations are between the levels of academic attainment and the full scale of the substance use variable. Correlations p<.05 shown in **bold**.

Table A.1.1b
Percentage Reporting Any Daily Smoking in the Last 30 Days
by Academic Attainment: Females

8th-Grade Classes 1991–1993 (combined)

Weighted N	210	399	454	675	1738	Pearson Product Moment Correlation*
% in Subgroups	12.1	23.0	26.1	38.8	100.0	
	H.S. Dropouts	H.S. Diploma	1–2 Years College	3+ Years College	Total	
Age 14	19.5	11.3	6.6	3.0	7.8	-.23
Age 16	39.5	21.6	15.4	8.9	17.2	-.27
Age 18	42.9	30.6	21.1	14.7	23.4	-.25
Age 20	48.1	32.6	26.7	19.1	27.7	-.21
Age 22	45.7	34.8	25.8	18.5	27.4	-.21

12th-Grade Classes 1988–1994 (combined)

Weighted N		924	1518	1612	4054	Pearson Product Moment Correlation*
% in Subgroups		22.8	37.4	39.8	100.0	
	H.S. Dropouts	H.S. Diploma	1–2 Years College	3+ Years College	Total	
Age 18		28.6	16.4	11.1	17.1	-.19
Ages 19–20		27.8	19.1	13.1	18.7	-.16
Ages 21–22		29.1	18.4	14.2	19.2	-.15
Ages 23–24		27.6	18.5	12.8	18.3	-.15
Ages 25–26		27.2	16.1	10.4	16.4	-.18
Ages 27–28		28.8	16.1	9.4	16.4	-.20

12th-Grade Classes 1976–1982 (combined)

Weighted N		1362	1441	928	3731	Pearson Product Moment Correlation*
% in Subgroups		36.5	38.6	24.9	100.0	
	H.S. Dropouts	H.S. Diploma	1–2 Years College	3+ Years College	Total	
Age 18		34.7	22.2	12.7	24.4	-.21
Ages 19–20		33.8	24.7	17.3	26.2	-.16
Ages 21–22		33.8	25.0	17.6	26.4	-.16
Ages 23–24		32.8	25.0	16.1	25.6	-.16
Ages 25–26		31.4	22.3	15.5	24.0	-.16
Ages 27–28		30.0	20.7	12.7	22.1	-.17
Ages 29–30		28.4	19.3	11.3	20.6	-.17
Ages 31–32		27.1	19.0	10.0	19.7	-.17
Age 35		25.6	17.9	9.9	18.7	-.17
Age 40		25.6	16.5	8.7	17.9	-.18

*Correlations are between the levels of academic attainment and the full scale of the substance use variable. Correlations p<.05 shown in **bold**.

Table A.1.2
Percentage Reporting Any Daily Smoking
in the Last 30 Days by Eighth-Grade GPA

Males
Any Daily Smoking in the Last 30 Days

	A	A-	B+ or B	B- or C+	C or C-	D or Below	Pearson*
Age 14	3.2	2.1	5.6	7.1	12.3	27.6	**-.18**
Age 16	5.6	6.4	9.4	17.6	22.3	34.2	**-.21**
Age 18	12.9	15.0	21.4	31.1	34.8	52.6	**-.22**
Age 20	17.6	21.4	25.1	33.7	43.6	57.9	**-.22**
Age 22	18.5	23.6	28.2	31.9	42.2	51.3	**-.17**

Females
Any Daily Smoking in the Last 30 Days

	A	A-	B+ or B	B- or C+	C or C-	D or Below	Pearson*
Age 14	1.2	3.2	4.5	11.2	15.0	29.5	**-.21**
Age 16	13.9	18.2	20.5	32.6	34.4	51.2	**-.21**
Age 18	22.5	30.6	33.3	41.3	42.2	53.5	**-.17**
Age 20	30.1	31.0	37.5	43.0	45.6	52.3	**-.16**
Age 22	30.1	31.6	35.3	44.4	43.3	52.3	**-.14**

*Correlations between 8th-grade GPA and the full scale of the substance use variable. Correlations $p<.05$ shown in **bold**.

Table A.1.3a
Percentage Reporting Any Marijuana Use in the Last 30 Days
by Academic Attainment at Age 22: Males

8th-Grade Classes 1991–1993 (combined)						Pearson Product Moment Correlation*
Weighted *N*	198	364	381	419	1362	
% in Subgroups	14.5	26.7	28.0	30.8	100.0	
	H.S. Dropouts	H.S. Diploma	1–2 Years College	3+ Years College	Total	
Age 14	12.1	4.4	2.9	2.6	4.6	-.12
Age 16	26.3	12.9	10.5	7.6	12.6	-.17
Age 18	38.9	25.5	21.5	16.5	23.6	-.18
Age 20	39.4	26.4	25.5	25.1	27.6	-.13
Age 22	36.4	22.5	23.1	24.4	25.3	-.08

12th-Grade Classes 1988–1994 (combined)						Pearson Product Moment Correlation*
Weighted *N*		778	1073	1046	2897	
% in Subgroups		26.9	37.0	36.1	100.0	
	H.S. Dropouts	H.S. Diploma	1–2 Years College	3+ Years College	Total	
Age 18		19.7	15.8	12.0	15.5	-.09
Ages 19–20		16.9	17.5	16.2	16.9	-.04
Ages 21–22		14.9	17.2	19.0	17.3	.02
Ages 23–24		16.5	17.0	13.8	15.7	-.03
Ages 25–26		17.1	14.9	14.1	15.2	-.05
Ages 27–28		13.9	12.3	11.4	12.4	-.05

12th-Grade Classes 1976–1982 (combined)						Pearson Product Moment Correlation*
Weighted *N*		1070	1018	808	2895	
% in Subgroups		37.0	35.2	27.9	100.0	
	H.S. Dropouts	H.S. Diploma	1–2 Years College	3+ Years College	Total	
Age 18		41.5	33.8	27.8	35.0	-.15
Ages 19–20		37.0	35.1	35.6	35.9	-.07
Ages 21–22		35.2	32.1	35.8	34.3	-.05
Ages 23–24		32.5	28.5	29.0	30.1	-.06
Ages 25–26		28.4	22.2	23.1	24.8	-.07
Ages 27–28		25.1	19.3	18.3	21.1	-.08
Ages 29–30		19.7	16.6	16.4	17.7	-.06
Ages 31–32		17.9	14.2	13.7	15.4	-.05
Age 35		16.4	13.7	12.9	14.5	-.04
Age 40		13.3	10.9	10.7	11.7	-.02

*Correlations are between the levels of academic attainment and the full scale of the substance use variable. Correlations p<.05 shown in **bold**.

Table A.1.3b
Percentage Reporting Any Marijuana Use in the Last 30 Days
by Academic Attainment at Age 22: Females

8th-Grade Classes 1991–1993 (combined)						Pearson Product Moment Correlation*
Weighted *N*	210	399	454	675	1738	
% in Subgroups	12.1	23.0	26.1	38.8	100.0	
	H.S. Dropouts	H.S. Diploma	1–2 Years College	3+ Years College	Total	
Age 14	11.4	5.0	4.4	1.9	4.4	**-.11**
Age 16	20.0	14.3	11.6	9.2	12.3	**-.12**
Age 18	23.2	18.3	18.1	13.8	17.1	**-.10**
Age 20	23.3	16.5	19.3	20.7	19.7	-.06
Age 22	22.7	14.8	16.0	16.9	16.9	-.05

12th-Grade Classes 1988–1994 (combined)						Pearson Product Moment Correlation*
Weighted *N*		924	1518	1612	4054	
% in Subgroups		22.8	37.4	39.8	100.0	
	H.S. Dropouts	H.S. Diploma	1–2 Years College	3+ Years College	Total	
Age 18		15.5	11.3	10.0	11.8	**-.07**
Ages 19–20		13.6	12.5	12.3	12.7	-.03
Ages 21–22		11.4	11.7	13.0	12.1	.00
Ages 23–24		10.1	10.5	8.8	9.7	-.02
Ages 25–26		8.8	8.4	8.0	8.3	-.03
Ages 27–28		9.6	8.1	6.1	7.7	-.06

12th-Grade Classes 1976–1982 (combined)						Pearson Product Moment Correlation*
Weighted *N*		1362	1441	928	3731	
% in Subgroups		36.5	38.6	24.9	100.0	
	H.S. Dropouts	H.S. Diploma	1–2 Years College	3+ Years College	Total	
Age 18		32.3	27.5	21.1	27.7	**-.12**
Ages 19–20		28.7	27.4	23.8	27.0	**-.07**
Ages 21–22		24.0	25.1	22.2	24.0	-.05
Ages 23–24		21.2	20.9	16.9	20.0	**-.07**
Ages 25–26		17.4	15.0	12.1	15.1	**-.07**
Ages 27–28		14.0	12.8	8.8	12.2	**-.08**
Ages 29–30		10.3	10.7	5.9	9.4	-.06
Ages 31–32		11.0	9.1	5.5	8.9	**-.08**
Age 35		8.7	7.6	4.1	7.2	**-.07**
Age 40		6.9	5.4	4.0	5.6	-.06

*Correlations are between the levels of academic attainment and the full scale of the substance use variable. Correlations p<.05 shown in **bold**.

Table A.1.4a
Percentage Reporting Any Heavy Drinking in the Last Two Weeks
by Academic Attainment at Age 22: Males

8th-Grade Classes 1991–1993 (combined)

	H.S. Dropouts	H.S. Diploma	1–2 Years College	3+ Years College	Total	Pearson Product Moment Correlation*
Weighted *N*	198	364	381	419	1362	
% in Subgroups	14.5	26.7	28.0	30.8	100.0	
Age 14	31.8	17.3	13.6	7.9	15.5	-.18
Age 16	37.9	26.1	22.6	15.3	23.5	-.16
Age 18	41.9	37.9	37.3	30.4	36.0	-.09
Age 20	49.0	44.8	45.1	51.9	47.7	.02
Age 22	55.1	49.7	52.8	55.4	53.1	.01

12th-Grade Classes 1988–1994 (combined)

	H.S. Dropouts	H.S. Diploma	1–2 Years College	3+ Years College	Total	Pearson Product Moment Correlation*
Weighted *N*		778	1073	1046	2897	
% in Subgroups		26.9	37.0	36.1	100.0	
Age 18		41.7	34.4	34.3	36.3	-.09
Ages 19–20		39.7	38.8	44.4	41.1	.01
Ages 21–22		47.9	47.6	54.2	50.1	.03
Ages 23–24		43.6	44.9	48.7	45.9	.01
Ages 25–26		41.9	40.1	43.3	41.7	-.01
Ages 27–28		41.6	42.0	43.6	42.5	-.04

12th-Grade Classes 1976–1982 (combined)

	H.S. Dropouts	H.S. Diploma	1–2 Years College	3+ Years College	Total	Pearson Product Moment Correlation*
Weighted *N*		1070	1018	808	2895	
% in Subgroups		37.0	35.2	27.9	100.0	
Age 18		54.9	48.4	42.9	49.3	-.15
Ages 19–20		53.2	51.3	51.0	51.9	-.05
Ages 21–22		55.7	53.9	55.6	55.1	-.03
Ages 23–24		51.5	49.4	47.4	49.6	-.07
Ages 25–26		47.9	43.8	45.5	45.8	-.06
Ages 27–28		44.2	39.7	38.3	41.0	-.09
Ages 29–30		41.2	37.9	34.4	38.2	-.09
Ages 31–32		39.8	34.3	31.9	35.7	-.09
Age 35		35.7	30.0	28.0	31.5	-.10
Age 40		33.8	28.2	25.6	29.5	-.10

*Correlations are between the levels of academic attainment and the full scale of the substance use variable. Correlations p<.05 shown in **bold**.

Table A.1.4b
Percentage Reporting Any Heavy Drinking in the Last Two Weeks
by Academic Attainment at Age 22: Females

8th-Grade Classes 1991–1993 (combined)

						Pearson Product Moment Correlation*
Weighted N	210	399	454	675	1738	
% in Subgroups	12.1	23.0	26.1	38.8	100.0	
	H.S. Dropouts	**H.S. Diploma**	**1–2 Years College**	**3+ Years College**	**Total**	
Age 14	28.1	16.8	15.9	7.6	14.3	-.17
Age 16	29.0	20.6	16.3	13.2	17.6	-.14
Age 18	26.7	27.6	26.2	23.0	25.3	-.05
Age 20	31.9	25.1	26.4	37.6	31.1	.06
Age 22	31.0	27.3	34.4	41.8	35.2	.05

12th-Grade Classes 1988–1994 (combined)

						Pearson Product Moment Correlation*
Weighted N		924	1518	1612	4054	
% in Subgroups		22.8	37.4	39.8	100.0	
	H.S. Dropouts	**H.S. Diploma**	**1–2 Years College**	**3+ Years College**	**Total**	
Age 18		24.8	21.6	19.4	21.5	-.06
Ages 19–20		22.0	25.3	31.8	27.1	.07
Ages 21–22		22.6	26.2	35.9	29.2	.12
Ages 23–24		22.9	22.8	28.2	25.0	.05
Ages 25–26		18.7	21.3	21.9	20.9	.03
Ages 27–28		18.8	19.5	21.4	20.1	.01

12th-Grade Classes 1976–1982 (combined)

						Pearson Product Moment Correlation*
Weighted N		1362	1441	928	3731	
% in Subgroups		36.5	38.6	24.9	100.0	
	H.S. Dropouts	**H.S. Diploma**	**1–2 Years College**	**3+ Years College**	**Total**	
Age 18		33.0	27.9	23.3	28.6	-.10
Ages 19–20		29.7	31.0	34.4	31.3	.01
Ages 21–22		27.6	29.3	32.9	29.6	.04
Ages 23–24		26.5	26.6	24.6	26.1	-.04
Ages 25–26		22.0	19.9	20.4	20.8	-.04
Ages 27–28		21.1	18.1	16.1	18.7	-.07
Ages 29–30		19.9	14.5	11.6	15.7	-.10
Ages 31–32		17.2	13.8	12.0	14.6	-.07
Age 35		16.4	12.6	8.7	13.0	-.08
Age 40		16.8	11.0	10.4	13.0	-.08

*Correlations are between the levels of academic attainment and the full scale of the substance use variable. Correlations p<.05 shown in **bold**.

Table A.3.1a
Response Rates at Each Survey Wave by Risk Group and Gender: Males

Risk Group	Wave 1, Modal Age 14		Wave 2, Modal Age 16			Wave 3, Modal Age 18		
	Raw N	Initial Selection Wtd. N	Raw N	Initial Selection Wtd. N	% of Age-14 Target (Init. Sel. Wt.)	Raw N	Initial Selection Wtd. N	% of Age-14 Target (Init. Sel. Wt.)
Low Risk: 1	656	1136.1	584	1011.6	89.0	463	801.9	70.6
2	693	719.7	549	570.4	79.3	411	427.0	59.3
3	771	560.2	551	400.4	71.5	408	296.6	52.9
High Risk: 4	941	469.4	540	269.9	57.5	380	189.8	40.4
Total Males	3061	2885.4	2224	2252.2	78.1	1662	1715.3	59.4

Risk Group	Wave 4, Modal Age 20			Wave 5, Modal Age 22			Participants at Wave 4 and/or Wave 5		
	Raw N	Initial Selection Wtd. N	% of Age-14 Target (Init. Sel. Wt.)	Raw N	Initial Selection Wtd. N	% of Age-14 Target (Init. Sel. Wt.)	Raw N	Initial Selection Wtd. N	% of Age-14 Target (Init. Sel. Wt.)
Low Risk: 1	440	761.6	67.0	400	693.2	61.0	492	851.4	74.9
2	381	395.9	55.0	349	362.7	50.4	442	459.2	63.8
3	358	259.7	46.4	307	223.0	39.8	424	307.8	54.9
High Risk: 4	338	168.6	35.9	283	141.3	30.1	400	200.2	42.6
Total Males	1517	1585.8	55.0	1339	1420.2	49.2	1758	1818.6	63.0

Table A.3.1b
Response Rates at Each Survey Wave by Risk Group and Gender: Females

		Wave 1, Modal Age 14		Wave 2, Modal Age 16			Wave 3, Modal Age 18		
Risk Group		Raw N	Initial Selection Wtd. N	Raw N	Initial Selection Wtd. N	% of Age-14 Target (Init. Sel. Wt.)	Raw N	Initial Selection Wtd. N	% of Age-14 Target (Init. Sel. Wt.)
Low Risk:	1	834	1446.5	765	1326.8	91.7	694	1202.8	83.1
	2	793	823.8	667	693.0	84.1	575	597.2	72.5
	3	705	514.1	518	377.8	73.5	424	308.8	60.1
High Risk:	4	529	266.0	335	169.7	63.8	257	130.6	49.1
Total Females		2861	3050.4	2285	2567.3	84.2	1950	2239.4	73.4

		Wave 4, Modal Age 20			Wave 5, Modal Age 22			Participants at Wave 4 and/or Wave 5		
Risk Group		Raw N	Initial Selection Wtd. N	% of Age-14 Target (Init. Sel. Wt.)	Raw N	Initial Selection Wtd. N	% of Age-14 Target (Init. Sel. Wt.)	Raw N	Initial Selection Wtd. N	% of Age-14 Target (Init. Sel. Wt.)
Low Risk:	1	666	1155.4	79.9	627	1087.4	75.2	714	1238.4	85.6
	2	566	588.2	71.4	522	542.7	65.9	612	636.1	77.2
	3	379	276.2	53.7	341	248.8	48.4	423	308.6	60.0
High Risk:	4	239	120.8	45.4	192	96.3	36.2	275	138.8	52.2
Total Females		1850	2140.6	70.2	1682	1975.1	64.7	2024	2322.0	76.1

Table A.3.1c
Response Rates at Each Survey Wave by Risk Group and Gender: Males and Females Combined

Risk Group	Wave 1, Modal Age 14 Raw N	Wave 1 Initial Selection Wtd. N	Wave 2, Modal Age 16 Raw N	Wave 2 Initial Selection Wtd. N	Wave 2 % of Age-14 Target (Init. Sel. Wt.)	Wave 3, Modal Age 18 Raw N	Wave 3 Initial Selection Wtd. N	Wave 3 % of Age-14 Target (Init. Sel. Wt.)
Low Risk: 1	1490	2582.6	1349	2338.4	90.5	1157	2004.7	77.6
2	1486	1543.4	1216	1263.4	81.9	986	1024.1	66.4
3	1476	1074.3	1069	778.2	72.4	832	605.3	56.3
High Risk: 4	1470	735.4	875	439.6	59.8	637	320.5	43.6
Total Sample	5922	5935.8	4509	4819.5	81.2	3612	3954.7	66.6

Risk Group	Wave 4, Modal Age 20 Raw N	Wave 4 Initial Selection Wtd. N	Wave 4 % of Age-14 Target (Init. Sel. Wt.)	Wave 5, Modal Age 22 Raw N	Wave 5 Initial Selection Wtd. N	Wave 5 % of Age-14 Target (Init. Sel. Wt.)	Participants at Wave 4 and/or Wave 5 Raw N	Initial Selection Wtd. N	% of Age-14 Target (Init. Sel. Wt.)
Low Risk: 1	1106	1916.9	74.2	1027	1780.5	68.9	1206	2089.9	80.9
2	947	984.0	63.8	871	905.4	58.7	1054	1095.3	71.0
3	737	535.9	49.9	648	471.8	43.9	847	616.4	57.4
High Risk: 4	577	289.5	39.4	475	237.6	32.3	675	339.0	46.1
Total Sample	3367	3726.4	62.8	3021	3395.3	57.2	3782	4140.6	69.8

Table A.3.2
Measures, Including Question Text and Response
Categories

Gender
What is your sex?
    1. Male
    2. Female

Race/Ethnicity
Race/Ethnicity is a recode of the variable below. Code 2 was coded "African-American"; Codes 3, 4, 8, and 9 were coded "Hispanic"; Codes 1, 5, 7 and missing data were coded "Other race"; and Code 6 was coded "White."

How do you describe yourself?
    2. Black or African American
    3. Mexican American or Chicano
    4. Cuban American
    8. Puerto Rican American
    9. Other Latin American
    5. Oriental or Asian American
    6. White (Caucasian)
    1. American Indian (Native American Indian)
    7. Other

Population Density
Population Density was created by combining data from the question below with information on self- and non-self-representing Metropolitan Statistical Areas (MSAs). Codes 1 and 2 in the question below were not changed. Code 3 was combined with the MSA data to create the following additional codes: 3. Non-MSA, small town or city, 4. Non-self-representing MSA, 5. Self-representing MSA.

Where did you grow up mostly?
    1. On a farm
    2. In the country, not on a farm
    3. In a city or town

Parents' Education Level Wave 1
Parents' Education Level is an average of the father and mother's data, recoded to whole numbers to produce a 1–11 scale. Missing data were allowed on one variable.

Table A.3.2 continued on next page.

Table A.3.2
Measures, Including Question Text and Response
Categories (continued)

For MCA analyses and related figures, the 11-category measure was bracketed to a 5-category measure to provide sufficient cases in all categories. The 11-category measure was bracketed in the following manner: 1–4 = 1, 5 = 2, 6–7 = 3, 8–9 = 4, 10–11 = 5.

The next three questions ask about your parents. If you were raised mostly by foster parents, stepparents, or others, answer for them. For example, if you have both a stepfather and a natural father, answer for the one that was the most important in raising you.

What is the highest level of schooling your father completed?
1. Completed grade school or less
2. Some high school
3. Completed high school
4. Some college
5. Completed college
6. Graduate or professional school after college
7. Don't know, or does not apply

What is the highest level of schooling your mother completed?
1. Completed grade school or less
2. Some high school
3. Completed high school
4. Some college
5. Completed college
6. Graduate or professional school after college
7. Don't know, or does not apply

Number of Parents in Home Wave 1
Number of Parents in the Home was recoded from the following variable. If father **or** mother were checked, 1 parent in home was coded; if father **and** mother were both checked, 2 parents in home was coded.

Which of the following people live in the same household with you? (Mark ALL that apply.)
A. Father (or stepfather)
B. Mother (or stepmother)

Table A.3.2 continued on next page.

Table A.3.2
Measures, Including Question Text and Response
Categories (continued)

    C. Brothers (or stepbrothers)
    D. Sisters (or stepsisters)
    E. Grandparent(s)
    F. Other relative(s)
    G. Nonrelative(s)
    H. I live alone

Number of Parents in Home Waves 2 and 3
Number of Parents in the Home was recoded from the
following variable. If father **or** mother were checked, 1 parent
in home was coded; if father **and** mother were both checked, 2
parents in home was coded.

Which of the following people live in the same household with
you? (Mark ALL that apply.)
    A. Father (or stepfather)
    B. Mother (or stepmother)
    C. Foster parent(s)
    D. Brothers (or stepbrothers)
    E. Sisters (or stepsisters)
    F. My husband/wife
    G. My partner of the opposite sex
    H. Spouse's parent(s)
    I. My children
    J. Grandparent(s)
    K. Other relative(s)
    L. Nonrelative(s)
    M. I live alone

Lived with 2 Parents Waves 1–3
Recoded from Number of Parents in Home variables above.
Indicates lived with two parents in home at all three waves. If
the respondent indicated two parents all three waves, then
lived with two parents was coded 1, otherwise it was coded 0.

Parent Involvement Index
Parent Involvement Index is an index of the next set of
variables, scaled 1–4.

Table A.3.2 continued on next page.

Table A.3.2
Measures, Including Question Text and Response
Categories (continued)

How often do your parents (or stepparents or guardians) do the following?

Check on whether you have done your homework
   1. Never
   2. Rarely
   3. Sometimes
   4. Often

Provide help with your homework when it's needed
   1. Never
   2. Rarely
   3. Sometimes
   4. Often

Require you to do work or chores around the home
   1. Never
   2. Rarely
   3. Sometimes
   4. Often

Limit the amount of time you can spend watching TV
   1. Never
   2. Rarely
   3. Sometimes
   4. Often

Held Back Grade 8 or Earlier Wave 1
Have you ever had to repeat a grade in school?
   1. No
   2. Yes, one time
   3. Yes, two or more times

Suspended/Expelled Grade 8 or Earlier Wave 1
Have you ever been suspended or expelled from school?
   1. No
   2. Yes, one time
   3. Yes, two or more times

Table A.3.2 continued on next page.

Table A.3.2
Measures, Including Question Text and Response
Categories (continued)

GPA Waves 1, 2, and 3
GPA was created by recoding the data (prior to imputation) in the following manner: Code 1 remained Code 1, Codes 2 and 3 were recoded to Code 2, Codes 4 and 5 were recoded to Code 3, Codes 6 and 7 were recoded to Code 4, Code 8 was recoded to Code 5, and Code 9 was recoded to Code 6.

Which of the following best describes your average grade in this school year?
- 9. A (93–100)
- 8. A- (90–92)
- 7. B+ (87–89)
- 6. B (83–86)
- 5. B- (80–82)
- 4. C+ (77–79)
- 3. C (73–76)
- 2. C- (70–72)
- 1. D (69 or below)

Mean Secondary School GPA
Mean Secondary School GPA is the mean of GPA at Waves 1, 2, and 3.

College Plans Wave 1
How likely is it that you will graduate from college (four-year program)?
- 1. Definitely won't
- 2. Probably won't
- 3. Probably will
- 4. Definitely will

College Plans Waves 2 and 3
Codes 4, 5, and 6 were combined.

How likely is it that you will graduate from college (four-year program)?
- 1. Definitely won't
- 2. Probably won't
- 3. Probably will
- 4. Definitely will

Table A.3.2 continued on next page.

Table A.3.2
Measures, Including Question Text and Response
Categories (continued)

    5.   I'm doing this now
    6.   I have done this

Mean Secondary School College Plans
Mean Secondary School College Plans is the mean of the preceding three items.

Held Back Waves 1, 2, and 3
Have you ever had to repeat a grade in school?
    1.   No
    2.   Yes, one time
    3.   Yes, two or more times

Held Back Wave 1 to Wave 2
Held Back Wave 1 to Wave 2 is a change score indicating the number of times the respondent reported having been held back at Wave 2 minus the number of times reported at Wave 1. Scale is 0, 1, and 2.

Held Back Wave 2 to Wave 3
Held Back Wave 2 to Wave 3 is a change score indicating the number of times the respondent reported having been held back at Wave 3 minus the number of times reported at Wave 2. Scale is 0, 1, and 2.

Suspended/Expelled Waves 1, 2, and 3
Have you ever been suspended or expelled from school?
    1.   No
    2.   Yes, one time
    3.   Yes, two or more times

Suspended/Expelled Wave 1 to Wave 2
Suspended/Expelled Wave 1 to Wave 2 is a change score indicating the number of times the respondent reported having been suspended/expelled at Wave 2 minus the number of times reported at Wave 1. Scale is 0, 1, and 2.

Suspended/Expelled Wave 3
Have you ever been suspended or expelled from school?
    1.   No

Table A.3.2 continued on next page.

Table A.3.2
Measures, Including Question Text and Response
Categories (continued)

    2. Yes, one time
    3. Yes, two or more times

Suspended/Expelled Wave 2 to Wave 3
Suspended/Expelled Wave 2 to Wave 3 is a change score indicating the number of times the respondent reported having been suspended/expelled at Wave 3 minus the number of times reported at Wave 2. Scale is 0, 1, and 2.

Serious Scholastic Setback Wave 1 to Wave 2
Serious Scholastic Setback Wave 1 to Wave 2 is a sum of the change scores in being held back between Wave 1 and Wave 2 and being suspended/expelled between Wave 1 and Wave 2 (scored 0, 1, 2, or more).

Serious Scholastic Setback Wave 2 to Wave 3
Serious Scholastic Setback Wave 2 to Wave 3 is a sum of the change scores in being held back between Wave 2 and Wave 3 and being suspended/expelled between Wave 2 and Wave 3 (scored 0, 1, 2, or more).

High School Dropout by Wave 3
High School Dropout by Wave 3 was created by dichotomizing the following data. Codes 1 and 2 were combined to create the "not a high school graduate" (dropout) category versus Codes 3–5.

Which of the following BEST describes your current high school situation?
    1. I left school WITHOUT graduating, but earned a GED
    2. I left school WITHOUT graduating (dropped out, was permanently expelled, etc.) and have not earned a GED
    3. I am still in high school, but I am on temporary suspension
    4. I am still in high school (or on vacation)
    5. I have graduated from high school (Do not count a GED)

Table A.3.2 continued on next page.

Table A.3.2
Measures, Including Question Text and Response
Categories (continued)

Sent to Office Waves 1, 2, and 3
Now thinking back over the past year in school, how often did
you get sent to the office, or have to stay after school, because
you misbehaved?
1. Never
2. Seldom
3. Sometimes
4. Often
5. Almost always

Days Cut School Wave 1
During the LAST FOUR WEEKS, how many whole days of
school have you missed because you skipped or "cut"?
1. None
2. 1 day
3. 2 days
4. 3 days
5. 4 to 5 days
6. 6 to 10 days
7. 11 or more

Days Cut School Waves 2 and 3
During the LAST FOUR WEEKS, how many whole days of
school have you missed because you skipped or "cut"?
1. None
2. 1 day
3. 2 days
4. 3 days
5. 4 to 5 days
6. 6 to 10 days
7. 11 to 19 days
8. 20 days

Days Skipped Classes Waves 1, 2, and 3
During the last four weeks, how often have you gone to school,
but skipped a class when you weren't supposed to?
1. Not at all
2. 1 or 2 times
3. 3–5 times
4. 6–10 times

Table A.3.2 continued on next page.

Table A.3.2
Measures, Including Question Text and Response
Categories (continued)

    5. 11–20 times
    6. More than 20 times

Delinquency Index Waves 1, 2, and 3
The Delinquency Index is based on the following set of variables. Each item was dichotomized into "not at all" versus all other responses prior to imputation. The index created (after imputation) is a sum of the seven items.

During the LAST 12 MONTHS, how often have you . . .

Gotten into a serious fight in school or at work
    1. Not at all
    2. Once
    3. Twice
    4. 3 or 4 times
    5. 5 or more times

Taken part in a fight where a group of your friends were against another group
    1. Not at all
    2. Once
    3. Twice
    4. 3 or 4 times
    5. 5 or more times

Hurt someone badly enough to need bandages or a doctor
    1. Not at all
    2. Once
    3. Twice
    4. 3 or 4 times
    5. 5 or more times

Taken something not belonging to you worth under $50
    1. Not at all
    2. Once
    3. Twice
    4. 3 or 4 times
    5. 5 or more times

Table A.3.2 continued on next page.

Table A.3.2
Measures, Including Question Text and Response
Categories (continued)

Taken something not belonging to you worth over $50
1. Not at all
2. Once
3. Twice
4. 3 or 4 times
5. 5 or more times

Gone into some house or building when you weren't supposed to be there
1. Not at all
2. Once
3. Twice
4. 3 or 4 times
5. 5 or more times

Damaged school property on purpose
1. Not at all
2. Once
3. Twice
4. 3 or 4 times
5. 5 or more times

Evenings Out Waves 1, 2, and 3
During a typical week, on how many evenings do you go out for fun and recreation? (Don't count things you do with your parents or other adult relatives.)
1. Less than one evening per week
2. One evening
3. Two evenings
4. Three evenings
5. Four or five evenings
6. Six or seven evenings per week

Hours Worked Wave 1
On the average over the school year, how many hours per week do you work in a paid job?
1. None
2. 5 or less hours per week
3. 6 to 10 hours per week
4. 11 to 15 hours per week

Table A.3.2 continued on next page.

Table A.3.2
Measures, Including Question Text and Response
Categories (continued)

    5. 16 to 20 hours per week
    6. 21 to 25 hours per week
    7. 26 to 30 hours per week
    8. More than 30 hours per week

Hours Worked Waves 2 and 3
On the average, how many hours PER WEEK do you work in your current paid job or jobs?
    1. I'm not working for pay
    2. 5 or less hours per week
    3. 6 to 10 hours per week
    4. 11 to 15
    5. 16 to 20
    6. 21 to 25
    7. 26 to 30
    8. 31 to 35
    9. 36 to 40
    10. 41 to 45
    11. 46 to 50
    12. 51 or more hours

Preferred Hours of Work Wave 1
Think about the kinds of paid jobs that people your age usually have. If you could work just the number of hours that you wanted, how many hours per week would you PREFER to work during the school year?
    1. None
    2. 5 or less hours per week
    3. 6–10
    4. 11–15
    5. 16–20
    6. 21–25
    7. 26–30
    8. More than 30 hours per week
    9. Don't know, can't say

Preferred Hours of Work Waves 2 and 3
Think about the kinds of paid jobs that people your age usually have. If you could work just the number of hours that you

Table A.3.2 continued on next page.

Table A.3.2
Measures, Including Question Text and Response
Categories (continued)

wanted, how many hours PER WEEK would you PREFER to
work?
1. None
2. 5 or less hours per week
3. 6 to 10 hours per week
4. 11 to 15
5. 16 to 20
6. 21 to 25
7. 26 to 30
8. 31 to 35
9. 36 to 40
10. 41 to 45
11. 46 to 50
12. 51 or more hours

Religious Attendance Waves 1, 2, and 3
How often do you attend religious services?
1. Never
2. Rarely
3. Once or twice a month
4. About once a week or more

Religious Importance Waves 1, 2, and 3
How important is religion in your life?
1. Not important
2. A little important
3. Pretty important
4. Very important

Self-Esteem Index Waves 1, 2, and 3
The Self-Esteem Index is based on the following set of
variables. The first four items were reverse coded, then all
eight items were dichotomized into "high self-esteem" (the top
two categories) versus all other responses prior to imputation.
The index created (after imputation) is a sum of all items (scale
0–8).

How much do you agree or disagree with each of the following
statements?

Table A.3.2 continued on next page.

Table A.3.2
Measures, Including Question Text and Response
Categories (continued)

I feel I do not have much to be proud of
1. Disagree
2. Mostly disagree
3. Neither
4. Mostly agree
5. Agree

Sometimes I think that I am no good at all
1. Disagree
2. Mostly disagree
3. Neither
4. Mostly agree
5. Agree

I feel that I can't do anything right
1. Disagree
2. Mostly disagree
3. Neither
4. Mostly agree
5. Agree

I feel that my life is not very useful
1. Disagree
2. Mostly disagree
3. Neither
4. Mostly agree
5. Agree

I take a positive attitude toward myself
1. Disagree
2. Mostly disagree
3. Neither
4. Mostly agree
5. Agree

I feel I am a person of worth, on an equal plane with others
1. Disagree
2. Mostly disagree
3. Neither

Table A.3.2 continued on next page.

Table A.3.2
Measures, Including Question Text and Response
Categories (continued)

    4. Mostly agree
    5. Agree

I am able to do things as well as most people
    1. Disagree
    2. Mostly disagree
    3. Neither
    4. Mostly agree
    5. Agree

On the whole, I'm satisfied with myself
    1. Disagree
    2. Mostly disagree
    3. Neither
    4. Mostly agree
    5. Agree

Cigarette Use Waves 1, 2, and 3
Data were recoded by subtracting one from code indicated
(creating a true zero).

How frequently have you smoked cigarettes during the past 30
days?
    1. Not at all
    2. Less than one cigarette per day
    3. One to five cigarettes per day
    4. About one-half pack per day
    5. About one pack per day
    6. About one and one-half packs per day
    7. Two packs or more per day

Marijuana Use Waves 1, 2, and 3
Data were recoded by subtracting one from code indicated
(creating a true zero).

On how many occasions (if any) have you used marijuana
(grass, pot) or hashish (hash, hash oil) during the last 30 days?
    1. 0 occasions
    2. 1–2
    3. 3–5

Table A.3.2 continued on next page.

Table A.3.2
Measures, Including Question Text and Response
Categories (continued)

4. 6–9
5. 10–19
6. 20–39
7. 40 or more

Cocaine Use Waves 1, 2, and 3
Data were recoded by subtracting one from code indicated (creating a true zero).

To create the cocaine-use variable, data from the two questions below (crack cocaine, and other cocaine) were combined.

On how many occasions (if any) have you used crack (cocaine in chunk or rock form) during the last 12 months?
1. 0 occasions
2. 1–2
3. 3–5
4. 6–9
5. 10–19
6. 20–39
7. 40 or more

On how many occasions (if any) have you used cocaine in any other form (like cocaine powder) during the last 12 months?
1. 0 occasions
2. 1–2
3. 3–5
4. 6–9
5. 10–19
6. 20–39
7. 40 or more

Alcohol Use Waves 1, 2, and 3
Data were recoded by subtracting one from code indicated (creating a true zero).

Table A.3.2 continued on next page.

Table A.3.2
Measures, Including Question Text and Response Categories (continued)

On how many occasions have you had alcoholic beverages to drink—more than just a few sips—during the last 30 days?
1. 0 occasions
2. 1–2
3. 3–5
4. 6–9
5. 10–19
6. 20–39
7. 40 or more

Data were recoded by subtracting one from code indicated (creating a true zero).

Think back over the LAST TWO WEEKS. How many times have you had five or more drinks in a row? (A "drink" is a glass of wine, a bottle of beer, a wine cooler, a shot glass of liquor, or a mixed drink.)
1. None
2. Once
3. Twice
4. Three to five times
5. Six to nine time
6. Ten or more times

Academic Attainment Wave 5
Academic attainment was created in the following manner: For the last year of school completed Codes 9 and 10 were combined. For the highest degree obtained Codes 5–7 were combined. A cross-tabulation was then performed which resulted in a variable with eight categories: 1. Dropout, 2. GED, 3. High school diploma, 4. One year of college, 5. Two years of college or associate's degree, 6. Three years of college, 7. Four years of college 8. Bachelor's degree or higher.

What is the last year of school that you COMPLETED?
1. 8th grade
2. 9th grade
3. 10th grade
4. 11th grade
5. 12th grade

Table A.3.2 continued on next page.

Table A.3.2
Measures, Including Question Text and Response
Categories (continued)

    6. One year of college
    7. Two years of college
    8. Three years of college
    9. Four years of college
  10. Five or more years of college

What is the HIGHEST degree you have earned?
  1. Less than high school
  2. GED
  3. High school diploma
  4. Associate's degree
  5. Bachelor's degree
  6. Master's degree
  7. Doctoral degree or equivalent

Table A.3.3a Males
Product-Moment Correlations Among the Major Variables
(Means and Standard Deviations Appear in Table 3.2)

	1	2	3	4	5	6	7	8	9	10	11	12	13	14	15	16
1 African-American																
2 Hispanic	-.122															
3 Other race	-.168	-.139														
4 White	-.489	-.405	-.558													
5 Large MSA	.027	.106	.041	-.112												
6 Other MSA	.010	-.051	-.027	.044	-.558											
7 Non-MSA	-.038	-.049	-.011	.063	-.375	-.560										
8 Parents' education level	-.060	-.217	-.052	.209	.050	.079	-.138									
9 Number of parents Wave 1	-.234	-.058	.001	.195	-.011	.034	-.027	.148								
10 Number of parents Wave 2	-.211	-.005	.028	.128	.020	.007	-.028	.085	.569							
11 Number of parents Wave 3	-.149	-.017	.015	.101	.020	.008	-.029	.132	.417	.519						
12 Lived with 2 parents Waves 1-3	-.186	-.037	.000	.150	.005	.011	-.017	.153	.658	.694	.754					
13 Parent involvement index Wave 1	-.003	-.080	-.010	.058	.001	.026	-.031	.193	.167	.076	.133	.160				
14 Parent involvement index Wave 2	.072	-.128	-.012	.036	-.038	.048	-.016	.150	.087	.081	.094	.096	.406			
15 Parent involvement index Wave 3	.076	-.081	-.012	.005	-.017	-.010	.028	.120	.068	.067	.081	.095	.302	.509		
16 Held back grade 8 or earlier	.116	.087	.055	-.173	-.040	-.039	.083	-.226	-.155	-.120	-.158	-.186	-.158	-.068	-.031	
17 Suspended/expell. gr. 8 or earlier	.148	.059	.036	-.165	.048	-.016	-.030	-.171	-.181	-.145	-.159	-.195	-.168	-.042	-.015	.317
18 GPA Wave 1	-.106	-.062	-.094	.181	.057	.000	-.056	.282	.176	.173	.146	.199	.149	.069	.087	-.315
19 GPA Wave 2	-.104	-.053	-.090	.171	.015	.006	-.022	.281	.118	.105	.136	.142	.132	.093	.066	-.242
20 GPA Wave 3	-.108	-.046	-.084	.165	.015	.005	-.021	.253	.117	.127	.116	.140	.117	.071	.070	-.207
21 Mean secondary school GPA	-.127	-.064	-.107	.206	.036	.004	-.040	.325	.165	.163	.159	.193	.159	.092	.089	-.306
22 College plans Wave 1	.002	-.074	-.084	.106	.041	.096	-.148	.312	.136	.094	.115	.135	.248	.123	.073	-.295
23 College plans Wave 2	.047	-.048	-.061	.042	.072	.073	-.153	.272	.090	.095	.124	.129	.187	.171	.090	-.223
24 College plans Wave 3	.008	-.038	-.079	.077	.098	.043	-.145	.278	.121	.122	.151	.167	.168	.110	.074	-.243
25 Mean secondary school coll. plans	.023	-.066	-.093	.093	.088	.087	-.185	.357	.144	.130	.163	.180	.249	.166	.098	-.315
26 Held back Wave 1 to Wave 2	-.001	.038	.027	-.042	.036	-.020	-.014	-.079	-.070	-.053	-.061	-.082	-.043	.001	-.025	-.048
27 Held back Wave 2 to Wave 3	.033	.060	.047	-.094	-.005	-.014	.021	-.065	-.068	-.090	-.085	-.092	-.043	-.012	-.010	.056
28 Suspended/expelled W1 to W2	.046	.033	.004	-.055	-.006	.000	.006	-.088	-.030	-.009	-.055	-.068	-.034	-.077	-.074	.046
29 Suspended/expelled W2 to W3	-.002	.004	.051	-.039	-.010	.004	.005	-.029	-.059	-.052	-.044	-.065	-.043	-.016	-.023	.024
30 Ser. scholastic setback W1 to W2	.035	.048	.019	-.067	.016	-.011	-.004	-.113	-.063	-.037	-.078	-.100	-.051	-.059	-.071	.008

Table A.3.3a Males

	1	2	3	4	5	6	7	8	9	10	11	12	13	14	15	16
31 Ser. scholastic setback W2 to W3	.018	.039	.066	-.086	-.010	-.005	.016	-.061	-.085	-.093	-.084	-.103	-.058	-.019	-.023	.052
32 High school dropout by Wave 3	.075	.065	.042	-.122	-.042	.000	.041	-.183	-.174	-.137	-.244	-.240	-.146	-.067	-.022	.320
33 Sent to the office Wave 1	.031	.039	.007	-.050	-.036	.021	.013	-.081	-.122	-.087	-.113	-.132	-.171	-.070	-.053	.185
34 Sent to the office Wave 2	.007	.045	-.008	-.026	-.012	.041	-.034	-.080	-.063	-.017	-.072	-.081	-.127	-.089	-.069	.144
35 Sent to the office Wave 3	.026	-.011	.027	-.032	-.011	.007	.003	-.093	-.083	-.039	-.093	-.109	-.105	-.034	-.046	.131
36 Days cut school Wave 1	.011	.056	.051	-.080	.030	.000	-.030	-.085	-.120	-.059	-.065	-.121	-.178	-.075	-.058	.207
37 Days cut school Wave 2	.015	.069	.043	-.084	.016	-.001	-.014	-.088	-.102	-.099	-.120	-.151	-.107	-.108	-.054	.132
38 Days cut school Wave 3	.023	.026	.043	-.063	-.033	.071	-.047	-.051	-.052	-.058	-.080	-.093	-.058	-.052	-.084	.065
39 Skipped classes Wave 1	.054	.067	.022	-.093	.058	.071	-.036	-.050	-.097	-.036	-.039	-.080	-.154	-.053	-.029	.170
40 Skipped classes Wave 2	.024	.076	.035	-.089	.065	-.006	-.057	-.079	-.072	-.073	-.077	-.092	-.097	-.107	-.041	.143
41 Skipped classes Wave 3	.025	.050	.015	-.058	.028	.033	-.064	.004	-.035	-.025	-.045	-.055	-.049	-.055	-.047	.026
42 Delinquency index Wave 1	.011	.082	.009	-.063	.063	-.020	-.040	-.112	-.095	-.060	-.092	.112	-.199	-.121	-.097	.190
43 Delinquency index Wave 2	-.019	.030	.010	-.012	.054	.014	-.069	-.011	-.055	-.030	-.068	-.071	-.125	-.130	-.081	.077
44 Delinquency index Wave 3	-.020	.031	.046	-.039	.045	.000	-.045	-.026	-.015	-.008	-.034	-.044	-.057	-.067	-.078	.010
45 Evenings out Wave 1	.001	.010	.026	-.026	.030	.005	-.036	.032	-.038	-.046	-.027	-.053	-.081	-.025	-.040	.026
46 Evenings out Wave 2	-.006	-.044	.007	.025	.015	.011	-.026	.001	-.040	-.030	-.069	-.065	-.060	-.099	-.052	.033
47 Evenings out Wave 3	-.059	-.060	-.012	.085	-.020	.030	-.013	.049	.030	.035	.066	.034	.001	-.003	-.032	-.074
48 Hours worked Wave 1	-.006	.014	.039	-.034	.003	-.032	.032	-.018	-.037	.002	.005	-.009	-.037	.006	.021	.115
49 Hours worked Wave 2	-.065	.004	.007	.037	-.027	-.011	.040	-.074	-.031	-.016	-.057	-.036	-.027	-.019	-.018	.115
50 Hours worked Wave 3	-.035	-.006	.007	.022	-.054	.021	.031	-.094	-.040	-.042	-.103	-.068	-.075	-.016	-.020	.096
51 Preferred hours of work Wave 1	-.029	.014	.015	.001	-.037	.001	.036	-.055	-.021	-.028	-.044	-.023	-.042	-.030	-.008	.061
52 Preferred hours of work Wave 2	-.007	.035	.029	-.038	-.045	-.018	.065	-.167	-.071	-.060	-.110	-.094	-.104	-.067	-.078	.144
53 Preferred hours of work Wave 3	.032	.072	.036	-.092	-.093	-.044	.143	-.206	-.071	-.074	-.107	-.100	-.087	-.042	.003	.123
54 Religious attendance Wave 1	.037	-.054	-.066	.056	-.018	.028	-.013	.159	.089	.064	.093	.095	.184	.163	.097	-.120
55 Religious attendance Wave 2	.039	-.040	-.063	.044	-.068	.059	.002	.156	.101	.085	.120	.129	.167	.218	.130	-.120
56 Religious attendance Wave 3	.076	-.042	-.051	.011	-.052	.016	.034	.106	.077.	.088	.105	.131	.169	.202	.169	-.108
57 Religious importance Wave 1	.136	.019	-.015	-.094	-.064	.055	.003	.035	-.005	-.031	.000	.004	.166	.156	.104	-.006
58 Religious importance Wave 2	.175	.017	-.078	-.072	-.038	.018	.018	.018	.010	.000	.020	.016	.128	.182	.137	-.023
59 Religious importance Wave 3	.169	-.005	-.051	-.075	-.034	-.009	.044	.006	.003	.024	.019	.018	.130	.158	.158	-.019
60 Self-esteem index Wave 1	-.028	-.033	-.038	.067	.036	.016	-.055	.104	.064	.054	.050	.074	.123	.057	.064	-.118

Table A.3.3a Males

	1	2	3	4	5	6	7	8	9	10	11	12	13	14	15	16
61 Self-esteem index Wave 2	.071	-.013	-.056	.001	.015	.008	-.023	.036	.015	.025	.002	.029	.119	.164	.103	-.045
62 Self-esteem index Wave 3	.039	-.041	-.068	.050	-.004	.004	-.001	.056	.029	.003	.038	.049	.099	.127	.154	-.037
63 30-day cigarette use Wave 1	-.071	-.011	.042	.024	-.021	.004	.016	-.094	-.062	-.026	-.045	-.077	-.191	-.069	-.050	.185
64 30-day cigarette use Wave 2	-.096	-.016	.032	.051	-.012	-.007	.021	-.077	-.041	-.062	-.094	-.097	-.131	-.099	-.062	.173
65 30-day cigarette use Wave 3	-.107	-.061	.037	.082	-.047	.024	.020	-.060	-.021	-.047	-.051	-.057	-.122	-.111	-.091	.116
66 30-day marijuana use Wave 1	.007	.031	.024	-.042	-.017	.024	-.010	-.081	-.051	-.020	-.049	-.049	-.140	-.054	-.020	.125
67 30-day marijuana use Wave 2	-.033	.013	.027	-.006	.030	.008	-.040	-.042	-.028	-.058	-.085	-.094	-.124	-.143	-.068	.096
68 30-day marijuana use Wave 3	-.033	.009	.028	-.003	.024	.019	-.046	-.016	.004	-.058	-.086	-.097	-.115	-.130	-.124	.031
69 Annual cocaine use Wave 1	.028	.025	-.003	-.031	-.004	.030	-.029	-.044	-.073	-.039	-.041	-.058	-.092	-.001	-.026	.084
70 Annual cocaine use Wave 2	-.018	.034	.017	-.020	-.015	.011	.002	-.061	.010	.003	-.004	-.013	-.049	-.035	-.026	.029
71 Annual cocaine use Wave 3	-.032	.035	.014	-.009	.008	-.003	-.004	-.013	.008	-.014	-.051	-.035	-.070	-.074	-.055	.008
72 30-day alcohol use Wave 1	-.007	.043	.010	-.028	-.014	.000	.014	-.090	-.100	-.020	-.041	-.074	-.207	-.049	-.036	.174
73 30-day alcohol use Wave 2	-.033	.036	-.037	.029	-.040	-.030	.074	-.066	-.073	-.084	-.104	-.099	-.165	-.133	-.098	.115
74 30-day alcohol use Wave 3	-.087	.002	-.008	.065	-.061	.026	.031	-.017	-.012	-.054	-.062	-.059	-.063	-.091	-.092	.053
75 Heavy drinking last 2 weeks W1	-.002	.040	.022	-.039	-.037	-.010	.049	-.118	-.155	-.057	-.068	-.114	-.194	-.055	-.037	.201
76 Heavy drinking last 2 weeks W2	-.044	.058	-.030	.019	-.036	-.024	.062	-.065	-.077	-.098	-.081	-.107	-.137	-.122	-.081	.109
77 Heavy drinking last 2 weeks W3	-.065	.025	.001	.029	-.061	.033	.024	-.040	-.029	-.058	-.067	-.069	-.068	-.096	-.101	.084
78 Academic attainment at age 22	-.077	-.109	-.070	.171	.082	.032	.118	.335	.182	.172	.232	.237	.152	.097	.071	-.287

Table A.3.3a Males

		17	18	19	20	21	22	23	24	25	26	27	28	29	30	31	32
18	GPA Wave 1	-.329															
19	GPA Wave 2	-.256	.572														
20	GPA Wave 3	-.228	.475	.608													
21	Mean secondary school GPA	-.326	.827	.863	.821												
22	College plans Wave 1	-.214	.394	.313	.263	.389											
23	College plans Wave 2	-.211	.359	.410	.299	.426	.468										
24	College plans Wave 3	-.222	.360	.381	.375	.444	.388	.545									
25	Mean secondary school coll. plans	-.269	.461	.459	.392	.524	.760	.827	.820								
26	Held back Wave 1 to Wave 2	.085	-.143	-.138	-.111	-.157	-.066	-.125	-.109	-.125							
27	Held back Wave 2 to Wave 3	.103	-.163	-.124	-.148	-.174	-.081	-.087	-.139	-.129	.010						
28	Suspended/expelled W1 to W2	-.129	-.115	-.176	-.145	-.172	-.094	-.125	-.137	-.148	.075	.043					
29	Suspended/expelled W2 to W3	.038	-.090	-.074	-.145	-.122	-.052	-.078	-.116	-.104	.070	.098	-.055				
30	Ser. scholastic setback W1 to W2	-.052	-.171	-.216	-.176	-.224	-.111	-.169	-.169	-.187	.633	.039	.819	-.003			
31	Ser. scholastic setback W2 to W3	.091	-.165	-.130	-.197	-.196	-.087	-.110	-.170	-.155	.057	.679	-.014	.797	.022		
32	High school dropout by Wave 3	.323	-.331	-.273	-.256	-.344	-.264	-.291	-.352	-.379	.183	.157	.112	.041	.192	.125	
33	Sent to the office Wave 1	.417	-.319	-.269	-.234	-.329	-.219	-.225	-.223	-.277	.072	.080	.082	.085	.105	.111	.215
34	Sent to the office Wave 2	.287	-.267	-.296	-.234	-.317	-.197	-.250	-.218	-.276	.085	.072	.168	.072	.179	.096	.236
35	Sent to the office Wave 3	.248	-.242	-.228	-.231	-.280	-.173	-.213	-.251	-.267	.087	.117	.120	.220	.143	.233	.258
36	Days cut school Wave 1	.268	-.187	-.135	-.133	-.182	-.230	-.140	-.094	-.190	.066	.077	.000	.050	.038	.084	.164
37	Days cut school Wave 2	.188	-.180	-.203	-.160	-.216	-.109	-.181	-.150	-.183	.125	.118	.091	.032	.143	.095	.217
38	Days cut school Wave 3	.148	-.146	-.155	-.179	-.191	-.060	-.109	-.156	-.137	.049	.136	.074	.106	.086	.161	.194
39	Skipped classes Wave 1	.263	-.125	-.097	-.096	-.127	-.154	-.093	-.062	-.126	.044	.032	.006	.030	.030	.042	.100
40	Skipped classes Wave 2	.231	-.169	-.212	-.162	-.216	-.116	-.165	-.143	-.176	.092	.116	.112	.046	.140	.104	.217
41	Skipped classes Wave 3	.110	-.087	-.103	-.167	-.141	-.024	-.073	-.117	-.091	.034	.104	.087	.107	.087	.142	.155
42	Delinquency index Wave 1	.373	-.249	-.193	-.158	-.241	-.187	-.194	-.165	-.226	.054	.104	.062	.075	.079	.118	.218
43	Delinquency index Wave 2	.260	-.148	-.170	-.162	-.191	-.091	-.151	-.096	-.140	.056	.063	.129	.070	.132	.090	.160
44	Delinquency index Wave 3	.155	-.095	-.124	-.152	-.147	-.048	-.105	-.087	-.100	.077	.066	.113	.137	.132	.141	.086
45	Evenings out Wave 1	.140	-.057	-.045	-.056	-.063	.009	-.017	-.025	-.015	.026	.041	.031	.016	.039	.037	.033
46	Evenings out Wave 2	.087	-.080	-.113	-.088	-.111	-.042	-.081	-.080	-.085	.017	.060	.112	.037	.097	.063	.096
47	Evenings out Wave 3	.003	-.005	-.054	-.063	-.047	.047	.005	.007	.024	.035	.016	.061	.042	.067	.041	-.007

Table A.3.3a Males

	17	18	19	20	21	22	23	24	25	26	27	28	29	30	31	32
48 Hours worked Wave 1	.152	-.060	-.072	-.063	-.077	-.072	-.100	-.100	-.113	.082	.039	.019	.062	.062	.069	.095
49 Hours worked Wave 2	.072	-.090	-.065	-.079	-.094	-.087	-.117	-.094	-.123	.032	.015	.019	.059	.033	.053	.101
50 Hours worked Wave 3	.097	-.138	-.102	-.123	-.145	-.093	-.115	-.149	-.150	.016	.002	.046	.067	.045	.050	.143
51 Preferred hours of work Wave 1	.086	-.075	-.081	-.055	-.084	-.069	-.104	-.095	-.111	.024	.018	.020	.041	.029	.041	.073
52 Preferred hours of work Wave 2	.149	-.187	-.178	-.153	-.207	-.166	-.197	-.199	-.234	.075	.036	.084	.047	.108	.057	.178
53 Preferred hours of work Wave 3	.142	-.213	-.190	-.200	-.241	-.176	-.193	-.231	-.251	.052	.095	.079	.100	.091	.132	.163
54 Religious attendance Wave 1	-.168	.183	.158	.163	.201	.182	.196	.196	.232	-.051	-.072	-.054	-.067	-.071	-.093	-.165
55 Religious attendance Wave 2	-.197	.197	.214	.207	.246	.180	.222	.229	.263	-.071	-.078	-.095	-.059	-.114	-.091	-.217
56 Religious attendance Wave 3	-.139	.175	.199	.188	.224	.172	.217	.205	.246	-.037	-.054	-.126	-.062	-.119	-.079	-.151
57 Religious importance Wave 1	-.084	.115	.129	.131	.149	.136	.152	.166	.189	-.035	-.023	-.018	-.055	-.034	-.055	-.104
58 Religious importance Wave 2	-.067	.103	.141	.145	.154	.138	.203	.170	.212	-.014	-.019	-.052	-.058	-.048	-.055	-.108
59 Religious importance Wave 3	-.070	.103	.123	.127	.140	.122	.139	.162	.177	-.014	-.003	-.056	-.057	-.052	-.044	-.054
60 Self-esteem index Wave 1	-.144	.177	.156	.127	.184	.154	.134	.159	.186	-.044	-.067	-.064	-.046	-.075	-.075	-.138
61 Self-esteem index Wave 2	-.077	.099	.195	.123	.165	.138	.177	.120	.179	-.048	-.042	-.055	-.012	-.071	-.035	-.049
62 Self-esteem index Wave 3	-.039	.088	.142	.150	.150	.096	.106	.128	.138	-.032	-.006	-.090	-.077	-.088	-.060	-.063
63 30-day cigarette use Wave 1	.253	-.196	-.146	-.135	-.191	-.208	-.142	-.156	-.210	.061	.095	.031	.064	.059	.105	.225
64 30-day cigarette use Wave 2	.227	-.219	-.220	-.176	-.245	-.190	-.235	-.198	-.258	.094	.120	.125	.041	.151	.103	.286
65 30-day cigarette use Wave 3	.182	-.207	-.228	-.228	-.263	-.156	-.218	-.220	-.248	.088	.112	.129	.096	.150	.139	.251
66 30-day marijuana use Wave 1	.174	-.142	-.091	-.059	-.118	-.133	-.114	-.085	-.136	.031	.054	-.006	.015	.013	.044	.172
67 30-day marijuana use Wave 2	.206	-.135	-.158	-.137	-.171	-.127	-.174	-.151	-.187	.054	.085	.099	.053	.108	.091	.206
68 30-day marijuana use Wave 3	.134	-.142	-.165	-.184	-.195	-.085	-.138	-.138	-.150	.098	.068	.130	.107	.157	.121	.150
69 Annual cocaine use Wave 1	.128	-.057	-.041	-.010	-.044	-.121	-.042	-.006	-.068	-.009	.018	-.013	.009	-.015	.018	.061
70 Annual cocaine use Wave 2	.097	-.095	-.071	-.040	-.083	-.068	-.069	-.059	-.081	.054	.028	.019	-.010	.046	.010	.135
71 Annual cocaine use Wave 3	.087	-.082	-.070	-.083	-.094	-.043	-.075	-.077	-.081	.076	.081	.075	.050	.102	.086	.125
72 30-day alcohol use Wave 1	.229	-.144	-.133	-.093	-.148	-.172	-.135	-.111	-.172	.007	.052	.064	.036	.053	.059	.182
73 30-day alcohol use Wave 2	.140	-.166	-.170	-.136	-.188	-.157	-.211	-.161	-.218	.044	.111	.118	.061	.116	.113	.181
74 30-day alcohol use Wave 3	.066	-.087	-.117	-.120	-.129	-.074	-.130	-.112	-.131	.032	.044	.090	.052	.088	.065	.086
75 Heavy drinking last 2 weeks W1	.258	-.177	-.155	-.125	-.183	-.204	-.160	-.155	-.215	.029	.067	.064	.027	.066	.060	.220
76 Heavy drinking last 2 weeks W2	.133	-.144	-.171	-.127	-.176	-.140	-.191	-.159	-.203	.023	.073	.098	.032	.089	.068	.177
77 Heavy drinking last 2 weeks W3	.073	-.091	-.117	-.120	-.130	-.081	-.120	-.114	-.131	.029	.057	.083	.049	.081	.071	.101
78 Academic attainment at age 22	-.291	.438	.465	.421	.527	.321	.411	.515	.523	-.141	-.190	-.169	-.125	-.212	-.208	-.454

Table A.3.3a Males

	33	34	35	36	37	38	39	40	41	42	43	44	45	46	47	48
31 Ser. scholastic setback W2 to W3																
32 High school dropout by Wave 3																
33 Sent to the office Wave 1																
34 Sent to the office Wave 2	.443															
35 Sent to the office Wave 3	.324	.442														
36 Days cut school Wave 1	.260	.155	.134													
37 Days cut school Wave 2	.166	.204	.152	.188												
38 Days cut school Wave 3	.146	.162	.208	.097	.154											
39 Skipped classes Wave 1	.254	.145	.123	.419	.113	.082										
40 Skipped classes Wave 2	.197	.274	.169	.204	.461	.111	.188									
41 Skipped classes Wave 3	.151	.168	.217	.071	.071	.424	.091	.187								
42 Delinquency index Wave 1	.342	.260	.219	.260	.170	.124	.283	.239	.132							
43 Delinquency index Wave 2	.296	.401	.240	.128	.232	.145	.160	.317	.185	.344						
44 Delinquency index Wave 3	.187	.270	.276	.074	.132	.163	.116	.198	.225	.273	.472					
45 Evenings out Wave 1	.168	.134	.085	.110	.052	.052	.093	.079	.054	.133	.108	.066				
46 Evenings out Wave 2	.140	.187	.118	.072	.103	.086	.047	.154	.079	.146	.172	.127	.310			
47 Evenings out Wave 3	.082	.133	.128	.019	.029	.107	.016	.048	.088	.059	.116	.179	.137	.201		
48 Hours worked Wave 1	.104	.059	.077	.094	.063	.060	.105	.062	.025	.088	.065	.089	.090	.065	.011	
49 Hours worked Wave 2	.076	.045	.046	.040	.050	.056	.017	.073	.040	.062	.029	.030	.024	.052	.028	.069
50 Hours worked Wave 3	.019	.052	.085	.064	.062	.071	.016	.059	.042	.061	.052	.065	.020	.036	.008	.110
51 Preferred hours of work Wave 1	.065	.079	.090	.047	.055	.066	.026	.044	.056	.061	.057	.033	.004	.077	-.012	.166
52 Preferred hours of work Wave 2	.128	.140	.107	.052	.094	.081	.044	.095	.055	.087	.061	.039	.029	.098	-.001	.086
53 Preferred hours of work Wave 3	.103	.114	.154	.060	.100	.101	.026	.076	.049	.061	.054	.020	.038	.037	.005	.075
54 Religious attendance Wave 1	-.131	-.079	-.086	-.069	-.116	-.081	-.050	-.128	-.095	-.139	-.044	-.068	-.023	-.038	.024	-.022
55 Religious attendance Wave 2	-.134	-.122	-.112	-.073	-.150	-.107	-.048	-.159	-.109	-.170	-.106	-.099	-.062	-.074	-.014	-.026
56 Religious attendance Wave 3	-.140	-.129	-.110	-.072	-.123	-.132	-.054	-.128	-.116	-.149	-.100	-.133	-.044	-.073	-.042	-.002
57 Religious importance Wave 1	-.131	-.083	-.091	-.037	-.050	-.034	-.055	-.072	-.056	-.123	-.079	-.108	-.006	-.012	-.014	-.015
58 Religious importance Wave 2	-.095	-.107	-.085	-.044	-.084	-.062	-.036	-.111	-.091	-.139	-.130	-.119	-.034	-.024	-.027	-.010
59 Religious importance Wave 3	-.112	-.098	-.097	-.033	-.063	-.085	-.038	-.092	-.094	-.109	-.099	-.132	-.012	-.041	-.020	.014
60 Self-esteem index Wave 1	-.146	-.098	-.095	-.126	-.072	-.054	-.099	-.076	-.051	-.130	-.086	-.060	-.029	-.050	-.004	-.071

Table A.3.3a Males

	33	34	35	36	37	38	39	40	41	42	43	44	45	46	47	48
61 Self-esteem index Wave 2	-.105	-.140	-.062	-.048	-.054	-.070	-.052	-.054	-.057	-.082	-.202	-.119	.013	.021	.011	.005
62 Self-esteem index Wave 3	-.075	-.093	-.128	-.036	-.050	-.073	-.043	-.056	-.078	-.079	-.101	-.173	.048	.053	.031	.006
63 30-day cigarette use Wave 1	.261	.207	.151	.231	.134	.068	.193	.156	.034	.295	.146	.089	.125	.120	.024	.118
64 30-day cigarette use Wave 2	.238	.283	.204	.130	.234	.130	.100	.265	.110	.265	.277	.179	.100	.146	.083	.074
65 30-day cigarette use Wave 3	.215	.274	.253	.083	.164	.179	.063	.154	.133	.216	.251	.226	.102	.138	.159	.068
66 30-day marijuana use Wave 1	.171	.100	.094	.211	.099	.050	.180	.101	.027	.219	.118	.041	.043	.060	-.010	.079
67 30-day marijuana use Wave 2	.170	.224	.161	.129	.248	.140	.088	.347	.156	.270	.339	.245	.097	.187	.056	.040
68 30-day marijuana use Wave 3	.194	.210	.223	.079	.172	.175	.079	.253	.203	.249	.281	.282	.105	.150	.183	.039
69 Annual cocaine use Wave 1	.098	.040	.032	.224	.019	.007	.260	.025	-.007	.137	.027	.011	.019	.009	-.004	.042
70 Annual cocaine use Wave 2	.096	.118	.056	.064	.112	.048	.039	.109	.045	.112	.125	.088	.016	.034	-.001	.012
71 Annual cocaine use Wave 3	.114	.124	.101	.039	.128	.102	.032	.132	.101	.149	.156	.203	.016	.076	.096	.056
72 30-day alcohol use Wave 1	.242	.189	.142	.210	.136	.091	.226	.143	.069	.322	.189	.116	.103	.095	.024	.141
73 30-day alcohol use Wave 2	.205	.238	.172	.122	.207	.142	.135	.227	.098	.259	.274	.167	.094	.155	.079	.073
74 30-day alcohol use Wave 3	.158	.206	.178	.070	.112	.159	.107	.117	.141	.190	.217	.269	.096	.159	.231	.068
75 Heavy drinking last 2 weeks W1	.239	.165	.137	.276	.135	.081	.259	.134	.057	.307	.179	.096	.090	.113	.029	.151
76 Heavy drinking last 2 weeks W2	.181	.216	.164	.109	.165	.114	.104	.232	.103	.209	.252	.159	.088	.161	.064	.064
77 Heavy drinking last 2 weeks W3	.160	.187	.175	.083	.086	.148	.100	.090	.118	.180	.187	.237	.091	.144	.211	.056
78 Academic attainment at age 22	-.222	-.218	-.259	-.133	-.198	-.175	-.077	-.192	-.147	-.209	-.158	-.123	-.055	-.081	.006	-.102

Table A.3.3a Males

		49	50	51	52	53	54	55	56	57	58	59	60	61	62	63	64
50	Hours worked Wave 4	.208															
51	Preferred hours of work Wave 1	.072	.089														
52	Preferred hours of work Wave 2	.268	.128	.158													
53	Preferred hours of work Wave 3	.120	.248	.096	.234												
54	Religious attendance Wave 1	-.009	-.035	-.037	-.046	-.101											
55	Religious attendance Wave 2	-.017	-.028	-.017	-.044	-.083	.657										
56	Religious attendance Wave 3	-.016	-.015	-.020	-.056	-.065	.556	.722									
57	Religious importance Wave 1	.023	-.023	-.003	-.012	-.006	.549	.500	.460								
58	Religious importance Wave 2	-.005	-.015	-.018	-.028	-.009	.472	.610	.553	.591							
59	Religious importance Wave 3	-.021	-.019	-.007	-.068	-.036	.425	.509	.587	.544	.682						
60	Self-esteem index Wave 1	-.036	-.058	-.045	-.108	-.103	.059	.053	.058	.053	.029	.043					
61	Self-esteem index Wave 2	.012	.007	-.032	-.034	-.016	.108	.131	.138	.120	.174	.139	.180				
62	Self-esteem index Wave 3	.036	.009	-.016	-.025	-.020	.090	.086	.127	.078	.107	.135	.124	.374			
63	30-day cigarette use Wave 1	.068	.092	.066	.114	.085	-.093	-.128	-.114	-.097	-.093	-.070	-.143	-.070	-.050		
64	30-day cigarette use Wave 2	.081	.103	.058	.113	.117	-.117	-.175	-.176	-.106	-.149	-.117	-.132	-.137	-.061	.404	
65	30-day cigarette use Wave 3	.058	.127	.058	.126	.153	-.123	-.174	-.193	-.126	-.145	-.163	-.142	-.148	-.095	.269	.499
66	30-day marijuana use Wave 1	.033	.048	.026	.074	.017	-.044	-.049	-.031	-.040	-.011	.001	-.063	.000	.023	.359	.168
67	30-day marijuana use Wave 2	.048	.024	.031	.072	.033	-.108	-.196	-.165	-.120	-.167	-.108	-.091	-.110	-.070	.222	.387
68	30-day marijuana use Wave 3	.059	.045	.039	.070	.051	-.133	-.182	-.198	-.124	-.161	-.138	-.097	-.118	-.093	.149	.272
69	Annual cocaine use Wave 1	.035	.035	.019	.057	-.018	.023	.002	-.019	.019	.005	-.001	-.069	.001	.013	.132	.024
70	Annual cocaine use Wave 2	.043	.027	.009	.071	.013	-.046	-.051	-.040	-.038	-.047	.002	-.064	-.051	-.033	.132	.184
71	Annual cocaine use Wave 3	.042	.080	.026	.032	.060	-.082	-.083	-.081	-.070	-.100	-.079	-.077	-.061	-.050	.103	.162
72	30-day alcohol use Wave 1	.078	.047	.068	.103	.066	-.063	-.108	-.099	-.079	-.100	-.084	-.117	-.066	-.009	.406	.205
73	30-day alcohol use Wave 2	.061	.076	.061	.069	.066	-.072	-.129	-.141	-.082	-.124	-.094	-.102	-.128	-.048	.224	.365
74	30-day alcohol use Wave 3	.061	.093	.043	.031	.039	-.068	-.110	-.136	-.087	-.122	-.089	-.062	-.078	-.053	.108	.205
75	Heavy drinking last 2 weeks W1	.093	.055	.084	.130	.068	-.065	-.096	-.083	-.055	-.077	-.025	-.104	-.065	-.014	.433	.226
76	Heavy drinking last 2 weeks W2	.042	.085	.055	.058	.064	-.074	-.123	-.131	-.067	-.113	-.084	-.091	-.120	-.054	.171	.333
77	Heavy drinking last 2 weeks W3	.031	.088	.038	.043	.059	-.070	-.096	-.107	-.070	-.124	-.072	-.050	-.048	-.046	.087	.165
78	Academic attainment at age 22	-.078	-.142	-.095	-.201	-.259	.231	.251	.212	.134	.153	.115	.171	.105	.141	-.186	-.247

Table A.3.3a Males

	65	66	67	68	69	70	71	72	73	74	75	76	77
66 30-day marijuana use Wave 1	.076												
67 30-day marijuana use Wave 2	.261	.184											
68 30-day marijuana use Wave 3	.333	.063	.402										
69 Annual cocaine use Wave 1	.026	.334	.059	.008									
70 Annual cocaine use Wave 2	.107	.145	.256	.093	.106								
71 Annual cocaine use Wave 3	.171	.047	.194	.316	.015	.206							
72 30-day alcohol use Wave 1	.145	.325	.180	.143	.187	.094	.090						
73 30-day alcohol use Wave 2	.257	.148	.329	.231	.052	.130	.141	.316					
74 30-day alcohol use Wave 3	.323	.015	.186	.313	.008	.055	.155	.171	.339				
75 Heavy drinking last 2 weeks W1	.147	.342	.171	.144	.233	.109	.086	.636	.277	.198			
76 Heavy drinking last 2 weeks W2	.223	.107	.309	.223	.035	.099	.109	.235	.670	.303	.234		
77 Heavy drinking last 2 weeks W3	.290	.023	.159	.252	.030	.042	.127	.148	.300	.771	.180	.271	
78 Academic attainment at age 22	-.245	-.108	-.155	-.175	-.030	-.074	-.089	-.123	-.163	-.093	-.173	-.152	-.097

Table A.3.3b Females
Product-Moment Correlations Among the Major Variables
(Means and Standard Deviations Appear in Table 3.2)

	1	2	3	4	5	6	7	8	9	10	11	12	13	14	15	16
1 African-American																
2 Hispanic	-.132															
3 Other race	-.168	-.141														
4 White	-.500	-.418	-.531													
5 Large MSA	.049	.047	.001	-.064												
6 Other MSA	-.052	.006	-.034	.058	-.581											
7 Non-MSA	.010	-.056	.038	-.001	-.355	-.554										
8 Parents' education level	-.078	-.214	-.030	.208	.054	.022	-.144									
9 Number of parents Wave 1	-.247	.026	.023	.141	-.026	.025	.001	.073								
10 Number of parents Wave 2	-.221	-.005	.009	.152	.000	.025	-.029	.100	.608							
11 Number of parents Wave 3	-.172	-.011	.007	.124	.010	.045	-.061	.153	.437	.587						
12 Lived with 2 parents Waves 1-3	-.223	-.016	.017	.155	.004	.024	-.032	.131	.633	.683	.793					
13 Parent involvement index Wave 1	.004	-.039	-.031	.044	.009	-.036	.032	.173	.134	.136	.149	.163				
14 Parent involvement index Wave 2	.024	-.025	-.006	.003	-.011	-.002	.013	.148	.101	.113	.117	.139	.504			
15 Parent involvement index Wave 3	.009	.006	-.009	-.003	-.015	-.018	.036	.107	.096	.093	.079	.104	.361	.509		
16 Held back gr. 8 or earlier	.147	.081	.001	-.154	-.042	.021	.018	-.183	-.121	-.138	-.194	-.174	-.117	-.053	.003	
17 Suspended/expell. gr. 8 or earlier	.239	.041	.030	-.215	.029	.019	-.052	-.157	-.167	-.200	-.190	-.214	-.143	-.103	-.036	.232
18 GPA Wave 1	-.098	-.063	-.082	.169	.036	-.049	.020	.273	.156	.179	.232	.224	.139	.110	.020	-.277
19 GPA Wave 2	-.094	-.072	-.065	.159	.007	-.055	.056	.269	.120	.155	.190	.194	.109	.104	.000	-.233
20 GPA Wave 3	-.111	-.074	-.041	.153	-.030	-.045	.082	.231	.116	.162	.192	.198	.098	.086	.018	-.205
21 Mean secondary school GPA	-.118	-.081	-.074	.188	.006	-.058	.060	.302	.153	.194	.240	.241	.136	.117	.014	-.280
22 College plans Wave 1	-.023	-.085	-.029	.090	.046	.016	-.065	.348	.118	.133	.173	.152	.184	.125	.036	-.190
23 College plans Wave 2	-.018	-.045	-.024	.058	.056	.025	-.087	.297	.083	.145	.200	.163	.145	.137	.030	-.181
24 College plans Wave 3	-.034	-.034	-.040	.074	.092	.010	-.106	.287	.080	.147	.237	.196	.121	.112	.025	-.202
25 Mean secondary school coll. plans	-.032	-.067	-.040	.093	.084	.021	-.111	.390	.117	.180	.260	.217	.187	.157	.038	-.242
26 Held back Wave 1 to Wave 2	.032	.050	.026	-.072	.007	-.002	-.005	-.099	-.066	-.080	-.124	-.124	-.054	-.054	-.005	.032
27 Held back Wave 2 to Wave 3	.079	.054	-.013	-.079	.031	-.024	-.004	-.089	-.039	-.046	-.093	-.088	-.011	.011	.034	.100
28 Suspended/expelled W1 to W2	.073	.040	.006	-.081	.029	-.026	.000	-.138	-.080	-.110	-.144	-.139	-.082	-.062	-.022	.054
29 Suspended/expelled W2 to W3	.080	.030	.006	-.079	.030	-.003	-.027	-.051	-.080	-.099	-.113	-.131	-.016	-.031	-.031	.065
30 Ser. scholastic setback W1 to W2	.074	.058	.019	-.102	.026	-.021	-.003	-.160	-.098	-.129	-.179	-.175	-.093	-.078	-.020	.059

Table A.3.3b Females

	1	2	3	4	5	6	7	8	9	10	11	12	13	14	15	16
31 Ser. scholastic setback W2 to W3	.107	.055	-.004	-.106	.041	-.017	-.022	-.091	-.083	-.101	-.140	-.150	-.019	-.016	-.002	.109
32 High school dropout by Wave 3	.032	.044	.020	-.065	-.033	.007	.026	-.234	-.148	-.223	-.370	-.300	-.132	-.091	.024	.221
33 Sent to the office Wave 1	.110	.083	.016	-.140	.011	.041	-.058	-.170	-.133	-.133	-.145	-.162	-.154	-.091	-.054	.132
34 Sent to the office Wave 2	.055	.008	.012	-.053	.022	-.001	-.022	-.139	-.118	-.123	-.155	-.161	-.128	-.113	-.051	.106
35 Sent to the office Wave 3	.033	.024	.022	-.054	.013	.004	-.018	-.109	-.095	-.089	-.121	-.126	-.089	-.082	-.025	.106
36 Days cut school Wave 1	.034	.046	.024	-.070	.028	.019	-.050	-.106	-.093	-.077	-.101	-.104	-.162	-.099	-.060	.067
37 Days cut school Wave 2	.052	.072	.018	-.095	.048	.003	-.053	-.107	-.099	-.075	-.112	-.127	-.142	-.146	-.049	.121
38 Days cut school Wave 3	.031	.035	.008	-.050	.015	-.001	-.013	-.102	-.075	-.074	-.126	-.125	-.096	-.098	-.080	.073
39 Skipped classes Wave 1	.071	.082	.051	-.138	.052	-.001	-.052	-.107	-.066	-.104	-.076	-.080	-.122	-.049	-.025	.063
40 Skipped classes Wave 2	.055	.074	.011	-.093	.095	-.031	-.061	-.078	-.048	-.049	-.061	-.072	-.109	-.106	-.056	.066
41 Skipped classes Wave 3	.023	.050	.001	-.047	.085	-.011	-.075	.014	-.023	-.018	-.036	-.033	-.041	-.046	-.062	.005
42 Delinquency index Wave 1	.031	.056	.064	-.104	.031	.039	-.077	-.124	-.101	-.104	-.139	-.144	-.174	-.119	-.054	.096
43 Delinquency index Wave 2	.010	.000	.054	-.047	.075	.001	-.078	-.068	-.073	-.087	-.095	-.106	-.126	-.148	-.071	.052
44 Delinquency index Wave 3	.026	.002	.010	-.027	.111	-.030	-.079	-.026	-.050	-.055	-.063	-.065	-.064	-.083	-.041	.013
45 Evenings out Wave 1	.012	.010	-.022	.001	.010	.004	-.014	-.025	-.043	-.036	-.050	-.081	-.062	-.020	-.043	.017
46 Evenings out Wave 2	-.153	-.031	-.057	.169	.001	.013	-.016	.034	.012	-.013	-.018	-.039	-.038	-.060	-.042	-.001
47 Evenings out Wave 3	-.172	-.045	-.053	.188	.032	.003	-.037	.085	.068	.071	.096	.069	-.012	-.023	-.048	-.133
48 Hours worked Wave 1	-.127	-.027	-.007	.111	.040	.013	-.056	.026	.033	.016	-.012	.001	.010	-.004	.004	-.028
49 Hours worked Wave 2	-.032	-.013	-.016	.042	-.017	.024	-.010	-.027	-.013	-.019	-.037	-.030	-.076	-.036	-.032	.073
50 Hours worked Wave 3	-.058	-.057	-.013	.086	-.015	.028	-.017	-.057	-.014	-.025	-.058	-.035	-.067	-.084	-.078	.024
51 Preferred hours of work Wave 1	.026	.009	.021	-.040	-.034	-.001	.035	-.071	-.015	-.020	-.045	-.034	-.027	-.015	-.005	.030
52 Preferred hours of work Wave 2	.105	.090	.021	-.144	-.057	-.026	.089	-.247	-.075	-.107	-.159	-.155	-.073	-.073	-.068	.095
53 Preferred hours of work Wave 3	.106	.080	.024	-.141	-.076	-.017	.098	-.244	-.087	-.141	-.212	-.201	-.073	-.077	-.032	.149
54 Religious attendance Wave 1	-.004	-.001	-.058	.046	-.018	-.004	.023	.151	.111	.100	.117	.145	.191	.146	.086	-.111
55 Religious attendance Wave 2	.046	.018	-.050	-.007	-.022	-.015	.040	.122	.091	.107	.115	.140	.180	.190	.090	-.087
56 Religious attendance Wave 3	.085	.031	-.023	-.062	-.048	-.004	.054	.114	.085	.082	.130	.149	.182	.212	.161	.030
57 Religious importance Wave 1	.131	.060	-.053	-.090	-.040	-.007	.049	.012	.023	.013	.011	.033	.150	.114	.066	-.007
58 Religious importance Wave 2	.137	.078	-.056	-.103	-.038	-.014	.055	-.003	.017	.025	.020	.029	.125	.151	.087	.012
59 Religious importance Wave 3	.169	.084	-.028	-.150	-.053	-.033	.092	-.018	.013	-.012	-.003	.011	.109	.141	.107	.002
60 Self-esteem index Wave 1	.025	-.020	-.060	.039	.000	-.019	.022	.122	.035	.055	.097	.079	.158	.128	.083	-.080

Table A.3.3b Females

		1	2	3	4	5	6	7	8	9	10	11	12	13	14	15	16
61	Self-esteem index Wave 2	.091	.017	-.030	-.053	.021	-.045	.030	.053	.029	.034	.042	.040	.102	.168	.101	-.030
62	Self-esteem index Wave 3	.043	-.001	-.039	.000	-.014	.017	-.005	.090	.046	.043	.049	.050	.038	.101	.099	-.056
63	30-day cigarette use Wave 1	-.094	-.006	.040	.040	-.013	.039	-.031	-.134	-.088	-.116	-.142	-.150	-.211	-.101	-.054	.134
64	30-day cigarette use Wave 2	-.122	-.053	-.010	.126	-.008	.016	-.011	-.087	-.082	-.103	-.158	-.152	-.140	-.123	-.044	.070
65	30-day cigarette use Wave 3	-.123	-.087	-.002	.142	-.010	.003	.006	-.092	-.063	-.112	-.143	-.145	-.112	-.120	-.061	.056
66	30-day marijuana use Wave 1	-.012	.047	.031	-.043	-.022	.057	-.043	-.072	-.037	-.064	-.082	-.078	-.117	-.037	-.036	.074
67	30-day marijuana use Wave 2	-.077	.001	-.007	.059	.041	.019	-.064	-.042	-.025	-.023	-.057	-.060	-.114	-.098	-.060	.021
68	30-day marijuana use Wave 3	-.062	-.021	.015	.045	.025	.024	-.053	-.009	-.046	-.054	-.096	-.085	-.113	-.071	-.068	-.006
69	Annual cocaine use Wave 1	-.036	.057	.042	-.040	-.017	.040	-.028	-.054	-.014	-.021	-.012	-.025	-.079	-.035	-.023	.057
70	Annual cocaine use Wave 2	-.041	.061	-.014	.001	-.013	.046	-.039	-.030	-.031	-.047	-.027	-.038	-.067	-.054	-.028	.012
71	Annual cocaine use Wave 3	-.059	.010	-.006	.039	.013	.013	-.028	-.042	-.005	-.025	-.073	-.062	-.077	-.076	-.030	.007
72	30-day alcohol use Wave 1	-.027	.067	.040	-.051	.003	.035	-.044	-.081	-.058	-.086	-.091	-.117	-.168	-.104	-.047	.080
73	30-day alcohol use Wave 2	-.053	.029	-.008	.025	-.008	.003	.004	-.040	-.042	-.057	-.099	-.090	-.072	-.101	-.047	.043
74	30-day alcohol use Wave 3	-.116	-.003	-.037	.111	.000	.000	-.026	.044	-.049	-.031	-.058	-.053	-.069	-.086	-.089	-.037
75	Heavy drinking last 2 weeks W1	.015	.074	.053	-.095	-.031	.056	-.032	-.100	-.079	-.104	-.103	-.125	-.143	-.087	-.038	.115
76	Heavy drinking last 2 weeks W2	-.059	.041	-.015	.028	-.023	-.002	.026	-.050	-.021	-.040	-.078	-.065	-.086	-.092	-.030	.042
77	Heavy drinking last 2 weeks W3	-.063	.009	-.011	.047	.000	.002	-.002	.005	-.039	-.045	-.058	-.057	-.066	-.061	-.060	.015
78	Academic attainment at age 22	-.126	-.124	-.016	.176	.100	-.026	-.072	.411	.169	.210	.327	.302	.141	.111	.028	-.269

Table A.3.3b Females

	17	18	19	20	21	22	23	24	25	26	27	28	29	30	31	32
18 GPA Wave 1	-.281															
19 GPA Wave 2	-.218	.614														
20 GPA Wave 3	-.221	.538	.633													
21 Mean secondary school GPA	-.282	.847	.878	.838												
22 College plans Wave 1	-.197	.367	.282	.200	.334											
23 College plans Wave 2	-.186	.345	.354	.261	.376	.472										
24 College plans Wave 3	-.154	.330	.325	.296	.371	.341	.494									
25 Mean secondary school coll. plans	-.225	.437	.407	.323	.457	.736	.829	.801								
26 Held back Wave 1 to Wave 2	.120	-.182	-.146	-.125	-.178	-.123	-.190	-.141	-.192							
27 Held back Wave 2 to Wave 3	.120	-.116	-.132	-.118	-.143	-.076	-.060	-.110	-.105	.049						
28 Suspended/expelled W1 to W2	-.002	-.171	-.199	-.150	-.203	-.115	-.157	-.116	-.163	.124	.101					
29 Suspended/expelled W2 to W3	.073	-.110	-.110	-.153	-.152	-.066	-.095	-.112	-.117	.045	.095	-.006				
30 Ser. scholastic setback W1 to W2	.064	-.232	-.233	-.184	-.254	-.156	-.225	-.167	-.231	.647	.105	.837	.020			
31 Ser. scholastic setback W2 to W3	.127	-.166	-.161	-.185	-.199	-.095	-.107	-.150	-.151	.063	.682	.058	.793	.079		
32 High school dropout by Wave 3	.268	-.322	-.304	-.281	-.354	-.275	-.328	-.383	-.420	.236	.155	.192	.133	.277	.193	
33 Sent to the office Wave 1	.454	-.318	-.256	-.226	-.314	-.219	-.161	-.121	-.207	.127	.101	.134	.119	.173	.149	.215
34 Sent to the office Wave 2	.270	-.286	-.333	-.246	-.338	-.195	-.257	-.184	-.267	.144	.111	.294	.092	.305	.136	.275
35 Sent to the office Wave 3	.215	-.212	-.234	-.270	-.278	-.162	-.176	-.181	-.219	.103	.092	.175	.228	.191	.224	.285
36 Days cut school Wave 1	.224	-.165	-.142	-.121	-.168	-.125	-.129	-.087	-.142	.085	.027	.040	.078	.077	.074	.164
37 Days cut school Wave 2	.180	-.182	-.248	-.166	-.233	-.133	-.177	-.131	-.186	.142	.112	.171	.068	.210	.119	.234
38 Days cut school Wave 3	.124	-.173	-.184	-.219	-.224	-.098	-.123	-.172	-.168	.116	.120	.091	.148	.134	.182	.236
39 Skipped classes Wave 1	.246	-.192	-.138	-.119	-.176	-.159	-.116	-.095	-.153	.089	.059	.070	.069	.103	.087	.123
40 Skipped classes Wave 2	.159	-.162	-.234	-.176	-.223	-.112	-.130	-.095	-.141	.082	.088	.142	.110	.154	.135	.177
41 Skipped classes Wave 3	.085	-.081	-.111	-.170	-.139	-.012	-.033	-.039	-.036	.051	.058	.039	.100	.058	.109	.044
42 Delinquency index Wave 1	.305	-.234	-.213	-.184	-.247	-.196	-.174	-.127	-.207	.106	.055	.117	.089	.149	.099	.225
43 Delinquency index Wave 2	.211	-.193	-.246	-.166	-.237	-.148	-.173	-.081	-.166	.107	.043	.210	.064	.220	.073	.179
44 Delinquency index Wave 3	.153	-.137	-.171	-.177	-.189	-.055	-.100	-.092	-.106	.045	.033	.098	.140	.100	.123	.082
45 Evenings out Wave 1	.131	-.060	-.059	-.075	-.075	-.015	-.005	-.024	-.019	.057	.007	.002	.047	.033	.039	.104
46 Evenings out Wave 2	-.004	-.046	-.048	-.014	-.043	.004	-.007	-.003	-.003	.027	-.013	.049	.039	.052	.021	.059
47 Evenings out Wave 3	-.057	.033	.013	.000	.018	.061	.057	.065	.078	-.039	-.020	-.012	-.008	-.031	-.018	-.071

Table A.3.3b Females

		17	18	19	20	21	22	23	24	25	26	27	28	29	30	31	32
48	Hours worked Wave 1	.010	-.013	.010	.002	-.001	.003	-.001	.013	.007	.020	-.018	-.016	.015	-.001	.000	.011
49	Hours worked Wave 2	.051	-.031	-.027	-.028	-.034	-.013	-.050	-.017	-.034	.003	.006	-.007	.021	-.004	.019	.038
50	Hours worked Wave 3	.026	-.052	-.046	-.087	-.071	-.023	-.064	-.046	-.057	.027	-.019	.042	.049	.047	.024	.079
51	Preferred hours of work Wave 1	.050	-.032	-.046	-.031	-.042	-.018	-.028	-.040	-.037	.019	-.005	.025	.011	.029	.005	.032
52	Preferred hours of work Wave 2	.184	-.157	-.177	-.140	-.185	-.125	-.149	-.193	-.200	.080	.057	.061	.063	.091	.081	.176
53	Preferred hours of work Wave 3	.166	-.222	-.245	-.240	-.276	-.146	-.190	-.191	-.224	.101	.079	.085	.085	.121	.110	.221
54	Religious attendance Wave 1	-.148	.163	.174	.137	.185	.165	.148	.120	.180	-.084	-.054	-.084	-.015	-.111	-.044	-.190
55	Religious attendance Wave 2	-.126	.166	.201	.155	.204	.143	.143	.135	.177	-.056	-.065	-.102	-.029	-.109	-.061	-.207
56	Religious attendance Wave 3	-.112	.162	.193	.181	.209	.114	.139	.136	.165	-.066	-.047	-.096	-.045	-.110	-.062	-.175
57	Religious importance Wave 1	-.078	.094	.103	.094	.114	.099	.056	.039	.079	.004	.006	-.037	-.017	-.026	-.009	-.088
58	Religious importance Wave 2	-.030	.094	.156	.116	.143	.076	.096	.046	.091	-.025	-.016	-.087	-.032	-.081	-.033	-.094
59	Religious importance Wave 3	-.023	.089	.113	.108	.120	.048	.068	.039	.065	-.015	-.010	-.038	-.016	-.037	-.017	-.037
60	Self-esteem index Wave 1	-.120	.189	.152	.125	.183	.182	.155	.121	.191	-.064	-.028	-.050	-.041	-.074	-.047	-.116
61	Self-esteem index Wave 2	-.050	.143	.226	.138	.198	.131	.137	.082	.145	-.055	-.009	-.068	.000	-.082	-.005	-.079
62	Self-esteem index Wave 3	-.047	.151	.183	.195	.206	.124	.134	.122	.160	-.013	-.015	-.035	-.060	-.034	-.054	-.083
63	30-day cigarette use Wave 1	.274	-.240	-.197	-.166	-.237	-.212	-.182	-.147	-.225	.103	.061	.089	.080	.125	.096	.264
64	30-day cigarette use Wave 2	.181	-.221	-.243	-.188	-.256	-.174	-.231	-.180	-.247	.162	.092	.179	.098	.226	.129	.325
65	30-day cigarette use Wave 3	.131	-.185	-.222	-.240	-.251	-.125	-.182	-.183	-.209	.061	.071	.131	.142	.134	.148	.277
66	30-day marijuana use Wave 1	.172	-.143	-.092	-.078	-.123	-.149	-.085	-.059	-.120	.037	.052	.084	.061	.085	.076	.149
67	30-day marijuana use Wave 2	.144	-.142	-.181	-.119	-.173	-.132	-.144	-.086	-.151	.055	.064	.139	.072	.137	.092	.174
68	30-day marijuana use Wave 3	.102	-.098	-.128	-.139	-.141	-.066	-.092	-.073	-.097	-.009	.050	.089	.077	.063	.088	.121
69	Annual cocaine use Wave 1	.118	-.071	-.058	-.035	-.065	-.142	-.081	-.039	-.106	.007	.034	.029	.079	.026	.079	.110
70	Annual cocaine use Wave 2	.118	-.066	-.086	-.063	-.084	-.099	-.086	-.041	-.093	.026	.001	.031	.017	.038	.013	.076
71	Annual cocaine use Wave 3	.071	-.068	-.085	-.102	-.099	-.048	-.064	-.087	-.086	.012	-.007	.066	.066	.057	.044	.090
72	30-day alcohol use Wave 1	.238	-.180	-.159	-.131	-.184	-.155	-.144	-.096	-.164	.110	.053	.073	.076	.117	.088	.209
73	30-day alcohol use Wave 2	.082	-.122	-.160	-.097	-.149	-.091	-.126	-.118	-.142	.099	.070	.112	.093	.141	.111	.187
74	30-day alcohol use Wave 3	.035	-.032	-.047	-.074	-.059	-.014	-.007	.012	-.003	-.021	-.010	.026	.054	.008	.034	.037
75	Heavy drinking last 2 weeks W1	.288	-.201	-.164	-.144	-.199	-.129	-.131	-.094	-.148	.112	.062	.071	.086	.116	.101	.195
76	Heavy drinking last 2 weeks W2	.094	-.112	-.159	-.096	-.144	-.069	-.124	-.079	-.115	.062	.044	.088	.085	.102	.089	.164
77	Heavy drinking last 2 weeks W3	.052	-.063	-.090	-.114	-.103	-.042	-.039	-.035	-.049	.003	.041	.039	.068	.032	.075	.061
78	Academic attainment at age 22	-.259	.454	.459	.420	.521	.336	.429	.534	.556	-.177	-.169	-.179	-.147	-.235	-.212	-.473

Table A.3.3b Females

		33	34	35	36	37	38	39	40	41	42	43	44	45	46	47	48
34	Sent to the office Wave 2	.358															
35	Sent to the office Wave 3	.259	.406														
36	Days cut school Wave 1	.255	.146	.108													
37	Days cut school Wave 2	.186	.314	.241	.176												
38	Days cut school Wave 3	.140	.172	.206	.138	.139											
39	Skipped classes Wave 1	.276	.165	.137	.288	.141	.117										
40	Skipped classes Wave 2	.216	.307	.229	.155	.425	.137	.185									
41	Skipped classes Wave 3	.132	.131	.142	.080	.108	.443	.114	.214								
42	Delinquency index Wave 1	.432	.303	.212	.269	.205	.138	.271	.215	.116							
43	Delinquency index Wave 2	.255	.485	.282	.159	.315	.161	.173	.358	.158	.363						
44	Delinquency index Wave 3	.177	.259	.338	.104	.196	.155	.136	.207	.212	.234	.430					
45	Evenings out Wave 1	.144	.106	.099	.113	.077	.067	.068	.087	.046	.145	.117	.096				
46	Evenings out Wave 2	.096	.104	.100	.053	.102	.083	.022	.120	.054	.071	.162	.099	.256			
47	Evenings out Wave 3	.042	.024	.107	.005	-.007	.070	.012	.027	.099	.018	.078	.132	.214	.345		
48	Hours worked Wave 1	-.018	-.010	.017	.028	.009	.006	.006	.007	.012	.042	.029	.029	.057	.080	.063	
49	Hours worked Wave 2	.026	.010	.044	.050	.064	.044	.027	.017	.016	.031	.039	.029	.010	.066	.027	.103
50	Hours worked Wave 3	.047	.036	.050	.066	.051	.072	.013	.052	.045	.060	.046	.049	.084	.072	.024	.127
51	Preferred hours of work Wave 1	.040	.026	.019	.031	.013	-.002	.036	-.005	.000	.046	.027	.017	.018	-.012	-.009	.077
52	Preferred hours of work Wave 2	.140	.118	.079	.079	.085	.083	.078	.080	.001	.106	.094	.052	.082	.035	-.016	.024
53	Preferred hours of work Wave 3	.122	.129	.128	.082	.110	.104	.086	.090	.024	.124	.087	.077	.105	.030	-.026	.030
54	Religious attendance Wave 1	-.102	-.093	-.065	-.089	-.108	-.116	-.073	-.072	-.047	-.109	-.094	-.042	-.050	.003	.039	.026
55	Religious attendance Wave 2	-.116	-.121	-.110	-.094	-.139	-.121	-.080	-.084	-.032	-.136	-.140	-.088	-.073	-.036	-.013	.003
56	Religious attendance Wave 3	-.110	-.130	-.108	-.085	-.130	-.128	-.044	-.103	-.072	-.115	-.141	-.116	-.092	-.070	-.077	-.033
57	Religious importance Wave 1	-.085	-.062	-.055	-.098	-.052	-.082	-.045	-.053	-.038	-.107	-.089	-.050	-.063	-.042	-.057	-.048
58	Religious importance Wave 2	-.061	-.118	-.086	-.070	-.102	-.098	-.045	-.093	-.071	-.094	-.172	-.075	-.046	-.078	-.077	-.042
59	Religious importance Wave 3	-.054	-.082	-.086	-.052	-.065	-.079	-.024	-.072	-.085	-.087	-.132	-.111	-.058	-.087	-.118	-.050
60	Self-esteem index Wave 1	-.135	-.112	-.107	-.093	-.079	-.057	-.097	-.057	-.034	-.154	-.112	-.086	.002	-.029	-.005	-.006

Table A.3.3b Females

	33	34	35	36	37	38	39	40	41	42	43	44	45	46	47	48
61 Self-esteem index Wave 2	-.075	-.174	-.093	-.058	-.094	-.061	-.048	-.106	-.048	-.110	-.212	-.093	.024	-.012	-.010	-.020
62 Self-esteem index Wave 3	-.060	-.107	-.151	-.051	-.072	-.054	-.015	-.065	-.070	-.087	-.139	-.162	.016	.001	.004	-.013
63 30-day cigarette use Wave 1	.334	.215	.168	.232	.126	.109	.213	.105	.048	.380	.185	.115	.166	.102	.048	.039
64 30-day cigarette use Wave 2	.252	.322	.227	.163	.200	.163	.133	.182	.077	.276	.292	.162	.145	.211	.097	.030
65 30-day cigarette use Wave 3	.179	.217	.240	.118	.138	.168	.109	.117	.127	.196	.212	.220	.101	.183	.177	.049
66 30-day marijuana use Wave 1	.196	.113	.099	.197	.102	.067	.160	.085	.047	.235	.117	.070	.078	.035	.017	.016
67 30-day marijuana use Wave 2	.195	.279	.197	.109	.232	.152	.086	.232	.130	.239	.338	.184	.103	.203	.107	.009
68 30-day marijuana use Wave 3	.122	.185	.198	.096	.126	.183	.102	.133	.177	.163	.200	.232	.063	.106	.178	-.002
69 Annual cocaine use Wave 1	.145	.069	.063	.199	.106	.062	.128	.120	.073	.205	.109	.068	.069	.015	.007	.012
70 Annual cocaine use Wave 2	.113	.116	.077	.083	.104	.042	.053	.119	.022	.138	.184	.110	.079	.043	.043	.057
71 Annual cocaine use Wave 3	.104	.116	.128	.082	.076	.091	.037	.081	.108	.114	.153	.200	.056	.076	.086	.027
72 30-day alcohol use Wave 1	.313	.185	.132	.245	.139	.109	.248	.130	.083	.388	.205	.139	.160	.064	.016	.058
73 30-day alcohol use Wave 2	.155	.234	.171	.096	.206	.142	.078	.182	.106	.190	.263	.140	.117	.196	.072	.029
74 30-day alcohol use Wave 3	.098	.087	.137	.060	.057	.118	.053	.094	.170	.115	.149	.210	.140	.113	.253	.050
75 Heavy drinking last 2 weeks W1	.288	.161	.148	.248	.124	.076	.251	.107	.053	.341	.177	.109	.141	.039	-.026	.043
76 Heavy drinking last 2 weeks W2	.170	.214	.169	.112	.210	.125	.108	.168	.116	.199	.262	.164	.080	.210	.075	.030
77 Heavy drinking last 2 weeks W3	.091	.085	.160	.069	.079	.115	.069	.098	.149	.103	.134	.202	.126	.117	.194	.022
78 Academic attainment at age 22	-.225	-.237	-.219	-.131	-.223	-.202	-.134	-.176	-.055	-.179	-.152	-.087	-.061	-.023	.064	.017

Table A.3.3b Females

		49	50	51	52	53	54	55	56	57	58	59	60	61	62	63	64
50	Hours worked Wave 3	.172															
51	Preferred hours of work Wave 1	.060	.043														
52	Preferred hours of work Wave 2	.158	.096	.106													
53	Preferred hours of work Wave 3	.080	.266	.103	.325												
54	Religious attendance Wave 1	-.002	.004	.004	-.085	-.079											
55	Religious attendance Wave 2	-.043	-.029	-.011	-.068	-.078	.660										
56	Religious attendance Wave 3	-.049	-.049	.007	-.090	-.101	.514	.679									
57	Religious importance Wave 1	.002	-.021	.012	-.008	-.009	.551	.488	.439								
58	Religious importance Wave 2	-.031	-.024	.006	.020	-.002	.446	.573	.509	.582							
59	Religious importance Wave 3	-.011	-.032	.009	.012	.011	.409	.494	.589	.551	.676						
60	Self-esteem index Wave 1	-.046	-.048	-.042	-.135	-.068	.074	.088	.093	.074	.071	.076					
61	Self-esteem index Wave 2	-.020	-.037	-.040	-.045	-.034	.039	.074	.097	.049	.111	.109	.232				
62	Self-esteem index Wave 3	-.043	-.046	-.030	-.063	-.066	.036	.062	.093	.037	.063	.112	.198	.448			
63	30-day cigarette use Wave 1	.041	.058	.053	.148	.122	-.149	-.177	-.153	-.150	-.141	-.112	-.159	-.104	-.053		
64	30-day cigarette use Wave 2	.074	.108	.028	.132	.129	-.169	-.223	-.205	-.160	-.199	-.153	-.147	-.164	-.085	.469	
65	30-day cigarette use Wave 3	.064	.116	.038	.125	.149	-.119	-.192	-.218	-.136	-.192	-.182	-.114	-.144	-.122	.351	.557
66	30-day marijuana use Wave 1	.014	.021	.016	.102	.057	-.079	-.084	-.069	-.082	-.058	-.054	-.091	-.047	-.047	.366	.192
67	30-day marijuana use Wave 2	.030	.040	.013	.050	.054	-.112	-.154	-.165	-.116	-.149	-.131	-.075	-.124	-.088	.251	.389
68	30-day marijuana use Wave 3	.025	.044	.014	.023	.067	-.099	-.130	-.169	-.118	-.142	-.140	-.050	-.091	-.082	.183	.275
69	Annual cocaine use Wave 1	.012	.017	.006	.052	.040	-.058	-.039	-.032	-.071	-.049	-.028	-.067	-.057	-.097	.234	.102
70	Annual cocaine use Wave 2	.032	.032	.007	.030	.044	-.048	-.047	-.019	-.058	-.063	-.019	-.018	-.048	-.051	.172	.161
71	Annual cocaine use Wave 3	.017	.030	.017	.020	.043	-.035	-.048	-.081	-.043	-.056	-.047	-.037	-.070	-.060	.115	.192
72	30-day alcohol use Wave 1	.061	.068	.046	.135	.105	-.128	-.166	-.145	-.171	-.117	-.100	-.166	-.097	-.060	.454	.282
73	30-day alcohol use Wave 2	.075	.069	.007	.069	.063	-.088	-.131	-.140	-.080	-.121	-.086	-.057	-.097	-.061	.186	.454
74	30-day alcohol use Wave 3	.085	.065	-.005	.013	.020	-.059	-.098	-.150	-.119	-.126	-.152	-.019	-.051	-.072	.115	.204
75	Heavy drinking last 2 weeks W1	.047	.067	.047	.126	.124	-.128	-.138	-.095	-.124	-.072	-.053	-.151	-.086	-.067	.434	.245
76	Heavy drinking last 2 weeks W2	.056	.083	.003	.055	.095	-.072	-.126	-.110	-.089	-.121	-.089	-.065	-.102	-.062	.176	.369
77	Heavy drinking last 2 weeks W3	.045	.060	-.013	.035	.064	-.052	-.089	-.108	-.078	-.085	-.114	-.035	-.056	-.068	.112	.158
78	Academic attainment at age 22	-.045	-.094	-.048	-.255	-.315	.181	.186	.191	.044	.051	.015	.161	.092	.103	-.213	-.243

Table A.3.3b Females

	65	66	67	68	69	70	71	72	73	74	75	76	77
66 30-day marijuana use Wave 1	.131												
67 30-day marijuana use Wave 2	.280	.183											
68 30-day marijuana use Wave 3	.371	.101	.404										
69 Annual cocaine use Wave 1	.093	.407	.155	.064									
70 Annual cocaine use Wave 2	.094	.176	.282	.120	.161								
71 Annual cocaine use Wave 3	.220	.088	.232	.306	.066	.166							
72 30-day alcohol use Wave 1	.207	.324	.212	.144	.244	.129	.110						
73 30-day alcohol use Wave 2	.255	.102	.349	.213	.082	.114	.125	.209					
74 30-day alcohol use Wave 3	.346	.079	.198	.384	.042	.095	.216	.148	.248				
75 Heavy drinking last 2 weeks W1	.165	.347	.176	.104	.252	.169	.077	.641	.163	.095			
76 Heavy drinking last 2 weeks W2	.248	.087	.318	.214	.074	.086	.162	.222	.606	.246	.193		
77 Heavy drinking last 2 weeks W3	.296	.075	.168	.334	.023	.088	.194	.113	.188	.676	.107	.224	
78 Academic attainment at age 22	-.234	-.102	-.107	-.104	-.062	-.060	-.093	-.151	-.129	.017	-.169	-.122	-.042

Table A.3.4
Factor Loadings Used in Structural Models

	Males	Females
African-American	1.000	1.000
Hispanic	1.000	1.000
Other race	1.000	1.000
Large MSA	1.000	1.000
Non-MSA	1.000	1.000
Parents' education level	1.000	1.000
Lived with 2 parents Waves 1–3	1.000	1.000
Parent involvement index		
Parents check homework	.535	.485
Parents help with homework	.552	.501
Parents give chores	.585	.534
Parents limit television viewing	.508	.459
Held back grade 8 or earlier	1.000	1.000
Suspended/expelled grade 8 or earlier	1.000	1.000
GPA Wave 1	.900	.900
GPA Wave 2	.900	.900
GPA Wave 3	.900	.900
College plans Wave 1	.900	.900
College plans Wave 2	.900	.900
College plans Wave 3	.900	.900
Serious scholastic setback W1 to W2	1.000	1.000
Serious scholastic setback W2 to W3	1.000	1.000
High school dropout by Wave 3	1.000	1.000
Delinquency Wave 1	.900	.900
Delinquency Wave 2	.900	.900
Delinquency Wave 3	.900	.900
30-day cigarette smoking Wave 1	.900	.900
30-day cigarette smoking Wave 2	.900	.900
30-day cigarette smoking Wave 3	.900	.900
30-day marijuana Wave 1	.803	.759
30-day marijuana Wave 2	.805	.766
30-day marijuana Wave 3	.803	.760
Annual cocaine Wave 1	.724	.722
Annual cocaine Wave 2	.724	.720
Annual cocaine Wave 3	.725	.721
30-day alcohol Wave 1	.829	.780
30-day alcohol Wave 2	.828	.779
30-day alcohol Wave 3	.828	.781
Heavy drinking Wave 1	.737	.672
Heavy drinking Wave 2	.734	.669
Heavy drinking Wave 3	.733	.666

Note: W1 = Wave 1 data collection (grade 8, modal age 14),
W2 = Wave 2 data collection (modal age 16),
W3 = Wave 3 data collection (modal age 18)

Table A.3.5
Model Fit Statistics for the Model Including 30-Day Alcohol Use and
the Model Including Heavy Drinking

Model Fit Statistics for the Model Including 30-Day Alcohol Use

	Males	Females
Bentler-Bonett Normed Fit Index	.991	.991
Bentler-Bonett Non-Normed Fit Index	.991	.988
Comparative Fit Index (CFI)	.996	.995
Bollen (IFI) Fit Index	.996	.995
McDonald (MFI) Fit Index	.918	.892
LISREL GFI Fit Index	.979	.979
LISREL AGFI Fit Index	.951	.951
Root Mean-Square Residual (RMR)	.029	.027
Standardized RMR	.023	.024
Root Mean-Square Error of Approximation (RMSEA)	.023	.027
Chi-Square	549.33	711.63
Degrees of Freedom	316	316

Model Fit Statistics for the Model Including Heavy Drinking

	Males	Females
Bentler-Bonett Normed Fit Index	.991	.991
Bentler-Bonett Non-Normed Fit Index	.990	.988
Comparative Fit Index (CFI)	.996	.995
Bollen (IFI) Fit Index	.996	.995
McDonald (MFI) Fit Index	.913	.893
LISREL GFI Fit Index	.979	.979
LISREL AGFI Fit Index	.950	.951
Root Mean-Square Residual (RMR)	.029	.027
Standardized RMR	.023	.024
Root Mean-Square Error of Approximation (RMSEA)	.024	.027
Chi-Square	562.82	710.23
Degrees of Freedom	316	316

Table A.3.6
Variance in Endogenous Factors (R²) Explained by
All Prior Causal Factors, Based on the Structural
Model Including 30-Day Alcohol Use

	Males	Females
GPA Wave 1	.268	.240
GPA Wave 2	.545	.613
GPA Wave 3	.590	.637
College plans Wave 1	.358	.301
College plans Wave 2	.455	.432
College plans Wave 3	.534	.448
Serious scholastic setback W1 to W2	.080	.110
Serious scholastic setback W2 to W3	.049	.075
High school dropout by Wave 3	.284	.311
Delinquency Wave 1	.247	.201
Delinquency Wave 2	.240	.267
Delinquency Wave 3	.365	.305
30-day cigarette smoking Wave 1	.219	.329
30-day cigarette smoking Wave 2	.362	.438
30-day cigarette smoking Wave 3	.440	.505
30-day marijuana Wave 1	.275	.308
30-day marijuana Wave 2	.395	.407
30-day marijuana Wave 3	.454	.492
Annual cocaine Wave 1	.069	.124
Annual cocaine Wave 2	.109	.185
Annual cocaine Wave 3	.260	.232
30-day alcohol Wave 1	.250	.353
30-day alcohol Wave 2	.329	.224
30-day alcohol Wave 3	.323	.284
Academic attainment at age 22	.478	.530

Note: W1 = Wave 1 data collection (grade 8, modal age 14), W2 =
Wave 2 data collection (modal age 16), W3 = Wave 3 data
collection (modal age 18)

Table A.3.7
Variance in Endogenous Factors (R^2) Explained by
All Prior Causal Factors, Based on the Structural
Model Including Heavy Drinking

	Males	Females
GPA Wave 1	.268	.240
GPA Wave 2	.545	.613
GPA Wave 3	.590	.637
College plans Wave 1	.358	.301
College plans Wave 2	.455	.432
College plans Wave 3	.535	.448
Serious scholastic setback W1 to W2	.083	.111
Serious scholastic setback W2 to W3	.047	.075
High school dropout by Wave 3	.285	.312
Delinquency Wave 1	.247	.201
Delinquency Wave 2	.239	.266
Delinquency Wave 3	.366	.306
30-day cigarette smoking Wave 1	.219	.328
30-day cigarette smoking Wave 2	.365	.439
30-day cigarette smoking Wave 3	.442	.514
30-day marijuana Wave 1	.275	.310
30-day marijuana Wave 2	.396	.408
30-day marijuana Wave 3	.456	.497
Annual cocaine Wave 1	.069	.123
Annual cocaine Wave 2	.109	.192
Annual cocaine Wave 3	.260	.239
Heavy drinking Wave 1	.311	.414
Heavy drinking Wave 2	.297	.296
Heavy drinking Wave 3	.317	.283
Academic attainment at age 22	.479	.527

Note: W1 = Wave 1 data collection (grade 8, modal age 14),
W2 = Wave 2 data collection (modal age 16),
W3 = Wave 3 data collection (modal age 18)

Table A.3.8
Bivariate Factor Correlations (BFC), Direct and Total Effects
of Each Predictor in the Model on Academic Attainment,
Based on the Structural Model Including 30-Day Alcohol Use*

	Males			Females		
	BFC	Direct	Total	BFC	Direct	Total
African-American	-.078	-.021	-.024	-.127	-.049	-.022
Hispanic	-.110	-.055	-.052	-.124	-.063	-.045
Other race	-.071	-.009	-.060	-.016	.008	-.016
Large MSA	.083	.031	.059	.100	.048	.076
Non-MSA	-.119	-.040	-.059	-.073	-.007	.000
Parents' education level	.338	.091	.227	.414	.145	.325
Lived with 2 parents Waves 1–3	.239	.057	.136	.305	.076	.207
Parent involvement index	.191	-.033	.047	.177	-.015	.021
Held back grade 8 or earlier	-.274	-.029	-.125	-.248	-.037	-.112
Suspended/expelled grade 8 or earlier	-.262	-.046	-.143	-.251	-.033	-.121
GPA Wave 1	.458		.314	.472		.310
GPA Wave 2	.529	.215	.375	.525	.189	.347
GPA Wave 3	.464	.024	.095	.470	.048	.106
College plans Wave 1	.354		.092	.372		.101
College plans Wave 2	.463		.201	.469		.209
College plans Wave 3	.548	.293	.295	.575	.327	.335
Serious scholastic setback W1 to W2	-.209	-.042	-.122	-.238	-.016	-.081
Serious scholastic setback W2 to W3	-.203	-.062	-.094	-.199	-.034	-.061
High school dropout by Wave 3	-.427	-.190	-.190	-.437	-.159	-.159
Delinquency Wave 1	-.204		-.027	-.201		-.018
Delinquency Wave 2	-.163		-.028	-.173		.004
Delinquency Wave 3	-.140	-.018	-.015	-.110	.031	.031
30-day cigarette smoking Wave 1	-.183		-.034	-.224		-.049
30-day cigarette smoking Wave 2	-.259		-.071	-.262		-.094
30-day cigarette smoking Wave 3	-.256	-.045	-.057	-.259	-.074	-.085
30-day marijuana Wave 1	-.134		-.001	-.152		-0.011
30-day marijuana Wave 2	-.206		-.030	-.174		-.023
30-day marijuana Wave 3	-.214	-.056	-.056	-.145	-.032	-.032
Annual cocaine Wave 1	-.074		.004	-.091		.008
Annual cocaine Wave 2	-.110		-.004	-.101		.001
Annual cocaine Wave 3	-.108	.028	.028	-.123	-.014	-.014
30-day alcohol Wave 1	-.155		.003	-.184		.003
30-day alcohol Wave 2	-.202		.019	-.164		.027
30-day alcohol Wave 3	-.116	.054	.054	.005	.080	.080

*Coefficients that are p<.05 (two-tailed) are shown in **bold**.

Note: W1 = Wave 1 data collection (grade 8, modal age 14), W2 = Wave 2 data collection
(modal age 16), W3 = Wave 3 data collection (modal age 18)

Table A.3.9
Bivariate Factor Correlations (BFC), Direct and Total Effects
of Each Predictor in the Model on Academic Attainment,
Based on the Structural Model Including Heavy Drinking*

	Males			Females		
	BFC	Direct	Total	BFC	Direct	Total
African-American	-.078	-.022	-.024	-.127	-.054	-.022
Hispanic	-.110	-.057	-.051	-.124	-.063	-.045
Other race	-.071	-.010	-.060	-.016	.005	-.016
Large MSA	.083	.032	.059	.100	.050	.076
Non-MSA	-.118	-.039	-.059	-.073	-.008	.000
Parents' education level	.338	.092	.226	.413	.146	.325
Lived with 2 parents Waves 1–3	.239	.057	.136	.304	.073	.207
Parent involvement index	.193	-.031	.049	.178	-.015	.021
Held back grade 8 or earlier	-.275	-.029	-.126	-.249	-.037	-.112
Suspended/expelled grade 8 or earlier	-.263	-.046	-.143	-.252	-.034	-.121
GPA Wave 1	.458		.313	.472		.310
GPA Wave 2	.529	.215	.374	.525	.191	.347
GPA Wave 3	.464	.025	.095	.469	.050	.105
College plans Wave 1	.354		.092	.372		.101
College plans Wave 2	.463		.201	.469		.208
College plans Wave 3	.548	.293	.295	.575	.332	.335
Serious scholastic setback W1 to W2	-.209	-.042	-.123	-.239	-.017	-.082
Serious scholastic setback W2 to W3	-.203	-.062	-.093	-.199	-.037	-.061
High school dropout by Wave 3	-.427	-.191	-.191	-.437	-.160	-.160
Delinquency Wave 1	-.205		-.028	-.201		-.018
Delinquency Wave 2	-.162		-.027	-.172		.006
Delinquency Wave 3	-.141	-.020	-.015	-.111	.033	.030
30-day cigarette smoking Wave 1	-.185		-.032	-.221		-.040
30-day cigarette smoking Wave 2	-.260		-.074	-.261		-.081
30-day cigarette smoking Wave 3	-.255	-.049	-.061	-.261	-.065	-.070
30-day marijuana Wave 1	-.134		.000	-.150		-0.008
30-day marijuana Wave 2	-.204		-.029	-.171		-.013
30-day marijuana Wave 3	-.213	-.055	-.055	-.146	-.017	-.017
Annual cocaine Wave 1	-.074		.006	-.090		.008
Annual cocaine Wave 2	-.111		-.004	-.100		-.001
Annual cocaine Wave 3	-.108	.028	.028	-.123	-.014	-.014
Heavy drinking Wave 1	-.215		-.004	-.235		-.005
Heavy drinking Wave 2	-.215		.024	-.187		.008
Heavy drinking Wave 3	-.131	.064	.064	-.084	.047	.047

*Coefficients that are p<.05 (two-tailed) are shown in **bold**.

Note: W1 = Wave 1 data collection (grade 8, modal age 14), W2 = Wave 2 data collection (modal age 16), W3 = Wave 3 data collection (modal age 18)

Table A.3.10, Part 1
Full Tabular Summary of SEM Including 30-Day Alcohol*

Dependent Factors

Predictors		GPA W1 Direct	GPA W1 Total	College Plans W1 Direct	College Plans W1 Total	Delinquency W1 Direct	Delinquency W1 Total
Held back by Wave 1	Males	-.192	-.192	-.125	-.193	.026	.062
	Females	-.196	-.196	-.041	-.104	-.044	-.005
Suspended or expelled by Wave 1	Males	-.244	-.244	-.016	-.102	.326	.366
	Females	-.189	-.189	-.064	-.124	.255	.294
African-American vs. all others	Males	-.050	-.050	.061	.044	-.060	-.054
	Females	-.006	-.006	.056	.054	-.034	-.038
Hispanic vs. all others	Males	-.013	-.013	.009	.004	.026	.028
	Females	-.008	-.008	.000	-.003	.027	.028
Other race/ethnicity vs. all others	Males	-.087	-.087	-.026	-.057	-.032	-.016
	Females	-.084	-.084	.023	-.004	.042	.055
Lived with 2 parents W1–3	Males	.090	.090	-.008	.024	-.001	-.015
	Females	.138	.138	.019	.063	-.041	-.068
Parents' education level Wave 1	Males	.189	.189	.147	.214	.029	-.007
	Females	.210	.210	.237	.304	.006	-.053
Parental involvement at Wave 1	Males	.049	.049	.207	.224	-.164	-.180
	Females	.048	.048	.141	.157	-.144	-.166
Large MSA vs. all others	Males	.062	.062	-.032	-.010	.050	.041
	Females	.043	.043	-.005	.009	.015	.008
Non-MSA vs. all others	Males	-.005	-.005	-.115	-.117	-.036	-.031
	Females	.066	.066	-.057	-.036	-.062	-.069
GPA Wave 1	Males			.353	.353	-.149	-.162
	Females			.319	.319	-.147	-.177
College plans Wave 1	Males					-.038	-.038
	Females					-.093	-.093
Delinquency index Wave 1	Males						
	Females						
30-day cigarette use Wave 1	Males						
	Females						
30-day marijuana use Wave 1	Males						
	Females						
Annual cocaine use Wave 1	Males						
	Females						
30-day alcohol use Wave 1	Males						
	Females						
R square	Males	.268		.358		.247	
	Females	.240		.301		.201	

*Notes to Table A.3.10 (Parts 1, 2, and 3) appear on pg. 356.

Table A.3.10, Part 1, continued
Full Tabular Summary of SEM Including 30-Day Alcohol*

Dependent Factors

30-Day Cigarettes W1		30-Day Marijuana W1		Annual Cocaine W1		30-Day Alcohol W1		Serious Scholastic Setback W1–W2	
Direct	Total	Direct	Total	Direct	Total	Direct	Total	Direct	Total
.076	**.117**	.008	.067	.044	.047	**.075**	**.104**	**-.070**	-.015
.036	**.059**	-.012	.018	.033	.030	-.002	.011	-.041	-.003
.120	.229	.018	.164	.085	.129	.060	.189	-.186	-.101
.151	.276	.038	.199	.066	.147	.111	.262	-.087	-.010
-.125	-.139	.045	-.018	.017	.009	-.027	-.048	.040	.036
-.203	-.217	.044	-.064	-.058	-.069	-.083	-.101	.052	.045
-.084	-.077	.032	.003	.005	.008	-.009	.000	.030	.030
-.095	-.085	.070	.033	.049	.057	.036	.050	.032	.035
-.011	-.005	.018	.015	-.006	-.010	-.008	-.012	.010	.027
-.049	-.021	.029	.025	.030	.045	-.005	.026	.009	.028
.005	-.006	.025	.018	-.019	-.019	.014	.009	-.071	-.090
-.054	-.094	.014	-.039	.032	.014	-.029	-.071	-.098	-.139
.013	-.016	-.013	-.022	-.001	.002	.016	.005	-.057	-.102
-.024	-.076	.025	-.025	-.003	-.017	.036	-.008	-.068	-.123
-.139	-.202	-.073	-.177	-.109	-.132	-.191	-.263	-.006	-.046
-.147	-.213	-.027	-.148	-.077	-.122	-.125	-.207	-.025	-.063
-.029	-.022	-.034	-.041	-.040	-.033	-.039	-.024	.023	.015
-.004	-.007	-.047	-.050	-.040	-.038	-.010	-.010	.038	.029
-.012	-.010	-.026	-.037	-.052	-.056	.001	-.004	-.020	-.014
.000	-.029	-.041	-.060	-.021	-.039	.000	-.036	.008	-.012
-.058	-.125	-.031	-.096	.024	.002	.008	-.064	-.194	-.225
-.109	-.180	-.002	-.112	.008	-.041	-.074	-.160	-.184	-.222
-.078	-.087	.022	-.019		-.005	-.045	-.058	-.039	-.046
-.033	-.065	-.026	-.066		-.026	-.011	-.053	-.033	-.046
.239	.239	.115	.218	.135	.135	.345	.345	.074	.085
.339	.339	.094	.254	.278	.278	.462	.462	.075	.092
		.428	.428					.042	.029
		.472	.472					.001	.046
								-.031	-.031
								.094	.094
								-.035	-.035
								-.098	-.098
								.036	.036
								.043	.043
.219		.275		.069		.250		.080	
.329		.308		.124		.353		.110	

Table A.3.10, Part 2
Full Tabular Summary of SEM Including 30-Day Alcohol*

Dependent Factors

Predictors		GPA W2 Direct	GPA W2 Total	College Plans W2 Direct	College Plans W2 Total	Delinquency W2 Direct	Delinquency W2 Total
Held back by Wave 1	Males		-.127		-.119		.041
	Females		-.144		-.081		.022
Suspended or expelled by Wave 1	Males		-.153		-.084		.158
	Females		-.138		-.088		.135
African-American vs. all others	Males	-.035	-.072	.102	.096	-.042	-.057
	Females	-.014	-.021	.044	.059	-.032	-.039
Hispanic vs. all others	Males	.009	-.003	.026	.025	-.013	.001
	Females	-.010	-.017	.037	.028	-.046	-.029
Other race/ethnicity vs. all others	Males	-.026	-.088	.026	-.027	-.014	-.008
	Females	-.009	-.073	.025	.003	.007	.043
Lived with 2 parents W1–3	Males	-.026	.044	.029	.059	-.011	-.033
	Females	.017	.126	.030	.102	.001	-.066
Parents' education level Wave 1	Males	.091	.228	.041	.208	.092	.049
	Females	.075	.236	.059	.264	.046	-.036
Parental involvement at Wave 1	Males	.028	.066	.042	.159	-.051	-.141
	Females	-.017	.021	.033	.115	-.050	-.129
Large MSA vs. all others	Males	-.019	.021	.021	.022	.012	.028
	Females	-.004	.026	.007	.014	.065	.067
Non-MSA vs. all others	Males	.022	.020	-.074	-.116	-.054	-.065
	Females	.057	.106	-.068	-.058	-.019	-.060
GPA Wave 1	Males	.671	.694		.379		-.170
	Females	.734	.746		.342		-.221
College plans Wave 1	Males		.005	.416	.420		-.036
	Females		.002	.452	.457		-.059
Delinquency index Wave 1	Males		-.009		-.008	.408	.417
	Females		-.005		-.010	.382	.395
30-day cigarette use Wave 1	Males		-.003		-.003		.003
	Females		-.002		-.005		.007
30-day marijuana use Wave 1	Males		.003		.003		-.003
	Females		-.005		-.010		.014
Annual cocaine use Wave 1	Males		.004		.003		-.004
	Females		.005		.011		-.014
30-day alcohol use Wave 1	Males		-.004		-.003		.004
	Females		-.002		-.005		.006
Serious scholastic setback W1–2	Males	-.105	-.105	-.061	-.094	.095	.109
	Females	-.052	-.052	-.098	-.111	.135	.147
GPA Wave 2	Males			.314	.314	-.099	-.111
	Females			.236	.236	-.148	-.157
College plans Wave 2	Males					-.036	-.036
	Females					-.038	-.038
Delinquency index Wave 2	Males						
	Females						
30-day cigarette use Wave 2	Males						
	Females						
30-day marijuana use Wave 2	Males						
	Females						
Annual cocaine use Wave 2	Males						
	Females						
30-day alcohol use Wave 2	Males						
	Females						
R square	Males	.545		.455		.240	
	Females	.613		.432		.267	

Table A.3.10, Part 2, continued
Full Tabular Summary of SEM Including 30-Day Alcohol*

Dependent Factors

30-Day Cigarettes W2		30-Day Marijuana W2		Annual Cocaine W2		30-Day Alcohol W2		Serious Scholastic Setback W2–W3		High School Dropout W3	
Direct	Total	Direct	Total	Direct	Total	Direct	Total	Direct	Total	Direct	Total
	.082		.056		.029		.068		.023	.158	.195
	.051		.034		.019		.021		.023	.080	.118
	.146		.123		.067		.121		.034	.156	.191
	.172		.138		.097		.114		.036	.116	.175
-.095	-.165	.001	-.082	-.024	-.033	-.048	-.085	.023	.012	.034	.002
-.147	-.253	-.051	-.166	-.049	-.082	-.091	-.126	.101	.071	-.040	-.095
-.045	-.077	.002	-.026	.021	.024	-.003	-.004	.044	.038	.030	.020
-.099	-.140	.000	-.056	.054	.058	-.005	.002	.060	.047	.002	-.025
-.025	-.015	.010	.006	.009	.014	-.071	-.068	.068	.070	.013	.026
-.091	-.083	-.042	-.054	-.048	-.029	-.061	-.036	.019	.016	.002	-.007
-.043	-.070	-.033	-.071	.021	.013	-.043	-.061	-.063	-.078	-.113	-.143
-.056	-.147	.037	-.045	-.003	-.027	-.043	-.098	-.086	-.118	-.160	-.234
.020	-.030	.020	.010	-.042	-.052	.042	.014	.008	-.013	.005	-.061
.030	-.069	.024	-.024	.033	.003	.035	-.009	-.021	-.059	-.062	-.158
.021	-.121	-.034	-.152	.022	-.053	-.044	-.198	-.009	-.043	-.014	-.067
.017	-.124	-.053	-.159	-.021	-.100	.024	-.072	.037	.016	.011	-.042
.003	-.003	.016	.018	-.023	-.029	-.017	-.022	-.013	-.014	-.036	-.042
.003	.011	.029	.045	-.036	-.037	-.015	.000	.033	.033	-.014	-.014
.008	.000	-.034	-.052	.003	-.017	.075	.070	.006	.009	-.009	.004
.020	-.011	-.023	-.056	-.023	-.053	.044	.013	-.011	-.021	.002	.000
	-.217		-.164		-.076		-.157		-.095		-.159
	-.246		-.199		-.100		-.175		-.117		-.202
	-.096		-.072	-.023	-.034		-.082		-.022		-.084
	-.084		-.063	-.053	-.083		-.050		-.022		-.102
	.198		.231		.119		.231		.037		.045
	.240		.242		.165		.229		.028		.055
.407	.410		.199		.086		.002		.018		.075
.465	.472		.241		.119		.005		.045		.103
	-.004	.123	.120	.198	.196		-.003		-.005		.016
	.014	.142	.150	.252	.251		.009		.002		.016
	-.004		-.003	.075	.073		-.003		-.004		.002
	-.015		-.009	.049	.049		-.010		-.004		-.017
	.004		.004		.002	.364	.367		.023		.002
	.006		.004		.000	.251	.255		.014		.008
.071	.116	.021	.101	.040	.059	.042	.085		.025	.113	.154
.108	.149	-.015	.087	-.039	-.005	.053	.100		.026	.119	-.171
-.098	-.160	.006	-.103	-.021	-.038	-.055	-.119	-.087	-.113	-.060	-.131
-.093	-.141	-.034	-.136	-.014	-.050	-.067	-.119	-.104	-.130	-.092	-.160
-.116	-.124	-.057	-.112		-.005	-.119	-.128	-.027	-.044	-.146	-.165
-.084	-.090	-.011	-.056		-.009	-.039	-.049	-.030	-.041	-.175	-.193
.223	.223	.315	.394	.150	.150	.240	.240	.029	.059	-.022	.030
.180	.180	.301	.368	.231	.231	.272	.272	-.028	.013	-.022	.018
		.353	.353					.035	.048	.144	.152
		.366	.366					.072	.095	.200	.204
								.037	.037	.023	.023
								.062	.062	.011	.011
								-.045	-.045	.092	.092
								-.037	-.037	-.005	-.005
								.061	.061	-.010	-.010
								.052	.052	.004	.004
	.362		.395		.109		.329		.049		.284
	.438		.407		.185		.224		.075		.311

Table A.3.10, Part 3a
Full Tabular Summary of SEM Including 30-Day Alcohol*

Dependent Factors

Predictors		GPA W3 Direct	GPA W3 Total	College Plans W3 Direct	College Plans W3 Total	Delinquency W3 Direct	Delinquency W3 Total
Held back by Wave 1	Males		-.094		-.087		.031
	Females		-.111		-.061		.025
Suspended or expelled by Wave 1	Males		-.114		-.072		.100
	Females		-.107		-.064		.082
African-American vs. all others	Males	-.032	-.085	.015	.050	-.011	-.038
	Females	-.028	-.047	.019	.037	.001	-.010
Hispanic vs. all others	Males	.000	-.006	.011	.021	.013	.017
	Females	-.013	-.029	.020	.027	-.010	-.019
Other race/ethnicity vs. all others	Males	-.018	-.088	-.021	-.059	.034	.040
	Females	.002	-.054	-.015	-.023	-.024	.004
Lived with 2 parents W1–3	Males	.017	.057	.055	.105	.007	-.022
	Females	.040	.142	.070	.152	.021	-.039
Parents' education level Wave 1	Males	.042	.207	.059	.218	-.009	.007
	Females	.021	.204	.086	.258	.038	-.012
Parental involvement at Wave 1	Males	.010	.061	.029	.132	.038	-.050
	Females	.000	.016	.005	.066	.002	-.065
Large MSA vs. all others	Males	.004	.021	.044	.061	.015	.029
	Females	-.023	-.005	.051	.056	.073	.108
Non-MSA vs. all others	Males	.002	.016	-.034	-.095	-.001	-.039
	Females	.037	.119	-.050	-.060	-.006	-.046
GPA Wave 1	Males		.509		.321		-.134
	Females		.574		.275		-.182
College plans Wave 1	Males		.006		.235		-.022
	Females		.003		.237		-.039
Delinquency index Wave 1	Males		-.010		-.009		.246
	Females		-.005		-.008		.199
30-day cigarette use Wave 1	Males		-.004		-.003		.004
	Females		-.004		-.006		.007
30-day marijuana use Wave 1	Males		.003		.002		-.003
	Females		-.004		-.006		.008
Annual cocaine use Wave 1	Males		.003		.003		-.003
	Females		-.004		.007		-.008
30-day alcohol use Wave 1	Males		-.005		-.004		.005
	Females		-.002		-.004		.005
Serious scholastic setback W1–2	Males		-.078		-.070		.069
	Females		-.041		-.065		.081

Table A.3.10, Part 3a, continued
Full Tabular Summary of SEM Including 30-Day Alcohol*

Dependent Factors

30-Day Cigarettes W3		30-Day Marijuana W3		Annual Cocaine W3		30-Day Alcohol W3		Academic Attainment at Age 22	
Direct	Total	Direct	Total	Direct	Total	Direct	Total	Direct	Total
	.066		.051		.028		.043	-.029	-.125
	.048		.032		.020		.012	-.037	-.112
	.110		.105		.063		.084	-.046	-.143
	.125		.111		.069		.059	-.033	-.121
-.083	-.168	-.010	-.080	-.029	-.054	-.100	-.142	-.021	-.024
-.112	-.252	.016	-.141	-.077	-.130	-.153	-.198	-.049	-.022
-.084	-.122	.011	-.022	.019	.031	-.029	-.028	-.055	-.052
-.100	-.178	.020	-.065	-.024	-.030	-.041	-.040	-.063	-.045
-.028	-.014	-.004	.011	-.010	.011	-.025	-.040	-.009	-.060
-.037	-.078	.032	-.018	-.024	-.039	-.076	-.089	.008	-.016
.022	-.034	-.038	-.086	-.010	-.024	-.030	-.064	.057	.136
-.039	-.153	-.019	-.088	-.046	-.073	-.051	-.084	.076	.207
.021	-.034	.056	.039	.057	.031	.022	.014	.091	.227
-.024	-.096	.053	.021	-.025	-.037	.056	.071	.145	.325
-.045	-.133	-.033	-.142	-.054	-.104	.043	-.059	-.033	.047
-.006	-.088	-.041	-.146	-.031	-.098	-.070	-.105	-.015	.021
-.038	-.043	.004	.006	.006	.002	-.063	-.067	.031	.059
-.003	.017	-.019	.023	-.010	.017	.009	.039	.048	.076
-.017	-.018	-.024	-.060	.013	-.005	-.016	.004	-.040	-.059
.027	.000	-.016	-.051	.007	-.032	.018	-.001	-.007	.000
	-.220		-.185		-.098		-.133		.314
	-.244		-.183		-.122		-.104		.310
	-.071		-.048		-.030		-.045		.092
	-.057		-.040		-.027		.002		.101
	.140		.175		.119		.162		-.027
	.165		.187		.127		.130		-.018
	.218		.136		.051		.002		-.034
	.278		.200		.080		.002		-.049
	-.003		.052		.078		-.002		-.001
	.010		.071		.080		.005		-.011
	-.003		-.003		.024		-.002		.004
	-.010		-.008		.004		-.005		.008
	.005		.004		.004		.157		.003
	.005		.004		.002		.099		.003
	.086		.081		.050		.059	-.042	-.122
	.103		.080		.036		.050	-.016	-.081

Table A.3.10, Part 3b
Full Tabular Summary of SEM Including 30-Day Alcohol*

Dependent Factors

Predictors		GPA W3 Direct	GPA W3 Total	College Plans W3 Direct	College Plans W3 Total	Delinquency W3 Direct	Delinquency W3 Total
GPA Wave 2	Males	.720	.732		.333		-.113
	Females	.762	.769		.252		-.168
College plans Wave 2	Males		.004	.552	.556		-.022
	Females		.002	.515	.518		-.038
Delinquency index Wave 2	Males		-.006		-.005	.579	.585
	Females		-.001		-.001	.497	.498
30-day cigarette use Wave 2	Males		-.005		-.004		.004
	Females		-.005		-.006		.008
30-day marijuana use Wave 2	Males		-.004		-.003		.003
	Females		-.003		-.004		.005
Annual cocaine use Wave 2	Males		.005		.004		-.004
	Females		.002		.002		-.003
30-day alcohol use Wave 2	Males		-.006		-.005		.006
	Females		-.003		-.003		.004
Serious scholastic setback W2–3	Males	-.101	-.101	-.062	-.083	.086	.092
	Females	-.049	-.049	-.058	-.065	.075	.082
High school dropout Wave 3	Males						
	Females						
GPA Wave 3	Males			.208	.208	-.056	-.055
	Females			.160	.160	-.094	-.099
College plans Wave 3	Males					.005	.005
	Females					-.032	-.032
Delinquency index Wave 3	Males						
	Females						
30-day cigarette use Wave 3	Males						
	Females						
30-day marijuana use Wave 3	Males						
	Females						
Annual cocaine use Wave 3	Males						
	Females						
30-day alcohol use Wave 3	Males						
	Females						
R square	Males	.590		.534		.365	
	Females	.637		.448		.305	

*Coefficients that are $p<.05$ (two-tailed) are shown in **bold**.

Note: W1 = Wave 1 data collection (grade 8, modal age 14), W2 = Wave 2 data collection (modal age 16), W3 = Wave 3 data collection (modal age 18)

Table A.3.10, Part 3b, continued
Full Tabular Summary of SEM Including 30-Day Alcohol*

Dependent Factors

30-Day Cigarettes W3		30-Day Marijuana W3		Annual Cocaine W3		30-Day Alcohol W3		Academic Attainment at Age 22	
Direct	Total	Direct	Total	Direct	Total	Direct	Total	Direct	Total
	-.216		-.174		-.082		-.124	.215	.375
	-.206		-.143		-.107		-.093	.189	.347
	-.108		-.069	-.012	-.032		-.070		.201
	-.064		-.025	.022	.000		.038		.209
	.198		.317		.219		.253		-.028
	.165		.281		.229		.212		.004
.527	.530		.271		.039		.000		-.071
.582	.588		.357		.090		-.001		-.094
	.002	.441	.443	.098	.101		.000		-.030
	.004	.447	.448	.244	.244		.000		-.023
	-.003		-.003	.344	.341		.000		-.004
	-.002		-.001	.166	.165		.000		.001
	.004		.004		.005	.426	.427		.019
	.003		.001		.001	.387	.387		.027
.037	.067	.021	.058	.058	.081	-.028	.003	-.062	-.094
.043	.060	-.006	.021	-.009	.010	-.019	-.007	-.034	-.061
								-.190	-.190
								-.159	-.159
-.124	-.145	-.090	-.127	-.034	-.045	-.056	-.074	.024	.095
-.125	-.138	-.009	-.059	-.050	-.070	-.058	-.060	.048	.106
-.067	-.066	.016	.003		.001	-.018	-.017	.293	.295
-.009	-.012	.049	.041		-.006	.124	.117	.327	.335
.132	.132	.169	.197	.213	.213	.260	.260	-.018	-.015
.119	.119	.125	.164	.203	.203	.215	.215	.031	.031
		.214	.214					-.045	-.057
		.330	.330					-.074	-.085
								-.056	-.056
								-.032	-.032
								.028	.028
								-.014	-.014
								.054	.054
								.080	.080
.440		.454		.260		.323		.478	
.505		.492		.232		.284		.530	

Table A.4.1a
Cross-Tabulation of Academic Attainment Reported at Age 22 with Academic Attainment Reported at Age 24[1]
Wave 5 (1999–2001) and Wave 6 (2001–2003): Males

Academic Attainment at Age 22	Wave 5	Academic Attainment at Age 24								Total	Wave 6
		High School Dropout	GED	High School Diploma	1 Yr Col	2 Yrs Col	3 Yrs Col	4 Yrs Col	Bachelor's		
Missing		15.3	22.8	52.2	34.0	29.8	12.4	18.3	50.6	1214.3	27.7
High School Dropout	Wtd. N*	24.2	5.2	4.7	3.1	0.0	0.0	1.0	0.0	38.2	30.6
	Row %	63.4	13.5	12.2	8.2	0.0	0.0	2.7	0.0		
GED	Wtd. N*	3.8	38.7	3.9	2.5	2.0	0.0	0.7	0.0	51.7	97.1
	Row %	7.3	74.8	7.6	4.9	4.0	0.0	1.4	0.0		
HS diploma	Wtd. N*	4.4	5.3	180.7	19.6	15.8	3.6	0.7	0.0	230.3	40.6
	Row %	1.9	2.3	78.5	8.5	6.9	1.6	0.3	0.0		
1 year college	Wtd. N*	0.0	3.0	15.0	65.2	31.0	8.1	0.0	1.0	123.3	33.7
	Row %	0.0	2.4	12.2	52.9	25.1	6.6	0.0	0.8		
2 years college	Wtd. N*	0.0	1.7	3.2	13.5	85.0	22.4	10.4	20.7	156.9	54.6
	Row %	0.0	1.1	2.1	8.6	54.2	14.3	6.6	13.2		
3 years college	Wtd. N*	0.0	1.0	1.7	5.6	8.2	22.3	40.8	167.8	247.5	37.3
	Row %	0.0	0.4	0.7	2.3	3.3	9.0	16.5	67.8		
4 years college	Wtd. N*	0.0	0.0	2.7	1.1	4.1	3.5	20.0	68.5	99.9	22.8
	Row %	0.0	0.0	2.7	1.1	4.1	3.5	20.0	68.6		
Bachelor's	Wtd. N*	0.0	0.0	0.5	1.7	2.5	0.0	5.7	100.3	110.8	
	Row %	0.0	0.0	0.5	1.6	2.2	0.0	5.2	90.6		
Total	Wtd. N	32.4	54.9	212.5	112.4	148.7	59.9	79.4	358.3	1058.5	

Pearson Correlation   0.864

[1] Main table and percentages limited to those who participated in both Wave 5 (modal age 22) and Wave 6 (modal age 24) surveys, and provided academic attainment data in both. The right-hand column shows weighted numbers of cases* who participated in Wave 5 but not in Wave 6.

*The weighted numbers of cases in this table are based on the initial selection weight only. The numbers of cases are not adjusted to correct for panel attrition.

Table A.4.1b

Cross-Tabulation of Academic Attainment Reported at Age 22 with Academic Attainment Reported at Age 24[1] Wave 5 (1999–2001) and Wave 6 (2001–2003): Females

Academic Attainment at Age 22	Wave 5	High School Dropout	GED	High School Diploma	1 Yr Col	2 Yrs Col	3 Yrs Col	4 Yrs Col	Bachelor's	Total	Wave 6
Missing		14.9	19.6	43.0	36.8	20.3	11.3	17.4	49.6	857.5	24.3
High School Dropout	Wtd. N*	**33.6**	8.5	4.1	3.4	0.0	0.0	0.7	0.5	50.8	24.3
	Row %	**66.1**	16.8	8.0	6.7	0.0	0.0	1.5	1.0		
GED	Wtd. N*	4.3	**45.3**	5.2	9.4	2.8	0.4	0.0	0.0	67.4	22.4
	Row %	6.3	**67.2**	7.8	13.9	4.1	0.7	0.0	0.0		
HS diploma	Wtd. N*	3.2	4.8	**254.7**	30.3	11.3	3.4	3.4	0.7	311.9	77.6
	Row %	1.0	1.6	**81.7**	9.7	3.6	1.1	1.1	0.2		
1 year college	Wtd. N*	0.0	0.7	23.1	**123.8**	45.8	7.0	1.1	0.0	201.5	42.6
	Row %	0.0	0.4	11.5	**61.5**	22.7	3.5	0.5	0.0		
2 years college	Wtd. N*	0.0	1.5	3.3	20.7	**99.4**	33.8	13.6	13.7	185.9	36.2
	Row %	0.0	0.8	1.8	11.1	**53.4**	18.2	7.3	7.4		
3 years college	Wtd. N*	0.0	3.4	4.2	1.7	30.1	**38.8**	45.7	305.0	428.8	52.5
	Row %	0.0	0.8	1.0	0.4	7.0	**9.1**	10.7	71.1		
4 years college	Wtd. N*	0.0	1.7	0.0	1.7	1.6	3.6	**24.0**	92.7	125.3	23.6
	Row %	0.0	1.4	0.0	1.4	1.3	2.8	**19.2**	74.0		
Bachelor's	Wtd. N*	0.0	0.0	3.5	0.0	0.0	2.7	23.6	**223.2**	252.9	24.7
	Row %	0.0	0.0	1.4	0.0	0.0	1.1	9.3	**88.2**		
Total	Wtd. N	41.0	66.1	298.0	190.9	190.9	89.7	112.2	635.7	1624.54	

Pearson Correlation 0.871

[1] Main table and percentages limited to those who participated in both Wave 5 (modal age 22) and Wave 6 (modal age 24) surveys, and provided academic attainment data in both. The right-hand column shows weighted numbers of cases* who participated in Wave 5 but not in Wave 6.

*The weighted numbers of cases in this table are based on the initial selection weight only.
The numbers of cases are *not* adjusted to correct for panel attrition.

Table A.4.2a

OLS Regressions Predicting Academic Attainment at Age 22 (8 Levels)[1]
Eighth-Grade Class Years 1991–1993: Males

Effective *N* = 1361	Column 1 Zero-Order Correlation	Column 2 Standardized Regression Coefficient	Column 3 Standardized Regression Coefficient	Column 4 Standardized Regression Coefficient
African-American	-.077	-.017	-.017	-.021
Hispanic	-.109	-.050	-.046	-.048
Other race	-.070	-.013	-.013	-.006
White	.171			
Large MSA	.082	.035	.029	.038
Other MSA	.032			
Non-MSA	-.118	-.034	-.038	-.033
Parents' education level	.336	.095	.098	.085
Number of parents Wave 1	.182			
Number of parents Wave 2	.172			
Number of parents Wave 3	.232			
Lived with 2 parents Waves 1–3	.237	.076	.055	.067
Parent involvement index Wave 1	.152	-.010	-.013	-.023
Parent involvement index Wave 2	.097			
Parent involvement index Wave 3	.071			
Held back grade 8 or earlier	-.287	-.058	-.027	-.055
Suspended/expelled grade 8 or earlier	-.291	-.087	-.052	-.066
GPA Wave 1	.438	.082	.066	.072
GPA Wave 2	.465	.138	.139	.139
GPA Wave 3	.421	.081	.076	.064
Mean secondary school GPA	.527			
College plans Wave 1	.321	-.008	-.014	-.004
College plans Wave 2	.411	.063	.054	.054
College plans Wave 3	.515	.262	.231	.239
Mean secondary school college plans	.523			
Held back Wave 1 to Wave 2	-.141			
Held back Wave 2 to Wave 3	-.190			
Suspended/expelled Wave 1 to Wave 2	-.169			
Suspended/expelled Wave 2 to Wave 3	-.125			
Serious scholastic setback W1 to W2	-.213	-.082	-.055	-.065
Serious scholastic setback W2 to W3	-.208	-.080	-.073	-.054
High school dropout by Wave 3	-.455		-.200	

[1] These OLS (ordinary least squares) regressions were run with SAS statistical analyses software. A covariance matrix constructed with pairwise deletion served as the input data, because of missing values on the variables described in Notes 2 and 3 below. Coefficients that are p<.05 (two-tailed) are shown in **bold**.

Table A.4.2a continued on next page.

Table A.4.2a (continued)
OLS Regressions Predicting Academic Attainment at Age 22 (8 Levels)[1]
Eighth-Grade Class Years 1991–1993: Males

Effective *N* = 1361	Column 1 Zero-Order Correlation	Column 2 Standardized Regression Coefficient	Column 3 Standardized Regression Coefficient	Column 4 Standardized Regression Coefficient
Sent to the office Wave 1	-.222			.027
Sent to the office Wave 2	-.218			.028
Sent to the office Wave 3	-.259			-.040
Days cut school Wave 1	-.136			.000
Days cut school Wave 2	-.197			-.013
Days cut school Wave 3	-.168			-.011
Skipped classes Wave 1	-.078			.031
Skipped classes Wave 2	-.190			-.011
Skipped classes Wave 3	-.138			-.031
Delinquency index Wave 1[2]	-.209			-.016
Delinquency index Wave 2	-.159			-.035
Delinquency index Wave 3	-.123			.004
Evenings out Wave 1	-.055			-.018
Evenings out Wave 2	-.081			.005
Evenings out Wave 3	.006			.015
Hours worked Wave 1	-.101			-.011
Hours worked Wave 2	-.079			.017
Hours worked Wave 3	-.142			-.012
Preferred hours of work Wave 1[3]	-.095			-.005
Preferred hours of work Wave 2	-.201			-.022
Preferred hours of work Wave 3	-.259			-.047
Religious attendance Wave 1	.231			.048
Religious attendance Wave 2	.251			.021
Religious attendance Wave 3	.212			.004
Religious importance Wave 1	.134			.003
Religious importance Wave 2	.153			.039
Religious importance Wave 3	.115			-.043
Self-esteem index Wave 1[2]	.171			.025
Self-esteem index Wave 2	.105			-.029
Self-esteem index Wave 3	.141			.042
Multiple *R*		.657	.679	.671
R Squared		.432	.461	.450
R Squared, adjusted		.431	.460	.448

[2] The items in this index appeared in only one of two forms randomly distributed to respondents in their schools. Effective *N* is thus only half of that shown.

[3] This item appeared in only one of two forms randomly distributed to respondents in their schools. Its first appearance was in 1992. Effective *N* is only one third of that shown.

Note: W1 = Wave 1 data collection (grade 8, modal age 14), W2 = Wave 2 data collection (modal age 16), W3 = Wave 3 data collection (modal age 18)

Table A.4.2b
OLS Regressions Predicting Academic Attainment at Age 22 (8 Levels)[1]
Eighth-Grade Class Years 1991–1993: Females

Effective *N* = 1739	Column 1 Zero-Order Correlation	Column 2 Standardized Regression Coefficient	Column 3 Standardized Regression Coefficient	Column 4 Standardized Regression Coefficient
African-American	**-.114**	-.025	**-.042**	-.022
Hispanic	**-.112**	-.045	**-.050**	-.037
Other race	-.014	.010	.006	.012
White	**.160**			
Large MSA	**.090**	**.057**	**.056**	**.053**
Other MSA	-.023			
Non-MSA	**-.065**	-.007	-.008	-.001
Parents' education level	**.370**	**.167**	**.159**	**.143**
Number of parents Wave 1	**.152**			
Number of parents Wave 2	**.190**			
Number of parents Wave 3	**.295**			
Lived with 2 parents Waves 1–3	**.272**	**.108**	**.080**	**.087**
Parent involvement index Wave 1	**.126**	-.007	-.008	-.020
Parent involvement index Wave 2	**.099**			
Parent involvement index Wave 3	.025			
Held back grade 8 or earlier	**-.244**	**-.046**	**-.035**	**-.039**
Suspended/expelled grade 8 or earlier	**-.233**	**-.054**	**-.030**	**-.038**
GPA Wave 1	**.409**	**.088**	**.081**	**.088**
GPA Wave 2	**.413**	**.109**	**.103**	**.093**
GPA Wave 3	**.379**	**.093**	**.085**	**.088**
Mean secondary school GPA	**.469**			
College plans Wave 1	**.303**	.004	-.003	.004
College plans Wave 2	**.385**	**.084**	**.073**	**.078**
College plans Wave 3	**.480**	**.289**	**.256**	**.277**
Mean secondary school college plans	**.500**			
Held back Wave 1 to Wave 2	**-.158**			
Held back Wave 2 to Wave 3	**-.153**			
Suspended/expelled W1 to W2	**-.162**			
Suspended/expelled W2 to W3	**-.133**			
Serious scholastic setback W1 to W2	**-.212**	**-.046**	-.019	-.029
Serious scholastic setback W2 to W3	**-.191**	**-.060**	**-.046**	**-.045**
High school dropout by Wave 3	**-.425**		**-.175**	

[1] These OLS (ordinary least squares) regressions were run with SAS statistical analyses software. A covariance matrix constructed with pairwise deletion served as the input data, because of missing values on the variables described in Notes 2 and 3 below. Coefficients that are $p<.05$ (two-tailed) are shown in **bold**.

Table A.4.2b continued on next page.

Table A.4.2b (continued)
OLS Regressions Predicting Academic Attainment at Age 22 (8 Levels)[1]
Eighth-Grade Class Years 1991–1993: Females

Effective N = 1739	Column 1 Zero-Order Correlation	Column 2 Standardized Regression Coefficient	Column 3 Standardized Regression Coefficient	Column 4 Standardized Regression Coefficient
Sent to the office Wave 1	-.202			-.005
Sent to the office Wave 2	-.213			.024
Sent to the office Wave 3	-.195			-.014
Days cut school Wave 1	-.125			.004
Days cut school Wave 2	-.203			-.040
Days cut school Wave 3	-.180			-.025
Skipped classes Wave 1	-.120			.004
Skipped classes Wave 2	-.147			-.030
Skipped classes Wave 3	-.029			.014
Delinquency index Wave 1[2]	-.163			.012
Delinquency index Wave 2	-.137			-.016
Delinquency index Wave 3	-.079			.033
Evenings out Wave 1	-.055			.005
Evenings out Wave 2	-.022			-.006
Evenings out Wave 3	.058			-.005
Hours worked Wave 1	.015			.007
Hours worked Wave 2	-.038			.003
Hours worked Wave 3	-.083			-.022
Preferred hours of work Wave 1[3]	-.044			.005
Preferred hours of work Wave 2	-.229			-.029
Preferred hours of work Wave 3	-.283			-.068
Religious attendance Wave 1	.162			.022
Religious attendance Wave 2	.167			.018
Religious attendance Wave 3	.172			.066
Religious importance Wave 1	.038			-.011
Religious importance Wave 2	.045			-.010
Religious importance Wave 3	.013			-.064
Self-esteem index Wave 1[2]	.145			.028
Self-esteem index Wave 2	.084			-.006
Self-esteem index Wave 3	.093			-.022
Multiple R		.697	.712	.711
R Squared		.485	.507	.505
R Squared, adjusted		.485	.506	.504

[2] The items in this index appeared in only one of two forms randomly distributed to respondents in their schools. Effective N is thus only half of that shown.

[3] This item appeared in only one of two forms randomly distributed to respondents in their schools. Its first appearance was in 1992. Effective N is thus only one third of that shown.

Note: W1 = Wave 1 data collection (grade 8, modal age 14), W2 = Wave 2 data collection (modal age 16), W3 = Wave 3 data collection (modal age 18)

Table A.4.3
Trends Over Time in Number of Times
Held Back a Grade
1991–2001: Males and Females
(Based on Eighth-Grade
Cross-Sectional Surveys)

Percentage of Males

	Never	Once	Two or more
1991	78.2	18.5	3.4
1992	76.5	20.0	3.5
1993	76.0	20.1	3.9
1994	79.2	17.8	3.0
1995	81.0	16.2	2.8
1996	81.5	16.3	2.2
1997	85.1	13.5	1.4
1998	85.0	13.1	1.9
1999	84.6	13.7	1.7
2000	85.0	13.0	2.0
2001	84.2	13.8	2.0

Percentage of Females

	Never	Once	Two or more
1991	86.4	12.4	1.2
1992	84.4	14.0	1.6
1993	84.3	14.4	1.3
1994	85.4	13.0	1.6
1995	86.6	12.0	1.4
1996	86.4	12.5	1.0
1997	89.2	9.9	1.0
1998	90.1	8.9	1.0
1999	90.3	8.7	1.0
2000	89.4	9.4	1.2
2001	91.4	7.8	0.8

Table A.4.4
Trends Over Time in Number of Times
Suspended or Expelled
1991–2001: Males and Females
(Based on Eighth-Grade
Cross-Sectional Surveys)

Percentage of Males

	Never	Once	Two or more
1991	73.5	14.1	12.5
1992	70.6	15.2	14.2
1993	69.2	15.2	15.7
1994	68.4	15.8	15.9
1995	68.1	15.7	16.2
1996	67.4	16.7	16.0
1997	67.5	17.5	15.0
1998	68.0	16.2	15.7
1999	67.7	16.6	15.8
2000	69.2	15.9	14.9
2001	69.8	15.8	14.4

Percentage of Females

	Never	Once	Two or more
1991	88.3	6.9	4.7
1992	85.3	9.2	5.5
1993	84.0	9.6	6.4
1994	84.2	9.3	6.5
1995	83.6	9.6	6.8
1996	83.2	9.9	6.9
1997	83.8	9.8	6.4
1998	84.0	9.4	6.6
1999	83.2	9.8	6.9
2000	84.3	9.4	6.3
2001	84.3	9.8	5.9

Table A.4.5
Basic Structural Equation Model of Academic Attainment
Model Fit Statistics

	Males	Females
Bentler-Bonett Normed Fit Index	.989	.988
Bentler-Bonett Non-Normed Fit Index	.978	.973
Comparative Fit Index (CFI)	.992	.991
Bollen (IFI) Fit Index	.992	.991
McDonald (MFI) Fit Index	.925	.909
LISREL GFI Fit Index	.981	.980
LISREL AGFI Fit Index	.945	.942
Root Mean-Square Residual (RMR)	.033	.036
Standardized RMR	.029	.032
Root Mean-Square Error of Approximation (RMSEA)	.040	.044
Chi-Square	309.4	427.4
Degrees of Freedom	97	97

Table A.4.6
Basic Structural Equation Model of Academic Attainment
Variance in Endogenous Factors (R^2) Explained
by All Prior Causal Factors in the Model

	Males	Females
GPA Wave 1	.268	.241
GPA Wave 2	.546	.615
GPA Wave 3	.590	.643
College plans Wave 1	.358	.300
College plans Wave 2	.456	.432
College plans Wave 3	.535	.449
Serious scholastic setback W1 to W2	.070	.096
Serious scholastic setback W2 to W3	.038	.059
High school dropout by Wave 3	.255	.281
Academic attainment at age 22	.474	.524

Note: W1 = Wave 1 data collection (grade 8, modal age 14),
W2 = Wave 2 data collection (modal age 16),
W3 = Wave 3 data collection (modal age 18)

Table A.4.7
Basic Structural Equation Model of Academic Attainment
Bivariate Factor Correlations (BFC), Direct and Total Effects of Each Predictor
in the Model on Academic Attainment*

	Males			Females		
	BFC	Direct	Total	BFC	Direct	Total
African-American	**-.078**	-.016	-.023	**-.127**	**-.041**	-.023
Hispanic	**-.110**	**-.049**	**-.051**	**-.124**	**-.052**	**-.045**
Other race	**-.071**	-.009	**-.060**	-.016	.009	-.016
Large MSA	**.083**	.028	**.059**	**.100**	**.052**	**.076**
Non-MSA	**-.118**	-.035	**-.059**	**-.073**	-.007	.000
Parents' education level	**.338**	**.087**	**.226**	**.413**	**.150**	**.324**
Lived with 2 parents Waves 1–3	**.239**	**.056**	**.136**	**.304**	**.077**	**.206**
Parent involvement index	**.191**	-.026	.047	**.185**	-.013	.024
Held back grade 8 or earlier	**-.274**	-.028	**-.123**	**-.247**	**-.037**	**-.111**
Suspended/expelled grade 8 or earlier	**-.267**	**-.054**	**-.149**	**-.250**	-.035	**-.120**
GPA Wave 1	**.457**	n/a	**.311**	**.471**	n/a	**.309**
GPA Wave 2	**.529**	**.217**	**.376**	**.526**	**.192**	**.353**
GPA Wave 3	**.464**	.035	**.096**	**.471**	.052	**.106**
College plans Wave 1	**.352**	n/a	**.090**	**.371**	n/a	**.099**
College plans Wave 2	**.462**	n/a	**.202**	**.469**	n/a	**.210**
College plans Wave 3	**.548**	**.296**	**.296**	**.576**	**.336**	**.336**
Serious scholastic setback Wave 1 to Wave 2	**-.210**	**-.048**	**-.126**	**-.238**	-.019	**-.083**
Serious scholastic setback Wave 2 to Wave 3	**-.200**	**-.067**	**-.095**	**-.195**	**-.038**	**-.062**
High school dropout by Wave 3	**-.427**	**-.196**	**-.196**	**-.438**	**-.169**	**-.169**

*Coefficients that are p<.05 (two-tailed) are shown in **bold**.

Note: W1 = Wave 1 data collection (grade 8, modal age 14), W2 = Wave 2 data collection (modal age 16), W3 = Wave 3 data collection (modal age 18)

Table A.5.1
Model Fit Statistics

	Males	Females
Bentler-Bonett Normed Fit Index	.991	.990
Bentler-Bonett Non-Normed Fit Index	.983	.980
Comparative Fit Index (CFI)	.994	.993
Bollen (IFI) Fit Index	.994	.993
McDonald (MFI) Fit Index	.913	.902
LISREL GFI Fit Index	.979	.979
LISREL AGFI Fit Index	.943	.944
Root Mean-Square Residual (RMR)	.035	.034
Standardized RMR	.028	.030
Root Mean-Square Error of Approximation (RMSEA)	.038	.040
Chi-Square	376.9	489.1
Degrees of Freedom	129	129

Table A.5.2
Variance in Endogenous Factors (R^2) Explained by
All Prior Causal Factors in the Model

	Males	Females
GPA Wave 1	.268	.241
GPA Wave 2	.546	.615
GPA Wave 3	.590	.640
College plans Wave 1	.357	.300
College plans Wave 2	.456	.432
College plans Wave 3	.535	.448
Serious scholastic setback W1 to W2	.076	.103
Serious scholastic setback W2 to W3	.042	.060
High school dropout by Wave 3	.255	.281
Delinquency Wave 1	.246	.201
Delinquency Wave 2	.234	.269
Delinquency Wave 3	.362	.308
Academic attainment at age 22	.475	.524

Note: W1 = Wave 1 data collection (grade 8, modal age 14),
W2 = Wave 2 data collection (modal age 16),
W3 = Wave 3 data collection (modal age 18)

Table A.5.3
Structural Equation Model Including Delinquency
Bivariate Factor Correlations (BFC), Direct and Total Effects
of Each Predictor in the Model on Academic Attainment

	Males			Females		
	BFC	Direct	Total	BFC	Direct	Total
African-American	-.078	-.018	-.023	-.127	-.040	-.023
Hispanic	-.109	-.049	-.051	-.124	-.051	-.045
Other race	-.070	-.009	-.060	-.016	.009	-.016
Large MSA	.083	.028	.059	.100	.049	.076
Non-MSA	-.118	-.036	-.059	-.073	-.007	.000
Parents' education level	.338	.088	.226	.414	.149	.324
Lived with 2 parents Waves 1–3	.239	.056	.136	.304	.077	.206
Parent involvement index	.193	-.025	.049	.185	-.012	.024
Held back grade 8 or earlier	-.275	-.029	-.125	-.247	-.035	-.109
Suspended/expelled grade 8 or earlier	-.266	-.051	-.147	-.251	-.038	-.121
GPA Wave 1	.458		.311	.471		.308
GPA Wave 2	.529	.218	.375	.526	.196	.353
GPA Wave 3	.464	.031	.094	.470	.054	.106
College plans Wave 1	.353		.090	.370		.098
College plans Wave 2	.462		.201	.468		.209
College plans Wave 3	.547	.295	.295	.576	.338	.337
Serious scholastic setback Wave 1 to Wave 2	-.210	-.046	-.126	-.238	-.021	-.083
Serious scholastic setback Wave 2 to Wave 3	-.201	-.065	-.094	-.196	-.041	-.063
High school dropout by Wave 3	-0.428	-.197	-.197	-.437	-.168	-.168
Delinquency Wave 1	-.200		-.021	-.190		-.005
Delinquency Wave 2	-.159		-.025	-.168		.007
Delinquency Wave 3	-.140	-.019	-.019	-.110	.026	.026

Coefficients that are p<.05 (two-tailed) are shown in bold.

Note: W1 = Wave 1 data collection (grade 8, modal age 14), W2 = Wave 2 data collection (modal age 16),
W3 = Wave 3 data collection (modal age 18)

Table A.5.4
Comparison of Bivariate Factor Correlations (BFC), Direct and Total Effects
of Each Predictor on Academic Attainment Between the Basic Structural Model
of Academic Attainment (Chapter 4) and the Structural Model of Academic
Attainment That Includes Delinquency and Substance Use (Chapters 6–9):
Males and Females

| | Bivariate Factor Correlations | | | |
| | Males | | Females | |
	Chapter 4	Chapters 6–9	Chapter 4	Chapters 6–9
African-American	-.078	-.078	-.127	-.127
Hispanic	-.110	-.110	-.124	-.124
Other race	-.071	-.071	-.016	-.016
Large MSA	.083	.083	.100	.100
Non-MSA	-.118	-.119	-.073	-.073
Parents' education level	.338	.338	.413	.414
Lived with 2 parents Waves 1–3	.239	.239	.304	.305
Parent involvement index	.191	.191	.185	.177
Held back grade 8 or earlier	-.274	-.274	-.247	-.248
Suspended/expelled grade 8 or earlier	-.267	-.262	-.250	-.251
GPA Wave 1	.457	.458	.471	.472
GPA Wave 2	.529	.529	.526	.525
GPA Wave 3	.464	.464	.471	.470
College plans Wave 1	.352	.354	.371	.372
College plans Wave 2	.462	.463	.469	.469
College plans Wave 3	.548	.548	.576	.575
Serious scholastic setback Wave 1 to Wave 2	-.210	-.209	-.238	-.238
Serious scholastic setback Wave 2 to Wave 3	-.200	-.203	-.195	-.199
High school dropout by Wave 3	-.427	-.427	-.438	-.437
Delinquency Wave 1		-.204		-.201
Delinquency Wave 2		-.163		-.173
Delinquency Wave 3		-.140		-.110
30-day cigarette smoking Wave 1		-.183		-.224
30-day cigarette smoking Wave 2		-.259		-.262
30-day cigarette smoking Wave 3		-.256		-.259
30-day marijuana Wave 1		-.134		-.152
30-day marijuana Wave 2		-.206		-.174
30-day marijuana Wave 3		-.214		-.145
Annual cocaine Wave 1		-.074		-.091
Annual cocaine Wave 2		-.110		-.101
Annual cocaine Wave 3		-.108		-.123
30-day alcohol Wave 1		-.155		-.184
30-day alcohol Wave 2		-.202		-.164
30-day alcohol Wave 3		-.116		.005

Table A.5.4 continued on next page.

Table A.5.4 (continued)
Comparison of Bivariate Factor Correlations (BFC), Direct and Total
Effects of Each Predictor on Academic Attainment Between the Basic
Structural Model of Academic Attainment (Chapter 4) and the
Structural Model of Academic Attainment That Includes Delinquency
and Substance Use (Chapters 6–9): Males and Females

| Direct Effects | | | | Total Effects | | | |
| Males | | Females | | Males | | Females | |
Chapter 4	Chapters 6–9	Chapter 4	Chapters 6–9	Chapter 4	Chapters 6–9	Chapter 4	Chapters 6–9
-.016	-.021	**-.041**	**-.049**	-.023	-.024	-.023	-.022
-.049	**-.055**	**-.052**	**-.063**	**-.051**	**-.052**	**-.045**	**-.045**
-.009	-.009	.009	.008	**-.060**	**-.060**	-.016	-.016
.028	.031	**.052**	**.048**	**.059**	**.059**	**.076**	**.076**
-.035	**-.040**	-.007	-.007	**-.059**	**-.059**	.000	.000
.087	**.091**	**.150**	**.145**	**.226**	**.227**	**.324**	**.325**
.056	**.057**	**.077**	**.076**	**.136**	**.136**	**.206**	**.207**
-.026	-.033	-.013	-.015	.047	.047	.024	.021
-.028	**-.029**	**-.037**	**-.037**	**-.123**	**-.125**	**-.111**	**-.112**
-.054	**-.046**	**-.035**	-.033	**-.149**	**-.143**	**-.120**	**-.121**
				.311	**.314**	**.309**	**.310**
.217	**.215**	**.192**	**.189**	**.376**	**.375**	**.353**	**.347**
.035	.024	.052	.048	**.096**	**.095**	**.106**	**.106**
				.090	**.092**	**.099**	**.101**
				.202	**.201**	**.210**	**.209**
.296	**.293**	**.336**	**.327**	**.296**	**.295**	**.336**	**.335**
-.048	-.042	**-.019**	-.016	**-.126**	**-.122**	**-.083**	**-.081**
-.067	**-.062**	**-.038**	-.034	**-.095**	**-.094**	**-.062**	**-.061**
-.196	**-.190**	**-.169**	**-.159**	**-.196**	**-.190**	**-.169**	**-.159**
					-.027		-.018
					-.028		.004
	-.018		.031		-.015		.031
					-.034		**-.049**
					-.071		**-.094**
	-.045		**-.074**		-.057		**-.085**
					-.001		-.011
					-.030		-.023
	-.056		-.032		-.056		-.032
					.004		.008
					-.004		.001
	.028		-.014		.028		-.014
					.003		.003
					.019		.027
	.054		**.080**		.054		**.080**

Coefficients that are p<.05 (two-tailed) are shown in **bold**.

Note: W1 = Wave 1 data collection (grade 8, modal age 14), W2 = Wave 2 data collection (modal age 16), W3 = Wave 3 data collection (modal age 18)

Table A.6.1
Selected Patterns of Daily Smoking in the Last 30 Days
Over Five Waves

		Pattern[a]	"Age of Initiation" Continuum	Percent of Total Sample	Males	Females
A. 57% of the sample	**Never a daily smoker**	NNNNN	(1)	57.0	54.5	59.0
B. 25.2% of the sample	**Initiated and then**	NNNNY	(2)	4.6	6.0	3.5
	continued daily smoking	NNNYY	(3)	5.7	6.5	5.1
		NNYYY	(4)	6.5	7.8	5.6
		NYYYY	(5)	5.4	5.2	5.5
		YYYYY	(6)	3.0	2.9	3.1
C. 12.3% of the sample	**Initiated daily smoking and**	NNNYN		2.6	2.5	2.8
	subsequently stopped	NNYNN		2.7	2.6	2.8
	daily smoking	NNYYN		1.3	1.7	1.0
		NYNNN		1.4	1.2	1.6
		NYYNN		0.8	0.7	0.8
		NYYYN		1.0	1.0	1.1
		YNNNN		1.2	1.3	1.0
		YYNNN		0.3	0.2	0.4
		YYYNN		0.3	0.3	0.3
		YYYYN		0.6	0.4	0.7
D. Remaining trajectories	**Initiated daily smoking,**	NNYNY		0.9	0.8	1.0
5.6% of the sample	**stopped daily smoking, and**	NYNNY		0.3	0.3	0.4
	reinitiated daily smoking	NYNYN		0.4	0.4	0.4
		NYNYY		0.9	0.5	1.2
		NYYNY		0.6	0.5	0.6
		YNNNY		0.2	0.1	0.2
		YNNYN		0.2	0.2	0.1
		YNNYY		0.3	0.4	0.1
		YNYNN		0.1	0.1	0.2
		YNYNY		0.1	0.2	0.1
		YNYYN		0.1	0.1	0.2
		YNYYY		0.5	0.8	0.2
		YYNYN		0.2	0.1	0.2
		YYNYY		0.5	0.6	0.5
		YYYNY		0.2	0.1	0.2
		YYNNY		0.1	0.0	0.1

[a] N = No, Y = Yes.

Wave 1 is represented in the first (left-most) entry in the sequence.
Wave 5 is represented in the last (right-most) entry in the sequence.

Table A.6.2a
OLS Regressions Predicting 30-Day Smoking
at Ages 14, 16, and 18: Males[1]

	Age 14		
	Column 1	Column 2	Column 3
Effective N = 1361	Zero-Order Correlation	Standardized Regression Coefficient	Standardized Regression Coefficient
African-American	**-.071**	**-.122**	**-.110**
Hispanic	-.011	**-.077**	**-.075**
Other race	.042	-.014	-.015
White	.024		
Large MSA	-.021	-.021	-.020
Other MSA	.004		
Non-MSA	.016	-.009	-.010
Parents' education level	**-.094**	.002	-.010
Number of parents Wave 1	**-.062**		
Number of parents Wave 2	-.026		
Number of parents Wave 3	-.045		
Lived with 2 parents Waves 1–3	**-.077**	.012	.019
Parent involvement index Wave 1	**-.191**	**-.095**	**-.071**
Parent involvement index Wave 2	**-.069**		
Parent involvement index Wave 3	-.050		
Held back grade 8 or earlier	**.185**	.059	.040
Suspended/expelled grade 8 or earlier	**.253**	**.118**	.054
GPA Wave 1	**-.196**	-.030	-.016
GPA Wave 2	**-.146**	-.001	.021
GPA Wave 3	**-.135**	-.010	-.010
Mean secondary school GPA	**-.191**		
College plans Wave 1	**-.208**	**-.089**	**-.067**
College plans Wave 2	**-.142**	.045	.058
College plans Wave 3	**-.156**	-.003	-.003
Mean secondary school college plans	**-.210**		
Held back Wave 1 to Wave 2	**.061**		
Held back Wave 2 to Wave 3	**.095**		
Suspended/expelled Wave 1 to Wave 2	.031		
Suspended/expelled Wave 2 to Wave 3	**.064**		
Serious scholastic setback Wave 1 to Wave 2	**.059**	.026	.005
Serious scholastic setback Wave 2 to Wave 3	**.105**	.050	.045
High school dropout by Wave 3	**.225**	**.096**	**.082**
Sent to the office Wave 1	**.261**		**.077**
Sent to the office Wave 2	**.207**		.055
Sent to the office Wave 3	**.151**		-.011
Days cut school Wave 1	**.231**		.078
Days cut school Wave 2	**.134**		.012
Days cut school Wave 3	**.068**		-.014
Skipped classes Wave 1	**.193**		.041
Skipped classes Wave 2	**.156**		.033
Skipped classes Wave 3	.034		-.060
Delinquency index Wave 1[2]	**.295**	**.186**	**.149**
Delinquency index Wave 2	**.146**	.012	-.025
Delinquency index Wave 3	**.089**	-.013	-.008
Evenings out Wave 1	**.125**		.045
Evenings out Wave 2	**.120**		.031
Evenings out Wave 3	.024		-.009
Hours worked Wave 1	**.118**		.041
Hours worked Wave 2	**.068**		.000
Hours worked Wave 3	**.092**		.029
Preferred hours of work Wave 1[3]	**.066**		.009
Preferred hours of work Wave 2	**.114**		.022
Preferred hours of work Wave 3	**.085**		.000
Religious attendance Wave 1	**-.093**		.041
Religious attendance Wave 2	**-.128**		-.032
Religious attendance Wave 3	**-.114**		-.025
Religious importance Wave 1	**-.097**		-.020
Religious importance Wave 2	**-.093**		-.008
Religious importance Wave 3	**-.070**		.033
Self-esteem index Wave 1[2]	**-.143**		-.049
Self-esteem index Wave 2	**-.070**		-.008
Self-esteem index Wave 3	-.050		-.008
Multiple R		.392	.432
R Squared		.153	.186
R Squared, adjusted		.143	.163

[1] These OLS (ordinary least squares) regressions were run with SAS statistical analyses software. A covariance matrix constructed with pairwise deletion served as the input data, because of missing values on the variables described in Notes 2 and 3 below. Coefficients that are p<.05 (two-tailed) are shown in **bold**.

Table A.6.2a continued on next page.

Table A.6.2a (continued)
OLS Regressions Predicting 30-Day Smoking
at Ages 14, 16, and 18: Males[1]

	Age 16			Age 18	
Column 4	Column 5	Column 6	Column 7	Column 8	Column 9
Zero-Order Correlation	Standardized Regression Coefficient	Standardized Regression Coefficient	Zero-Order Correlation	Standardized Regression Coefficient	Standardized Regression Coefficient
-.096	-.150	-.134	-.107	-.157	-.134
-.016	-.084	-.082	-.061	-.120	-.113
.032	-.035	-.033	.037	-.043	-.037
.051			.082		
-.012	-.003	.001	-.047	-.035	-.022
-.007			.024		
.021	.003	.007	.020	-.012	-.008
-.077	.025	.019	-.060	.027	.023
-.041			-.021		
-.062			-.047		
-.094			-.051		
-.097	-.011	-.002	-.057	.021	.029
-.131	-.025	-.015	-.122	-.041	-.022
-.099			-.111		
-.062			-.091		
.173	.054	.049	.116	.014	.022
.227	.069	.036	.182	.049	.018
-.219	-.019	-.009	-.207	-.015	.000
-.220	-.063	-.027	-.228	-.055	-.022
-.176	-.001	.002	-.228	-.078	-.060
-.245			-.263		
-.190	-.030	-.030	-.156	-.004	-.007
-.235	-.062	-.040	-.218	-.038	-.026
-.198	.004	.015	-.220	-.045	-.016
-.258			-.248		
.094			.088		
.120			.112		
.125			.129		
.041			.096		
.151	.073	.044	.150	.068	.040
.103	.031	.019	.139	.058	.037
.286	.150	.126	.251	.128	.109
.238		.031	.215		.013
.283		.070	.274		.066
.204		.006	.253		.052
.130		-.020	.083		-.029
.234		.046	.164		.030
.130		.003	.179		.046
.100		-.018	.063		-.024
.265		.099	.154		-.003
.110		-.025	.133		.003
.265	.104	.091	.216	.065	.062
.277	.144	.084	.251	.097	.058
.179	.030	.020	.226	.103	.063
.100		.026	.102		.035
.146		.029	.138		.012
.083		.023	.159		.084
.074		-.002	.068		.000
.081		.002	.058		-.017
.103		.029	.127		.046
.058		-.004	.058		-.006
.113		.000	.126		.017
.117		.025	.153		.055
-.117		.025	-.123		.012
-.175		-.013	-.174		-.014
-.176		-.061	-.193		-.065
-.106		.015	-.126		.006
-.149		-.026	-.145		.043
-.117		.019	-.163		-.053
-.132		-.042	-.142		-.055
-.137		-.051	-.148		-.056
-.061		.023	-.095		.008
	.446	.499		.441	.503
	.199	.249		.194	.253
	.189	.228		.184	.231

[2] The items in this index appeared in only one of two forms randomly distributed to respondents in their schools. Effective N is thus only half of that shown.

[3] This item appeared in only one of two forms randomly distributed to respondents in their schools. Its first appearance was in 1992. Effective N is thus only one third of that shown.

Note: W1 = Wave 1 data collection (grade 8, modal age 14), W2 = Wave 2 data collection (modal age 16), W3 = Wave 3 data collection (modal age 18)

Table A.6.2b
OLS Regressions Predicting 30-Day Smoking
at Ages 14, 16, and 18: Females[1]

	Age 14		
	Column 1	Column 2	Column 3
Effective N = 1739	Zero-Order Correlation	Standardized Regression Coefficient	Standardized Regression Coefficient
African-American	-.094	-.187	-.178
Hispanic	-.006	-.085	-.089
Other race	.040	-.037	-.036
White	.040		
Large MSA	-.013	-.007	-.001
Other MSA	.039		
Non-MSA	-.031	-.010	-.011
Parents' education level	-.134	-.022	-.006
Number of parents Wave 1	-.088		
Number of parents Wave 2	-.116		
Number of parents Wave 3	-.142		
Lived with 2 parents Waves 1–3	-.150	-.041	-.030
Parent involvement index Wave 1	-.211	-.100	-.078
Parent involvement index Wave 2	-.101		
Parent involvement index Wave 3	-.054		
Held back grade 8 or earlier	.134	.034	.044
Suspended/expelled grade 8 or earlier	.274	.150	.083
GPA Wave 1	-.240	-.061	-.036
GPA Wave 2	-.197	-.019	-.007
GPA Wave 3	-.166	.004	-.001
Mean secondary school GPA	-.237		
College plans Wave 1	-.212	-.052	-.040
College plans Wave 2	-.182	-.004	-.009
College plans Wave 3	-.147	.020	.017
Mean secondary school college plans	-.225		
Held back Wave 1 to Wave 2	.103		
Held back Wave 2 to Wave 3	.061		
Suspended/expelled Wave 1 to Wave 2	.089		
Suspended/expelled Wave 2 to Wave 3	.080		
Serious scholastic setback Wave 1 to Wave 2	.125	.022	.011
Serious scholastic setback Wave 2 to Wave 3	.096	.027	.020
High school dropout by Wave 3	.264	.095	.079
Sent to the office Wave 1	.334		.114
Sent to the office Wave 2	.215		.008
Sent to the office Wave 3	.168		.006
Days cut school Wave 1	.232		.071
Days cut school Wave 2	.126		-.019
Days cut school Wave 3	.109		-.006
Skipped classes Wave 1	.213		.057
Skipped classes Wave 2	.105		-.037
Skipped classes Wave 3	.048		-.013
Delinquency index Wave 1[2]	.380	.269	.209
Delinquency index Wave 2	.185	-.008	-.017
Delinquency index Wave 3	.115	.003	.001
Evenings out Wave 1	.166		.071
Evenings out Wave 2	.102		.013
Evenings out Wave 3	.048		.008
Hours worked Wave 1	.039		-.002
Hours worked Wave 2	.041		-.012
Hours worked Wave 3	.058		-.014
Preferred hours of work Wave 1[3]	.053		.018
Preferred hours of work Wave 2	.148		.062
Preferred hours of work Wave 3	.122		.007
Religious attendance Wave 1	-.149		.005
Religious attendance Wave 2	-.177		-.034
Religious attendance Wave 3	-.153		.015
Religious importance Wave 1	-.150		-.023
Religious importance Wave 2	-.141		-.042
Religious importance Wave 3	-.112		.021
Self-esteem index Wave 1[2]	-.159		-.035
Self-esteem index Wave 2	-.104		-.021
Self-esteem index Wave 3	-.053		.027
Multiple R		.478	.513
R Squared		.228	.263
R Squared, adjusted		.220	.245

[1] These OLS (ordinary least squares) regressions were run with SAS statistical analyses software. A covariance matrix constructed with pairwise deletion served as the input data, because of missing values on the variables described in Notes 2 and 3 below. Coefficients that are p<.05 (two-tailed) are shown in **bold**.

Table A.6.2b continued on next page.

Table A.6.2b (continued)
OLS Regressions Predicting 30-Day Smoking
at Ages 14, 16, and 18: Females[1]

	Age 16			Age 18	
Column 4	Column 5	Column 6	Column 7	Column 8	Column 9
Zero-Order Correlation	Standardized Regression Coefficient	Standardized Regression Coefficient	Zero-Order Correlation	Standardized Regression Coefficient	Standardized Regression Coefficient
-.122	-.215	-.171	-.123	-.218	-.161
-.053	-.128	-.110	-.087	-.161	-.137
-.010	-.097	-.079	-.002	-.084	-.063
.126			.142		
-.008	-.001	.002	-.010	-.002	-.001
.016			.003		
-.011	.013	.011	.006	.026	.025
-.087	.020	.032	-.092	-.019	-.012
-.082			-.063		
-.103			-.112		
-.158			-.143		
-.152	-.044	-.026	-.145	-.063	-.049
-.140	-.044	-.011	-.112	-.036	-.012
-.123			-.120		
-.044			-.061		
.070	-.018	-.015	.056	-.016	-.003
.181	.072	.026	.131	.037	.013
-.221	-.015	.002	-.185	.023	.031
-.243	-.080	-.038	-.222	-.046	-.021
-.188	-.010	-.012	-.240	-.125	-.096
-.256			-.251		
-.174	-.007	-.002	-.125	.011	.011
-.231	-.057	-.051	-.182	-.025	-.023
-.180	.003	.000	-.183	-.023	-.022
-.247			-.209		
.162			.061		
.092			.071		
.179			.131		
.098			.142		
.226	.101	.069	.134	.026	.013
.129	.059	.044	.148	.078	.063
.325	.166	.126	.277	.144	.133
.252		.059	.179		.028
.322		.089	.217		.016
.227		.014	.240		.047
.163		.029	.118		.009
.200		.020	.138		-.005
.163		-.006	.168		.021
.133		.012	.109		.027
.182		.001	.117		-.038
.077		-.014	.127		.049
.276	.124	.085	.196	.067	.045
.292	.138	.071	.212	.055	.020
.162	.012	.004	.220	.123	.083
.145		.031	.101		-.013
.211		.103	.183		.067
.097		.021	.177		.102
.030		-.021	.049		-.005
.074		.019	.064		.007
.108		.028	.116		.030
.028		.003	.038		.012
.132		.043	.125		.048
.129		.011	.149		.036
-.169		-.009	-.119		.035
-.223		-.063	-.192		-.040
-.205		-.004	-.218		-.038
-.160		-.019	-.136		.004
-.199		-.049	-.192		-.053
-.153		.030	-.182		-.017
-.147		-.036	-.114		-.009
-.164		-.058	-.144		-.046
-.085		.025	-.122		-.003
	.511	.562		.442	.442
	.261	.316		.195	.195
	.253	.299		.186	.186

[2] The items in this index appeared in only one of two forms randomly distributed to respondents in their schools. Effective *N* is thus only half of that shown.

[3] This item appeared in only one of two forms randomly distributed to respondents in their schools. Its first appearance was in 1992. Effective *N* is thus only one third of that shown.

Note: W1 = Wave 1 data collection (grade 8, modal age 14), W2 = Wave 2 data collection (modal age 16), W3 = Wave 3 data collection (modal age 18)

Table A.7.1a

OLS Regressions Predicting Marijuana Use in the Last 30 Days
at Ages 14, 16, and 18: Males[1]

	Age 14		
	Column 1	Column 2	Column 3
Effective *N* = 1361	Zero-Order Correlation	Standardized Regression Coefficient	Standardized Regression Coefficient
African-American	.007	-.009	-.013
Hispanic	.031	-.001	.001
Other race	.024	.013	.013
White	-.042		
Large MSA	-.017	-.034	-.036
Other MSA	.024		
Non-MSA	-.010	-.029	-.023
Parents' education level	**-.081**	-.012	-.019
Number of parents Wave 1	-.051		
Number of parents Wave 2	-.020		
Number of parents Wave 3	-.049		
Lived with 2 parents Waves 1–3	-.049	.025	.030
Parent involvement index Wave 1	**-.140**	**-.078**	**-.065**
Parent involvement index Wave 2	**-.054**		
Parent involvement index Wave 3	-.020		
Held back grade 8 or earlier	**.125**	.024	.002
Suspended/expelled grade 8 or earlier	**.174**	.055	.008
GPA Wave 1	**-.142**	-.048	-.040
GPA Wave 2	**-.091**	.007	.001
GPA Wave 3	**-.059**	.040	.035
Mean secondary school GPA	**-.118**		
College plans Wave 1	**-.133**	-.040	-.019
College plans Wave 2	**-.114**	-.020	-.021
College plans Wave 3	**-.085**	.027	.013
Mean secondary school college plans	**-.136**		
Held back Wave 1 to Wave 2	.031		
Held back Wave 2 to Wave 3	**.054**		
Suspended/expelled Wave 1 to Wave 2	-.006	.	
Suspended/expelled Wave 2 to Wave 3	.015		
Serious scholastic setback W1 to W2	.013	-.022	-.027
Serious scholastic setback W2 to W3	.044	.007	.002
High school dropout by Wave 3	**.172**	**.099**	**.089**
Sent to the office Wave 1	**.171**		.052
Sent to the office Wave 2	**.100**		-.025
Sent to the office Wave 3	**.094**		.016
Days cut school Wave 1	**.211**		**.120**
Days cut school Wave 2	**.099**		.004
Days cut school Wave 3	.050		.034
Skipped classes Wave 1	**.180**		.060
Skipped classes Wave 2	**.101**		.015
Skipped classes Wave 3	.027		-.045
Delinquency index Wave 1[2]	**.219**	**.155**	**.121**
Delinquency index Wave 2	**.118**	.046	.047
Delinquency index Wave 3	.041	-.041	-.031
Evenings out Wave 1	.043		-.013
Evenings out Wave 2	**.060**		.016
Evenings out Wave 3	-.010		-.020
Hours worked W1	**.079**		.035
Hours worked W2	.033		-.005
Hours worked W3	.048		.017
Preferred hours work Wave 1[3]	.026		-.016
Preferred hours work Wave 2	**.074**		.030
Preferred hours work Wave 3	.017		-.050
Religious attendance Wave 1	-.044		.014
Religious attendance Wave 2	-.049		-.016
Religious attendance Wave 3	-.031		.001
Religious importance Wave 1	-.040		-.035
Religious importance Wave 2	-.011		.035
Religious importance Wave 3	.001		.028
Self-esteem index Wave 1[2]	**-.063**		.000
Self-esteem index Wave 2	.000		.022
Self-esteem index Wave 3	.023		.042
Multiple *R*		.320	.372
R Squared		.102	.138
R Squared, adjusted		.091	.113

[1] These OLS (ordinary least squares) regressions were run with SAS statistical analyses software. A covariance matrix constructed with pairwise deletion served as the input data, because of missing values on the variables described in Notes 2 and 3 below. Coefficients that are p<.05 (two-tailed) are shown in **bold**.

Table A.7.1a continued on next page.

Table A.7.1a (continued)
OLS Regressions Predicting Marijuana Use in the Last 30 Days
at Ages 14, 16, and 18: Males[1]

	Age 16			Age 18	
Column 4	Column 5	Column 6	Column 7	Column 8	Column 9
Zero-Order Correlation	Standardized Regression Coefficient	Standardized Regression Coefficient	Zero-Order Correlation	Standardized Regression Coefficient	Standardized Regression Coefficient
-.033	-.051	-.039	-.033	-.052	-.028
.013	-.027	-.030	.009	-.023	-.020
.027	-.006	-.012	.028	-.006	-.004
-.006			-.003		
.030	.006	-.011	.024	-.002	-.002
.008			.019		
-.040	-.030	-.018	-.046	-.030	-.017
-.042	.027	.020	-.016	.054	.038
-.028			.004		
-.058			-.058		
-.085			-.086		
-.094	-.025	-.011	-.097	-.044	-.036
-.124	-.034	-.025	-.115	-.049	-.033
-.143			-.130		
-.068			-.124		
.096	-.002	-.003	.031	-.044	-.036
.206	.054	.047	.134	.001	-.023
-.135	.033	.016	-.142	-.002	-.007
-.158	-.036	.008	-.165	-.026	.008
-.137	-.003	.001	-.184	-.078	-.053
-.171			-.195		
-.127	-.018	-.026	-.085	.010	.001
-.174	-.045	-.023	-.138	-.018	-.002
-.151	-.022	-.021	-.138	-.025	-.008
-.187			-.150		
.054			.098		
.085			.068		
.099			.130		
.053			.107		
.108	.032	.014	.157	.080	.057
.091	.021	.012	.121	.044	.024
.206	.092	.067	.150	.044	.037
.170		-.031	.194		.023
.224		.001	.210		-.024
.161		-.004	.223		.062
.129		.011	.079		-.026
.248		.073	.172		.016
.140		.033	.175		.044
.088		-.047	.079		-.024
.347		.201	.253		.118
.156		.015	.203		.076
.270	.112	.091	.249	.125	.102
.339	.208	.135	.281	.118	.070
.245	.080	.064	.282	.149	.088
.097		.014	.105		.027
.187		.080	.150		.022
.056		-.021	.183		.098
.040		-.012	.039		-.005
.048		.013	.059		.024
.024		-.030	.045		-.007
.031		-.013	.039		.000
.072		.001	.070		.004
.033		-.020	.051		-.004
-.108		.060	-.133		-.007
-.196		-.078	-.182		-.014
-.165		-.019	-.198		-.073
-.120		-.026	-.124		.001
-.167		-.059	-.161		-.028
-.108		.058	-.138		.023
-.091		-.021	-.097		-.033
-.110		-.021	-.118		-.034
-.070		.002	-.093		.003
	.440	.519		.444	.507
	.193	.270		.197	.257
	.183	.249		.187	.236

[2] The items in this index appeared in only one of two forms randomly distributed to respondents in their schools. Effective N is thus only half of that shown.

[3] This item appeared in only one of two forms randomly distributed to respondents in their schools. Its first appearance was in 1992. Effective N is thus only one third of that shown.

Note: W1 = Wave 1 data collection (grade 8, modal age 14), W2 = Wave 2 data collection (modal age 16), W3 = Wave 3 data collection (modal age 18)

Table A.7.1b
OLS Regressions Predicting Marijuana Use in the
Last 30 Days at Ages 14, 16, and 18: Females[1]

	Age 14		
	Column 1	Column 2	Column 3
Effective N = 1739	Zero-Order Correlation	Standardized Regression Coefficient	Standardized Regression Coefficient
African-American	-.012	-.047	-.044
Hispanic	.047	.018	.011
Other race	.031	.007	.003
White	-.043		
Large MSA	-.022	-.042	-.043
Other MSA	.057		
Non-MSA	-.043	-.038	-.036
Parents' education level	-.072	.008	.018
Number of parents Wave 1	-.037		
Number of parents Wave 2	-.064		
Number of parents Wave 3	-.082		
Lived with 2 parents Waves 1–3	-.078	-.004	-.003
Parent involvement index Wave 1	-.117	-.054	-.035
Parent involvement index Wave 2	-.037		
Parent involvement index Wave 3	-.036		
Held back grade 8 or earlier	.074	.009	.020
Suspended/expelled grade 8 or earlier	.172	.090	.049
GPA Wave 1	-.143	-.056	-.042
GPA Wave 2	-.092	.026	.031
GPA Wave 3	-.078	.020	.021
Mean secondary school GPA	-.123		
College plans Wave 1	-.149	-.079	-.071
College plans Wave 2	-.085	.020	.020
College plans Wave 3	-.059	.035	.035
Mean secondary school college plans	-.120		
Held back Wave 1 to Wave 2	.037		
Held back Wave 2 to Wave 3	.052		
Suspended/expelled Wave 1 to Wave 2	.084		
Suspended/expelled Wave 2 to Wave 3	.061		
Serious scholastic setback W1 to W2	.085	.027	.027
Serious scholastic setback W2 to W3	.076	.037	.032
High school dropout by Wave 3	.149	.060	.056
Sent to the office Wave 1	.196		.039
Sent to the office Wave 2	.113		-.013
Sent to the office Wave 3	.099		.007
Days cut school Wave 1	.197		.116
Days cut school Wave 2	.102		.010
Days cut school Wave 3	.067		-.010
Skipped classes Wave 1	.160		.045
Skipped classes Wave 2	.085		-.008
Skipped classes Wave 3	.047		.012
Delinquency index Wave 1[2]	.235	.163	.119
Delinquency index Wave 2	.117	.006	.000
Delinquency index Wave 3	.070	.004	-.007
Evenings out Wave 1	.078		.020
Evenings out Wave 2	.035		-.009
Evenings out Wave 3	.017		.016
Hours worked Wave 1	.016		.000
Hours worked Wave 2	.014		-.017
Hours worked Wave 3	.021		-.007
Preferred hours work Wave 1[3]	.016		-.003
Preferred hours work Wave 2	.102		.063
Preferred hours work Wave 3	.057		-.014
Religious attendance Wave 1	-.079		.004
Religious attendance Wave 2	-.084		-.010
Religious attendance Wave 3	-.069		.014
Religious importance Wave 1	-.082		-.027
Religious importance Wave 2	-.058		-.002
Religious importance Wave 3	-.054		-.006
Self-esteem index Wave 1[2]	-.091		-.013
Self-esteem index Wave 2	-.047		.008
Self-esteem index Wave 3	-.047		-.018
Multiple R		.311	.351
R Squared		.097	.123
R Squared, adjusted		.087	.102

[1] These OLS (ordinary least squares) regressions were run with SAS statistical analyses software. A covariance matrix constructed with pairwise deletion served as the input data, because of missing values on the variables described in Notes 2 and 3 below. Coefficients that are p<.05 (two-tailed) are shown in **bold**.

Table A.7.1b continued on next page.

Table A.7.1b (continued)
OLS Regressions Predicting Marijuana Use in the
Last 30 Days at Ages 14, 16, and 18: Females[1]

	Age 16			Age 18	
Column 4	Column 5	Column 6	Column 7	Column 8	Column 9
Zero-Order Correlation	Standardized Regression Coefficient	Standardized Regression Coefficient	Zero-Order Correlation	Standardized Regression Coefficient	Standardized Regression Coefficient
-.077	-.118	-.082	-.062	-.098	-.059
.001	-.041	-.030	-.021	-.044	-.030
-.007	-.061	-.042	.015	-.021	-.006
.059			.045		
.041	.015	.008	.025	-.007	-.015
.019			.024		
-.064	-.021	-.022	-.053	-.020	-.021
-.042	.027	.023	-.009	.037	.031
-.025			-.046		
-.023			-.054		
-.057			-.096		
-.060	.014	.022	-.085	-.041	-.036
-.114	-.044	-.022	-.113	-.071	-.047
-.098			-.071		
-.060			-.068		
.021	-.033	-.031	-.006	-.047	-.032
.144	.054	.037	.102	.033	.023
-.142	.005	.004	-.098	.022	.020
-.181	-.082	-.042	-.128	-.027	-.005
-.119	.018	.031	-.139	-.069	-.028
-.173			-.141		
-.132	-.033	-.035	-.066	-.004	-.004
-.144	-.027	-.028	-.092	-.018	-.017
-.086	.014	.014	-.073	.003	.004
-.151			-.097		
.055			-.009		
.064			.050		
.139			.089		
.072			.077		
.137	.037	.014	.063	-.008	-.024
.092	.049	.028	.088	.044	.024
.174	.064	.037	.121	.043	.034
.195		.023	.122		-.018
.279		.062	.185		.049
.197		.020	.198		.052
.109		-.006	.096		.010
.232		.061	.126		.008
.152		.039	.183		.077
.086		-.030	.102		.024
.232		.056	.133		-.001
.130		.032	.177		.075
.239	.093	.079	.163	.057	.049
.338	.237	.159	.200	.072	.027
.184	.023	-.005	.232	.157	.106
.103		.004	.063		-.025
.203		.111	.106		.009
.107		.024	.178		.125
.009		-.026	-.002		-.035
.030		-.002	.025		.001
.040		-.007	.044		.001
.013		.010	.014		.010
.050		-.004	.023		-.018
.054		-.005	.067		.026
-.112		-.001	-.099		-.003
-.154		-.027	-.130		.009
-.165		-.044	-.169		-.068
-.116		-.014	-.118		-.021
-.149		-.010	-.142		-.027
-.131		.014	-.140		.006
-.075		.010	-.050		.018
-.124		-.016	-.091		-.020
-.088		-.014	-.082		-.009
	.406	.458		.331	.401
	.165	.210		.110	.161
	.156	.190		.100	.140

[2] The items in this index appeared in only one of two forms randomly distributed to respondents in their schools. Effective N is thus only half of that shown.

[3] This item appeared in only one of two forms randomly distributed to respondents in their schools. Its first appearance was in 1992. Effective N is thus only one third of that shown.

Note: W1 = Wave 1 data collection (grade 8, modal age 14), W2 = Wave 2 data collection (modal age 16), W3 = Wave 3 data collection (modal age 18)

Table A.8.1

Percentage of Annual Cocaine Use at Age 18
Correlated With 30-Day Marijuana Use
at Ages 16 and 18

30-Day Marijuana Use at Age 16	Percentage of Any Annual Cocaine Use at Age 18	
	Males	Females
No use	3.9	2.1
1–5 times	17.0	14.5
6–19 times	25.0	24.0
20 or more times	33.3	30.8
Total	6.2	4.1
Pearson r	.266	.291
eta	.268	.293

30-Day Marijuana Use at Age 18	Percentage of Any Annual Cocaine Use at Age 18	
	Males	Females
No use	1.5	1.5
1–5 times	14.0	9.4
6–19 times	16.7	16.9
20 or more times	35.4	37.7
Total	6.2	4.1
Pearson r	.388	.360
eta	.394	.369

Table A.8.2a

OLS Regressions Predicting Cocaine Use in the Last 12 Months at Ages 14, 16, and 18: Males[1]

	Age 14		
	Column 1	Column 2	Column 3
Effective N = 1361	Zero-Order Correlation	Standardized Regression Coefficient	Standardized Regression Coefficient
African-American	.028	.009	.010
Hispanic	.025	.004	.003
Other race	-.003	-.006	-.009
White	-.031		.000
Large MSA	-.004	-.032	-.033
Other MSA	.030		.000
Non-MSA	-.029	-.046	-.037
Parents' education level	-.044	.000	-.011
Number of parents Wave 1	-.073		
Number of parents Wave 2	-.039		
Number of parents Wave 3	-.041		
Lived with 2 parents Waves 1–3	-.058	-.023	-.016
Parent involvement index Wave 1	-.092	-.046	-.026
Parent involvement index Wave 2	-.001		
Parent involvement index Wave 3	-.026		
Held back grade 8 or earlier	.084	.025	-.008
Suspended/expelled grade 8 or earlier	.128	.076	.033
GPA Wave 1	-.057	.019	.021
GPA Wave 2	-.041	-.018	-.030
GPA Wave 3	-.010	.036	.036
Mean secondary school GPA	-.044		
College plans Wave 1	-.121	-.113	-.076
College plans Wave 2	-.042	.008	.008
College plans Wave 3	-.006	.065	.042
Mean secondary school college plans	-.068		
Held back Wave 1 to Wave 2	-.009		
Held back Wave 2 to Wave 3	.018		
Suspended/expelled Wave 1 to Wave 2	-.013		
Suspended/expelled Wave 2 to Wave 3	.009		
Serious scholastic setback W1 to W2	-.015	-.015	-.016
Serious scholastic setback W2 to W3	.018	.007	.012
High school dropout by Wave 3	.061	.008	.011
Sent to the office Wave 1	.098		.007
Sent to the office Wave 2	.040		-.008
Sent to the office Wave 3	.032		-.003
Days cut school Wave 1	.224		.132
Days cut school Wave 2	.019		-.020
Days cut school Wave 3	.007		-.006
Skipped classes Wave 1	.260		.188
Skipped classes Wave 2	.025		-.034
Skipped classes Wave 3	-.007		-.035
Delinquency index Wave 1[2]	.137	.103	.057
Delinquency index Wave 2	.027	-.030	-.020
Delinquency index Wave 3	.011	-.012	-.004
Evenings out Wave 1	.019		-.018
Evenings out Wave 2	.009		-.008
Evenings out Wave 3	-.004		.005
Hours worked Wave 1	.042		.003
Hours worked Wave 2	.035		.013
Hours worked Wave 3	.035		.029
Preferred hours of work Wave 1[3]	.019		.002
Preferred hours of work Wave 2	.057		.040
Preferred hours of work Wave 3	-.018		-.052
Religious attendance Wave 1	.023		.056
Religious attendance Wave 2	.002		.007
Religious attendance Wave 3	-.019		-.044
Religious importance Wave 1	.019		.031
Religious importance Wave 2	.005		-.008
Religious importance Wave 3	-.001		-.007
Self-esteem index Wave 1[2]	-.069		-.030
Self-esteem index Wave 2	.001		.015
Self-esteem index Wave 3	.013		.020
Multiple R		.237	.353
R Squared		.056	.124
R Squared, adjusted		.044	.099

[1] These OLS (ordinary least squares) regressions were run with SAS statistical analyses software. A covariance matrix constructed with pairwise deletion served as the input data, because of missing values on the variables described in Notes 2 and 3 below. Coefficients that are $p<.05$ (two-tailed) are shown in **bold**.

Table A.8.2a continued on next page.

Table A.8.2a (continued)
OLS Regressions Predicting Cocaine Use in the Last 12 Months at Ages 14, 16, and 18: Males[1]

	Age 16				Age 18		
	Column 4	Column 5	Column 6		Column 7	Column 8	Column 9
	Zero-Order Correlation	Standardized Regression Coefficient	Standardized Regression Coefficient		Zero-Order Correlation	Standardized Regression Coefficient	Standardized Regression Coefficient
	-.018	-.019	-.016		-.032	-.033	-.014
	.034	.015	.012		.035	.017	.018
	.017	.008	.007		.014	-.001	.000
	-.020				-.009		
	-.015	-.022	-.021		.008	.000	.011
	.011	.000	.000		-.003	.000	.000
	.002	-.004	-.001		-.004	.009	.012
	-.061	-.031	-.031		-.013	.029	.023
	.010				.008		
	.003				-.014		
	-.004				-.051		
	-.013	.029	.036		-.035	.005	.009
	-.049	-.009	-.003		**-.070**	-.036	-.028
	-.035				**-.074**		
	-.026				**-.055**		
	.029	-.043	-.050		.008	-.042	-.038
	.097	.029	.018		**.087**	.015	.007
	-.095	-.047	-.043		**-.082**	-.021	-.018
	-.071	-.015	.000		**-.070**	.016	.034
	-.040	.042	.041		**-.083**	-.017	-.005
	-.083				**-.094**		
	-.068	-.013	-.009		-.043	.017	.013
	-.069	.002	.019		**-.075**	-.005	.007
	-.059	.008	.002		**-.077**	-.009	.002
	-.081				**-.081**		
	.054				.076		
	.028				.081		
	.019				.075		
	-.010				.050		
	.046	.007	-.002		**.102**	.057	.047
	.010	-.022	-.021		**.086**	.039	.032
	.135	**.107**	.097		**.125**	**.082**	**.076**
	.096		.016		**.114**		.030
	.118		.042		**.124**		.010
	.056		-.020		**.101**		-.022
	.064		.017		.039		-.023
	.112		.067		**.128**		.073
	.048		.013		**.102**		.038
	.039		-.017		.032		-.026
	.109		.023		**.132**		.015
	.045		-.014		**.101**		.022
	.112	.046	.038		**.149**	.065	.059
	.125	**.073**	.045		**.156**	.035	.005
	.088	.030	.033		**.203**	**.143**	**.119**
	.016		-.007		.016		-.035
	.034		.001		**.076**		.021
	-.001		-.023		**.096**		.051
	.012		-.010		**.056**		.024
	.043		.023		.042		.013
	.027		.002		**.080**		.044
	.009		-.019		.026		-.004
	.071		.041		.032		-.022
	.013		-.028		**.060**		.023
	-.046		-.011		**-.082**		-.035
	-.051		.014		**-.083**		.028
	-.040		-.017		**-.081**		.010
	-.038		-.016		**-.070**		.016
	-.047		-.053		**-.100**		-.064
	.002		**.088**		**-.079**		-.001
	-.064		-.027		**-.077**		-.039
	-.051		-.011		**-.061**		-.016
	-.033		-.005		**-.050**		.008
		.212	.249			.266	.310
		.045	.062			.071	.096
		.033	.035			.059	.070

[2] The items in this index appeared in only one of two forms randomly distributed to respondents in their schools. Effective *N* is thus only half of that shown.

[3] This item appeared in only one of two forms randomly distributed to respondents in their schools. Its first appearance was in 1992. Effective *N* is thus only one third of that shown.

Note: W1 = Wave 1 data collection (grade 8, modal age 14), W2 = Wave 2 data collection (modal age 16), W3 = Wave 3 data collection (modal age 18)

Table A.8.2b
OLS Regressions Predicting Cocaine Use in the Last 12 Months at Ages 14, 16, and 18: Females[1]

Age 14

Effective N = 1739	Column 1 Zero-Order Correlation	Column 2 Standardized Regression Coefficient	Column 3 Standardized Regression Coefficient
African-American	-.036	-.039	-.043
Hispanic	**.057**	.037	.024
Other race	.042	.027	.019
White	-.040		
Large MSA	-.017	-.034	-.043
Other MSA	.040	.000	.000
Non-MSA	-.028	-.025	-.022
Parents' education level	-**.054**	.010	.014
Number of parents Wave 1	-.014		
Number of parents Wave 2	-.021		
Number of parents Wave 3	-.012		
Lived with 2 parents Waves 1–3	-.025	.027	.023
Parent involvement index Wave 1	-**.079**	-.028	-.006
Parent involvement index Wave 2	-.035		
Parent involvement index Wave 3	-.023		
Held back 8 or earlier	.057	.016	.026
Suspended/expelled grade 8 or earlier	**.118**	.047	.017
GPA Wave 1	-**.071**	.017	.022
GPA Wave 2	-**.058**	.003	.013
GPA Wave 3	-.035	.031	.043
Mean secondary school GPA	-**.065**		
College plans Wave 1	-**.142**	-**.100**	-**.092**
College plans Wave 2	-**.081**	-.007	-.005
College plans Wave 3	-.039	.038	.032
Mean secondary school college plans	-**.106**		
Held back Wave 1 to Wave 2	.007		
Held back Wave 2 to Wave 3	.034		
Suspended/expelled Wave 1 to Wave 2	.029		
Suspended/expelled Wave 2 to Wave 3	**.079**		
Serious scholastic setback W1 to W2	.026	-.022	-.012
Serious scholastic setback W2 to W3	**.079**	.056	.052
High school dropout by Wave 3	**.110**	**.055**	**.059**
Sent to the office Wave 1	**.145**		.022
Sent to the office Wave 2	**.069**		-.039
Sent to the office Wave 3	**.063**		-.021
Days cut school Wave 1	**.199**		**.142**
Days cut school Wave 2	**.106**		.022
Days cut school Wave 3	**.062**		-.009
Skipped classes Wave 1	**.128**		.020
Skipped classes Wave 2	**.120**		.054
Skipped classes Wave 3	**.073**		.040
Delinquency index Wave 1[2]	**.205**	**.157**	**.115**
Delinquency index Wave 2	**.109**	.023	.007
Delinquency index Wave 3	**.068**	.014	.000
Evenings out Wave 1	**.069**		.034
Evenings out Wave 2	.015		-.026
Evenings out Wave 3	.007		.008
Hours worked W1	.012		-.003
Hours worked W2	.012		-.009
Hours worked W3	.017		-.007
Preferred hours work W1[3]	.006		-.007
Preferred hours work W2	**.052**		.020
Preferred hours work W3	.040		-.002
Religious attendance Wave 1	-**.058**		-.021
Religious attendance Wave 2	-.039		.039
Religious attendance Wave 3	-.032		.015
Religious importance Wave 1	-**.071**		-.037
Religious importance Wave 2	-**.049**		-.029
Religious importance Wave 3	-.028		.029
Self-esteem index Wave 1[2]	-**.067**		-.002
Self-esteem index Wave 2	-**.057**		.013
Self-esteem index Wave 3	-**.097**		-**.082**
Multiple R		.240	.297
R Squared		.058	.088
R Squared, adjusted		.047	.066

[1] These OLS (ordinary least squares) regressions were run with SAS statistical analyses software. A covariance matrix constructed with pairwise deletion served as the input data, because of missing values on the variables described in Notes 2 and 3 below. Coefficients that are p<.05 (two-tailed) are shown in **bold**.

Table A.8.2b continued on next page.

Table A.8.2b (continued)
OLS Regressions Predicting Cocaine Use in the
Last 12 Months at Ages 14, 16, and 18: Females[1]

Age 16			Age 18		
Column 4	Column 5	Column 6	Column 7	Column 8	Column 9
Zero-Order Correlation	Standardized Regression Coefficient	Standardized Regression Coefficient	Zero-Order Correlation	Standardized Regression Coefficient	Standardized Regression Coefficient
-.041	-.055	-.051	-.059	-.089	-.073
.061	.046	.046	.010	-.017	-.014
-.014	-.030	-.027	-.006	-.033	-.024
.001			.039		
-.013	-.039	-.041	.013	-.007	-.008
.046	.000	.000	.013	.000	.000
-.039	-.028	-.030	-.028	-.011	-.010
-.030	.024	.023	-.042	-.012	-.018
-.031			-.005		
-.047			-.025		
-.027			-.073		
-.038	-.006	-.008	-.062	-.033	-.031
-.067	-.021	-.019	-.077	-.039	-.032
-.054			-.076		
-.028			-.030		
.012	-.026	-.022	.007	-.021	-.014
.118	.076	.068	.071	.023	.012
-.066	.026	.024	-.068	.022	.021
-.086	-.028	-.020	-.085	.004	.010
-.063	-.006	-.008	-.102	-.055	-.039
-.084			-.099		
-.099	-.054	-.053	-.048	.006	.005
-.086	-.025	-.026	-.064	.013	.012
-.041	.014	.007	-.087	-.047	-.052
-.093			-.086		
.026			.012		
.001			-.007		
.031			.066		
.017			.066		
.038	-.017	-.018	.057	.007	.002
.013	-.016	-.019	.044	.005	-.003
.076	.014	.002	.090	.023	.023
.113		.019	.104		.027
.116		.000	.116		.004
.077		-.013	.128		.023
.083		.025	.082		.041
.104		.005	.076		-.012
.042		.001	.091		.005
.053		-.024	.037		-.032
.119		.058	.081		-.004
.022		-.035	.108		.064
.138	.049	.038	.114	.033	.021
.184	.129	.112	.153	.055	.042
.110	.031	.037	.200	.152	.135
.079		.038	.056		.001
.043		-.016	.076		.017
.043		.028	.086		.039
.057		.042	.027		.005
.032		.014	.017		.000
.032		.005	.030		-.007
.007		-.004	.017		.009
.030		-.010	.020		-.018
.044		.008	.043		.006
-.048		-.021	-.035		-.002
-.047		-.004	-.048		.032
-.019		.056	-.081		-.043
-.058		-.027	-.043		-.004
-.063		-.054	-.056		-.022
-.019		.054	-.047		.041
-.018		.029	-.037		.011
-.048		.013	-.070		-.027
-.051		-.031	-.060		.004
	.252	.286		.264	.294
	.064	.082		.070	.086
	.053	.059		.059	.064

[2] The items in this index appeared in only one of two forms randomly distributed to respondents in their schools. Effective N is thus only half of that shown.

[3] This item appeared in only one of two forms randomly distributed to respondents in their schools. Its first appearance was in 1992. Effective N is thus only one third of that shown.

Note: W1 = Wave 1 data collection (grade 8, modal age 14), W2 = Wave 2 data collection (modal age 16), W3 = Wave 3 data collection (modal age 18)

Table A.8.3a
Multiple Classification Analyses Predicting
Percentage Who Report Dropping Out of
High School by Age 18
in 1995–1997: Males

Grand Mean = 15.7

Variable		Percentage Reporting Dropping Out of High School by Age 18	
Effective *N* = 1361		Column 1	Column 2
	Wtd. *N*	Bivariate	Multivariate
Race/ethnicity			
African-American	175	22.8	16.6
White	842	12.2	14.8
Hispanic	125	23.2	19.1
Other race	219	19.2	16.3
Population density			
Large MSA	372	18.1	16.3
Other MSA	619	15.7	16.5
Non-MSA	371	13.2	13.6
Parents' education level			
1 (Low)	204	26.1	14.9
2	262	21.2	17.1
3	358	16.3	17.1
4	351	9.4	13.7
5 (High)	187	7.2	15.6
Parent involvement index (grade 8)			
1 (Low)	137	30.8	19.4
2	319	17.8	15.4
3	538	14.0	15.2
4 (High)	367	10.7	15.3
Held back grade 8 or earlier			
Never	1034	9.6	12.5
Once	271	31.2	23.3
More than once	56	53.4	36.9
Suspended/expelled grade 8 or earlier			
Never	967	8.7	12.2
Once	182	24.0	19.6
More than once	213	40.2	28.0
GPA Wave 2			
D or below	63	49.4	32.6
C- or C	242	28.5	19.6
C+ or B-	402	16.6	15.2
B or B+	432	8.2	12.4
A-	124	5.2	13.7
A	97	4.4	13.8

Table A.8.3a continued on next page.

Table A.8.3a (continued)
Multiple Classification Analyses Predicting
Percentage Who Report Dropping Out of
High School by Age 18
in 1995–1997: Males

Grand Mean = 15.7
Effective *N* = 1361

		Percentage Reporting Dropping Out of High School by Age 18	
Variable		Column 1	Column 2
	Wtd. *N*	Bivariate	Multivariate
College plans Wave 2			
Definitely won't	88	42.3	27.5
Probably won't	192	29.5	23.0
Probably will	468	17.2	15.6
Definitely will	614	6.4	11.8
Delinquency Wave 2			
No incidents	497	11.5	14.7
1 incident	293	13.5	15.6
2 incidents	221	14.9	14.8
3 incidents	136	20.2	18.3
4 incidents	92	17.0	12.8
5 incidents	60	28.1	19.2
6 incidents	39	34.2	23.1
7 incidents	24	44.4	20.5
Any annual cocaine Wave 2			
Yes	22	58.4	40.4
No	1339	15.0	15.3
Multiple *R*			.495
R Squared			.245

Factor Summary*

	eta	beta
Race/ethnicity	**.320**	**.169**
Population density	**.323**	**.162**
Parents' education level	**.126**	.036
Parent involvement index (grade 8)	.050	.034
Held back grade 8 or earlier	**.179**	.039
Suspended/expelled grade 8 or earlier	**.155**	.034
GPA Wave 2	**.300**	**.123**
College plans Wave 2	**.292**	**.133**
Delinquency Wave 2	**.175**	.056
Any annual cocaine use Wave 2	**.149**	**.086**

*Coefficients that are p<.05 are shown in **bold**.

Note: W1 = Wave 1 data collection (grade 8, modal age 14),
W2 = Wave 2 data collection (modal age 16),
W3 = Wave 3 data collection (modal age 18)

Table A.8.3b
Multiple Classification Analyses Predicting
Percentage Who Report Dropping Out of
High School by Age 18
in 1995–1997: Females

Grand Mean = 14.4
Effective *N* = 1739

Variable	Wtd. *N*	Percentage Reporting Dropping Out of High School by Age 18	
		Column 1 Bivariate	Column 2 Multivariate
Race/ethnicity			
African-American	237	17.3	8.1
White	1065	12.6	15.8
Hispanic	173	19.1	13.9
Other race	263	16.1	15.0
Population density			
Large MSA	439	16.0	14.7
Other MSA	828	14.7	14.8
Non-MSA	471	12.5	13.5
Parents' education level			
1 (Low)	337	30.1	22.8
2	351	16.5	13.2
3	448	13.2	14.0
4	391	5.4	9.6
5 (High)	211	5.5	13.0
Parent involvement index (grade 8)			
1 (Low)	156	25.6	14.8
2	432	18.7	15.8
3	759	11.9	13.5
4 (High)	391	10.1	14.5
Held back grade 8 or earlier			
Never	1455	11.1	13.2
Once	258	29.8	20.1
More than once	26	47.6	27.7
Suspended/expelled grade 8 or earlier			
Never	1476	10.5	12.5
Once	151	32.9	22.0
More than once	112	41.8	29.2
GPA Wave 2			
D or below	53	58.9	39.3
C- or C	261	31.2	22.5
C+ or B-	451	16.7	13.8
B or B+	554	8.4	11.0
A-	242	4.9	11.8
A	178	2.5	10.9

Table A.8.3b continued on next page.

Table A.8.3b (continued)
Multiple Classification Analyses Predicting
Percentage Who Report Dropping Out of
High School by Age 18
in 1995–1997: Females

Grand Mean = 14.4
Effective *N* = 1739

Variable		Percentage Reporting Dropping Out of High School by Age 18	
		Column 1	Column 2
	Wtd. *N*	Bivariate	Multivariate
College plans Wave 2			
Definitely won't	84	50.6	34.4
Probably won't	191	34.6	24.3
Probably will	514	15.1	13.6
Definitely will	950	6.8	11.1
Delinquency Wave 2			
No incidents	874	10.6	13.5
1 incident	400	13.0	13.5
2 incidents	231	16.5	15.6
3 incidents	119	28.3	21.3
4 incidents	61	22.3	11.5
5 incidents	29	36.6	18.8
6 incidents	15	40.0	18.6
7 incidents	9	49.7	26.8
Any annual cocaine use Wave 2			
Yes	35	38.7	21.8
No	1704	13.9	14.3
Multiple *R*			.518
R Squared			.268

Factor Summary*

	eta	beta
Race/ethnicity	**.221**	**.084**
Population density	**.272**	**.134**
Parents' education level	**.068**	**.073**
Parent involvement index (grade 8)	.036	.015
Held back grade 8 or earlier	**.249**	**.126**
Suspended/expelled grade 8 or earlier	**.135**	.026
GPA Wave 2	**.340**	**.168**
College plans Wave 2	**.337**	**.171**
Delinquency Wave 2	**.190**	.067
Any annual cocaine use Wave 2	**.098**	.030

*Coefficients that are p<.05 are shown in **bold**.

Note: W1 = Wave 1 data collection (grade 8, modal age 14),
W2 = Wave 2 data collection (modal age 16),
W3 = Wave 3 data collection (modal age 18)

Table A.9.1a
OLS Regressions Predicting Alcohol Use in the Last 30 Days at Ages 14, 16, and 18: Males[1]

| | Age 14 | | |
| | Column 1 | Column 2 | Column 3 |
Effective _N_ = 1361	Zero-Order Correlation	Standardized Regression Coefficient	Standardized Regression Coefficient
African-American	-.007	-.031	-.015
Hispanic	.043	-.006	-.006
Other race	.010	-.010	-.011
White	-.028		
Large MSA	-.014	-.029	-.028
Other MSA	.000	.000	.000
Non-MSA	.014	.003	.006
Parents' education level	**-.090**	.004	-.017
Number of parents Wave 1	**-.100**		
Number of parents Wave 2	-.020		
Number of parents Wave 3	-.041		
Lived with 2 parents Waves 1–3	**-.074**	.012	.016
Parent involvement index Wave 1	**-.207**	**-.118**	**-.101**
Parent involvement index Wave 2	-.049		
Parent involvement index Wave 3	-.036		
Held back grade 8 or earlier	**.174**	.063	.045
Suspended/expelled grade 8 or earlier	**.229**	**.080**	.022
GPA Wave 1	**-.144**	.023	.026
GPA Wave 2	**-.133**	-.036	-.022
GPA Wave 3	**-.093**	.027	.033
Mean secondary school GPA	**-.148**		
College plans Wave 1	**-.172**	-.062	-.044
College plans Wave 2	**-.135**	.006	.023
College plans Wave 3	**-.111**	.026	.027
Mean secondary school college plans	**-.172**		
Held back Wave 1 to Wave 2	.007		
Held back Wave 2 to Wave 3	.052		
Suspended/expelled W1 to W2	**.064**		
Suspended/expelled W2 to W3	.036		
Serious scholastic setback W1 to W2	.053	.016	.001
Serious scholastic setback W2 to W3	.059	.007	-.002
High school dropout by Wave 3	**.182**	**.062**	.054
Sent to the office Wave 1	**.242**		.058
Sent to the office Wave 2	**.189**		.029
Sent to the office Wave 3	**.142**		.007
Days cut school Wave 1	**.210**		.049
Days cut school Wave 2	**.136**		.040
Days cut school Wave 3	**.091**		.020
Skipped classes Wave 1	**.226**		.081
Skipped classes Wave 2	**.143**		-.012
Skipped classes Wave 3	**.069**		-.004
Delinquency index Wave 1[2]	**.322**	**.225**	**.188**
Delinquency index Wave 2	**.189**	.061	.029
Delinquency index Wave 3	**.116**	.001	-.006
Evenings out Wave 1	**.103**		.025
Evenings out Wave 2	**.095**		.009
Evenings out Wave 3	.024		-.010
Hours worked Wave 1	**.141**		.079
Hours worked Wave 2	**.078**		.034
Hours worked Wave 3	.047		-.014
Preferred hours of work Wave 1[3]	**.068**		.012
Preferred hours of work Wave 2	**.103**		.019
Preferred hours of work Wave 3	**.066**		.000
Religious attendance Wave 1	**-.063**		.064
Religious attendance Wave 2	**-.108**		-.021
Religious attendance Wave 3	**-.099**		-.007
Religious importance Wave 1	**-.079**		-.006
Religious importance Wave 2	**-.100**		-.037
Religious importance Wave 3	**-.084**		-.017
Self-esteem index Wave 1[2]	**-.117**		-.032
Self-esteem index Wave 2	**-.066**		-.014
Self-esteem index Wave 3	-.009		.045
Multiple _R_		.406	.454
_R_ Squared		.165	.206
_R_ Squared, adjusted		.154	.183

[1] These OLS (ordinary least squares) regressions were run with SAS statistical analyses software. A covariance matrix constructed with pairwise deletion served as the input data, because of missing values on the variables described in Notes 2 and 3 below. Coefficients that are p<.05 (two-tailed) are shown in **bold**.

Table A.9.1a continued on next page.

Table A.9.1a (continued)
OLS Regressions Predicting Alcohol Use in the Last 30 Days at Ages 14, 16, and 18: Males[1]

| | Age 16 | | | Age 18 | |
Column 4	Column 5	Column 6	Column 7	Column 8	Column 9
Zero-Order Correlation	Standardized Regression Coefficient	Standardized Regression Coefficient	Zero-Order Correlation	Standardized Regression Coefficient	Standardized Regression Coefficient
-.033	-.051	-.034	-.087	-.100	-.071
.036	-.009	-.005	.002	-.028	-.013
-.037	-.067	-.067	-.008	-.045	-.035
.029			.065		
-.040	-.022	-.018	-.061	-.062	-.051
-.030	.000	.000	.026	.000	.000
.074	.062	.075	.031	.011	.027
-.066	.033	.015	-.017	.032	.012
-.073			-.012		
-.084			-.054		
-.104			-.062		
-.099	-.029	-.018	-.059	-.040	-.034
-.165	-.077	-.064	-.063	-.007	.010
-.133			-.091		
-.098			-.092		
.115	.018	.011	.053	.023	.028
.140	-.021	-.056	.066	-.038	-.071
-.166	-.010	-.010	-.087	.020	.023
-.170	-.044	-.007	-.117	-.035	-.010
-.136	.004	.008	-.120	-.045	-.020
-.188			-.129		
-.157	-.018	-.020	-.074	.003	-.003
-.211	-.080	-.058	-.130	-.039	-.024
-.161	-.001	.005	-.112	-.021	-.010
-.218			-.131		
.044			.032		
.111			.044		
.118			.090		
.061			.052		
.116	.042	.017	.088	.025	.002
.113	.052	.038	.065	.005	-.012
.181	.056	.031	.086	.006	-.001
.205		.024	.158		.019
.238		.049	.206		.051
.172		.012	.178		.030
.122		-.012	.070		-.022
.207		.074	.112		.035
.142		.058	.159		.093
.135		.032	.107		.055
.227		.076	.117		-.015
.098		-.022	.141		.014
.259	.141	.115	.190	.104	.074
.274	.176	.112	.217	.075	.036
.167	.017	-.002	.269	.195	.136
.094		.018	.096		.018
.155		.058	.159		.057
.079		.017	.231		.148
.073		.015	.068		.022
.061		.016	.061		.023
.076		.026	.093		.054
.061		.010	.043		.004
.069		-.025	.031		-.029
.066		-.020	.039		-.013
-.072		.051	-.068		.013
-.129		.000	-.110		-.004
-.141		-.059	-.136		-.060
-.082		.008	-.087		-.007
-.124		-.038	-.122		-.049
-.094		.012	-.089		.046
-.102		-.021	-.062		-.016
-.128		-.057	-.078		-.013
-.048		.030	-.053		.010
	.411	.457		.367	.427
	.169	.209		.135	.183
	.158	.187		.124	.159

[2] The items in this index appeared in only one of two forms randomly distributed to respondents in their schools. Effective N is thus only half of that shown.

[3] This item appeared in only one of two forms randomly distributed to respondents in their schools. Its first appearance was in 1992. Effective N is thus only one third of that shown.

Note: W1 = Wave 1 data collection (grade 8, modal age 14), W2 = Wave 2 data collection (modal age 16), W3 = Wave 3 data collection (modal age 18)

Table A.9.1b
OLS Regressions Predicting Alcohol Use in the
Last 30 Days at Ages 14, 16, and 18: Females[1]

Age 14

Effective N = 1739	Column 1 Zero-Order Correlation	Column 2 Standardized Regression Coefficient	Column 3 Standardized Regression Coefficient
African-American	-.027	**-.070**	-.051
Hispanic	.067	.031	.030
Other race	.040	.003	.000
White	**-.051**		
Large MSA	.003	-.015	-.018
Other MSA	.035	.000	.000
Non-MSA	-.044	-.009	-.002
Parents' education level	**-.081**	.029	.046
Number of parents Wave 1	**-.058**		
Number of parents Wave 2	**-.086**		
Number of parents Wave 3	**-.091**		
Lived with 2 parents Waves 1–3	**-.117**	-.017	-.006
Parent involvement index Wave 1	**-.168**	**-.078**	-.041
Parent involvement index Wave 2	**-.104**		
Parent involvement index Wave 3	**-.047**		
Held back grade 8 or earlier	**.080**	-.008	.002
Suspended/expelled grade 8 or earlier	**.238**	**.109**	.035
GPA Wave 1	**-.180**	-.028	.003
GPA Wave 2	**-.159**	-.017	-.007
GPA Wave 3	**-.131**	.011	.012
Mean secondary school GPA	**-.184**		
College plans Wave 1	**-.155**	-.028	-.010
College plans Wave 2	**-.144**	-.018	-.023
College plans Wave 3	**-.096**	.031	.028
Mean secondary college plans	**-.164**		
Held back Wave 1 to Wave 2	**.110**		
Held back Wave 2 to Wave 3	**.053**		
Suspended/expelled W1 to W2	**.073**		
Suspended/expelled W2 to W3	**.076**		
Serious scholastic setback W1 to W2	**.117**	.021	.018
Serious scholastic setback W2 to W3	**.088**	.024	.018
High school dropout by Wave 3	**.209**	**.078**	**.068**
Sent to the office Wave 1	**.313**	.000	**.104**
Sent to the office Wave 2	**.185**	.000	-.012
Sent to the office Wave 3	**.132**	.000	-.023
Days cut school Wave 1	**.245**	.000	**.082**
Days cut school Wave 2	**.139**	.000	-.003
Days cut school Wave 3	**.109**	.000	-.003
Skipped classes Wave 1	**.248**	.000	**.095**
Skipped classes Wave 2	**.130**	.000	-.015
Skipped classes Wave 3	**.083**	.000	.010
Delinquency index Wave 1[2]	**.388**	**.298**	**.225**
Delinquency index Wave 2	**.205**	.024	.016
Delinquency index Wave 3	**.139**	.025	.019
Evenings out Wave 1	**.160**		**.077**
Evenings out Wave 2	**.064**		-.007
Evenings out Wave 3	.016		-.019
Hours worked Wave 1	**.058**		.028
Hours worked Wave 2	**.061**		.016
Hours worked Wave 3	**.068**		.011
Preferred hours of work Wave 1[3]	.046		.011
Preferred hours of work Wave 2	**.135**		.052
Preferred hours of work Wave 3	**.105**		-.001
Religious attendance Wave 1	**-.128**		.043
Religious attendance Wave 2	**-.166**		-.053
Religious attendance Wave 3	**-.145**		-.015
Religious importance Wave 1	**-.171**		**-.108**
Religious importance Wave 2	**-.117**		.015
Religious importance Wave 3	**-.100**		.023
Self-esteem index Wave 1[2]	**-.166**		-.064
Self-esteem index Wave 2	**-.097**		-.020
Self-esteem index Wave 3	**-.060**		.008
Multiple R		.463	.529
R Squared		.214	.280
R Squared, adjusted		.206	.262

[1] These OLS (ordinary least squares) regressions were run with SAS statistical analyses software. A covariance matrix constructed with pairwise deletion served as the input data, because of missing values on the variables described in Notes 2 and 3 below. Coefficients that are p<.05 (two-tailed) are shown in **bold**.

Table A.9.1b continued on next page.

Table A.9.1b (continued)
OLS Regressions Predicting Alcohol Use in the
Last 30 Days at Ages 14, 16, and 18: Females[1]

	Age 16			Age 18	
Column 4	Column 5	Column 6	Column 7	Column 8	Column 9
Zero-Order Correlation	Standardized Regression Coefficient	Standardized Regression Coefficient	Zero-Order Correlation	Standardized Regression Coefficient	Standardized Regression Coefficient
-.053	-.082	-.037	-.116	-.152	-.094
.029	.003	.019	-.003	-.029	-.006
-.008	-.044	-.020	-.037	-.075	-.050
.025			.111		
-.008	-.014	-.017	.026	.005	-.006
.003	.000	.000	.000	.000	.000
.004	.028	.028	-.026	.018	.023
-.040	.041	.038	.044	.050	.042
-.042			-.049		
-.057			-.031		
-.099			-.058		
-.090	-.020	-.005	-.053	-.062	-.059
-.072	-.016	.009	-.069	-.048	-.023
-.101			-.086		
-.047			-.089		
.043	-.008	-.011	-.037	-.036	-.016
.082	-.011	-.037	.035	.011	-.011
-.122	.010	.016	-.032	.011	.013
-.160	-.086	-.056	-.047	.000	.003
-.097	.037	.043	-.074	-.068	-.018
-.149			-.059		
-.091	.009	.004	-.014	-.011	-.015
-.126	-.010	-.006	-.007	.019	.011
-.118	-.031	-.033	.012	.040	.035
-.142			-.003		
.099			-.021		
.070			-.010		
.112			.026		
.093			.054		
.141	.044	.013	.008	-.024	-.023
.111	.066	.045	.034	.015	.001
.187	.089	.045	.037	.008	.016
.155		.028	.098		.028
.234		.058	.087		-.012
.171		.017	.137		.037
.096		.006	.060		.001
.206		.072	.057		-.022
.142		.018	.118		.041
.078		-.005	.053		.004
.182		.013	.094		.009
.106		.026	.170		.101
.190	.087	.068	.115	.054	.035
.263	.192	.125	.149	.053	.033
.140	.017	-.003	.210	.168	.110
.117		.030	.140		.065
.196		.128	.113		-.030
.072		-.001	.253		.177
.029		.001	.050		.003
.075		.042	.085		.064
.069		.027	.065		.021
.007		-.006	-.005		-.008
.069		.003	.013		.000
.063		-.018	.020		-.005
-.088		.007	-.059		.017
-.131		-.022	-.098		.006
-.140		-.058	-.150		-.061
-.080		-.012	-.119		-.039
-.121		-.030	-.126		-.006
-.086		.042	-.152		-.025
-.057		.011	-.019		.022
-.097		-.026	-.051		.003
-.061		-.001	-.072		-.029
	.326	.413		.289	.399
	.106	.171		.084	.160
	.096	.150		.074	.139

[2] The items in this index appeared in only one of two forms randomly distributed to respondents in their schools. Effective N is thus only half of that shown.

[3] This item appeared in only one of two forms randomly distributed to respondents in their schools. Its first appearance was in 1992. Effective N is thus only one third of that shown.

Note: W1 = Wave 1 data collection (grade 8, modal age 14), W2 = Wave 2 data collection (modal age 16), W3 = Wave 3 data collection (modal age 18)

Table A.9.2a

OLS Regressions Predicting Heavy Drinking in the Last Two Weeks at Ages 14, 16, and 18: Males[1]

	Age 14		
	Column 1	Column 2	Column 3
Effective N = 1361	Zero-Order Correlation	Standardized Regression Coefficient	Standardized Regression Coefficient
African-American	-.002	-.038	-.029
Hispanic	.040	-.010	-.007
Other race	.022	-.003	-.008
White	-.039		
Large MSA	-.037	-.038	-.038
Other MSA	-.010	.000	.000
Non-MSA	.049	.026	.027
Parents' education level	-.118	-.005	-.020
Number of parents Wave 1	-.155		
Number of parents Wave 2	-.057		
Number of parents Wave 3	-.068		
Lived with 2 parents Waves 1–3	-.114	-.020	-.013
Parent involvement index Wave 1	-.194	-.089	-.071
Parent involvement index Wave 2	-.055		
Parent involvement index Wave 3	-.037		
Held back grade 8 or earlier	.201	.066	.039
Suspended/expelled grade 8 or earlier	.258	.106	.052
GPA Wave 1	-.177	.016	.014
GPA Wave 2	-.155	-.023	-.019
GPA Wave 3	-.125	.007	.009
Mean secondary school GPA	-.183		
College plans Wave 1	-.204	-.074	-.047
College plans Wave 2	-.160	.013	.031
College plans Wave 3	-.155	.001	-.016
Mean secondary school college plans	-.215		
Held back Wave 1 to Wave 2	.029		
Held back Wave 2 to Wave 3	.067		
Suspended/expelled W1 to W2	.064		
Suspended/expelled W2 to W3	.027		
Serious scholastic setback W1 to W2	.066	.025	.014
Serious scholastic setback W2 to W3	.060	.001	-.007
High school dropout by Wave 3	.220	.078	.071
Sent to the office Wave 1	.239		.042
Sent to the office Wave 2	.165		-.010
Sent to the office Wave 3	.137		.000
Days cut school Wave 1	.276		.125
Days cut school Wave 2	.135		.028
Days cut school Wave 3	.081		.003
Skipped classes Wave 1	.259		.101
Skipped classes Wave 2	.134		-.031
Skipped classes Wave 3	.057	.000	-.019
Delinquency index Wave 1[2]	.307	.195	.150
Delinquency index Wave 2	.179	.058	.044
Delinquency index Wave 3	.096	-.018	-.014
Evenings out Wave 1	.090		.002
Evenings out Wave 2	.113		.038
Evenings out Wave 3	.029		.006
Hours worked Wave 1	.151		.075
Hours worked Wave 2	.093		.037
Hours worked Wave 3	.055		-.017
Preferred hours of work Wave 1[3]	.084		.021
Preferred hours of work Wave 2	.130		.041
Preferred hours of work Wave 3	.068		-.019
Religious attendance Wave 1	-.065		.037
Religious attendance Wave 2	-.096		.001
Religious attendance Wave 3	-.083		-.021
Religious importance Wave 1	-.055		.000
Religious importance Wave 2	-.077		-.068
Religious importance Wave 3	-.025		.071
Self-esteem index Wave 1[2]	-.104		-.001
Self-esteem index Wave 2	-.065		-.016
Self-esteem index Wave 3	-.014		.031
Multiple R		.412	.467
R Squared		.170	.218
R Squared, adjusted		.160	.196

[1] These OLS (ordinary least squares) regressions were run with SAS statistical analyses software. A covariance matrix constructed with pairwise deletion served as the input data, because of missing values on the variables described in Notes 2 and 3 below. Coefficients that are p<.05 (two-tailed) are shown in **bold**.

Table A.9.2a continued on next page.

Table A.9.2a (continued)
OLS Regressions Predicting Heavy Drinking in the
Last Two Weeks at Ages 14, 16, and 18: Males[1]

| | Age 16 | | | Age 18 | |
Column 4	Column 5	Column 6	Column 7	Column 8	Column 9
Zero-Order Correlation	Standardized Regression Coefficient	Standardized Regression Coefficient	Zero-Order Correlation	Standardized Regression Coefficient	Standardized Regression Coefficient
-.044	-.062	-.049	-.065	-.077	-.053
.058	.020	.024	.025	-.004	.013
-.030	-.055	-.056	.001	-.029	-.021
.019			.029		
-.036	-.021	-.018	-.061	-.068	-.053
-.024	.000	.000	.033	.000	.000
.062	.051	.065	.024	.000	.011
-.065	.031	.016	-.040	.017	.001
-.077			-.029		
-.098			-.058		
-.081			-.067		
-.107	-.050	-.042	-.069	-.039	-.037
-.137	-.054	-.043	-.068	-.010	.004
-.122			-.096		
-.081			-.101		
.109	.016	.011	.084	.049	.058
.133	-.012	-.044	.073	-.036	-.066
-.144	.012	.010	-.091	.026	.034
-.171	-.076	-.042	-.117	-.033	-.018
-.127	.008	.013	-.120	-.040	-.016
-.176			-.130		
-.140	-.014	-.014	-.081	-.002	-.006
-.191	-.061	-.043	-.120	-.022	-.012
-.159	-.020	-.012	-.114	-.023	-.013
-.203			-.131		
.023			.029		
.073			.057		
.098			.083		
.032			.049		
.089	.013	-.010	.081	.023	.005
.068	.008	-.007	.071	.014	-.003
.177	.068	.045	.101	.017	.009
.181		.023	.160		.039
.216		.032	.187		.035
.164		.028	.175		.038
.109		-.004	.083		-.002
.165		.021	.086		.005
.114		.053	.148		.095
.104		.012	.100		.040
.232		.111	.090		-.028
.103		-.015	.118		-.008
.209	.090	.065	.180	.099	.070
.252	.166	.107	.187	.055	.030
.159	.033	.011	.237	.172	.124
.088		.016	.091		.017
.161		.078	.144		.053
.064		.005	.211		.143
.064		.013	.056		.007
.042		-.006	.031		-.015
.085		.042	.088		.052
.055		.007	.038		.000
.058		-.027	.043		-.009
.064		-.014	.059		.005
-.074		.029	-.070		-.009
-.123		-.002	-.096		.009
-.131		-.053	-.107		-.017
-.067		.024	-.070		.015
-.113		-.040	-.124		-.107
-.084		.020	-.072		.059
-.091		-.016	-.050		-.003
-.120		-.051	-.048		.015
-.054		.017	-.046		.004
	.375	.419		.337	.397
	.140	.176		.113	.157
	.130	.152		.102	.133

[2] The items in this index appeared in only one of two forms randomly distributed to respondents in their schools. Effective N is thus only half of that shown.

[3] This item appeared in only one of two forms randomly distributed to respondents in their schools. Its first appearance was in 1992. Effective N is thus only one third of that shown.

Note: W1 = Wave 1 data collection (grade 8, modal age 14), W2 = Wave 2 data collection (modal age 16), W3 = Wave 3 data collection (modal age 18)

Table A.9.2b
OLS Regressions Predicting Heavy Drinking in the
Last Two Weeks at Ages 14, 16, and 18: Females[1]

Age 14

Effective N = 1739	Column 1 Zero-Order Correlation	Column 2 Standardized Regression Coefficient	Column 3 Standardized Regression Coefficient
African-American	.015	-.039	-.035
Hispanic	.074	.043	.038
Other race	.053	.025	.016
White	-.095		
Large MSA	-.031	-.051	-.050
Other MSA	.056	.000	.000
Non-MSA	-.032	-.014	-.008
Parents' education level	-.100	.009	.027
Number of parents Wave 1	-.079		
Number of parents Wave 2	-.104		
Number of parents Wave 3	-.103		
Lived with 2 parents Waves 1–3	-.125	-.016	-.008
Parent involvement index Wave 1	-.143	-.054	-.025
Parent involvement index Wave 2	-.087		
Parent involvement index Wave 3	-.038		
Held back grade 8 or earlier	.115	.017	.021
Suspended/expelled grade 8 or earlier	.288	.174	.114
GPA Wave 1	-.201	-.053	-.028
GPA Wave 2	-.164	-.007	-.006
GPA Wave 3	-.144	.004	.004
Mean secondary school GPA	-.199		
College plans Wave 1	-.129	.011	.030
College plans Wave 2	-.131	-.012	-.014
College plans Wave 3	-.094	.032	.027
Mean secondary school college plans	-.148		
Held back Wave 1 to Wave 2	.112		
Held back Wave 2 to Wave 3	.062		
Suspended/expelled W1 to W2	.071		
Suspended/expelled W2 to W3	.086		
Serious scholastic setback W1 to W2	.116	.033	.034
Serious scholastic setback W2 to W3	.101	.036	.032
High school dropout by Wave 3	.195	.053	.039
Sent to the office Wave 1	.288		.064
Sent to the office Wave 2	.161		-.034
Sent to the office Wave 3	.148		.023
Days cut school Wave 1	.248		.103
Days cut school Wave 2	.124		-.008
Days cut school Wave 3	.076		-.032
Skipped classes Wave 1	.251		.103
Skipped classes Wave 2	.107		-.029
Skipped classes Wave 3	.053		.000
Delinquency index Wave 1[2]	.341	.238	.174
Delinquency index Wave 2	.177	.018	.025
Delinquency index Wave 3	.109	.003	-.004
Evenings out Wave 1	.141		.067
Evenings out Wave 2	.039		-.003
Evenings out Wave 3	-.026		-.039
Hours worked Wave 1	.043		.022
Hours worked Wave 2	.047		.005
Hours worked Wave 3	.067		.019
Prefered hours of work Wave 1[3]	.047		.007
Prefered hours of work Wave 2	.126		.030
Prefered hours of work Wave 3	.124		.014
Religious attendance Wave 1	-.128		-.007
Religious attendance Wave 2	-.138		-.052
Religious attendance Wave 3	-.095		.028
Religious importance Wave 1	-.124		-.072
Religious importance Wave 2	-.072		.023
Religious importance Wave 3	-.053		.026
Self-esteem index Wave 1[2]	-.151		-.055
Self-esteem index Wave 2	-.086		-.020
Self-esteem index Wave 3	-.067		-.008
Multiple R		.411	.457
R Squared		.169	.209
R Squared, adjusted		.160	.190

[1] These OLS (ordinary least squares) regressions were run with SAS statistical
analyses software. A covariance matrix constructed with pairwise deletion served
as the input data, because of missing values on the variables described in Notes 2
and 3 below. Coefficients that are p<.05 (two-tailed) are shown in **bold**.

Table A.9.2b continued on next page.

Table A.9.2b (continued)
OLS Regressions Predicting Heavy Drinking in the Last Two Weeks at Ages 14, 16, and 18: Females[1]

	Age 16			Age 18	
Column 4	Column 5	Column 6	Column 7	Column 8	Column 9
Zero-Order Correlation	Standardized Regression Coefficient	Standardized Regression Coefficient	Zero-Order Correlation	Standardized Regression Coefficient	Standardized Regression Coefficient
-.059	-.084	-.039	-.063	-.096	-.054
.041	.016	.029	.009	-.011	.001
-.015	-.051	-.031	-.011	-.037	-.018
.028			.047		
-.023	-.024	-.026	.000	-.015	-.021
-.002	.000	.000	.002	.000	.000
.026	.054	.057	-.002	.029	.031
-.050	.021	.017	.005	.041	.036
-.021			-.039		
-.040			-.045		
-.078			-.058		
-.065	-.001	.010	-.057	-.037	-.033
-.086	-.034	-.010	-.066	-.041	-.022
-.092			-.061		
-.047			-.060		
.042	-.003	-.006	.015	-.002	.012
.094	.007	-.021	.052	.008	-.007
-.112	.013	.024	-.063	.026	.027
-.159	-.094	-.063	-.090	-.020	-.015
-.096	.027	.034	-.114	-.083	-.044
-.144			-.103		
-.069	.038	.038	-.042	-.019	-.022
-.124	-.041	-.038	-.039	.016	.009
-.079	.021	.016	-.035	.017	.015
-.115			-.049		
.062			.003		
.044			.041		
.088			.039		
.085			.068		
.102	.011	-.014	.032	-.010	-.009
.089	.049	.027	.075	.044	.027
.164	.083	.051	.061	.008	.001
.170		.046	.091		.006
.214		.030	.085		-.034
.169		.023	.160		.059
.112		.012	.069		.012
.210		.089	.079		-.004
.125		.003	.115		.027
.108		.025	.069		.016
.168		-.006	.098		.009
.116		.042	.149		.082
.199	.095	.065	.103	.033	.016
.262	.175	.115	.134	.036	.019
.164	.050	.027	.202	.164	.112
.080		-.018	.126		.056
.210		.150	.117		.011
.075		-.005	.194		.132
.030		.003	.022		-.008
.056		.015	.045		.022
.083		.036	.060		.018
.003		-.015	-.013		-.023
.055		-.013	.035		.004
.095		.028	.064		.023
-.072		.032	-.052		.014
-.126		-.058	-.089		-.031
-.110		.003	-.108		-.008
-.089		-.033	-.078		-.014
-.121		-.024	-.085		.021
-.089		.016	-.114		-.043
-.065		.001	-.035		.011
-.102		-.031	-.056		-.012
-.062		.004	-.068		-.012
	.341	.397		.256	.343
	.116	.158		.065	.118
	.106	.137		.055	.096

[2] The items in this index appeared in only one of two forms randomly distributed to respondents in their schools. Effective N is thus only half of that shown.

[3] This item appeared in only one of two forms randomly distributed to respondents in their schools. Its first appearance was in 1992. Effective N is thus only one third of that shown.

Note: W1 = Wave 1 data collection (grade 8, modal age 14), W2 = Wave 2 data collection (modal age 16), W3 = Wave 3 data collection (modal age 18)

Table A.9.3
Direct and Total Effects of Predictors on Heavy Drinking at Wave 1, Wave 2, and Wave 3*

	Heavy Drinking Wave 1				Heavy Drinking Wave 2				Heavy Drinking Wave 3			
	Males		Females		Males		Females		Males		Females	
	Direct	Total	Direct	Total	Direct	Total	Direct	Total	Direct	Total	Direct	Total
African-American	-.042	-.062	-.051	-.063	-.071	**-.108**	**-.122**	**-.153**	-.070	**-.122**	**-.092**	**-.143**
Hispanic	-.015	-.006	.064	**.076**	.034	.030	.004	.017	-.012	.004	-.024	-.015
Other race	-.001	-.001	.030	.063	**-.073**	-.064	**-.095**	-.057	-.011	-.022	-.031	-.048
Large MSA	-.057	-.043	-.067	-.069	-.018	-.027	-.012	-.011	**-.079**	**-.086**	-.015	.010
Non-MSA	.033	.032	-.009	-.049	.061	.064	**.090**	.049	-.027	-.009	.025	.016
Parents' education level	.000	-.021	.005	-.023	.048	.011	.035	-.012	.003	-.005	.054	.043
Lived with 2 parents Waves 1–3	-.034	-.042	-.034	**-.076**	-.062	**-.094**	-.005	-.063	-.025	**-.075**	-.039	**-.078**
Parent involvement index	**-.166**	**-.244**	**-.105**	**-.171**	-.034	**-.165**	-.016	**-.113**	.013	-.074	-.049	**-.102**
Held back grade 8 or earlier	.097	**.135**	.031	.046		.073		.035		.045		.026
Suspended/expelled grade 8 or earlier	**.113**	**.245**	**.223**	**.364**		**.133**		**.161**		**.087**		**.087**
GPA Wave 1	-.012	**-.094**	**-.121**	**-.176**		**-.197**				**-.138**		**-.156**
GPA Wave 2					-.084	**-.148**	-.084	**-.144**		**-.133**		**-.155**
GPA Wave 3									-.050	-.067	**-.102**	**-.112**
College plans Wave 1	-.078	-.091	.067	.027		**-.083**		-.027		**-.045**		-.002
College plans Wave 2					**-.110**	**-.120**	-.031	-.044		**-.067**		.012
College plans Wave 3									-.019	-.017	.074	.066
Serious scholastic setback W1 to W2					.013	.061	.004	.061		**.048**		**.041**
Serious scholastic setback W2 to W3									.006	.035	.027	.045
Delinquency Wave 1	**.332**	**.332**	**.430**	**.430**		**.208**		**.253**		**.148**		**.141**
Delinquency Wave 2					**.264**	**.264**	**.332**	**.332**		**.256**		**.236**
Delinquency Wave 3									**.247**	**.247**	**.218**	**.218**
30-day cigarette smoking Wave 1						.000		.001		.001		.002
30-day cigarette smoking Wave 2										.003		.004
30-day cigarette smoking Wave 3												
30-day marijuana Wave 1						-.002		.004		-.002		.003
30-day marijuana Wave 2										.002		.002
30-day marijuana Wave 3												
Annual cocaine Wave 1						-.003		-.006		-.002		-.004
Annual cocaine Wave 2										-.002		-.001
Annual cocaine Wave 3												
Heavy drinking Wave 1					**.287**	**.293**	**.281**	**.287**		**.124**		**.112**
Heavy drinking Wave 2									**.417**	**.417**	**.381**	**.384**
Heavy drinking Wave 3												

Direct and Total Effects of Heavy Drinking at Wave 1, Wave 2, and Wave 3 on Education Factors*

		GPA Wave 2 Total	College Plans Wave 2 Total	Serious Scholastic Setback W1 to W2 Direct	Serious Scholastic Setback W1 to W2 Total	GPA Wave 3 Total	College Plans Wave 3 Total	Serious Scholastic Setback W2 to W3 Direct	Serious Scholastic Setback W2 to W3 Total	High School Dropout Wave 3 Direct	High School Dropout Wave 3 Total	Academic Attainment Wave 5 Direct	Academic Attainment Wave 5 Total
Heavy drinking Wave 1	Males	-.010	-.009	.094	.094	-.007	-.006		-.002		.020		-.004
	Females	-.005	-.010	.093	.093	-.005	-.007		.024		.025		-.005
Heavy drinking Wave 2	Males					.002	.001	-.016	-.016	.020	.020		.024
	Females					-.004	-.005	.078	.078	.032	.032		.008
Heavy drinking Wave 3	Males											.064	.064
	Females											.047	.047

*Coefficients that are p<.05 (two-tailed) are shown in **bold**.

Note: W1 = Wave 1 data collection (grade 8, modal age 14), W2 = Wave 2 data collection (modal age 16), W3 = Wave 3 data collection (modal age 18)

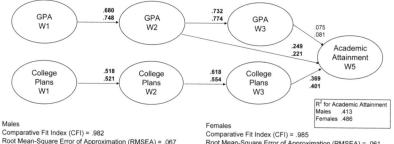

Males
Comparative Fit Index (CFI) = .982
Root Mean-Square Error of Approximation (RMSEA) = .067
Chi-Square = 562.891 Based on 79 Degrees of Freedom

Females
Comparative Fit Index (CFI) = .985
Root Mean-Square Error of Approximation (RMSEA) = .061
Chi-Square = 473.767 Based on 79 Degrees of Freedom

Males
Comparative Fit Index (CFI) = .987
Root Mean-Square Error of Approximation (RMSEA) = .058
Chi-Square = 420.856 Based on 75 Degrees of Freedom

Females
Comparative Fit Index (CFI) = .989
Root Mean-Square Error of Approximation (RMSEA) = .054
Chi-Square = 372.712 Based on 75 Degrees of Freedom

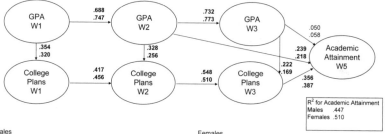

Males
Comparative Fit Index (CFI) = .993
Root Mean-Square Error of Approximation (RMSEA) = .042
Chi-Square = 257.558 Based on 76 Degrees of Freedom

Females
Comparative Fit Index (CFI) = .993
Root Mean-Square Error of Approximation (RMSEA) = .043
Chi-Square = 264.616 Based on 76 Degrees of Freedom

Coefficients for male sample shown above coefficients for female sample. Coefficients that are p<.05 (two-tailed) are shown in **bold**.

Eight exogenous factors have direct casual paths to each endogenous factor shown: African-American, Hispanic, Other race, presence of two parents in the home at Waves 1–3, parents' education level, parental involvement index, large MSA, and non-MSA

Two exogenous factors have direct causal paths to Wave 1 endogenous factors only: Held back grade 8 or earlier and suspended or expelled grade 8 or earlier

Note: W1 = Wave 1 data collection (grade 8, modal age 14), W2 = Wave 2 data collection (modal age 16), W3 = Wave 3 data collection (modal age 18), W5 = Wave 5 data collection (modal age 22)

Figure A.4.1. Comparison of simple models of the relationship between GPA at three waves and college plans at three waves.

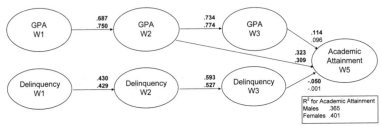

Males
Comparative Fit Index (CFI) = .991
Root Mean-Square Error of Approximation (RMSEA) = .047
Chi-Square = 315.438 Based on 79 Degrees of Freedom

Females
Comparative Fit Index (CFI) = .990
Root Mean-Square Error of Approximation (RMSEA) = .049
Chi-Square = 341.118 Based on 79 Degrees of Freedom

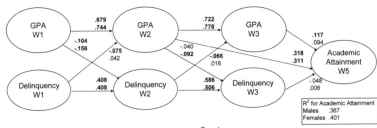

Males
Comparative Fit Index (CFI) = .992
Root Mean-Square Error of Approximation (RMSEA) = .046
Chi-Square = 294.790 Based on 75 Degrees of Freedom

Females
Comparative Fit Index (CFI) = .991
Root Mean-Square Error of Approximation (RMSEA) = .047
Chi-Square = 302.444 Based on 75 Degrees of Freedom

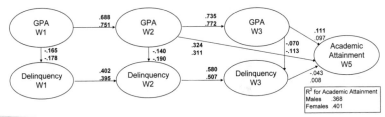

Males
Comparative Fit Index (CFI) = .993
Root Mean-Square Error of Approximation (RMSEA) = .043
Chi-Square = 267.065 Based on 76 Degrees of Freedom

Females
Comparative Fit Index (CFI) = .993
Root Mean-Square Error of Approximation (RMSEA) = .043
Chi-Square = 263.464 Based on 76 Degrees of Freedom

Coefficients for male sample shown above coefficients for female sample. Coefficients that are p<.05 (two-tailed) are shown in **bold**.

Eight exogenous factors have direct casual paths to each endogenous factor shown: African-American, Hispanic, Other race, presence of two parents in the home at Waves 1–3, parents' education level, parental involvement index, large MSA, and non-MSA

Two exogenous factors have direct causal paths to Wave 1 endogenous factors only: Held back grade 8 or earlier and suspended or expelled grade 8 or earlier

Note: W1 = Wave 1 data collection (grade 8, modal age 14), W2 = Wave 2 data collection (modal age 16), W3 = Wave 3 data collection (modal age 18), W5 = Wave 5 data collection (modal age 22)

Figure A.5.1. Comparison of simple models of the relationship between GPA at three waves and delinquency at three waves.

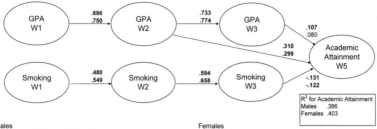

Males
Comparative Fit Index (CFI) = .990
Root Mean-Square Error of Approximation (RMSEA) = .050
Chi-Square = 342.713 Based on 79 Degrees of Freedom

Females
Comparative Fit Index (CFI) = .989
Root Mean-Square Error of Approximation (RMSEA) = .051
Chi-Square = 358.744 Based on 79 Degrees of Freedom

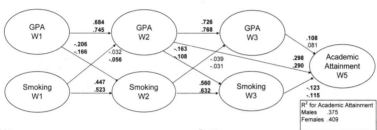

Males
Comparative Fit Index (CFI) = .993
Root Mean-Square Error of Approximation (RMSEA) = .043
Chi-Square = 266.063 Based on 75 Degrees of Freedom

Females
Comparative Fit Index (CFI) = .991
Root Mean-Square Error of Approximation (RMSEA) = .048
Chi-Square = 306.438 Based on 75 Degrees of Freedom

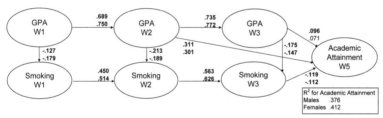

Males
Comparative Fit Index (CFI) = .994
Root Mean-Square Error of Approximation (RMSEA) = .040
Chi-Square = 242.422 Based on 76 Degrees of Freedom

Females
Comparative Fit Index (CFI) = .993
Root Mean-Square Error of Approximation (RMSEA) = .042
Chi-Square = 255.467 Based on 76 Degrees of Freedom

Coefficients for male sample shown above coefficients for female sample. Coefficients that are p<.05 (two-tailed) are shown in **bold**.

Eight exogenous factors have direct casual paths to each endogenous factor shown: African-American, Hispanic, Other race, presence of two parents in the home at Waves 1–3, parents' education level, parental involvement index, large MSA, and non-MSA

Two exogenous factors have direct casual paths to Wave 1 endogenous factors only: Held back grade 8 or earlier and suspended or expelled grade 8 or earlier

Note: W1 = Wave 1 data collection (grade 8, modal age 14), W2 = Wave 2 data collection (modal age 16), W3 = Wave 3 data collection (modal age 18), W5 = Wave 5 data collection (modal age 22)

Figure A.6.1. Comparison of simple models of the relationship between GPA at three waves and smoking at three waves.

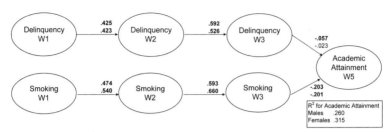

Males
Comparative Fit Index (CFI) = .986
Root Mean-Square Error of Approximation (RMSEA) = .058
Chi-Square = 443.098 Based on 80 Degrees of Freedom

Females
Comparative Fit Index (CFI) = .984
Root Mean-Square Error of Approximation (RMSEA) = .061
Chi-Square = 490.780 Based on 80 Degrees of Freedom

Males
Comparative Fit Index (CFI) = .989
Root Mean-Square Error of Approximation (RMSEA) = .053
Chi-Square = 365.204 Based on 76 Degrees of Freedom

Females
Comparative Fit Index (CFI) = .985
Root Mean-Square Error of Approximation (RMSEA) = .060
Chi-Square = 452.473 Based on 76 Degrees of Freedom

Males
Comparative Fit Index (CFI) = .992
Root Mean-Square Error of Approximation (RMSEA) = .043
Chi-Square = 273.576 Based on 77 Degrees of Freedom

Females
Comparative Fit Index (CFI) = .992
Root Mean-Square Error of Approximation (RMSEA) = .043
Chi-Square = 272.514 Based on 77 Degrees of Freedom

Coefficients for male sample shown above coefficients for female sample. Coefficients that are p<.05 (two-tailed) are shown in **bold**.

Eight exogenous factors have direct casual paths to each endogenous factor shown: African-American, Hispanic, Other race, presence of two parents in the home at Waves 1–3, parents' education level, parental involvement index, large MSA, and non-MSA

Two exogenous factors have direct causal paths to Wave 1 endogenous factors only: Held back grade 8 or earlier and suspended or expelled grade 8 or earlier

Note: W1 = Wave 1 data collection (grade 8, modal age 14), W2 = Wave 2 data collection (modal age 16),
W3 = Wave 3 data collection (modal age 18), W5 = Wave 5 data collection (modal age 22)

Figure A.6.2. Comparison of simple models of the relationship between delinquency at three waves and smoking at three waves.

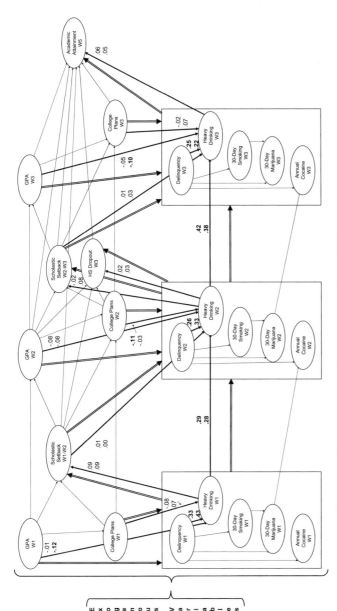

Coefficients for male sample shown above coefficients for female sample. Coefficients that are p<.05 (two-tailed) are shown in **bold**.

Note: W1 = Wave 1 data collection (grade 8, modal age 14), W2 = Wave 2 data collection (modal age 16), W3 = Wave 3 data collection (modal age 18), W5 = Wave 5 data collection (modal age 22)

Model Fit Statistics

	Males	Females
Comparative Fit Index (CFI)	.996	.995
Root Mean-Square Error of Approximation	.024	.027
Chi-Square	563	710
Degrees of Freedom	316	316

Figure A.9.1. Structural equation model of academic attainment and substance use, focusing on heavy drinking.

References

Allison, P. (2003). Missing data techniques for structural equation modeling. *Journal of Abnormal Psychology, 112,* 545–557.

Amato, P. R., & Keith, B. (1991a). Parental divorce and adult well-being: A meta-analysis. *Journal of Marriage and the Family, 53*(1), 43–58.

Amato, P. R., & Keith, B. (1991b). Parental divorce and the well-being of children: A meta-analysis. *Psychological Bulletin, 110*(1), 26–46.

Andrews, F. M., Morgan, J. N., & Sonquist, J. A. (1967). *Multiple classification analysis, a report on a computer program for multiple regression using categorical predictors.* Ann Arbor, MI: The University of Michigan.

Andrews, J. A., & Duncan, S. C. (1997). Examining the reciprocal relation between academic motivation and substance use: Effects of family relationships, self-esteem, and general deviance. *Journal of Behavioral Medicine, 20*(6), 523–549.

Arbeau, K. J., Galambos, N. L., & Jansson, M. S. (in press). Dating, sex, and substance use as correlates of adolescent's subjective experience of age. *Journal of Adolescence.*

Arif, A. (1987). *Adverse health consequences of cocaine abuse.* Albany, NY: World Health Organization.

Arnett, J. J. (2001). Conceptions of the transition to adulthood: Perspectives from adolescence through midlife. *Journal of Adult Development, 8*(2), 133–143.

Bachman, J. G. (1970). *Youth in transition: Vol. 2. The impact of family, background and intelligence on tenth-grade boys.* Ann Arbor, MI: Institute for Social Research.

*Bachman, J. G., Freedman-Doan, P., O'Malley, P. M., Schulenberg, J. E., Johnston, L. D., & Messersmith, E. E. (2006). *Substance use and academic success: Analyses of adjustments for panel attrition in three longitudinal panels* (Monitoring the Future Occasional Paper No. 62). Ann Arbor, MI: Institute for Social Research.

Bachman, J. G., Johnston, L. D., & O'Malley, P. M. (1990). Explaining the recent decline in cocaine use among young adults: Further evidence that perceived risks and disapproval lead to reduced drug use. *Journal of Health and Social Behavior, 31,* 173–184.

Bachman, J. G., Johnston, L. D., & O'Malley, P. M. (1991). How changes in drug use are linked to perceived risks and disapproval: Evidence from national studies that youth and young adults respond to information about the consequences of drug use. In R. L. Donohew, H. Sypher, & W. Bukoski (Eds.), *Persuasive communication and drug abuse prevention* (pp. 133–156). Hillsdale, NJ: Lawrence Erlbaum Associates.

---

*This document, or a more recent version, is available on the Monitoring the Future Web site (http://www.monitoringthefuture.org) under "Publications."

Bachman, J. G., Johnston, L. D., & O'Malley, P. M. (1998). Explaining the recent increases in students' marijuana use: Impacts of perceived risks and disapproval, 1976 through 1996. *American Journal of Public Health, 88,* 887–892.

Bachman, J. G., Johnston, L. D., & O'Malley, P. M. (2005). *Monitoring the Future: Questionnaire responses from the nation's high school seniors, 2004.* Ann Arbor, MI: Institute for Social Research.

Bachman, J. G., Johnston, L. D., O'Malley, P. M., & Humphrey, R. H. (1988). Explaining the recent decline in marijuana use: Differentiating the effects of perceived risks, disapproval, and general lifestyle factors. *Journal of Health and Social Behavior, 29,* 92–112.

*Bachman, J. G., Johnston, L. D., O'Malley, P. M., & Schulenberg, J. E., (2006). The Monitoring the Future project after thirty-two years: Design and procedures (Monitoring the Future Occasional Paper No. 64). Ann Arbor, MI: Institute for Social Research.

Bachman, J. G., O'Malley, P. M., & Johnston, J. (1978). *Youth in transition: Vol. 6. Adolescence to adulthood: A study of change and stability in the lives of young men.* Ann Arbor, MI: Institute for Social Research.

Bachman, J. G., O'Malley, P. M., Johnston, L. D., Schulenberg, J. E., & Freedman-Doan, P. (2001). *The Monitoring the Future eighth grade panel survey data: Sample design, adjustments for panel attrition biases, and assessment of measurement bias.* (Monitoring the Future Occasional Paper No. 55). Ann Arbor, MI: Institute for Social Research.

Bachman, J. G., O'Malley, P. M., Schulenberg, J. E., Johnston, L. D., Bryant, A. L., & Merline, A. C. (2002). *The decline of substance use in young adulthood: Changes in social activities, roles, and beliefs.* Mahwah, NJ: Lawrence Erlbaum Associates.

Bachman, J. G., Safron, D. J., Sy, S. R., & Schulenberg, J. E. (2003). Wishing to work: New perspectives on how adolescents' part-time work intensity is linked to educational disengagement, substance use, and other problem behaviours. *International Journal of Behavioral Development, 27*(4), 301–315.

Bachman, J. G., & Schulenberg, J. (1993). How part-time work intensity relates to drug use, problem behavior, time use, and satisfaction among high school seniors: Are these consequences, or merely correlates? (ERIC Document No. EJ464472). *Developmental Psychology, 29,* 220–235.

Bachman, J. G., Wadsworth, K. N., O'Malley, P. M., Johnston, L. D., & Schulenberg, J. (1997). *Smoking, drinking and drug use in young adulthood: The impacts of new freedoms and new responsibilities.* Mahwah, NJ: Lawrence Erlbaum Associates.

Baum-Baicker, C. (1985). The psychological benefits of moderate alcohol consumption: A review of the literature. *Drug and Alcohol Dependence, 15,* 305–322.

Beauvais, F. C., Chavez, E. L., Oetting, E. R., & Deffenbacher, J. L. (1996). Drug use, violence, and victimization among White American, Mexican American, and American Indian dropouts, students with academic problems, and students in good standing. *Journal of Counseling Psychology, 43*(3), 292–299.

Becker, H. S., Hughes, E. C., Geer, B., & Strauss, A. L. (1961). *Boys in white.* Chicago: University of Chicago Press.

Bentler, P. M. (1995). *EQS Structural equations program manual.* Encino, CA: Multivariate Software.

*This document, or a more recent version, is available on the Monitoring the Future Web site (http://www.monitoringthefuture.org) under "Publications."

Block, R. I., Erwin, W. J., & Ghoneim, M. M. (2002). Chronic drug use and cognitive impairments. *Pharmacology, Biochemistry, and Behavior, 73*, 491–504.

Braggio, J. T., Pishkin, V., Gameros, T. A., & Brooks, D. L. (1993). Academic achievement in substance-abusing and conduct-disordered adolescents. *Journal of Clinical Psychology, 49*(2), 282–291.

Brook, J. S., & Newcomb, M. D. (1995). Childhood aggression and unconventionality: Impact on later academic achievement, drug use, and workforce involvement. *Journal of Genetic Psychology, 156*, 393–410.

Brunswick, A. F., & Messeri, P. A. (1983). Causal factors in onset of adolescents' cigarette smoking: A prospective study of urban Black youth. *Advances in Alcohol and Substance Abuse, 3*(1–2), 35–52.

Brunswick, A. F., & Messeri, P. A. (1984). Origins of cigarette smoking in academic achievement, stress, and social expectations: Does gender make a difference? *Journal of Early Adolescence, 4*(4), 353–370.

Bryant, A. L., Schulenberg, J. E., Bachman, J. S., O'Malley, P. M., & Johnston, L. D. (2000). Understanding the links among school misbehavior, academic achievement, and cigarette use: A national panel study of adolescents. *Prevention Science, 1*(2), 71–87.

Bryant, A. L., Schulenberg, J. E., O'Malley, P. M., Bachman, J. G., & Johnston, L. D. (2003). How academic achievement, attitudes, and behaviors relate to the course of substance use during adolescence: A 6-year, multiwave national longitudinal study. *Journal of Research on Adolescence, 13*(3), 361–397.

Bryant, A. L., & Zimmerman, M. A. (2002). Examining the effects of academic beliefs and behaviors on changes in substance use among urban adolescents. *Journal of Educational Psychology, 94*(3), 621–637.

Butler, R. (1999). Information seeking and achievement motivation in middle childhood and adolescence: The role of conceptions of ability. *Developmental Psychology, 35*(1), 146–163.

Bynner, J., O'Malley, P. M., & Bachman, J. G. (1981). Self-esteem and delinquency revisited. *Youth and Adolescence, 10*, 407–441.

Byrne, B. M. (2006). *Structural equation modeling with EQS: Basic concepts, applications, and programming* (2nd ed.). Mahwah, NJ: Lawrence Erlbaum Associates.

Cagney, K. A., & Lauderdale, D. S. (2002). Education, wealth, and cognitive function in later life. *Journals of Gerontology: Series B: Psychological Sciences and Social Sciences, 57B*(2), 163–172.

Carvajal, S. C., Hanson, C., Downing, R. A., Coyle, K. K., & Pederson, L. L. (2004). Theory-based determinants of youth smoking: A multiple influence approach. *Journal of Applied Social Psychology, 34*(1), 59–84.

Caspers, K. M., Cadoret, R. J., Langbehn, D., Yucuis, R., & Troutman, B. (2005). Contributions of attachment style and perceived social support of lifetime use of illicit substances. *Addictive Behaviors, 30*(5), 1007–1011.

Caspi, A., Wright, B. R. E., Moffitt, T. E., & Silva, P. A. (1998). Early failure in the labor market: Childhood and adolescent predictors of unemployment in the transition to adulthood. *American Sociological Review, 63*(3), 424–451.

Chang, J., & Le, T. N. (2005). The influence of parents, peer delinquency, and school attitudes on academic achievement in Chinese, Cambodian, Laotian or Mien, and Vietnamese youth. *Crime and Delinquency, 51*(2), 238–264.

Chassin, L., Presson, C. C., Pitts, S. C., & Sherman, S. J. (2000). The natural history of cigarette smoking from adolescence to adulthood in a Midwestern community sample: Multiple trajectories and their psychosocial correlates. *Health Psychology, 19*(3), 223-231.

Chassin, L., Presson, C. C., Rose, J. S., & Sherman, S. J. (1996). The natural history of cigarette smoking from adolescence to adulthood: Demographic predictors of continuity and change. *Health Psychology, 15*(6), 478–484.

Chassin, L., Presson, C. C., Rose, J., Sherman, S. J., Davis, M. J., & Gonzalez, J. L. (2005). Parenting style and smoking-specific parenting practices as predictors of adolescent smoking onset. *Journal of Pediatric Psychology, 30*(4), 334–344.

Chen, Z., & Kaplan, H. B. (2003). School failure in early adolescence and status attainment in middle adulthood: A longitudinal study. *Sociology of Education, 76*(2), 110–127.

Clausen, J. A. (1991). Adolescent competence and the shaping of the life course. *American Journal of Sociology, 96*, 805–842.

Conwell, L. S., O'Callaghan, M. J., Andersen, M. J., Bor, W., Najman, J. M., & Williams, G. M. (2003). Early adolescent smoking and a web of personal and social disadvantage. *Journal of Paediatrics & Child Health, 39*(8), 580–585.

Cooper, M. L., Wood, P. K., Orcutt, H. K., & Albino, A. (2003). Personality and the predisposition to engage in risky or problem behaviors during adolescence. *Journal of Personality and Social Psychology, 84*(2), 390–410.

Costa, F. M., Jessor, R., & Donovan, J. E. (1989). Value on health and adolescent conventionality: A construct validation of a new measure in Problem-Behavior Theory. *Journal of Applied Social Psychology, 19*(10), 841–861.

Crosnoe, R. (2002). High school curriculum track and adolescent association with delinquent friends. *Journal of Adolescent Research, 17*(2), 143–167.

Crum, R. M., Ensminger, M. E., Ro, M. J., & McCord, J. (1998). The association of educational achievement and school dropout with risk of alcoholism: A twenty-five-year prospective study of inner-city children. *Journal of Studies on Alcohol, 59*, 318–326.

Day, J. C., & Newburger, E. C. (2002). *The big payoff: Educational attainment and synthetic estimates of work-life earnings* (Current Population Reports P23-210). Washington, DC: U.S. Census Bureau.

Dewey, J. D. (1999). Reviewing the relationship between school factors and substance use for elementary, middle, and high school students. *The Journal of Primary Prevention, 19*(3), 177–225.

Diener, C., & Dweck, C. (1978). An analysis of learned helplessness: Continuous changes in performance, strategy, and achievement cognitions following failure. *Journal of Personality and Social Psychology, 36*, 940–952.

Donovan, J. E., & Jessor, R. (1985). Structure of problem behavior in adolescence and young adulthood. *Journal of Consulting and Clinical Psychology, 53*, 890–904.

Donovan, J. E., Jessor, R., & Costa, F. M. (1988). Syndrome of problem behavior in adolescence: A replication. *Journal of Consulting and Clinical Psychology, 56*(5), 762–765.

Duchesne, S., Larose, S., Guay, F., Vitaro, F., & Tremblay, R. E. (2005). The transition from elementary to high school: The pivotal role of mother and child characteristics in explaining trajectories of academic functioning. *International Journal of Behavioral Development, 29*(5), 409–417.

Duncan, S. C., Duncan, T. E., & Strycker, L. A. (2000). Risk and protective factors influencing adolescent problem behavior: A multivariate latent growth curve analysis. *Annals of Behavioral Medicine, 22*(2), 103–109.

Ellickson, P. L., & Hays, R. D. (1991). Antecedents of drinking among young adolescents with different alcohol use histories. *Journal of Studies on Alcohol, 52*(5), 398–408.

Ellickson, P. L., Hays, R. D., & Bell, R. M. (1992). Stepping through the drug use sequence: Longitudinal scalogram analysis of initiation and regular use. *Journal of Abnormal Psychology, 101*(3), 441–451.

Ellickson, P. L., Tucker, J. S., & Klein, D. J. (2001). High-risk behaviors associated with early smoking: Results from a 5-year follow-up. *Journal of Adolescent Health, 28*, 465–473.

Ellickson, P. L., Tucker, J. S., Klein, D. J., & Saner, H. (2004). Antecedents and outcomes of marijuana use initiation during adolescence. *Preventive Medicine: An International Journal Devoted to Practice and Theory, 39*(5), 976–984.

Elliott, E. S., & Dweck, C. S. (1988). Goals: An approach to motivation and achievement. *Journal of Personality and Social Psychology, 54*(1), 5–12.

Ensminger, M. E., Juon, H. S., & Fothergill, K. E. (2002). Childhood and adolescent antecedents of substance use in adulthood. *Addiction, 97*, 833–844.

Ferguson, P., Jimerson, S. R., & Dalton, M. J. (2001). Sorting out successful failures: Exploratory analyses of factors associated with academic and behavioral outcomes of retained students. *Psychology in the Schools, 38*(4), 327–341.

Fergusson, D. M., Horwood, L. J., & Beautrais, A. L. (2003). Cannabis and educational achievement. *Addiction, 98*, 1681–1692.

Feshbach, N. D., & Feshbach, S. (1987). Affective processes and academic achievement. *Child Development, 58*(5), 1335–1347.

Fredricks, J. A., Blumenfeld, P. C., & Paris, A. H. (2004). School engagement: Potential of the concept, state of the evidence. *Review of Educational Research, 74*(1), 59–109.

Giskes, K., Kunst, A. E., Benach, J., Borrell, C., Costa, G., Dahl, E., et al. (2005). Trends in smoking behaviour between 1985 and 2000 in nine European countries by education. *Journal of Epidemiology and Community Health, 59*(5), 395–401.

Greenberger, E., & Steinberg, L. (1986). *When teenagers work: The psychological and social costs of adolescent employment.* New York: Basic Books.

Griffin, K. W., Botvin, G. J., Doyle, M. M., Diaz, T., & Epstein, J. A. (1999). A six-year follow-up study of determinants of heavy cigarette smoking among high-school seniors. *Journal of Behavioral Medicine, 22*(3), 271–284.

Guagliardo, M. F., Huang, Z., Hicks, J., & D'Angelo, L. (1998). Increased drug use among old-for-grade and dropout urban adolescents. *American Journal of Preventive Medicine, 15*(1), 42–48.

Harackiewicz, J. M., Barron, K. E., Tauer, J. M., & Elliot, A. J. (2002). Predicting success in college: A longitudinal study of achievement goals and ability measures as predictors of interest and performance from freshman year through graduation. *Journal of Educational Psychology, 94*(3), 562–575.

Hawkins, J. D., Catalano, R. F., & Miller, J. Y. (1992). Risk and protective factors for alcohol and other drug problems in adolescence and early adulthood: Implications for substance abuse prevention. *Psychological Bulletin, 112*(1), 64–105.

Hawkins, J. D., Hill, K. G., Guo, J., & Battin-Pearson, S. R. (2002). Substance use norms and transitions in substance use: Implications for the Gateway Hypothesis. In D. B. Kandel (Ed.), *Stages and pathways of drug involvement: Examining the Gateway Hypothesis* (pp. 42–64). New York: Cambridge University Press.

Helmke, A., & van Aken, M. A. G. (1995). The causal ordering of academic achievement and self-concept of ability during elementary school: A longitudinal study. *Journal of Educational Psychology, 87*(4), 624–637.

Hetherington, E. M., Cox, M., & Cox, R. (1982). Effects of divorce on parents and children. In M. Lamb (Ed.), *Nontraditional families: Parenting and child development* (pp. 223–288). Hillsdale, NJ: Lawrence Erlbaum Associates.

Hetherington, E. M., & Stanley-Hagan, M. (1999). The adjustment of children with divorced parents: A risk and resiliency perspective. *Journal of Child Psychology and Psychiatry, 40*(1), 129–140.

Hollar, D., & Moore, D. (2004). Relationship of substance use by students with disabilities to long-term educational, employment, and social outcomes. *Substance Use & Misuse, 39*(6), 931–962.

Hong, Y., Chiu, C., & Dweck, C. S. (1999). Implicit theories, attributions, and coping: A meaning system approach. *Journal of Personality and Social Psychology, 77*(3), 588–599.

Hops, H., Davis, B., & Lewin, L. M. (1999). The development of alcohol and other substance use: A gender study of family and peer context. *Journal of Studies on Alcohol, 13*, 22–31.

Hu, T.-W., Lin, Z., & Keeler, T. E. (1998). Teenage smoking, attempts to quit, and school performance. *American Journal of Public Health, 88*, 940–943.

Jacobsen, L. K., Krystal, J. H., Mencl, W. E., Westerveld, M., Frost, S. J., & Pugh, K. R. (2005). Effects of smoking and smoking abstinence on cognition in adolescent tobacco smokers. *Biological Psychiatry, 57*(1), 56–66.

Jaffee, S. R. (2002). Pathways to adversity in young adulthood among early childbearers. *Journal of Family Psychology, 16*(1), 38–49.

Jang, S. J., & Thornberry, T. P. (1998). Self-esteem, delinquent peers, and delinquency: A test of the self-enhancement thesis. *American Sociological Review, 63*, 586-598.

Jessor, R., Donovan, J. E., & Costa, F. M. (1991). *Beyond adolescence: Problem behavior and young adult development*. New York: Cambridge University Press.

Jessor, R., & Jessor, S. L. (1977). *Problem behavior and psychosocial development: A longitudinal study of youth*. New York: Academic Press.

Jeynes, W. H. (2002). The relationship between the consumption of various drugs by adolescents and their academic achievement. *American Journal of Drug and Alcohol Abuse, 28*(1), 15–35.

Jimerson, S. R. (1999). On the failure of failure: Examining the association between early grade retention and education and employment outcomes during late adolescence. *Journal of School Psychology, 37*(3), 243–272.

Johnson, R. A., & Hoffmann, J. P. (2000). Adolescent cigarette smoking in U.S. racial/ethnic subgroups: Findings from the national education longitudinal study. *Journal of Health and Social Behavior, 41*(4), 392–407.

Johnston, L. D., Bachman, J. G., & O'Malley, P. M. (2005). *Monitoring the Future: Questionnaire responses from the nation's high school seniors, 2003*. Ann Arbor, MI: Institute for Social Research.

*Johnston, L. D., O'Malley, P. M., Bachman, J. G., & Schulenberg, J. E. (2005a). *Monitoring the Future national results on adolescent drug use: Overview of key findings, 2004* (NIH Publication No. 05-5726). Bethesda, MD: National Institute on Drug Abuse.

*Johnston, L. D., O'Malley, P. M., Bachman, J. G., & Schulenberg, J. E. (2005b). *Monitoring the Future national survey results on drug use, 1975–2004: Volume I. Secondary school students* (NIH Publication No. 05-5727). Bethesda, MD: National Institute on Drug Abuse.

*Johnston, L. D., O'Malley, P. M., Bachman, J. G., & Schulenberg, J. E. (2005c). *Monitoring the Future national survey results on drug use, 1975–2004: Volume II. College students and adults ages 19–45* (NIH Publication No. 05-5728). Bethesda, MD: National Institute on Drug Abuse.

Johnston, L. D., O'Malley, P. M., Delva, J., Bachman, J. G., & Schulenberg, J. E. (2005). *YES results on School Policies and Programs: Overview of key findings, 2004*. Ann Arbor, MI: Institute for Social Research.

Jussim, L., Soffin, S., Brown, R., Ley, J., & Kohlhepp, K. (1992). Understanding reactions to feedback by integrating ideas from symbolic interactionism and cognitive evaluation theory. *Journal of Personality and Social Psychology, 62*, 402–421.

Kalton, G. (1983). *Compensating for missing survey data*. Ann Arbor, MI: Institute for Social Research.

---

*This document, or a more recent version, is available on the Monitoring the Future Web site (http://www.monitoringthefuture.org) under "Publications."

Kandel, D. B. (1988). Issues of sequencing of adolescent drug use and other problem behaviors. *Drugs and Society, 3,* 55–76.

Kandel, D. B., & Yamaguchi, K. (2002). Stages of drug involvement in the U.S. population. In D. B. Kandel (Ed.), *Stages and pathways of drug involvement: Examining the Gateway Hypothesis* (pp. 65–89). New York: Cambridge University Press.

Kaplan, H. B. (2001). Self-esteem and deviant behavior: A critical review and theoretical integration. In T. J. Owens, S. Stryker, & N. Coodman (Eds.), *Extending self-esteem theory and research: Sociological and psychological currents* (pp. 375–399). New York: Cambridge University Press.

Ketterlinus, R. D., Lamb, M. E., & Nitz, K. A. (1994). Adolescent nonsexual and sex-related problem behaviors: Their prevalence, consequences, and co-occurrence. In R. D. Ketterlinus & M. E. Lamb (Eds.), *Adolescent problem behaviors: Issues and research* (pp.17–39). Hillsdale, NJ: Lawrence Erlbaum Associates.

Kish, L. (1965). *Survey sampling.* New York: John Wiley & Sons.

Klatsky, A. L. (1999). Moderate drinking and reduced risk of heart disease. *Alcohol Research and Health, 23,* 15–24.

Lareau, A. (2003). *Unequal childhoods: Class, race, and family life.* Berkeley, CA: University of California Press.

Li, K. H., Raghunathan, T. E., & Rubin, D. B. (1991). Large sample significant levels from multiply imputed data using moment-based statistic and an F reference distribution. *Journal of the American Statistical Association, 86,* 1065–1073.

Luthar, S. S., & Ansary, N. S. (2005). Dimensions of adolescent rebellion: Risks for academic failure among high- and low-income youth. *Development and Psychopathology, 17*(1), 231–250.

Luthar, S. S., & Cushing, G. (1997). Substance use and personal adjustment among disadvantaged teenagers: A six-month prospective study. *Journal of Youth and Adolescence, 26*(3), 353–372.

Maehr, M. L., & Midgley, C. (1996). *Transforming school cultures.* Boulder, CO: Westview.

Maggs, J. L., Frome, P. M., Eccles, J. S., & Barber, B. L. (1997). Psychosocial resources, adolescent risk behaviour and young adult adjustment: Is risk taking more dangerous for some than others? *Journal of Adolescence, 20*(1), 103–119.

Mantzicopoulos, P. (1997). How do children cope with school failure? A study of social/emotional factors related to children's coping strategies. *Psychology in the Schools, 34*(3), 229–237.

Mauss, A. L. (1969). Anticipatory socialization toward college as a factor in adolescent marijuana use. *Social Problems, 16,* 357–364.

McCoy, A. R., & Reynolds, A. J. (1999). Grade retention and school performance: An extended investigation. *Journal of School Psychology, 37*(3), 273–298.

McDonald, R. P. H., & Ho, M. R. (2002). Principles and practices in reporting structural equation analyses. *Psychological Methods, 7,* 64–82.

McGuigan, K. A., Ellickson, P. L., Hays, R. D., & Bell, R. M. (1997). Adjusting for attrition in school-based samples: Bias, precision, and cost trade-off of three methods. *Evaluation Review, 21,* 554–567.

McLanahan, S., & Sandefur, G. (1994). *Growing up with a single parent: What hurts, what helps.* Cambridge, MA: Harvard University Press.

Meece, J. L., Blumenfeld, P. C., & Hoyle, R. H. (1988). Students' goal orientations and cognitive engagement in classroom activities. *Journal of Educational Psychology, 80,* 514–523.

Meisels, S. J., & Liaw, F. (1993). Failure in grade: Do retained students catch up? *Journal of Educational Research, 87*(2), 69–77.

Miech, R. A., & Shanahan, M. J. (2000). Socioeconomic status and depression over the life course. *Journal of Health and Social Behavior, 41*(2), 162–176.

Miller, A. (1986). Performance impairment after failure: Mechanism and sex differences. *Journal of Educational Psychology, 78,* 486–491.

Miller, T. Q., & Volk, R. J. (2002). Family relationships and adolescent cigarette smoking: Results from a national longitudinal survey. *Journal of Drug Issues, 32*(3), 945–972.

Mott, F. L. (1994). Sons, daughters, and fathers' absence: Differentials in father-leaving possibilities and in home environments. *Journal of Family Issues, 15*(1), 97–128.

Mullis, R. L., Rathge, R., & Mullis, A. K. (2003). Predictors of academic performance during early adolescence: A contextual view. *International Journal of Behavioral Development, 27*(6), 541–548.

Murrell, S. A., & Meeks, S. (2002). Psychological, economic, and social mediators of the education–health relationship in older adults. *Journal of Aging and Health, 14*(4), 527–550.

Newcomb, M. D., & Bentler, P. M. (1988). *Consequences of adolescent drug use: Impact on the lives of young adults.* Thousand Oaks, CA: Sage.

Nonnemaker, J. M., McNeely, C. A., & Blum, R. W. (2003). Public and private domains of religiosity and adolescent health risk behaviors: Evidence from the National Longitudinal Study of Adolescent Health. *Social Science and Medicine, 57*(11), 2049–2054.

O'Malley, P. M., Bachman, J. G., & Johnston, L. D. (1983). Reliability and consistency of self-reports of drug use. *International Journal of the Addictions, 18,* 805–824.

O'Malley, P. M., & Wagenaar, A. C. (1991). Effects of minimum drinking age laws on alcohol use, related behaviors, and traffic crash involvement among American youth: 1976–1987. *Journal of Studies on Alcohol, 52,* 478–491.

Osgood, D. W., Anderson, A. L., & Shaffer, J. N. (2005). Unstructured leisure in the after-school hours. In J. L. Mahoney, R. W. Reed, & J. S. Eccles (Eds.), *Organized activities as contexts of development: Extracurricular activities, after-school and community programs* (pp. 45–64). Mahwah, NJ: Lawrence Erlbaum Associates.

Osgood, D. W., Johnston, L. D., O'Malley, P. M., & Bachman, J. G. (1988). The generality of deviance in late adolescence and early adulthood. *American Sociological Review, 53,* 81–93.

Osgood, D. W., Wilson, J. K., O'Malley, P. M., Bachman, J. G., & Johnston, L. D. (1996). Routine activities and individual deviant behaviors. *American Sociological Review, 61,* 635–674.

Perkins, D. F., & Borden, L. M. (2003). Positive behaviors, problem behaviors, and resiliency in adolescence. In R. M. Lerner, M. A. Easterbrooks, & J. Mistry (Eds.), *Handbook of psychology: Vol. 6. Developmental psychology* (pp. 373–394). New York: Wiley.

Peters, J. F. (1991). Parental contributions to adolescents' possessions and educational expenses: Gender differences. *Adolescence, 26*(103), 649–657.

Pierret, C. R. (2001). The effect of family structure on youth outcomes in the NLSY97. In R. T. Robert (Ed.), *Social awakening: Adolescent behavior as adulthood approaches* (pp. 25–48). New York: Russell Sage Foundation.

Pierson, L. H., & Connell, J. P. (1992). Effect of grade retention on self-system processes, school engagement, and academic performance. *Journal of Educational Psychology, 84*(3), 300–307.

Pintrich, P. R. (2000). Multiple goals, multiple pathways: The role of goal orientation in learning and achievement. *Journal of Educational Psychology, 92*(3), 544–555.

Pintrich, P. R. (2003). Motivation and classroom learning. In W. M. Reynolds & G. E. Miller (Eds.), *Handbook of psychology: Educational psychology* (Vol. 7, pp. 103–122). Hoboken, NJ: Wiley.

Pope, H. G., Jr., Gruber, A. J., & Yurgelun-Todd, D. (2001). Residual neuropsychologic effects of cannabis. *Current Psychiatry Reports, 3*(6), 507–512.

Pope, H. G., Jr., & Yurgelun-Todd, D. (1996). The residual cognitive effects of heavy marijuana use in college students. *Journal of the American Medical Association, 275*(7), 521–527.

Powell, B., & Steelman, L. C. (1989). The liability of having brothers: Paying for college and the sex composition of family. *Sociology of Education, 62*(2), 134–147.

Powers, R. S., & Wojtkiewicz, R. A. (2004). Occupational aspirations, gender, and educational attainment. *Sociological Spectrum, 24*(5), 601–622.

Raghunathan, T. E., Lepkowski, J. M., Van Hoewyk, J., & Solenberger, P. (2001). A multivariate technique for multiply imputing missing values using a sequence of regression models. *Survey Methodology, 27*(1), 85–95.

Raghunathan, T. E., Solenberger, P. W., & Van Hoewyk, J. (2002). *IVEware: Imputation and variance estimation software user guide.* Retrieved June 29, 2006, from http://www.isr. umich.edu/src/smp/ive/

Reynolds, A. J., Temple, J. A., Robertson, D. L., & Mann, E. A. (2001). Long-term effects of an early childhood intervention on educational achievement and juvenile arrest: A 15-year follow-up of low-income children in public schools. *Journal of the American Medical Association, 285*(18), 2339–2346.

Reynolds, K., Lewis, B. L., Nolen, J. D. L., Kinney, G. L., Sathya, B., & He, J. (2003). Alcohol consumption and risk of stroke: A meta-analysis. *Journal of the American Medical Association, 289*, 579–588.

Riala, K., Isohanni, I., Jokelainen, J., Jones, P. B., & Isohanni, M. (2003). The relationship between childhood family background and educational performance, with special reference to single-parent families: A longitudinal study. *Social Psychology of Education, 6*, 349–365.

Roderick, M. (1994). Grade retention and school dropout: Investigating the association. *American Educational Research Journal, 31*(4), 729–759.

Roeser, R. W., Eccles, J. S., & Freedman-Doan, C. (1999). Academic functioning and mental health in adolescence: Patterns, progressions, and routes from childhood. *Journal of Adolescent Research, 14*(2), 135–174.

Rubin, D. B. (1987). *Multiple imputation for nonresponse in surveys.* New York: Wiley.

Ryan, R. M., & Deci, E. L. (2000). Self-determination theory and the facilitation of intrinsic motivation, social development, and well-being. *American Psychologist, 55*(1), 68–78.

Safron, D. J., Schulenberg, J. E., & Bachman, J. G. (2001). Part-time work and hurried adolescence: The links among work intensity, social activities, health behaviors, and substance use. *Journal of Health and Social Behavior, 42*, 425–449.

Schoon, I., Parsons, S., & Sacker, A. (2004). Socioeconomic adversity, educational resilience, and subsequent levels of adult adaptation. *Journal of Adolescent Research, 19*(4), 383–404.

Schulenberg, J. E., Bachman, J. G., O'Malley, P. M., & Johnston, L. D. (1994). High school educational success and subsequent substance use: A panel analysis following adolescents into young adulthood. *Journal of Health and Social Behavior, 35*, 45–62.

Schulenberg, J. E., & Maggs, J. L. (2002). A developmental perspective on alcohol use and heavy drinking during adolescence and the transition to young adulthood. *Journal of Studies on Alcohol* (Suppl.), *14*, 54–70.

Schulenberg, J. E., Merline, A. C., Johnston, L. D., O'Malley, P. M., Bachman, J. G., & Laetz, V. B. (2005). Trajectories of marijuana use during the transition to adulthood: The big picture based on national panel data. *Journal of Drug Issues, 35*, 255–279.

Schulenberg, J. E., O'Malley, P. M., Bachman, J. G., & Johnston, L. D. (2005). Early adult transitions and their relation to well-being and substance use. In R. A. Settersten, Jr., F. F. Furstenberg, Jr., & R. G. Rumbaut (Eds.), *On the frontier of adulthood: Theory, research, and public policy* (pp. 417–453). Chicago: University of Chicago Press.

Schulenberg, J. E., Wadsworth, K. N., O'Malley, P. M., Bachman, J. G., & Johnston, L. D. (1996). Adolescent risk factors for binge drinking during the transition to young adulthood: Variable- and pattern-centered approaches to change. *Developmental Psychology, 32*(4), 659–674.

Schulenberg, J. E., & Zarrett, N. R. (2006). Mental health during emerging adulthood: Continuity and discontinuity in courses, causes, and functions. In J. J. Arnett & J. L. Tanner (Eds.), *Emerging adults in America: Coming of age in the 21st century* (pp. 135–172). Washington DC: American Psychological Association.

Schunk, D. H., & Ertmer, P. A. (2000). Self-regulation and academic learning: Self-efficacy enhancing interventions. In M. Boekarts, P. R. Pintrich, & M. Zeidner (Eds), *Handbook of self-regulation* (pp. 631–649). San Diego: Academic Press.

Shepard, L. A., & Smith M. L. (1990). Synthesis of research on grade retention. *Educational Leadership, 47*(8), 84–88.

Simons-Morton, B. (2004). Prospective association of peer influence, school engagement, drinking expectancies, and parent expectations with drinking initiation among sixth graders. *Addictive Behaviors, 29*(2), 299–309.

Stipek, D. J., & Kowalski, P. S. (1989). Learned helplessness in task-orienting versus performance-orienting testing conditions. *Journal of Educational Psychology, 81*(3), 384–391.

Stronski, S. M., Ireland, M., Michaud, P.-A., Narring, F., & Resnick, M. D. (2000). Protective correlates of stages in adolescent substance use: A Swiss national study. *Journal of Adolescent Health, 26,* 420–427.

Sutherland, I., & Shepherd, J. P. (2001). The prevalence of alcohol, cigarette, and illicit drug use in a stratified sample of English adolescents. *Addiction, 96,* 637–640.

Tanner, J., Davies, S., & O'Grady, B. (1999). Whatever happened to yesterday's rebels? Longitudinal effects of youth delinquency on education and employment. *Social Problems, 46*(2), 250–274.

Tibbetts, S. G., & Whittimore, J. N. (2002). The interactive effects of low self-control and commitment to school on substance abuse among college students. *Psychological Reports, 90,* 327–337.

Tubman, J. G., Gil, A. G., & Wagner, E. F. (2004). Co-occurring substance use and delinquent behaviour during early adolescence: Emerging relations and implications for intervention strategies. *Criminal Justice and Behavior, 31*(4), 463–488.

U.S. Department of Health and Human Services. (2004). *The health consequences of smoking: A report of the Surgeon General.* Atlanta, GA: U.S. Department of Health and Human Services, Centers for Disease Control and Prevention, National Center for Chronic Disease Prevention and Health Promotion, Office on Smoking and Health.

U.S. Department of Health and Human Services and U.S. Department of Agriculture. (1995). *Dietary guidelines for Americans, 2005* (6th ed.). Washington, DC: U.S. Government Printing Office.

van den Bree, M. B. M., & Pickworth, W. B. (2005). Risk factors predicting changes in marijuana involvement in teenagers. *Archives of General Psychiatry, 62,* 311–319.

Vazsonyi, A. T., & Flannery, D. J. (1997). Early adolescent delinquent behaviors: Associations with family and school domains. *Journal of Early Adolescence, 17*(3), 271–293.

Vermeiren, R., Bogaerts, J., Ruchkin, V., Deboutte, D., & Schwab-Stone, M. (2004). Subtypes of self-esteem and self-concept in adolescent violent and property offenders. *Journal of Child Psychology and Psychiatry, 45*(2), 405–411.

Wallace, J. M., Jr., Brown, T. N., Bachman, J. G., & LaVeist, T. A. (2003). The influence of race and religion on abstinence from alcohol, cigarettes and marijuana among adolescents. *Journal of Studies on Alcohol, 64*(6), 843–848.

Wallace, J. M., Jr., & Forman, T. A. (1998). Religion's role in promoting health and reducing risk among American youth. *Health Education & Behavior, 25*(6), 721–741.

Wallace, J. M., Jr., & Muroff, J. R. (2002). Preventing substance abuse among African American children and youth: Race differences in risk factor exposure and vulnerability. *The Journal of Primary Prevention, 22*(3), 235–261.

Wallace, J. M., Jr., & Williams, D. R. (1997). Religion and adolescent health-compromising behaviors. In J. Schulenberg, J. L. Maggs, & K. Hurrelmann (Eds.), *Health risks and developmental transitions during adolescence* (pp. 444–468). New York: Cambridge University Press.

Wallerstein, J. S., & Lewis, J. (1998). The long-term impact of divorce on children: A first report from a 25-year study. *Family and Conciliation Courts Review, 36*(3), 368–383.

Wang, M. Q., Fitzhugh, E. C., Green, B. L., Turner, L. W., Eddy, J. M., & Westerfield, R. C. (1999). Prospective social-psychological factors of adolescent smoking progression. *Journal of Adolescent Health, 24*, 2–9.

Wells, J. E., Horwood, L. J., & Fergusson, D. M. (2004). Drinking patterns in mid-adolescence and psychosocial outcomes in late adolescence and early adulthood. *Addiction, 99*(12), 1529–1541.

Werch, C. E., Dunn, M., & Woods, R. (1997). A pilot study of alcohol and cigarette consumption among adolescent and young adult females attending health clinics. *Journal of Alcohol & Drug Education, 42*(3), 27–39.

Wetter, D. W., Cofta-Gunn, L., Fouladi, R. T., Irvin, J. E., Daza, P., Mazas, C., et al. (2005). Understanding the associations among education, employment characteristics, and smoking. *Addictive Behaviors, 30*(5), 905–914.

Whalley, L. J., Fox, H. C., Deary, I. J., & Starr, J. M. (2005). Childhood IQ, smoking, and cognitive change from age 11 to 64 years. *Addictive Behaviors, 30*(1), 77–88.

Wiesner, M., & Windle, M. (2004). Assessing covariates of adolescent delinquency trajectories: A latent growth mixture modeling approach. *Journal of Youth and Adolescence, 33*(5), 431–442.

Wills, T. A., Yaeger, A. M., & Sandy, J. M. (2003). Buffering effect of religiosity for adolescent substance use. *Psychology of Addictive Behaviors, 17*(1), 24–31.

Wirt, J., Choy, S., Rooney, P., Provasnik, S., Sen, A., & Tobin, R. (2004). *The Condition of Education 2004* (NCES 2004-077). *U.S. Department of Education, National Center for Education Statistics*. Washington, DC: U.S. Government Printing Office.

Wright, D. R., & Fitzpatrick, K. M. (2004). Psychosocial correlates of substance use behaviors among African American youth. *Adolescence, 39*(156), 653–667.

Zhan, M., & Pandey, S. (2002). Postsecondary education and the well-being of women in retirement. *Social Work Research, 26*(3), 171–184.

Zimmerman, M. A., & Schmeelk-Cone, K. H. (2003). A longitudinal analysis of adolescent substance use and school motivation among African American youth. *Journal of Research on Adolescence, 13*(2), 185–210.

Author Index

Subject Index

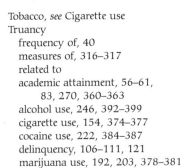